P9-CEO-057

STANISLAVSKY

STANISLAVSKY

A life

DAVID MAGARSHACK

faber and faber
LONDON · BOSTON

First published in 1950
by Macgibbon and Kee, London
First published in the USA in 1975
by Greenwood Press
This edition first published in 1986
by Faber and Faber Limited
3 Queen Square London WC1N 3AU

Printed in Great Britain by
Redwood Burn Limited
Trowbridge Wiltshire
All rights reserved

Copyright   David Magarshack 1950
Foreword © Irving Wardle 1986

*This book is sold subject to the condition that it shall not, by way of trade
or otherwise, be lent, resold, hired out or otherwise circulated without the
publisher's prior consent in any form of binding or cover other than that
in which it is published and without a similar condition including
this condition being imposed on the subsequent purchaser.*

British Library Cataloguing in Publication Data

Magarshack, David
Stanislavsky.
1. Theatrical producers and directors—
Soviet Union—Biography
I. Title
792'.092'4   PN2728.S78

ISBN 0–571–13791–1

Library of Congress Cataloging in Publication Data

Magarshack, David.
Stanislavsky: a life.

Reprint. Originally published: London: Macgibbon &
Kee, 1950.
Includes index.
1. Stanislavsky, Konstantin, 1863–1938. 2. Moscow.
Moskovski i khudozhestvenny i akademicheski i teatr.
3. Theatrical producers and directors—Soviet Union—
Biography. 4. Actors—Soviet Union—Biography.
I. Title.
[PN2728.S78M33   1986]   791.43'.028'0924 [B]   85–16208

ISBN 0–571–13791–1

CONTENTS

FOREWORD
by Irving Wardle

To those who view the modern theatre as a new faith that arose to fill the gap left vacant by orthodox religion, the Moscow Art Theatre figures as its principal shrine and Stanislavsky as its greatest prophet. A shrine, however, is something less than a human habitation, and a prophet less than a living man.

No director ever left a more painstaking record of his life's work than Stanislavsky; but thanks to his idealistic cast of mind, the effect of his books has been still more to shroud him in mystique. He was writing to spread the good news and to set a noble example; and he disdained to mention professional rivalries or any of the other petty human failings that beset any collaborative enterprise. The result, despite his personal humility, was to set himself and his company apart as a monastic élite beyond the scope of outside judgement.

To quote Jerzy Grotowski, a director who imposed monastic discipline with a severity much exceeding Stanislavsky's, "The main thing is not to be too noble." The Moscow Art Theatre paid the price for ignoring this principle when it went on tour in the 1960s and was discovered to be in an advanced state of institutional paralysis. Stanislavsky's own reputation remained unscathed by this exposure: worse, it became more saintly than ever. For the past twenty years, he has hovered over the scene as an ancestral shade, sniffing the incense of his true-believers, remote from the theatrical battlefield.

In England, where stage-directing has traditionally ranked (in Tyrone Guthrie's phrase) as "a semi-creative profession", his name has been most apt either to arouse vague reverence, or a robust rejection of the "system" along with the "Emperor's New Clothes". Stanislavsky never set foot in Britain, and it was not until 1958 – two years after the visit of the Berliner Ensemble – that London first saw the Moscow Art Theatre. The impact of that Chekhov season was breathtaking: but to the generation that had just discovered Brecht, it appeared in the guise of a stupendous anachronism. There is a further comparison to be drawn. Brecht has remained a vital presence partly because there were so many people around to document his human failings as well as his genius. No such chorus of candid friends rallied round the memory of Stanislavsky, who has either been idolized beyond recognition by his disciples, or caricatured beyond recognition by disgruntled colleagues (as by Bulgakov in *Black Snow*).

David Magarshack's biography first appeared in 1950, since when Stanislavsky scholarship has moved on. To note two obvious omissions: it gives no detailed picture of Stanislavsky's rehearsal procedures (such as appear in Nikolai M. Gorchakov's *Stanislavsky Directs*); nor any discussion of how this palpable class enemy and his élitist organization survived and adapted to post-revolutionary Russia. More on this subject in a moment.

The first point to make is that Magarshack has no personal axe to grind. He is that rare creature in the field of Stanislavsky studies – a disinterested observer, solely intent on delivering a faithful account of the facts. What he offers is a vigorous, highly readable narrative that succeeds in demystifying the workings of the MAT, and in removing Stanislavsky from his pedestal without cutting him down to size. To *My Life in Art*, Magarshack supplies the companion-piece – *A Life* – and as such it remains unsuperseded.

The personal characteristics it reveals are often those of a child who never grew up: a little boy, prone to catching colds, confined to the playroom and to the make-believe world of pushing cardboard heroes round the stage of a toy theatre. What Magarshack shows is that weaknesses were the source of Stanislavsky's power. Had he been less of a dreamer he would not have become an arch-realist. Had be been a naturally gifted actor, he would never have hammered out the system. If he has anything to teach us, it is not because he was blessed with inspired insight, but because he began as blind as everybody else.

In everything from its graphic descriptions of Stanislavsky's landmark productions to his enraptured first encounter with the American grapefruit, Magarshack's narrative carries the ring of truth. There is, however, a falling-off in candour and vividness in its foreshortened treatment of the later years: particularly in its guarded approach to politics, and to the relationship between Stanislavsky and his co-director, Nemirovich-Danchenko.

In 1969 I interviewed Magarshack and raised these points with him. His response was anything but guarded, and I quote it in the belief that, had he lived to undertake a revised edition of the book, he would have spoken his mind as he did to me!

Nemirovich-Danchenko was a typical academic; a toady towards the authorities. He went completely over to the Bolsheviks and they made him director of the classical theatres throughout Russia over Stanislavsky's head. So Stanislavsky finished with him: never spoke to him again. On the occasion of the thirtieth anniversary of the MAT they had a banquet and the two directors had to sit side by side. In Russian weddings when the guests get a bit tiddly they shout a toast as a sign for the bride and groom to kiss. This happened at the banquet, even though everybody knew that Stanislavsky and Nemirovich-Danchenko never spoke to each other, and the two poor chaps had to get up and kiss. After which they had the special performance of scenes from Chekhov with Stanislavsky playing Vershinin, and of course he collapsed in the middle of it and had his thrombosis.

His family firm was taken over by the State after the Revolution, but there was no evident change in the MAT during Stanislavsky's lifetime. There was trouble over Bulgakov's *Days of the Turbins*. They were going to ban it because it was fair to the Whites. So Stanislavsky went to the great boss himself, and Stalin said, "Well, why not? Put it on." But at the same time, the State gave Stanislavsky a secretary who followed him around everywhere, a CHEKA agent. He was always under surveillance; he couldn't move without the secretary's permission. The joke is that the same thing happened to Gorky. After the Kirov assassination Gorky wasn't even let out for a walk and in the end Stalin bumped him off by getting his doctors to light a bonfire in the garden and the smoke killed him. Then they executed the doctors for killing Gorky. Stalin always did that: he got someone executed, and then executed the executioner.

Stanislavsky was against dictatorship. He remembered the terrible days when he simply screamed at the actor. In the end he tried to produce without using a text. "This is the situation. Show me what you can do with it." He would just explain without imposing his will. He had great feelings of guilt for what he'd done to actors in the early days. He was obsessed, a man obsessed, that's all.

Part One

FIRST STEPS

CHAPTER I

KONSTANTIN ALEXEYEV, who under the stage name of Stanislavsky was to become famous as an actor and even more as a producer, was born on January 18th, 1863. In the same year occurred the death of one of the greatest actors on the Russian stage—Mikhail Shchepkin—whose principles of stage acting and production Stanislavsky was later to make into the corner-stone of his own system of acting and production.

Stanislavsky was the second son of a rich Moscow business man, the owner of a factory for making gold and silver thread. On his father's side his ancestors were peasants, and in the rigid pre-revolutionary Russian caste system Stanislavsky never belonged to the more privileged class of the nobility. His great-great-grandfather, Alexey Petrovich (he had no surname), was a serf in the village of Kostinaya in the province of Yaroslav. He was granted his freedom by his mistress and married a freed serf girl. In the late forties of the eighteenth century he migrated to Moscow where he is said to have obtained employment in a factory and invented a machine for the manufacture of gold thread, which laid the foundation of his family fortune. At any rate, his son, Semyon Alexeyevich, was in fact the owner of a gold and silver thread-making factory ; he was also the first to be given a surname, being known as Serebrennikov, a worker in silver ; but that surname did not descend to his children, who derived their surname of Alexeyev from the first known member of their family. Semyon Alexeyevich was already a man of substance, a Councillor of Commerce, who contributed as much as fifty thousand roubles (a huge sum in those days) to the war fund of 1812.

His son, Vladimir Semyonovich, was the founder of the firm of Alexeyev and Co., and his son, Sergey Vladimirovich, was Stanislavsky's father.

On his mother's side Stanislavsky's family antecedents are less well known. His mother's father, Vassily Yakovlev, was a rich man who owned quarries in Finland and who was responsible for supplying the big granite column for the memorial of Alexander I in Petersburg. During a visit to Paris he met a young French light comedy actress, Marie Varlet, and he brought her back to Petersburg as his mistress. He never married her, and after the birth of their second daughter, Stanislavsky's mother, she left him and went on the stage of the Mikhailovsky Theatre, the permanent French theatre in Petersburg. Stanislavsky's mother was first christened Adèle (her godfather was the famous Russian actor Sosnitsky), but after his separation from Marie Varlet Yakovlev legitimized his two daughters (quite a usual procedure in those days) and gave them different Christian names, Stanislavsky's mother being re-christened Yelisaveta. Yakovlev afterwards married a rich Moscow girl, Alexandra Bostanjoglo, but omitted to inform her that he was already the father of two daughters, which fact seems to have contributed to the strained relations between the two girls and their stepmother. Their relationship worsened considerably after Yakovlev's death and, unable to put up with her stepmother's treatment any longer, Yelisaveta, accompanied by her governess, ran away from home and joined her elder sister Maria in Moscow. Maria had by that time married her stepmother's brother. It was at their house that Yelisaveta first met Sergey Alexeyev, whom she married in 1859. She was eighteen at the time and Stanislavsky's father was twenty-three. The romance found little favour in the eyes of Stanislavsky's grandfather, as was perhaps to be expected, but nevertheless after his son's marriage the old man became reconciled to him and grew fond of his daughter-in-law.

According to the patriarchal customs of those days, Sergey Alexeyev and his bride set up house in his father's large Moscow mansion in Great Alexeyev Street, now Great Communist Street. In this house their first son Vladimir was born in 1861, and their second son Konstantin two years later. Altogether they had ten children, most of whom had inherited their French grandmother's love for the stage and later became members of Stanislavsky's amateur theatrical company known as the "Alexeyev Circle". After the October Revolution Vladimir worked with Stanislavsky in the opera studio of the Moscow Opera House (Bolshoy Theatre) and subsequently became a producer at the Stanislavsky Opera

House. Zinaida (Zina), Stanislavsky's eldest sister, who was born in 1865, became Stanislavsky's chief assistant and later a producer at the Stanislavsky Opera House. His second sister Anna, born in 1866, played the leading parts in the Alexeyev Circle. His third brother George, born in 1869, played the parts of old men in the Alexeyev Circle and later became the producer of the Kharkov People's Theatre. His fourth brother Boris, born in 1871, also played in the Alexeyev Circle and, for a time, in the Moscow Art Theatre. His third sister Maria, born in 1878, became an opera singer.

In view of all this dramatic talent in the family, it is surprising that so little is known of Marie Varlet herself. She seems to have been a rather quarrelsome, impulsive and flighty woman. After the death of his father, which was shortly after the birth of his first son Vladimir, Sergey Alexeyev invited her to stay in his family mansion. Her stay, however, was very short. What happened is not known, but it must have been something pretty unconventional, for so shocked was Stanislavsky's father that he drove her out of his home and forbade his wife to have anything to do with her ; and though she only died in 1885, she was never again admitted to her daughter's house and, as Stanislavsky's sister Anna records, "the relations of our parents towards her were surrounded by a kind of mystery."

Stanislavsky's father belonged to the merchant class, but in his time the life of the rich Moscow merchant was indistinguishable from the life of the Moscow nobility. Certain patriarchal customs were still observed : all church holidays and fasts were strictly kept, the whole family went to church regularly, and the children were given a strictly religious education. Stanislavsky, like the rest of his family, was extremely superstitious. Anna records that when Stanislavsky's elder brother was born and christened Vladimir after his grandfather, the old man observed that it meant that his grandson would soon take his place. And, to be sure, he died shortly afterwards. "After this occurrence," Anna writes in her memoir of Stanislavsky, "my father dared not christen any of the children after their parents. We were, generally speaking," Anna adds, "a terribly superstitious family, and all sorts of omens, dreams, and presentiments played a great part in the life of all of us."

Another of Stanislavsky's peculiarities that can be traced back to his early childhood was his dread of catching cold. This dread, which became almost a physical horror to him all through his life, was due to his mother's insistence that, when taken out for their regular morning walk, the children should be warmly wrapped up. The result was that even before leaving the house they were all covered with perspiration, and caught cold the moment they went out into the street. "Our morning walks," Anna records, "were a veritable torture to us. We· were always coughing, we always had bad colds, but we could do nothing with mother. She persisted in her belief that if a child was warmly dressed, it would not catch a cold." A close friend of his, the woman dramatic critic Lyubov Gurevich, writing of this peculiarity of Stanislavsky's character, tells of a case when, seeing a man sitting on a stone on a chilly day, he at once went up to him and said : "Why do you sit on this stone ? You're sure to catch sciatica." "Trained as a child to be afraid of catching colds," this friend adds, "Stanislavsky felt any drop in temperature as a danger signal not only for himself, but also for others, and many a time while walking with him, he would interrupt an interesting conversation with the question, 'Are you sure you're not cold ? Shall I run back for a shawl for you ?'" He was, Lyubov Gurevich adds, "very sweet in these little considerations for the health of his friends."

In spite of his splendid physique, Stanislavsky was a valetudinarian by nature, and this was no doubt due to the fact that he was a very sickly child. He suffered from rickets, was very often ill, and, in his mother's words, was "a difficult child". He started talking very late, and till the age of ten he could not pronounce the letters l and r. The clear enunciation of words gave him great trouble on the stage, too. As a baby he had difficulty in keeping his head up, and at the age of about nine months, when about to be vaccinated, his head suddenly dropped on the doctor's lancet, pricking his lower eyelid, on which the vaccination mark remained all his life. From the age of seven, however, he began to grow stronger, and by the time he was nine he became a thin but healthy child, with beautiful hair, cheerful and happy when playing games, though very shy and reserved in company. As his nurse Obukhova, who had nursed all the Alexeyev children, used to say, "He was nothing to boast about."

In 1863, the Alexeyevs moved from their family mansion in Great Alexeyev Street to a large house at the Red Gates, where Stanislavsky was to spend the next forty years of his life. It was at that house that his two sisters, Zina and Anna, who were to become his most enthusiastic assistants at the beginning of his stage career, were born. It was there, too, that the woman who probably exerted the most powerful influence on the development of Stanislavsky's imagination was engaged as a governess for the two elder Alexeyev boys. Stanislavsky was only four years old when Miss Snopov, a twenty-two year old girl who had just completed her studies at one of the Moscow high schools for girls, was interviewed by his mother, who decided that she was too young to be entrusted with the care of the children. The two boys, however, took a liking to the net made out of painted melon seeds she wore on her head, as was the fashion in those days, and Vladimir especially was vociferous in demanding the engagement of "the young lady with the pretty net". Mrs. Alexeyev, whose favourite little Vladimir was, changed her mind and engaged Miss Snopov, who stayed with the Alexeyevs for the next seven years. She seems to have possessed great imaginative powers herself and did much to develop them in Stanislavsky. She invented all sorts of games for the children and later on, when they began to take an interest in theatrical performances, she dramatised all sorts of stories for them. Anna mentions the occasion when the four elder children first realized that sooner or later they would have to die and were terribly upset about it. Miss Snopov, whom the children called Papusha, at once assured them that there existed "an elixir of life" which a person had only to find and take a few drops of at a time and he would never die or even grow old. So convincingly did she tell the children about this "elixir" that, in Anna's words, "it quietened and comforted us and we no longer thought of death as something terrible, for we were convinced that we could escape it if only we found the magic elixir."

It was Papusha, too, to whom Stanislavsky owed his first appearance on the stage. In *My Life in Art*, Stanislavsky refers to this incident of his childhood as "one of the most vivid memories of my far-away past," and states that he was about three or four years old at the time. Actually, he must have been at least six years old, since the "performance" took place in a dilapidated shed on his father's country estate of Lyubimovka which was only bought in 1869. It was Papusha who had thought of preparing a surprise for Stanislavsky's mother on her birthday on September 5th, by making the four elder children take part in a *tableau vivant* representing the four seasons. Little Konstantin was given the part of Winter. He was dressed in a long white coat covered with cotton-wool, and he wore a long beard also made of cotton-wool, and a white hat. Beside him was a real Christmas tree, also covered with bits of cotton-wool, and the floor round him, too, was covered thickly with this imaginary snow. To lend greater realism to the scene, Miss Snopov put a lighted end of a candle on a saucer near little Konstantin. But during the performance an unfortunate accident happened. According to Anna's account of it, Stanislavsky accidentally overturned the candle, and the cotton-wool on the floor and on his dress caught fire. Fortunately, the fire was immediately put out and the children were carried to the house. "Poor Papusha," Anna adds, "got a severe scolding, but then mother had such a terrible fright."

In recounting this incident about sixty years after it had taken place, Stanislavsky seems to ascribe to himself as a little boy feelings that could only have occurred to him much later in life. "I sat on the floor," he writes, "wrapped in a fur coat and wearing a fur cap and a long white beard and moustache which kept getting into my eyes, and I did not understand where to look or what to do. This feeling of awkwardness at senseless inaction on the stage, of which I was probably unconsciously aware even then, is something I am afraid of even now. After the applause, which I liked very much, I was put in a different position. In front of me a candle, hidden among fir-branches, was lighted to represent a camp-fire, and I was given a stick which I had to pretend to put on the fire. 'Just pretend to put it into the fire,' I was told. 'Just pretend! Understand?' And I was severely warned against putting the stick in the fire. But to me this seemed silly. Why pretend, if I could put the stick really and truly on the fire? The moment the curtain was drawn, I was filled with curiosity and wonder and stretched out my hand with the stick to the fire! It seemed to me to be a most logical and natural action, an action which had some sense. But what was even more natural was that the cotton-wool caught fire. I was seized and carried across the yard to the nursery, where I cried bitterly."

That evening, Stanislavsky claims, left two impressions on his mind : the pleasant feeling of success and of the satisfaction of behaving naturally on the stage, and the unpleasant feeling of failure and of the awkwardness of sitting on the stage without doing anything.

The main reason for his first "failure" on the stage Stanislavsky ascribes to his "stubbornness". He goes on to point out that this "inborn stubbornness" of his had both a good and a bad influence on his artistic development. He had always to fight against it. To illustrate his stubbornness as a child, Stanislavsky tells of his first serious quarrel with his father over his aunt Vera, his father's elder sister. After the death of her mother, Vera had practically brought up her brother and was the only member of Stanislavsky's father's family who was a great favourite with the Alexeyev children. Reprimanded at the breakfast table for being naughty, little Konstantin, who wanted to show that he was not afraid of his father, uttered the senseless threat that he would not let him see "Auntie Vera". His father told him that his threat was silly because he could not possibly prevent him from seeing his sister. Realizing that what he had said was silly and getting even angrier with himself, Konstantin kept repeating the same phrase over and over again, getting more and more emphatic as his father grew more and more angry with him. His father at last stopped answering him and resumed reading his paper. But noticing how irritated his father really was, Konstantin kept repeating the phrase, "And I shan't let you see Auntie Vera," till his father lost his temper and threatened to make him go without dinner. "And I shan't let you see Auntie Vera!" Konstantin repeated in despair, mimicking his father's tone. "Think what you're saying!" his father shouted, throwing the newspaper on the table. "And I shan't let you see Auntie Vera!" Konstantin went on repeating, in the belief that by repeating that phrase he would at any rate bring the scene to a close. His father flushed, his lips began to quiver, but, Stanislavsky writes, he controlled himself and left the room quickly, uttering "the terrible phrase,"— "You're not my son!" But the moment his father had left the room and he had won the fight, Konstantin relented and burst into tears, shouting, "I'm sorry, father, I shan't do it again!" But his father had already gone out and did not hear his words.

"I can remember all the inner steps of my childish ecstasy during that scene," Stanislavsky writes, "as though it happened yesterday ; and in recalling them I again experience a nagging pain in my heart."

But such scenes with his father were very rare. Sergey Alexeyev was an exceedingly gentle and kind-hearted man whom his children did not fear. His wife, on the other hand, was very much

7

feared by the children. She was very quick-tempered, made scenes on the slightest provocation, shouted at the children and scolded them ; but her anger was of short duration and she usually felt sorry for not controlling her temper. As a child, Konstantin was a great worry to her with his never-ending illnesses, his gawky manners, his shyness, and his obstinacy. Vladimir, on the other hand, was a much more sociable child, who never refused to entertain the guests by reciting poems or playing the piano. Mrs. Alexeyev was a very good pianist, and her musical abilities seemed to have been inherited by her eldest son. The first music master of the two boys was a Swede by the name of Wilborg, who joined the nursemaids, governesses and tutors with whom the house at the Red Gates seemed to swarm. He began giving music lessons to Vladimir and Konstantin when they were only seven and six years old respectively. But Konstantin used every possible opportunity to scamp his music lessons. What he seemed particularly to dislike was practising on the piano. When left alone with the elderly Swiss governess of his sisters, Mme. Schmidt, with whom he was supposed to play piano duets, he would begin by pestering her to let him go, and when the conscientious governess refused, he would blow out the candles and rush out of the room, leaving the old lady to grope her way to the door in the dark. He was almost as bad at learning poems by heart, although the children were expected to recite poems at the special family gatherings during the holidays. Thus, when Miss Snopov once chose one of Krylov's fables, *The Two Casks*, for him to learn by heart, Konstantin stubbornly refused to do so. The governess tried again and again to make him say the first line of the fable, but all she got out of him was, "There were two casks, one full of wine, the other empty—well that's enough, isn't it ? " He never learnt it.

Stanislavsky retained this aversion for learning things by heart to the very end of his life. For an actor this was a great handicap, but he never overcame it.

But if he hated learning things by heart and playing the piano, the two things his elder brother excelled in, he very soon found something in which he, too, excelled and in which he became the undisputed ringleader among the other children. For where games and play-acting were concerned, there was no trace of his usual reserve. At first, the children imitated the tricks of the boy acrobats accompanying the hurdy-gurdy men who came to play and perform in their courtyard. Then there were the trained dogs, or the old Italian organ-grinder who sang arias from Italian operas, or the Persian with his tambourine and his little performing monkey, who went through a whole repertoire of different characters, from a Cossack to an old woman fetching water from a well. All this was eagerly watched by the children, who then went through the different "items" one by one in their nursery or the yellow drawing-room. Very soon the children were taken to the Italian opera, the circus and the ballet. This considerably increased their repertoire. There was no longer any question of performing all sorts of "silly things". Now they were going to have "real" performances just as at the Bolshoy Theatre (the Moscow opera house) or at Ciniselli's Circus, or at the ballet. The children were usually taken to a show at Easter and Christmas, and those days were real red-letter days for them. Stanislavsky remembered every detail of those marvellous days to the end of his life. The excitement of the children before the announcement of the visit to the theatre came, the terrible suspense of waiting for their mother to dress (their father did not as a rule accompany them), the endless preparations, the baskets of food and the cannisters of hot tea, the arrival of the large carriage, the constant badgering of the footman to run into the house to see what time it was, the arrival at last of their mother, who had been kept supervising the feeding of baby. "Oh dear, mummy has stopped on the stairs again talking to nurse ! What are they talking about ? " At last their mother takes her seat in the carriage, but instead of telling the driver to start, she begins adjusting their clothes and making sure that their fur coats are properly buttoned up. On arrival at the Bolshoy Theatre, there is another delay. The governess takes such a long time getting the younger children out, and even when they are at last in their box, a lot of precious time is wasted in taking off their hats, coats, shawls and so on. The elder children knew the dancers and ballerinas by name. Each of them had his own favourite. "Yours has come ! " they would announce the arrival in a whisper, nudging the lucky one. The opera or ballet was watched with silent concentration ; for it was not only a question of enjoying the dancing or the performance : they had also to remember the scenery, the costumes, and the plot, and at the same time find their own favourites among the actors, circus performers, and dancers. Stanislavsky had two particular

9

favourites : Elvira, the equestrienne at the circus, and Stanislav-skaya, one of the ballerinas at the opera, from whom his stage-name was derived, though—as will appear—not directly. But his first public tribute of admiration he paid to Elvira. Stanis-lavsky was only eight or nine at the time. He and his brother liked to sit in the box overlooking the arena, from which they could see what was happening behind the scenes and get "a personal bow" from the artist as he or she was running off the arena. At one of the performances, Stanislavsky rushed out of the box on to the arena just as Elvira was running off it after taking her last bow, seized the hem of her short tarlatan dress, kissed it and, looking confused and flushed, rushed back to his seat. The other children could not help envying this heroic deed of his, while his parents could not get over their astonish-ment and kept asking him "What's the matter, Kostya ? What did you do that for, Kostya ? "

In *My Life in Art*, Stanislavsky describes the scene at some length. "The band," he writes, "struck up the familiar polka—it is *her* turn. *Danse de châle* will be performed by the whole com-pany and Miss Elvira on her horse. Here she is herself. My friends know my secret : it is my special item, my girl, and all the privileges are mine, too : the best opera-glasses, more room, everyone whispering congratulations in my ear. And, to be sure, she is very sweet today. At the end of her act, Elvira comes out to take her bow and runs past me. This proximity excites me, and I feel I have to do something out of the ordinary ; I rush out of the box, kiss her dress, run back quickly to my seat and sit down like one sentenced to death, afraid to stir and ready to burst into tears. My friends congratulate me, but behind me father laughs. "Congratulations ! It's all settled ! Kostya is engaged ! When's the wedding ? "

In recounting this incident, Stanislavsky is again rather vague about the time when it took place. He seems to place it at least seven years later than when it actually occurred.

CHAPTER II

THE OPERA, THE BALLET, and the circus played a great role in the development of Stanislavsky's stage career. They supplied him with the first impetus to apply his experiences as a spectator to the more difficult discipline of a performer. At first, of course, his attempts were purely imitative. He blindly copied the actors he admired, whether it was a circus performer, a dancer, or a singer. With the legitimate stage (in those early days there was only one dramatic theatre—the Maly or Little Theatre—in Moscow) Stanislavsky became acquainted later. But the first private theatrical performance in the house at the Red Gates was organized not by Stanislavsky, but by his parents. It took place when Stanislavsky was only about seven, and both his mother and father took part in it. His father played a batman and his mother the wife of an army officer. The scenery, the rehearsals and the performance itself made a great impression on the children and no doubt stimulated their desire to do something of the kind themselves. It was not till after the two elder boys had been sent to school, however, that the actual performances in the Alexeyev family began in earnest.

Stanislavsky was sent to school, the Fourth Classical Secondary School in Moscow, at the age of twelve. Before that he had been educated in the conventional manner of the sons of rich people. At first he was put in the charge of Papusha, then different tutors made their appearance in the classroom on the ground floor of the house. Teachers of music and dancing were engaged. The dancing master, Yermolov, a former dancer of the ballet and an uncle of the famous Russian actress Yermolova, a tall, spare old man, wearing a frock-coat and white gloves, with a red nose which was always covered in snuff, used to bring with him an ancient fiddler who could only play a very limited number of tunes. Stanislavsky was not particularly fond of dancing, but the lessons came in useful for his first fancy-dress ball. As usual, it was his elder brother who was dressed in the more resplendent costume of a Greek evzone, while Konstantin had to go dressed as a stevedore, and his mother's unfairness in choosing such a splendid rig-out for her favourite son was only emphasized by the fact that Vladimir also sported a little dagger. All the same, Stanislavsky was a much better dancer than his brother, which to a certain extent restored the balance and also raised him in his mother's estimation.

When they were still young children, Stanislavsky and his elder brother shared a bedroom with their two sisters and the nurse. The bedroom was dimly lit by the little lamp burning in front of the icon and shaded by a green lampshade. The children used to get up at about nine o'clock, and after seeing off their father and watching him being driven off to the office they went to their nursery. About twelve o'clock, they were taken out for their daily walk, when the ritual of being warmly wrapped up in fur coats and shawls was religiously observed. They were accompanied on their walks by two governesses and two nursemaids. Later on they got up an hour earlier and immediately after breakfast went to their classroom. At twelve o'clock they had lunch, and after lunch went for a walk, usually to Kusnetsky Bridge where they bought the pictures of their favourite actors. Stanislavsky had a whole album of picture postcards of the famous Italian actor, Ernesto Rossi, who played a great part in his artistic life.

Next to the classroom, the two boys had a well-equipped gymnasium, where they spent hours with their games masters. The gymnasium was also the place where Stanislavsky loved to do his homework. He would climb up to the very top of one of the ladders and sit there for hours. The two boys were also taught fencing, Vladimir finding it very difficult to fence with Stanislavsky, who was much taller than he and always held his rapier too high. All these bodily exercises, so necessary for an actor, Stanislavsky was fortunate enough to learn at a time when he hardly dreamt of the stage as his future career. In those early days, too, Stanislavsky and his brother began to learn riding, and Stanislavsky became a particularly proficient rider, which also did not fail to restore him in the estimation of his mother, who was an excellent horsewoman herself.

It was during this early period that the incident with the two "armies" described by Stanislavsky in *My Life in Art* occurred.

Stanislavsky seems to connect this incident with the introduction of conscription in Russia. His brother, however, ascribes it to the stories their father used to tell them about how as a little boy he played at soldiers with peasant children. Both Konstantin and Vladimir were overjoyed when they were given permission to organize their own "army" in the country. Stanislavsky was about nine or ten at the time. They organized two "armies" of about a dozen "soldiers" each. As Stanislavsky points out, he looked on this game, too, as a kind of performance, an attempt to create an imaginary kind of life which did not resemble the life he was used to at home. When the two boys grew up, Miss Snopov, their governess, was replaced by a Swiss tutor, Eugene Vincent, an excellent fencer, rider, and sportsman. He became a general favourite, and he taught the two boys riding and shooting. Stanislavsky was never fond of hunting, and he did not take any part in the shooting expeditions organized in the country. Vincent also supervised the education of the boys at home and taught them French and German. Stanislavsky hated German and never became proficient in it.

Stanislavsky's actual preoccupation with the theatre only began after he had been sent to school. Classical subjects were in the ascendant in the school curriculum of those days and they were taught in a way that was least likely to appeal to Stanislavsky. The headmaster and the second master in his first school were Germans and both of them severe disciplinarians and pedants. The headmaster had a curious manner of interspersing his broken Russian with "sirs". "You, sir, what, sir, did you do that for, sir?" was the way he talked. He enjoyed no authority among the pupils, partly because they soon discovered that his knowledge of Latin, which he was supposed to teach them, was not particularly deep, and partly because he had all sorts of extraordinary mannerisms, such as scratching his left ear from behind his neck with the back of a penholder which he held in his right hand. The second master seems to have had the manners of a typical German sergeant-major, and the scarifying figure of a villain in a melodrama. His favourite pastime was to steal up noiselessly to a boy, his left hand in his pocket and his right hand grasping his long black beard, and bowl him over with a tremendous barrack-room shout. On entering the classroom he would roar at the top of his voice for the boys to stand up and then roar at them to sit down, and all this they had to do just as if they were carrying out an order on a parade-ground. He would repeat these orders ten or more times just by way of amusement.

Stanislavsky hated both the rigid school discipline and the pedantic teaching of the classical languages. The Latin irregular verbs, in particular, he could not master. He used to write out pages and pages of these irregular verbs, but he could never learn them, and in the end they became a real bugbear to him. Fortunately, the two boys were removed from this school after three years and placed in a more humane establishment. But Stanislavsky never overcame his hatred of Latin irregular verbs. His brother remembered him as "a giant among dwarfs, handsome, his cheeks glowing with colour, in a black uniform, with the tie protruding from under his stiff collar, looking frightened and confused. Konstantin," his brother adds, "was always shy and timid at school. He had no friends in his form and only made friends with pupils from my form, such as Fedya Kashdamanov and Shidlovsky."

Of these two friends, Fedya Kashdamanov, or "Fif", as Stanislavsky called him, was to exert the greatest influence on Stanislavsky. Reserved by nature, Stanislavsky never throughout his life made any real friends. There were only two exceptions to this rule : Fedya Kashdamanov and, many years later, Leopold Sulerzhitsky.

Fedya was the son of a teacher of the Fourth Moscow Secondary School, who was engaged as a Russian tutor to the two Alexeyev boys, and became a friend of the family. Through him the two boys later became acquainted with his two sons, Fedya becoming a great friend of Stanislavsky's, and Sergey a friend of Vladimir's. Fedya was a sickly boy (he died of consumption at the age of twenty-six), and as it was nearer for him to go to school from Alexeyev's house, Stanislavsky's mother invited him to live with them and sleep in the same room as Stanislavsky and his brother. Fedya was not of very prepossessing appearance, but he was a good musician. He played the violin and the piano, and he took an active part in all the performances at the home of the Alexeyevs, which Stanislavsky usually produced.

The first performances of the Alexeyev children were devoted to the ballet. The "production" of the scenes from the different ballets was at first mostly in the hands of their governess, Miss Snopov. One of them was *The Naiad and the Fisherman*. The scenery was provided by the different plants—palms, fig-trees and other exotic trees—in the house, which were brought to the yellow drawing-room to represent a wood. A long piece of blue muslin represented a brook, and a pile of logs a well. Stanislavsky's elder sister, Zina, acted the naiad and Stanislavsky himself the fisherman. Zina, squatting on her haunches, wore a thin white dress, and flowers in her loose hair. Stanislavsky wore white stockings, slippers, silk knickerbockers, dark blue and yellow, red and black ribbons, a white shirt with a soft collar, a black amulet on a black ribbon on his chest, and a pointed blue hat on his head. Over one of his shoulders was thrown a fisherman's net. The naiad appeared from the well, and the fisherman declared his love for her in dumb-show, expressing his suffering in the way ballet dancers do, that is to say, by theatrical gestures. The naiad would not be wooed by him, but did her best to increase his suffering by neither rejecting him outright nor accepting him. This scene was highly popular among the spectators, but in recalling this first appearance of his as an actor, Stanislavsky declared that he did not like it. "I had to pretend to be in love," he writes, "I had to kiss my sister, and I felt ashamed. It was much jollier to have to kill, or save someone, or sentence someone to death. But the chief trouble was that in this ballet a dance was put in which had nothing to do with it, a dance which we were just at the time trying to learn with our dancing master. That was too much like a lesson and that is why I disliked it."

Other ballet scenes the children performed in the yellow drawing-room were taken from *The Magic Flute*, a fairy tale in which the low-born suitor of a rich peasant possessed himself of a magic flute and made the reluctant parents of his sweetheart dance till they consented to his marriage with their daughter ; and *Satanilla* or *Love and Hell*, in which Stanislavsky played Count Fabio, a young man who was always in love. Being fond of money, Fabio never had enough of it, and eventually he sold his soul to the devil—a she-devil, as it happens—who stayed with him as his page. One of the scenes in this last ballet was a slave market where Fabio's beloved, a peasant girl by the name of Lily, is bought by Fabio with the help of Satanilla. After the performances there were usually dances, some of them invented by the children themselves. In one of them Stanislavsky helped his sister Zina to jump up into the air. He held her by the waist, while she stretched out her hands, stood on one foot, and held the other suspended backwards in the air. Stanislavsky had to turn her round by the waist. Then Zina stood on her toes, just like a real ballerina, and in the end assumed some ballet pose, while Stanislavsky released her and himself stood in the pose of a "cherub". To take their bow they all ran out "just as they did in the Bolshoy Theatre."

But the ballet was altogether too artificial an art to satisfy the boy who was later to become one of the great originators of realism on the stage. After striking up his friendship with Fedya Kashdamanov, in whom he at once divined a kindred spirit, Stanislavsky turned his attention to circus performances. Before that, he had been on the stage for the first time. A friend of the family who was a ballerina once invited the four Alexeyev children and their mother to go on the stage and get acquainted with its wonders. That visit had left a great impression on the nine-year-old Konstantin. There he could examine the scenery at close quarters, he could see the enormous "whale" from the ballet of *The Hunchback Horse*, he actually saw the trapdoor open and someone appear from the mysterious regions which he was wont to associate with the magic appearances of hobgoblins and devils. He could reproduce nothing of the kind in the yellow-drawing-room of his home. It was much easier to create the illusion of a circus arena. So he and Fedya a few years later began taking careful notes of the different circus turns and "performing" some of them at home. There was one such turn with a barrel. One of them hid in the barrel, the barrel was overturned and then rolled out of the room. Konstantin and Fedya also represented clowns (Stanislavsky was a great admirer of clowns), acrobats and performing horses. The imaginary performing horse was given the task of finding a buried handkerchief, and it reared and pranced round the room. Its trainer touched its knees with his riding-whip and it seemed to bow rather reluctantly. Then Fedya and Konstantin pretended to be a wheelbarrow, a turn in which the latest tricks of circus clowns were faithfully copied. Another of their turns was that of an engine driver (the railways were still being built in Russia at the time). These turns were varied by others performed by Zina and Anna, representing equestriennes jumping through hoops covered with paper. Stanislavsky's elder brother accompanied all these turns on the piano, and he sometimes also did juggling turns. To Stanislavsky's great disgust, however, he was highly unreliable. In the middle of his turn he would shatter the illusion of a circus performance by bursting into loud laughter and shouting : "What silly fools ! They imagine it's a circus ! Why, have you ever seen an equestrienne riding on a chair and then running round the arena ? Do you really think you're deceiving anyone ?" Poor Stanislavsky stood behind the curtains of the yellow drawing-room doing his best by gesture and mimicry to persuade his brother not to ruin the "real" performance, and afterwards threatening never to let him do any turn at all. "We've worked a whole week on this performance," he would tell him, "and you —why, it's disgraceful ! I've spent two or three days writing the handbills in block capitals and—and think of the time I've wasted on your moustache ! And you did nothing at all ! "

But the truth, of course, was that Vladimir was right. It was not a "real" performance. The whole thing demanded the exercise of too much imagination on the part of the audience, and if the performers themselves did not believe in the reality of what they were doing, how could one expect the audience to do so ? Thus, even as a child, Stanislavsky was preoccupied with one of the chief principles of what was later to be known as his "system": truth, that is, artistic truth, and belief. Without truth and belief there could be no stage art. It was not enough for him to believe that a chair was really a horse : everyone—performer and spectator—had to believe in it, for it was only then that the performance ceased to be a game and became "the real thing".

"The real thing ! " In those early years it merely meant a faithful reproduction of the scenery and costumes of the opera and ballet stage, and that was out of the question in the yellow drawing-room of his home. There was one way, though, in which it could be done even in the yellow drawing-room ; it could be done with puppets ! So, paradoxically enough, the boy Stanis-lavsky in his search for real stage illusion turned to the puppet theatre.

Here Stanislavsky's school-friend Fedya came in very useful. He had friends who already had a well-equipped puppet theatre, and it was from those friends that he obtained some of the scenery for Stanislavsky's puppet stage. Stanislavsky, as he himself records, made it quite clear to Fedya that the puppet theatre did not by any means signify a betrayal of the circus, for he still hoped one day to be the owner of his own real circus. "It is merely," he said, "a sad necessity."

The puppet theatre was a great success, for now Stanislavsky could not only reproduce real stage effects, such as a sinking ship, or the escape of thieves from prison, or a storm scene with real thunder and lightning (all these scenes were taken from different ballets), but also have a real box-office with the sale of tickets and an audience which, though it still consisted of his brothers and sisters, his governesses, and relations and acquaintances, was a real audience inasmuch as they had to pay for their seats. Besides, there was all the excitement of a "real" theatre : scenery had to be copied from the theatre and made, tickets had to be printed, a box-office had to be constructed, the puppet theatre had to be built and negotiations had to be conducted with the carpenter who did odd jobs at the Alexeyev house. There was so much to do and, as Stanislavsky himself relates, there were "the damned lessons at school" which somehow or other had to be sacrificed to the cause of dramatic art. Stanislavsky soon found a way of doing it. His book was on his desk, but inside the drawer were the bits of paper on which the scenery for the next production had to be drawn. The bits of paper were carefully covered up with the book or put inside it, and the moment the teacher came into the classroom a page was turned and everything was hidden. He used the margins of the textbooks to draw his first *mise-en-scènes* : if the teacher caught him, he pretended that they were just geometrical drawings.

On the puppet stage, Stanislavsky put on a large number of operas and ballets, or rather, as he explains, scenes from them. One act from the opera *Corsair*, for instance, in which the sinking of a ship in a storm was realistically reproduced, enjoyed particular popularity. At the beginning of the act the sea was calm and the sun was shining, but as night drew on a storm rose, the ship sank, the heroes swam about in the raging waves, a lighthouse suddenly loomed out of the darkness, throwing a bright light, they were saved, the storm passed, the clouds dispersed, the moon shone, a prayer was said, and the sun rose again. In a scene from *Don Juan*, flames shot out of the trap-door when the hero was precipitated into hell, the house was wrecked, and the whole scene became transformed into a blazing inferno with clouds of smoke and flames of fire. Very often the scenery got burnt in the process, and as Stanislavsky's brother records, there was so much smoke in the room after the performance that the audience had to leave ; but "the satisfaction was general".

The puppet theatre was placed on a large table in the doorway leading to another room, so that the audience in the drawing-room was kept quite separate from the "performers". The box-office was opened a few minutes before the beginning of the performance, the cashier being one of Stanislavsky's sisters.

But the puppet theatre did not entirely oust the ballet. Stanislavsky, who at that time seemed to be fond of classical dances, often gave special performances with his brother in the yellow drawing-room, each of them specialising in a different kind of figure, Stanislavsky hurling himself into the air and at the same time performing a particularly difficult body-twist.

Very soon Stanislavsky gave up these theatrical games, which undoubtedly had a great influence on the later development of his genius, in favour of "the real thing". The man who played one of the most important parts in attracting Stanislavsky to the stage was a young student by the name of Lvov, who had been engaged as a tutor for the two elder Alexeyev boys when they first began to go to school. It was Lvov, a mathematician and an amateur actor, who was the first to discover Stanislavsky's talent for the stage and who awakened in Stanislavsky the love for drama. Lvov was known to be a "red" and Stanislavsky's parents were rather apprehensive of his influence on their sons, but they respected him as an intelligent and well-read man and they grew attached to him. Lvov and his friends ran their own amateur theatre, the tiny Secretaryov Theatr in a Moscow suburb. Stanislavsky often visited this theatre, the repertoire of which included serious plays as well as farces. The acting of these amateurs was atrocious, so bad indeed that, according to Stanislavsky's elder brother, "it was difficult to restrain oneself from laughing when watching a play or from crying when watching a farce." However, among these amateurs there was a medical student who seemed to possess a spark of genuine talent and whom Stanislavsky greatly admired. This actor's name was Markov, but as he was, like Stanislavsky, a great admirer of the ballerina Stanislavskaya, he assumed the stage name of Stanislavsky. Later on, when Stanislavsky began to appear regularly on the amateur stage, playing chiefly in light French operettas, he felt the need of a stage name so as to dissociate his family from the rather outrageous parts he played, and remembering the actor he had once admired in the Secretaryov Theatre, who was no longer acting by that time, he, too, assumed the stage name of Stanislavsky.

It was Lvov who organized the first amateur theatrical performance at the Alexeyev country house in Lyubimovka in which Stanislavsky appeared on the stage for the first time. At that time Stanislavsky's father had built a theatre on the site of the old shed where Stanislavsky's appearance in the *tableau vivant* had had such a disastrous finale. The auditorium had a gallery which ran along two sides of it. The building also had four rooms—the dressing-rooms—with a special entrance.

CHAPTER III

THE FIRST PERFORMANCE at the theatre in Lyubimovka, which was to play so important a part in what was soon to be known as the Alexeyev Circle, took place on September 5th, 1877, the birthday of Stanislavsky's mother. Four plays were put on : *The Provincial Lady*, a two-act comedy by Turgenev, *Which of the Two*, a one-act comedy, *The Old Mathematician* or *The Appearance of a Comet in a Provincial Town*, a one-act farce, and *A Cup of Tea*, another one-act farce. The plays were produced by Lvov. The actors included Stanislavsky's father, Stanislavsky himself, his two brothers and sisters, his two cousins Bostanjoglo, Lvov, and a few friends. Stanislavsky played in *The Old Mathematician* and *A Cup of Tea*.

According to Stanislavsky's sister Anna, his début as an actor was very successful. Stanislavsky himself, however, was even at the time highly dissatisfied with his performance in the two plays. On the night of the performance he wrote down his first criticism of his acting in what was afterwards to be known as his *Artistic Notes*. "In the part of the Mathematician I played coldly and languidly, without a spark of talent, though I was not worse than the others. In *A Cup of Tea* I was successful. The audience laughed, but that was not because I had made them laugh. It was Muzil[1] who had made them laugh, for I had copied even his voice." This first note Stanislavsky made of his own acting is significant, for it laid the foundations of his future work on the stage. He kept up this regular criticism of his own acting all through his career as an actor, and it was this habit of unsparing self-criticism which gradually led him to examine analytically the laws of acting and eventually to evolve his famous "system". His first début on the stage, therefore, is doubly important : it heralded the first appearance on the footboards of an actor who was to become one of the foremost actors on the Russian stage, and it

[1] A comic actor of the Maly Theatre whom Stanislavsky admired.

brought to light that constant dissatisfaction with his artistic attainments which was in the end to make Stanislavsky into one of the greatest reformers of the art of acting.

At first, during the whole period of his appearance on the amateur stage in fact, Stanislavsky went on copying one actor after another, in spite of his growing conviction that to copy the acting of a famous player was one of the deadly sins of the stage. Only gradually did he shift the emphasis from copying the living actor to copying living men, that is, from blind imitation of life on the stage to the direct observation of life and the re-embodiment of the observed facts in the character he was representing on the stage. It was only when he had subconsciously learnt to rely on direct observation that he noticed to his surprise that the externally observed facts led him by some unknown process to an inner conception of the stage character. Having reached this second step in his evolution as an actor, Stanislavsky then spent the rest of his life in trying to find a way of solving the much more difficult problem of achieving the miracle of stage embodiment by reversing this process and going from the internal to the external. But at the very beginning of his career as an actor and producer, Stanislavsky could not help being impressed by the fact that when copying his favourite actor in *A Cup of Tea*, everything seemed easy to him, while when he had no one to copy in *The Old Mathematician* everything seemed to go wrong. In such parts he had to think of many different actors he knew for the different situations in the play, and his part was, therefore, made up of a host of different and very often incompatible mannerisms of the actors he copied.

"My part," he writes, "was transformed into a quilt sewn of different bits of material and I felt wretched on the stage." In that first period of his work on the stage, the art of acting sometimes seemed to him easy, but at other times very difficult ; sometimes it gave him joy, at other times it became unbearable. "I was not mistaken," he writes in *My Life in Art*, "for there is no greater happiness than to feel yourself at home on the stage, and there is nothing worse than to feel yourself a stranger on it. There is nothing more painful than the duty of embodying at all costs what is unfamiliar to you, what you are only vaguely aware of, what exists outside you. Even today these contradictions alternately delight and distress me."

What is so significant in Stanislavsky's accounts of his début on the stage is the passionate love of the theatre which he showed even at that early age. Though in his account of that performance in *My Life in Art* he makes the mistake of anticipating by five years his meeting with Gremislavsky, the future make-up man of the Moscow Art Theatre, whom he only met for the first time in July, 1882, there can be little doubt of the authenticity of his description of his own exeitement on the night of the performance. The very smell of the stage made him dizzy. He would certainly have understood Ellen Terry's words : "Come through one of the doors and sniff the perfume of our altars—the dust of our Divine Stage—and you shall be happy and be our real servant." He nearly fell out of the carriage on his way to Lyubimovka from Moscow as he inhaled the smell of the theatrical wigs and make-up he was carrying in a big hat-box on his knees. Then the hubbub in the dressing-rooms, the screams of laughter of the excited amateur actors as they failed to recognize each other in their make-up, their friends who were always in the way and who filled the little rooms with cigarette smoke, and, finally, the brass-band playing a march, to the strains of which the invited spectators, carrying lanterns, made their way to the little newly built theatre. A sudden stillness fell in the dressing-rooms ; the actors exchanged uneasy smiles. "But," writes Stanislavsky, "inside me everything seemed to seethe and rejoice. I rushed about, getting in everybody's way. My heart thumped. . . . At last I was on the stage, where I felt excellently. Something inside me seemed to drive me on, to inspire me, and I took the bit between my teeth and rushed through the whole of the play. I did not attempt to create my part. I was creating my own art, my own stage action. I was making a present of my genius to the spectators. I thought myself a great actor, displaying his genius for the admiration of the crowd. . . . Words and gestures flew out of me with amazing rapidity. My breath failed me, I could hardly utter the words of my part, and I mistook this over-ebullient nervousness and lack of control for real inspiration. While playing, I was convinced that the audience was entirely in my power."

At the end of the play, however, Stanislavsky was surprised to find that all the other actors seemed to avoid him. He had to swallow his pride and go "fishing for compliments" from the producer.

"It wasn't so bad," said Lvov. "Quite nice, in spite of everything."

What, Stanislavsky asked himself, did "in spite of everything" mean?

"From that moment," he declares, "I understood the meaning of artistic doubt."

After his performance in the second comedy, *The Old Mathematician*, in which he did not feel at his ease at all, the producer, to his surprise, congratulated him, saying "That's much better!"

What did it mean? When he felt all right on the stage he got no praise at all, but when he felt distinctly ill at ease he was congratulated! There must, therefore, be some difference between the actor's state of mind on the stage and the impression the audience got of his playing. That was the first discovery Stanislavsky claims to have made during his début on the stage. Another discovery was that it was not at all easy to recognize one's own artistic faults. To be able to gauge the effect one's acting had on the audience seemed to be a science in itself. It was only after a great number of enquiries that Stanislavsky found out that, in spite of his "inspiration", he had spoken in so low a voice that the spectators wanted to shout at him, "Louder!" and so fast that they wanted to shout, "Slower, please!" Besides, he flung his hands about with such rapidity and his feet carried him with such terrific speed from one end of the stage to the other, that no one on the stage or in the audience could make out what he was doing. The last thing he had learnt that night was the meaning of an actor's vanity, which gave rise to hatred, gossip and envy.

It seems hardly likely that Stanislavsky should have learnt it all at the very first performance in the Lyubimovka theatre. He was always very vague about dates, and it is much more probable that, in summarizing his first impressions of the stage, he had in mind the whole of the first period of his acting in what was soon to be known as the Alexeyev Circle of amateur actors. He did his best to overcome his shortcomings during the subsequent performances in which he took part. He tried to speak in a loud voice and not to wave his arms about, but he made things worse : he was accused of grimacing, of overacting, of showing no sense of proportion. In trying to control his hands, he seemed to lose control of the muscles of his face. As for the sense of proportion, of course he understood what it meant, but he was unable to achieve it.

In the meantime, he left his first school for the Lazarevsky

Institute, where he continued to be plagued with Latin irregular verbs. He paid visits to the theatre, the opera, the ballet, and, of course, Lvov's private theatricals at the Secretaryov Theatre. Occasionally, though very rarely, a play was put on at Lyubimovka. To while away the time between these rare performances at home, he and his friend Fedya dressed up as drunken beggars and frightened the passengers at the railway station, or as gipsies, or—and this time it was more than a lark—as monks tempted by the devil. A description of Stanislavsky in the part of the devil—Mephistopheles—has been preserved by Sergey Mamontov, the son of the Russian millionaire Savva Mamontov, a railway magnate with a taste for opera, who had his own private opera theatre. "A whole crowd of people in fancy dress invaded our house one evening. A long line of Capuchin monks, their faces hidden in their cowls, entered our drawing-room. Suddenly, a man dressed in red, with two feathers stuck in his cap, appeared among the black cassocks of the monks and—Mephistopheles stood before us. The monks went on walking quietly in procession round the room, while Mephistopheles was thrown into terrible contortions as he tried to get nearer to the holy men in an attempt to seduce them. His youthful figure was amazingly slender and supple, and every movement was carefully thought out, expressive and beautiful. The artistic taste of the Muscovites at that time was far below that of today, but even then they could not help feeling something out of the common in the acting of Mephistopheles, and followed breathlessly every movement of the clever devil. Soon a certain hesitation could be observed among the monks : the spell cast by the devil was evidently beginning to work. Suddenly Mephistopheles drew himself up to his full height and stretched out his hand in an imperious, magic gesture. The black hoods fell off the faces of the monks, some of them being transformed into pretty ballerinas in short muslin dresses, and the rest into young swells. They all began to dance, and gradually the ballet turned into a bacchanalian gallop which threw the spectators into a frenzy of admiration. Even at the time I felt that the whole mime had been devised by a highly talented producer. Soon the tired Mephistopheles threw off his mask and we all recognized Konstantin Alexeyev, a relation of ours and a student of the Lazarevsky Institute . . . "

At this time Stanislavsky was already sporting a moustache. It was still small, but he was rather proud of it, and as many years later this moustache is going to play rather an important role in one of his Shakespearean parts, it is worth mentioning it here. He was sixteen, very tall, and with a large, heavy nose, and full lips. He still retained a certain hesitancy in speech, and he was now a regular visitor at symphony concerts and balls. He was just on the threshold of his career as a young man-about-town. A year later he left school without finishing it and went to work in his father's factory, where he was to remain for the next thirty years or more. He did a lot of riding in the country in summer, and visited a riding academy in Moscow in winter. In Lyubimovka he was fond of spending the evenings on the large balcony over the verandah of their two-storied wooden country house. He sat there for hours, "listening to the stillness of the night". There was a stream near the house, winding leisurely through marshland, and as he listened to the interminable croaking of the frogs and the occasional cry of the corncrake, he seemed to become more and more aware of the great silence that brooded over the world. Twenty years later, as director of the Moscow Art Theatre, Stanislavsky was to win his overwhelming success as the producer of *The Seagull* by reproducing on the stage this "stillness" of a summer night in the country that is to be perceived through the different noises made by frogs and the corncrake. So powerful an impression did these evenings on the balcony of the Lyubimovka house leave on Stanislavsky that whenever he had to produce a summer night on the stage there inevitably came the croaking of frogs and the cry of the corncrake. He put them in even in *The Cherry Orchard*, and it was only after Chekhov had pointed out to him that at that time of the year the frogs no longer croaked and the corncrakes were silent that he agreed to dispense with these sound-effects of a summer night. Later still, when writing some of the *mise-en-scènes* of *Julius Cæsar*, he got in his frogs again, though that time Nemirovich-Danchenko, who was responsible for the production, over-ruled him. But Stanislavsky never forgot the lessons he had learnt on the balcony of his father's country house : stillness on the stage always meant to him the stillness that is perceived through the ordinary noises that are natural in the given circumstances.

Stanislavsky went to work at his father's factory at his own express wish, and he regarded it as a release from the classical education which he hated. The work at the factory demanded great accuracy and precision, and was highly responsible. At first he spent all his time there weighing small ingots of gold and silver and calculating their cost at the same time. Later on, when the theatre began to take up more and more of his time, he completely reorganized the work at the factory, but by then he was already a director of the company and was working in the office and not in the factory itself.

It was during his first years at the factory that Stanislavsky became a balletomane and did not miss a single ballet performance. He had begun going to the ballet, as he himself put it, in order to enjoy the sight of some of his friends "making fools of themselves", but in the end he, too, fell under its spell ; or, rather, under the spell of a young girl of the corps-de-ballet with whom he fell in love and whom he "abducted" one night. What an abduction meant, Stanislavsky described in *My Life in Art*. After the performance, it was the accepted rule for each balletomane to see his particular "flame" to the carriage which took her and the other young ballet dancers to their hostel. The girls were usually accompanied by a duenna, but while they trooped into the huge carriage the enterprising balletomane ran round to the other side of it and, if particularly favoured, had time to kiss the hand of his adored through the other window of the carriage. But the most intrepid of the balletomanes were not satisfied with that. They "abducted" the girls, that is, they made them leave the stage-door before the other girls, then put them into a cab and went for a quick ride through the streets. By the time the other girls arrived at the hostel, the "abducted" girl and her escort were already there, and to escape detection the girl was usually smuggled into the carriage while the others were coming out of it. It was supposed to be a highly daring and dangerous enterprise, and it required the bribing of the driver and of the doorkeeper of the hostel. The whole adventure, innocent though it was, had to be kept dark ; so that only a few friends knew about Stanislavsky's escapade and, as Anna records, they kept it "a dead secret".

During his visits to the hostel of the unmarried ballet dancers, Stanislavsky was present at the many discussions on the intricacies of ballet dancing and many a time he had to support a ballerina who was anxious to demonstrate her point. "I often let go of them," Stanislavsky writes, "and my awkwardness helped to reveal to me in practice the mystery of ballet technique. And if I add to this the eternal discussions of the balletomanes in their smoking den in the theatre, where I had the right of entry and where I met a great number of intelligent, well-read and sensitive æsthetes who discussed ballet dancing not from the point of view of mere technique, but from that of the æsthetic impression it evoked or from that of creative art, it will be clear that I had more than enough material for a thorough study of the art."

CHAPTER IV

IN THE SUMMER of 1881, about two years after Stanislavsky's first appearance on the stage, another four comedies were performed at the Lyubimovka theatre. This time the plays, all one-act comedies, were produced by Stanislavsky himself, with the assistance of Fedya Kashdamanov. Two of them, *A Woman's Secret* and *Her Weak Point*, were translations from the French. The plot of the second comedy was very simple. Two students are in love with two grisettes. They try to find their weak points so as to be able to gain their favours, and in the end the two girls fall in love with them and they get married. The plot of *A Woman's Secret* was also simple : an artist and a student by the name of Meriot, played by Stanislavsky, are paying court to the same grisette. The artist wants to marry her and the student is helping him. But to their horror they discover a bottle of rum in her room and jump to the conclusion that the girl drinks. Then it transpires that she only uses the rum to wash her hair. The rum is finally drunk by the student and the porter of the girl's house, and the artist marries the grisette.

Stanislavsky, his two sisters, Zina and Anna, and Kashdamanov spent the whole summer rehearsing these two plays. The problem Stanislavsky was particularly keen on solving was how to achieve the sense of proportion he was told he lacked at his first performance. But all he achieved was that the actors became so keenly aware of the need for a sense of proportion that they could hardly breathe, and the spectators at the rehearsals fell asleep from sheer boredom. "It's all right," the anxious producer was told, "except that it's a bit quiet." Quiet ? Ah, that meant that they had to play louder. More rehearsals ; but now the spectators found that they were shouting too much. Again the elusive sense of proportion seemed to have been lost sight of. This simple problem Stanislavsky was at that time unable to

29

solve. Someone then told him that speed was very important in a light comedy, and he tried to cut down by half the forty minutes it took them to act the play. But at a later rehearsal, the same man said that he was quite unable to make out what they were saying or doing on the stage. "All I could see," he told them, "was that you were rushing about like mad." Very well, if the trouble was that they were rushing about like mad, then all they had to do was to make sure that, even so, the audience could see their movements and hear what they were saying. "If," Stanislavsky adds, "we could have carried out this very difficult task, we should have become great actors ; but we did not succeed in carrying it out." However, the performance of the four one-act plays took place as arranged, and so successful was Stanislavsky in the part of the student, Meriot, that he played it many times later at the performances of the Society of Art and Literature.

It was in the same year that Stanislavsky figured in the only public procession he ever took part in. It was at the funeral of the principal of the Moscow Conservatoire, Nicolai Rubinstein. Stanislavsky's cousin, Nicolai Alexeyev, was a director of the Conservatoire and he asked Stanislavsky and his elder brother to help him supervise the procession on horseback, as large crowds were expected. When it came to mounting the horses, however, Stanislavsky's brother and cousin found that they had more important duties to perform, but Stanislavsky, who never went back on a promise, mounted his horse and rode in front of the procession as arranged. He was eighteen at the time, but his active participation in so grandiose a "crowd scene" must have been very useful to him later on when he was producing crowd scenes on the stage. It was also the first occasion on which Stanislavsky became the butt of the Moscow humorous journals, which published caricatures of him in the part of a "herald".

In November of the same year Stanislavsky appeared for the first time on the stage of Lvov's amateur theatre in a light comedy by the popular playwright, V. Krylov. About four years later, on January 27th, 1885, Stanislavsky again played in the same play and the same theatre, when he appeared for the first time under his stage name.

In his next performance at the theatre in Lyubimovka, Stanislavsky appeared for the first time in a Molière play, the one-act comedy *Marriage Forcé*. This play had made a tremendous impression on him when he saw it performed at the Maly Theatre at the age of thirteen, six years earlier, and one day he recited the speeches of Dr. Pancrace by heart to his brother. At first he pretended that he had remembered them, but his brother soon discovered that he had obtained a copy of the play and had learnt almost the whole of it by heart. At Lyubimovka he played the part of Dr. Pancrace, but he was greatly dissatisfied with himself. "Pancrace I played badly," he wrote in his *Artistic Notes*. "I tried to copy Buldin, a student at the Conservatoire, but nothing came of it. I wore my costume tolerably well, though, and my make-up reminded me of Peter the Great. There was a lot of ranting."

Stanislavsky's father played Marforius, in *Marriage Forcé*.

Two more plays were given on the same evening, *The Monster*, a two-act comedy by Krylov, and *The Love Potion* or *The Versifying Barber*, a translation from the French. Stanislavsky scored his first great success in the part of the versifying barber, Lavergé, which remained one of his favourite parts for many years. He played it for the last time ten years later, in 1892, and two photographs of Stanislavsky in this role show the great progress he had made as an actor. In the first photograph he looks like a tailor's dummy, while in the second he seems to have completely mastered the art of representing an individual type whose whole figure is alive and characteristic of the man.

The Love Potion was the first play Stanislavsky produced without any outside help, and, in the words of his sister Zina, it was the first play that deserved the name of a real, serious performance given by the Alexeyev Circle.

It was at about this time that Stanislavsky's father, who acquired his taste for amateur acting from his children, converted the red drawing-room of his house at the Red Gates into a theatre. When his children were small, he rarely accompanied them to the theatre. On returning home from the play, the children used to find him asleep on the sofa, in front of the tea-table, in the passage which connected the main building with the wing of the house where the red drawing-room was. He used to wake up and ask, "Well, did you enjoy the show? Did you meet many fools there?" And the reply he usually got was, "No, all the fools stayed at home. Only the clever ones were at the theatre." But the enthusiasm with which his children devoted themselves to the theatre finally infected him too. After building the little theatre at Lyubimovka, he converted the red drawing-room in the wing of his Moscow house into a theatre. The room was connected by an arch with a smaller room, the smoking-room, which was easily converted into a stage when required by placing gas footlights in the wide doorway and pulling aside the "gorgeous red and gold embroidered curtain" which concealed the footboards. Behind the smaller room all the necessary arrangements for dressing-rooms, etc., were made.

In the autumn of 1883, Stanislavsky had been for a short holiday to Vienna and he brought back with him a new operetta, *Giavotta*, which he thought had two merits : it had never been performed in Moscow and it had more or less suitable parts for all the members of the Alexeyev Circle. The chief part of the Duke, however, had to be given to a professional singer, a fine baritone, who was just completing his course at the Conservatoire, but whose looks were not particularly prepossessing. According to Stanislavsky, he had besides all the mannerisms of a bad opera singer and not a spark of dramatic talent. It was this baritone, however, who was the only success of the performance, in spite of the fact that Stanislavsky had, as usual, spent weeks in rehearsing the musical play with the members of his amateur company.

This was the second musical play Stanislavsky had put on. Earlier in the year, at Lyubimovka, unable to find a suitable play they decided to write their own musical comedy. It was written by Fedya Kashdamanov and performed on August 24th, 1883. Fedya called his operetta by the Russian proverb "every cricket must know its hearth," because the whole idea of it was that every member of the Alexeyev Circle should choose a part he or she would like to play. But the result of it was that while several scenes were extremely jolly and contained good dramatic material both for the producer and for the actor, it proved impossible to fit all these scenes together to make a play. It lacked a general, all-embracing idea and it was foredoomed to failure.

What was Stanislavsky's own ideal of an actor at that time ? First of all, of course, he wanted to appear on the stage as a handsome man. He wanted to sing love arias and be a favourite with the ladies. (It was just then that he and his elder brother fell in love with the younger daughter of a neighbouring landowner and pretended to ride off in different directions and look surprised when they met again half an hour later at the same house). He

wanted to resemble one of his own favourite singers whose stage
deportment and voice he could copy. He was, in short, only
interested in a part which would show him off to the best advantage ; he was not interested in looking for a part which suited him
best.

Kashdamanov's musical comedy was a failure, but on the
same evening Stanislavsky had put on *A Practical Gentleman,* a
one-act comedy by a popular Russian playwright, which had led
him to the discovery of a device which he found very useful even
after he became a professional actor. His idea was that while
rehearsing the play, the actors should try to live all the time not
as themselves but as its characters. Whatever they did, whether
they went for a country walk, or for a walk in the woods to gather
mushrooms, or for a sail on the river, they had to behave in
accordance with the conditions laid down in the play, and in accordance with the character of each person in the play. For instance,
in the play the parents of Stanislavsky's fiancée forbade him to
have anything to do with their daughter because he was a poor
student while she was a rich and beautiful young lady. Stanislavsky had to devise all sorts of schemes in order to arrange a
meeting with his supposed fiancée without the knowledge of her
supposed parents. One day, when he was out for a walk with his
sister, who played his fiancée, he saw in the distance one of his
friends, who played his fiancée's father. He had, therefore,
either to disappear before his fiancée's father had noticed him, or
to find some excuse if he should have seen them together. Stanislavsky's friend, on the other hand, had to act not as he would have
acted in real life but as "the practical gentleman" in the play
would, in his opinion, have acted in a similar contingency. The
difficulty of such an exercise, Stanislavsky discovered, was that
one had not only to be an actor, but also to be the author of all
sorts of impromptu actions. That was not easy, and indeed they
had often to interrupt their "rehearsals" for a quick conference
to decide how the characters in the play would have acted or what
they would have said to one another in the new and unexpected
circumstances, what thoughts, words and actions were logically
necessary for them, and only then would they resume their parts
and go on with their "rehearsal".

This unusual exercise led Stanislavsky to seek a faithful representation of the inner life of a part by concentrating on its external
characteristics, a method he persisted in for many years ; and as

late as 1900, during the visit of the Moscow Art Theatre to Chekhov, in the Crimea, holiday-makers on the beach in Yalta were amused to see him and two other actors every morning taking a walk "in character".

CHAPTER V

IN PRODUCING the musical comedy *Giavotta*, with the professional baritone, Stanislavsky applied the two lessons he had learnt from the production of *A Woman's Secret* and *Her Weak Point*, in 1881, and *A Practical Gentleman*, in the summer of 1883. He tried to get the actors to be so word-perfect that the moment they heard their cues, the words just poured out of their mouths ; then he made them live "in character" off stage. The combination of these two methods, however, proved disastrous to the parts because, as Stanislavsky explains, the method of living a part in ordinary life demanded continual impromptu acting, while the purely technical method of learning the parts by heart made impromptu acting impossible. "As usually happens," Stanislavsky writes, "the mechanical habit of learning the dialogue by heart got the better of me, and the moment I heard my cue I went on with my piece of dialogue, with the result that feeling could not keep pace with the words." However, this sort of technique did create "an illusion" of technical skill, and rather showed up the lack of dramatic training of the baritone. And yet, whenever the baritone took a high note the audience forgot all about the actors and clapped the man they felt was an expert.

"But he can't act !" Stanislavsky protested indignantly.

"Quite right," was the reply he got from the members of the audience, "but just listen to his voice ! What power ! What training !"

But Stanislavsky's disappointment with the lack of appreciation of his acting, though it drove him to enter a Moscow school of acting for a short time, did not make him abandon the production of musical comedies. He produced two French musical comedies in 1884 : he put on Lecocq's *La Comtesse de la Frontière* on January 28th, and *Mlle Nitouche* on August 18th. Earlier that summer he had put on the first act of the musical comedy *Mascotta*, an open-air performance arranged in imitation of the then popular open-air entertainments in the Moscow amusement park "The Hermitage," owned by M. Lentovsky, one of the first successful Russian private theatrical *entrepreneurs*. In *Mascotta*, Stanislavsky sang the part of the handsome shepherd Pipo. Writing of it in *My Life in Art*, he adds characteristically : "Today I feel ashamed to look at my photographs in this part. My make-up seems to express everything that is vulgar in a chocolate-box picture. A little turned-up moustache, carefully waved hair, legs in tights. And all that to represent a simple shepherd ! What absurdities an actor commits when he uses the theatre for self-display ! This time I was smitten with a passion for opera gestures and the dead-as-mutton acting technique of the opera stage. I sang, needless to say, like an amateur."

Stanislavsky's harshness to his own mistakes as an actor was the driving force that kept him searching constantly for perfection ; it is interesting that in writing of the other actors in the same musical comedy, he goes so far as to say that they were all very "sweet" in their parts. On the whole, however, this open-air entertainment was a great success. The country house was full of visitors. There was night bathing in the river, all sorts of impromptu entertainments and games which went on till the early hours of the morning, circus performances, gymnastic exercises on the roof of the house, constant shouts of laughter.

Musical comedy and farces, Stanislavsky thought, were "a good school for the actor". For voice, diction, gesture, movements, light rhythm, cheerful tempo, high spirits, were all necessary in that type of play. In addition, the actor required elegance and grace to add piquancy to such a play. Another advantage of this sort of light entertainment was that while demanding thorough external technique from the actor and training him to acquire it, it did not overburden him with powerful and complex feelings and hence did not confront him with the necessity of solving inner creative problems he could not be expected to tackle because of his inexperience.

All this Stanislavsky understood very well at the time, particularly as he had before him the example of a large number of professional actors who excelled in this genre.

Unfortunately, he was tall, ungraceful, still hesitant in speech and, above all, clumsy. When he entered a small room, his host immediately removed all the vases and little porcelain figures from it, for he was sure to knock them down. Once, at a ball, he overturned a palm-tree in a tub. Another time, dancing with a girl, he slipped, caught hold of the grand piano which had a broken leg, and crashed to the floor with it.

All these comic incidents made his clumsiness known all over Moscow and he dared not even hint that he wanted to become an actor, as it immediately provoked jocular remarks from his friends. He therefore made up his mind to overcome his physical faults and work on his voice, diction, gestures. It was a hard fight, but Stanislavsky was so determined to become an actor that this self-imposed process of training for the stage became a mania with him.

CHAPTER VI

THE SUMMER OF THE following year was very hot, but Stanislavsky decided to spend all his free time in town so as to be able to carry out his exercises in his father's empty house. There he spent hours before the large looking glass in the entrance-hall perfecting his gestures and movements, and particularly his diction, the acoustic properties of the marble walls and the large staircase being very good. During the whole of that summer and autumn he kept up this programme of training on his return from the office at seven o'clock in the evening till three o'clock in the morning. Later on he was to condemn this particular method of self-training before a looking-glass as harmful to the development of the actor's art, but it helped him at any rate to get to know his body and its faults and the best way of overcoming them.

On the election of his cousin, Nicolai Alexeyev, as Mayor of Moscow in November, 1885, he took his cousin's place as director of the Moscow branch of the Russian Musical Society and the Moscow Conservatoire. One of the reasons which induced him to accept this position, for which he was in no way suited, was that he could now resign from all sorts of charitable societies whose committees he had been persuaded to join on the ground that his position made it necessary for him to do some public and social work. It was much better, he reflected, to spend his free time in artistic circles than in charitable institutions.

As a director of the Moscow Musical Society and Conservatoire, Stanislavsky had an excellent opportunity of meeting the musical celebrities of the day, including Chaykovsky, Anton Rubinstein, and others. On one occasion, during a performance of Rubinstein's opera *The Demon*, he and one of his fellow-directors of the Musical Society had to present a large wreath to the famous composer, who was already sitting at the conductor's desk in front

of the stage and with his back to the orchestra as was the custom
in those days. This was Stanislavsky's first appearance on a large
stage and, unaccustomed to the strong glare of the footlights, he
and his fellow-director were almost immediately blinded. They
could see nothing in front of them, as though a mist, rising from
the footlights, covered up everything on the other side. They
walked and walked, and Stanislavsky had a feeling that they had
already been walking for miles when suddenly he heard a noise
in the auditorium which soon turned into loud laughter. They
continued to walk without realizing what was happening, until
from the mist there loomed up the box of the director of the
theatre, which jutted out on to the stage. It seemed that they
had lost their way on the stage under the eyes of thousands of
people : they had walked past the centre of it where, by the
prompter's box, the conductor was sitting. Shielding their
eyes from the footlights and forgetful of the enormous wreath
with all its ribbons which they were dragging along the floor, they
presented an extremely comic group. Rubinstein was roaring
with laughter and kept striking the desk with his baton to show
them where he was. At last they found him, presented the wreath,
and practically rushed off the stage. This experience on the stage
of the Bolshoy Theatre during the performance of *The Demon*
must have given Stanislavsky a better idea of what he always
called "the terrible hole of the proscenium" than any of his
appearances on the stage before or after it.

CHAPTER VII

THE YEAR 1885 was notable for an event which left its mark on the Russian theatre and, particularly, on the Moscow Art Theatre. It was during that year that the Company of the Duke of Meiningen, under its producer Kronegk, paid its first visit to Moscow. At the time, Stanislavsky who, as we have seen, was chiefly preoccupied with musical comedy and who would very soon be making his only attempt to gatecrash into opera as a singer, seems not to have paid much attention to this rather remarkable company. It was five years later, during the Meiningen Company's second visit to Moscow, that he received the full impact of those ideas on dramatic production which were to become so characteristic of his own first productions at the Moscow Art Theatre and which led to the impression that he was addicted to the extreme faults of the naturalistic school of producers.

Alexander Ostrovsky, on the other hand, was not in the least impressed by Kronegk's methods. The great Russian playwright was more than anyone responsible for building up the remarkable company of great actors of the Maly Theatre, which had contributed so greatly to Stanislavsky's artistic development and, as he himself confessed, had taught him " to see and to observe the beautiful ". On April 5th, 1885, Ostrovsky wrote in his diary this penetrating verdict on the acting of the Meiningen Company : "Their acting does not leave you with that satisfied feeling which you receive from a work of art ; what we saw at their theatre was not art but skill or, in other words, craftsmanship. Those were not the plays of Shakespeare, but a series of *tableaux vivants* from his plays. But all the same during the performance the impression the spectator received was both powerful and pleasant : I was, for instance, entirely carried away by the last scene of the third act of *Julius Cæsar*. But on thinking it over, I can see that the impression I got was not more

40

powerful than the impression I would have got from the march past of a well-drilled regiment or the dancing of a well-trained *corps-de-ballet* : what impressed me was the quick, easy and skilful way in which the orders of the producer had been carried out. It was obvious to me that Kronegk was a highly educated man who possessed good taste. But the trouble with the Meiningen actors is that the hand of the producer is seen in whatever they do ; it was indeed quite apparent that even the leading actors always played at the word of command. As it is impossible, however, to endow the leading players with talent and feeling merely by shouting orders at them, their acting becomes less interesting than the acting of the extras in crowd scenes. For all that is required from a crowd on the stage is external truth, while from the leading actors it is chiefly inner truth that is needed and inner truth is not so easy to acquire. For an actor to give us both external and inner truth, he must be able to grasp the meaning of his part, he must have talent, he must possess the necessary physical means and he must have been trained in the right kind of school. In the Meiningen company, on the other hand, the leading actors are bad and the leading actresses are worse. The actor who played Antony in *Julius Cæsar* delivered his speech very weakly, while the cleverly drilled crowd grew excited and carried away as though the speech had been said in a powerful and enthusiastic manner."

Ostrovsky found a great deal that was good in the Meiningen company. He particularly liked the grouping of the actors and the extras on the stage, both when in repose and when in movement. When in repose the crowd, he pointed out, remained one motionless mass which gazed at the audience with a hundred eyes ; its disposition on the stage was very beautiful and effective. But it was even better in movement. What struck him so forcibly about Kronegk's crowd scenes in *Julius Cæsar*, was that the crowd was alive and that it held the attention of the audience much more than Antony. The battle in the last act was also very well contrived : the soldiers of different detachments and arms came down from the mountains into a gorge which looked very beautiful and natural ; then they entered a small wood, where the battle began and the clashing of swords was heard ; then the soldiers retreated and, while retreating, fought on the stage with such fury that sparks flew from their swords ; the stage was strewn with dead and wounded men. The spectators were horrified ; the ladies in the audience turned away and covered their eyes with their hands.

Ostrovsky was further struck by the fact that the Meiningen producer was an excellent master of lighting effects and all sorts of other naturalistic stage effects, which were quite a novelty for the Moscow stage at the time : scudding clouds, pouring rain, lightning, moonlight—everything Ostrovsky found to be most effectively reproduced. The moonlight in Brutus's garden, for instance, cut through the deep shadows of the trees and fell on a white marble seat, which produced a very effective spot in the dark greenery of the garden and was at the same time highly natural ; the appearance of Cæsar's ghost in Brutus's tent sent a shiver down the backs of the spectators.

All these stage effects were unheard of on the Moscow stage at the time, but, as Ostrovsky pointed out, no particular credit was due to the Meiningen company for them, since every well-run theatre ought to have had them. As for the excellent scenery and props on the Meiningen stage, that, too, was something that the Moscow theatre ought not to have found so difficult to introduce ; though in fact they waited for Stanislavsky to lead the way. But Ostrovsky criticised the Meiningen company for the unnecessary pedantry of their productions, or, in other words, for their addiction to naturalism. They put on the stage an exact copy of Pompey's statue, exact copies of Roman wine-goblets. This, Ostrovsky found (and here he certainly showed a better understanding of the art of the stage than Stanislavsky did in his first productions at the Moscow Art Theatre) was quite unnecessary, since an exact replica of antique furniture, etc., would only be appreciated by the expert, and even an expert could not be expected to appreciate the exact reproduction of such small objects as wine-goblets. "For the spectator," Ostrovsky wrote, "it is quite sufficient if the scenery and props do not violate the historic truth of the epoch represented—absolute faithfulness is in fact pedantry. In the Meiningen company," he added, "even Julius Cæsar is nothing but a prop. The first entry of Cæsar among the crowd on the Forum, surrounded by his lictors, was very striking : the resemblance was amazing—you could not help feeling you were seeing the real, living Cæsar. But the moment he opened his mouth, and all through the rest of the play, this languid and lifeless actor was more like some third-rate provincial schoolmaster than the mighty Cæsar."

When this was pointed out to Kronegk, he justified himself by saying that he could not find a talented actor who looked like Cæsar, and that he was afraid to let an actor who did not resemble Cæsar play the part, because everyone knew what Cæsar looked like. "Kronegk," Ostrovsky remarked, "forgot that he was not showing us an exhibition of wax figures or *tableaux vivants*, that he was not showing us scenes from Roman history, but that his actors were acting in a play by Shakespeare, and it is impossible to play Shakespeare's *Julius Cæsar* without possessing talent."

The first appearance of the Meiningen company in Moscow produced a tremendous sensation and it seems incredible that Stanislavsky should not have been to see them. But, as already pointed out, he did not at the time seem to be interested in straight plays. He was still too much absorbed in the production of musical comedies and, as it becomes clear from his own statements, he was not sure that the stage was after all the right career for him.

What seems even more surprising in view of the fact that he would so soon be producing a large number of plays by Ostrovsky, is that he did not make any attempt to meet the great Russian playwright who died in 1886, two years before the foundation of the Society of Art and Literature. But Stanislavsky had always been extremely shy of famous literary men, and besides, such a meeting at that particular time would hardly have been pleasant, for Ostrovsky had an intense dislike of the amateur, and especially the rich amateur. And he certainly had no patience with people who wasted their time on plays of no real dramatic importance. As for musical comedies, he abhorred them.

CHAPTER VIII

In 1886, STANISLAVSKY produced the French musical comedy *Lili*, which was one of his most successful productions in that genre and which was revived during the next two years, being the last play performed by the Alexeyev Circle. The musical comedy was of a new type. It was a straight comedy, the dialogue of which was interlarded with songs. It was introduced on the French stage by the famous French comédienne, Anna Judic. It was this play that brought Stanislavsky one step nearer to drama.

Stanislavsky's elder brother Vladimir first saw *Lili* while honeymooning in Paris in 1882. Stanislavsky and his sisters saw it in Moscow during Anna Judic's visit in 1883. In his own account of the play in *My Life in Art*, Stanislavsky seems to be wrong in stating that it was his sisters who had seen it in Paris. Anyway, the comedy impressed them all so much that it was decided that it should be put on by the Alexeyev Circle. Vladimir remembered the dialogue by heart (he had seen the play several times) and he copied it out from memory "almost *verbatim*". Only the third act gave him some trouble, but he got over the difficulty by adding bits of his own dialogue with the help of the tutor of his younger brothers. Some places in the play had to be toned down "in view of the domestic censorship".

Stanislavsky is more explicit about the "writing" of the play than his brother. According to his account, it was decided that the text of the play should consist of short sentences, which should be no longer than French sentences. Each sentence was then checked by the performer with the rather curious idea that he or she should be able to pronounce it in "the French way".

"Fortunately," Stanislavsky writes, "every member of our family not only spoke French, but also understood the music of the language. It was not for nothing," he adds, referring to the unhappy Marie Varlet, who died in 1885, unrecognized and still

44

in disfavour, "that we all had French blood in our veins." It was Stanislavsky's sister Zina, who played Lili, the heroine of the French comedy, who so excelled everybody in this unusual innovation of speaking Russian as though it were really French that it was impossible to tell whether it was Russian or French that she was speaking. "It is true," Stanislavsky explains, "that we had to disregard the meaning of the sentences and use them mostly for the sake of their sound and their French intonation. And that was why the spectator, listening to Russian dialogue, at times thought that the play was being performed in a foreign language." Stanislavsky also found a typical French rhythm and tempo for the movements and the action in this play. The scenery, needless to say, was a faithful copy of the French production.

This almost complete elimination of the dialogue from the play, made possible by its simple plot, concentrated the whole attention of the producer and performers on its action, in which *Lili* was particularly rich. Thus in the first act Zina appeared as the young daughter of a middle-class family and Stanislavsky as a young soldier—a trumpeter *piou-piou*. In the second act, Zina was a *grande dame*, and Stanislavsky an army officer of twenty-five. In the third and last act Zina was an old woman and Stanislavsky a retired general. Zina seems to have been particularly success-ful in her difficult part. Though she had no voice, she sang her songs so "marvellously" that the famous tenor Kommissarzhevsky, who was present at one of the performances, rushed on to the stage during an interval, knelt down before her and kissed her hand. Stanislavsky, according to his elder brother, who provided the musical accompaniment on the piano, was an excellent Planchard, especially in the last act, singing his songs in "a masterly fashion". Of the other members of the cast, Sokolov, Zina's husband, seemed to have been adequate in the part of the baron, and Stanislavsky's younger brother George, who was seventeen at the time, played an ancient deaf vicomte so well that "it was impossible to believe that it was played by a boy."

In a notice of the comedy which appeared in the *Russian Courier,* the "good taste" of the production was highly praised. The critic found that the playing by Zina of the main part was inimitable and that "the talented" Konstantin Alexeyev (Stanis-lavsky did not use his stage name when acting at home) was also "very good both as actor and singer in the part of the soldier

Antoine Planchard, especially in the third act, in which he appeared as an old man."

Stanislavsky himself ascribed his success in *Lili* to the fact that in this part he was no longer copying a well-known actor, but something he had himself observed in life. "The moment I felt that national characteristic of my part," he writes, "I could easily justify the tempo and rhythm of my movements and speeches. This was no longer tempo for the sake of tempo, or rhythm for the sake of rhythm, but an inner rhythm, though of a general nature, characteristic of all Frenchmen and not of the individual person I was representing." As for the contribution this part made to his subsequent development as an actor, Stanislavsky thought that it lay in his concentrating on the external characteristics of his part, for "sometimes it is possible to arrive at the inner characteristics of a part by way of its outer characteristics. This is not the best but a possible method of the creative art of the stage. At all events, it helped me now and again to live my part, as had happened earlier in my part of the young student in *A Practical Gentleman*."

The only other musical production of the Alexeyev Circle before its dissolution was *The Mikado*, which Stanislavsky called "a Japanese operetta with music by the English composer Sullivan". He had obviously never heard of W. S. Gilbert, and the real point of *The Mikado* escaped him completely. But as at that particular period a play existed for Stanislavsky merely as a vehicle for external display, it is not surprising that he should have engaged the services of a family of Japanese acrobats who were providentially appearing at a circus in Moscow just then, and immediately made everybody learn the Japanese way of walking, bowing, dancing, and manipulating the fan. The Japanese were also responsible for the costumes in that production. Stanislavsky, who was anything but slipshod in his methods even in those early days, made the women in the cast walk with tied legs in order to learn the way Japanese ladies walked ; and so proficient had everybody become in the manipulation of the fan that they began using it even when talking to one another, "according to the Japanese custom". The fans were, indeed, the chief attraction of the light opera. "In the crowd scenes," Stanislavsky writes, "each member of the chorus was given his or her own sequence of gestures and movements of the fan with every beat of the music. Poses with the fan were so arranged that there was an incessant kaleidoscope of changing and intermingling groups : while some flung up their fans, others flung them down to their very feet, while others still did the same to the right and others to the left, and so on. And when in the big *ensemble* scenes the whole of this kaleidoscope of red, green and yellow fans of every size, large, medium, and small, was flying in the air, the people who watched this effective theatrical scene were breathless with excitement." Stanislavsky grouped the chorus on small rising platforms (his first attempt to "mould" the floor of the stage), so that the whole stage was covered with the fans as with a curtain. "Add to this," he goes on, "the picturesque costumes, many of which were genuine, the ancient Japanese armour of the Samurais, the original and genuine Japanese plastic poses, the dexterity of the actors, the acrobatic tricks, the rhythm, the dances, the pretty faces of the girls, the enthusiasm and vitality of the players—and the success of *The Mikado* becomes intelligible."

There was, however, a fly in the ointment : Stanislavsky himself, who was responsible for the new "tone and style" of the production, could not as an actor rid himself of the most banal, operatic, picture-postcard conception of beauty. Having worked out his plastic poses in front of the mirror in the empty entrance-hall in summer, he found it impossible to abandon them in this "Japanese production" and did his best to appear in it as a pretty-pretty Italian singer (he played Nanki-Poo). "How was I," he writes, "to bend my tall figure in the Japanese manner when my chief concern was to keep it straight ? So that this time, too, I was, as an actor, only getting more and more confirmed in my old mistakes and in the banal operatic traditions."

If Stanislavsky had known, when he wrote these lines almost forty years after his production of *The Mikado*, what the light opera was about, he would not have been so critical of himself for his failure to act "in the Japanese manner".

The Mikado was a great success for all that, and was given by the Alexeyev Circle four times : on April 18th, 22nd and 25th, and on May 2nd, 1887.

The Alexeyev Circle was now beginning to disintegrate. The friends and relations who took part in it were getting married and dispersing. Before its final dissolution, however, Stanislavsky put on a light comedy, for, as he writes, by that time "we were beginning to be sick of operettas." In this light comedy

Stanislavsky for the first time appeared in a dramatic role, a fact that had a certain influence on his future artistic career. The title of the play was *A Misfortune of a Special Kind*, and its plot revolved round a lesson a husband tried to teach his wife by pretending to take poison. In this comedy Stanislavsky wanted to try out his powers as a dramatic actor, but only succeeded in achieving a number of highly comic scenes.

"Does this produce any impression ? " he asked a friend, after playing the part at a rehearsal.

"I don't know—I don't think it made any particular impression on me," his friend replied candidly.

"Well—and now ? " he asked, running on to the stage again and starting all over again, exerting himself even more, which produced an even more deplorable result.

But his make-up, his youth, his strong voice, the scenic effectiveness of his acting, the good models he copied, did appeal to some people, and quite naturally he considered them to be competent judges of his acting and dismissed those who criticised his acting as "envious fools". Actually his mistakes in this dramatic part were greater than in any previous performance. "When one sings out of tune in a whisper, the result is unpleasant, but when one sings out of tune at the top of one's voice, it is a hundred times more unpleasant," Stanislavsky writes. "This time I was singing out of tune at the top of my voice. However, in this play I played a tragic part for the first time."

The final curtain on the Alexeyev Circle fell with the last curtain on the musical comedy *Lili* on January 9th, 1888.

CHAPTER IX

HIS SUCCESS IN musical comedy, in which his singing of love duets seems to have been greatly appreciated, made Stanislavsky dream of becoming an opera singer. There was the additional reason that he wished to emulate the railway magnate Mamontov and organize opera performances at his theatre at home. He had at the time already become a great friend of Theodore Kommissarzhevsky, a somewhat improvident and flamboyant tenor whose only claim to fame today rests on the fact that he was the father of Vera Kommissarzhevsky, one of Russia's great actresses, and of Theodore Kommissarzhevsky, a producer of international repute. Kommissarzhevsky had attended Stanislavsky's musical comedy production and his chivalrous appreciation of Zina's singing has already been described. Now he became Stanislavsky's singing master. Whenever Stanislavsky got a new idea into his head, he carried it out to the bitter end. Every day, on finishing his work at the factory, he rushed to the other end of the town to his music lesson. When he thought that he had acquired sufficient vocal technique to try his hand at opera, he decided to put on a few scenes from different operas. Kommissarzhevsky himself was not averse from appearing on the Alexeyev stage, and so they began to rehearse two opera scenes, a duet between Mephistopheles and Faust from Gounod's opera, and the first act from Dargomiszky's opera *The Water Maiden*, in which the part of the miller was taken by Stanislavsky and the part of the prince by Kommissarzhevsky. But already at the second rehearsal, Stanislavsky became hoarse, and his voice got worse and worse as the rehearsals went on and gave out completely at the dress rehearsal. The idea of an opera performance had to be given up : Stanislavsky realized that he would never make an operatic singer, and he felt very sorry about it, for it was operatic singers that he found so easy to copy. Further than copying, his ideas of acting did not go at the time.

But his abortive attempt at opera was not entirely wasted. Indeed, the remarkable fact about Stanislavsky's development as an artist is that he knew how to turn even his greatest failures to good account. What struck him, in rehearsing the opera scenes with Kommissarzhevsky, was the marvellous way in which different rhythms could be combined in opera. He began talking to Kommissarzhevsky about the need for opera singers to cultivate physical rhythm. He was already dreaming of becoming Kommissarzhevsky's assistant in a rhythm class at the Moscow Conservatoire. He and Kommissarzhevsky engaged a pianist who was good at improvising, and spent hours in moving about and sitting still "rhythmically". All these exercises and experiences came in very useful to Stanislavsky when, twenty-five years later, he undertook to teach his "system" to opera singers.

Having failed in opera, Stanislavsky was for a time at a loss what to do. His enthusiasm for musical comedies had gone and, besides, by that time, the Alexeyev Circle had come to a natural end. He was still taking part in all sorts of amateur theatricals, but that, too, no longer satisfied him. The only thing that remained was drama, but he realized how poor his training for it was, and he could not face another failure. Luckily, chance came to his rescue : several famous actresses of the Maly Theatre took part in a charitable performance at his home of a play by Nemirovich-Danchenko, a popular playwright and novelist who was beginning to be talked of as the successor of Ostrovsky. The play had already been put on by the Maly Theatre, and had, indeed, had quite a long run there. It was a heaven-sent opportunity for Stanislavsky, for now he could measure his strength against professional actors or, at any rate, find out whether his friends and relations who sneered at him for wanting to become an actor were right or not.

The first thing he noticed about the great actresses of the Maly Theatre was that, unlike the amateurs of the Alexeyev Circle (with perhaps the sole exception of himself), they were all present at least half an hour before the beginning of the rehearsals, although they had scored a success in that particular play and presumably knew it inside out. They spoke their lines "in full tone", while the amateurs were hardly audible and had to read their lines from their books. As he stood beside the professional actors, Stanislavsky could not help feeling nervous. He pretended to understand what the producer was telling him, though actually he was merely anxious to copy what was shown to him. He did, in fact, the opposite of what was necessary from the point of view of the creative art of the stage ! He was waiting for something outside him to arouse his enthusiasm, and he depended on the audience to supply him with the necessary amount of energy to carry on with his part, while the professional actors knew how to act their parts in such a way that the spectators had to respond to them.

What was the matter ? He turned to the famous actress Fedotova for an explanation.

"The trouble with you is that you don't know from which end to begin," Fedotova told him. "And," the old actress could not refrain from twitting the rich dilettante, "you don't want to learn. No training, no perseverance, no discipline. An actor can't do without discipline."

"But," Stanislavsky asked, "how am I to train myself in discipline ? "

"Work with us," was the old lady's answer. "We're not always as kind as we are today. We know how to be severe, too. Young actors seem to prefer to wait for inspiration from Apollo. That's a waste of time. He has enough to do as it is."

This was the first time Stanislavsky heard a great actress speak so disparagingly of "inspiration," on which he had hitherto relied almost entirely. He never forgot it. As his art grew and developed he, too, came to hold the same opinion : "inspiration" became his *bête noire*.

At the actual performance the professional actors dragged the amateurs after them. Stanislavsky himself thought that he played with inspiration. "But, alas," he adds, "it only seemed so. My part was far from perfect."

However, the professional actors were not apparently entirely disappointed with his playing, for on his return from abroad the same year, he found Fedotova's son, who was a friend of his, waiting for him at the station. The Maly Theatre company was due to leave for Ryazan for a performance of the same Nemirovich-Danchenko play and they wanted him to help them out, as the actor who had to play the part he had played at the charitable performance had fallen ill. Stanislavsky could not miss such a chance of appearing again on the stage with professional actors, and he agreed to go. By then he had completely forgotten his part and he had no time to learn it by heart again. He had to rely on the prompter ; and it was then that he realized what a nightmare it was to be on the stage without being word-perfect in one's part. He never forgot that dreadful experience of his, and in the future he always insisted on an absolute knowledge of their parts by his actors—a practice more honoured in the breach than in the observance on the Russian stage in those days.

They missed their train after the performance and had to stay in Ryazan till next morning. At the dinner given to Fedotova and the other actors of the Maly Theatre by their Ryazan admirers, Stanislavsky felt utterly worn out, while Fedotova, who was old enough to be his mother, was, he observed enviously, fresh, young, flirtatious and talkative. When he apologised afterwards for falling asleep at the dinner as he had had no proper rest after his return from abroad, Fedotova's son told him that his mother had had a temperature of over 100 all that day. "So that's the meaning of training and discipline," Stanislavsky reflected ruefully.

Training and discipline were only two of the principles of acting which Stanislavsky picked up from Fedotova and later adopted as part of his "system". It was Fedotova who used to say, "Look your partner straight in the eyes, read his thoughts in his eyes, and reply to him in accordance with the expression of his eyes and face." Stanislavsky later developed this into one of the elements of his "system," which he called *communication*.

It was, indeed, during those early days of his stage career that Stanislavsky showed an insatiable curiosity about the methods of the great actors. One of the great celebrities of the time, Tommaso Salvini, who was to become Stanislavsky's ideal actor, visited Moscow for the first time in 1882, and after that Stanislavsky made a point of finding out all he could about him. The same was true of every other great foreign actor who visited Moscow or whom he saw during his frequent journeys abroad. The great actors, Stanislavsky discovered, were too busy with their art to talk about it. But by analyzing their methods he could catch a glimpse of something they all seemed to possess in common. And it was that "something" that Stanislavsky set about analyzing till it provided him with a key to what was to become his "system".

But in 1888 Stanislavsky was still very far from realizing that the facts he was even then collecting would one day grow into a world-famous system of acting. By then he had become well known as an amateur actor. He played in all sorts of plays and on all sorts of stages, in cold and filthy little amateur theatres. He had to put up with constant changes in the time of the rehearsals ; he had to appear on the stage with men to whom acting was merely an opportunity for flirtations and dancing. These hastily contrived amateur theatricals could not even offer a decent dressing-room for their actors, and before the beginning of the performance and during the intervals Stanislavsky had to take a cab to his sister's flat, which was near the theatre where he usually played, change his costume, and hurry back to the theatre in the same cab. Very often he appeared in plays which would have shocked his family, but, fortunately, his stage name helped to cover up his tracks, though he was not altogether safe. Indeed, one night when he was playing a Parisian man-about-town in a highly improper French farce, he rushed out on to the stage with a large bouquet in his hand only to be faced in the box opposite by his father and mother and his mother's old governess (who had helped her to run away from her step-mother and spent the rest of her life in their house). In that farce he had to play scenes which would certainly not have passed the "domestic censorship". He felt so embarrassed that instead of a man-about-town he played a well-behaved, shy young man. On returning home that night, he dared not show his face to his parents. Next morning his father merely said to him, "If you insist on acting anywhere else, then get yourself a decent company of amateurs and don't play any sort of rubbish with goodness knows whom." And his mother's old governess, who had dandled him as a baby, cried in a horrified voice : "I never, never thought that such a pure young man as our dear Konstantin would be capable of appearing in public in such a—oh dear, it was dreadful, dreadful ! I wish I'd never seen it ! "

However, as Stanislavsky himself remarks in describing this incident, there is no evil but good may come of it. It was during those days of his indiscriminate appearances on the amateur stage in Moscow that he met several of the future famous actors of the Moscow Art Theatre, including his own wife Maria Lilina.

The theatrical performance at which Stanislavsky first met Lilina was given in aid of some Conservatoire charity, and as Stanislavsky was still a director of the Conservatoire at the time, he must have taken an active part in its organization. That night—it was February 29th, 1888—the programme included a three-act light comedy by the then popular playwright Krylov, and two one-act farces. The leading parts in the comedy were played by Stanislavsky and Lilina. It was Lilina's first appearance on the stage. She was at the time a schoolmistress in a select Moscow high school for girls. Her real name was Maria Perevoshchikova. She had assumed the stage name of Lilina in order to conceal the fact of her taking part in private theatricals from the headmistress of her school. She was not successful in that innocent trick and eventually had to leave her school. At the time, according to a description of her left by the dramatic critic Efros, she was a small, slender girl, very young, "enchantingly naïve, enchantingly simple and as enchantingly talented, with large bright eyes and beautiful hair." Having lost her job, she received an invitation from Stanislavsky towards the end of the same year to join the Society of Art and Literature he had just founded. Next April, Lilina played Luisa in Schiller's *Kabale und Liebe* opposite Stanislavsky's Ferdinand, and, to quote Stanislavsky, "it seems we were in love with one another without knowing it ourselves. But the audience told us about it. We kissed too naturally, and our secret was revealed from the stage. In this play," he adds, "it was intuition rather than technique that inspired my playing. But it is not difficult to guess who really inspired us : Apollo or Hymen." On July 5th of the same year they got married, and their whole subsequent life was a shining example of real comradeship in art.

CHAPTER X

SHORTLY AFTER his first appearance on the stage with Lilina, Stanislavsky was again asked to take part in an amateur theatrical performance. This time it was his friend Alexander Fedotov, son of the famous actress Fedotova, who asked him to help out his father, a well-known producer, playwright and actor, who had just returned to Moscow (he was divorced from his wife) and wished to remind the Muscovites of his existence. The main play of the evening was Racine's *Les Plaideurs* in Fedotov's own translation and, as a curtain raiser, Gogol's one-act comedy *The Card Players*, was included in the programme. The chief part in Racine's play was taken by the well-known artist and æsthete, Fyodor Sollogub, and Stanislavsky played the main part in Gogol's curtain-raiser.

The young Stanislavsky was tremendously impressed by Fedotov as a producer, and Fedotov, too, seems to have taken a fancy to Stanislavsky. Many years later Stanislavsky often asserted that his rehearsals with Fedotov were his best school, and that after him he could no longer go back to his former amateur performances.

Stanislavsky proposed to Fedotov and Sollogub that they should found a society to unite all amateurs in a dramatic circle and all professional actors and artists in an "artistic club without card games". He had already discussed the idea several times with his friend and mentor Theodore Kommissarzhevsky, and now it seemed that all that remained to be done was to introduce Kommissarzhevsky to Fedotov and go ahead with the foundation of the society. If he had had more experience of human nature, he would have realized that Fedotov, who in his way was a genuine artist, would never have got along with Kommissarzhevsky, a rather unstable and superficial personality who possessed all the well-known weaknesses of a famous operatic tenor. However, at first everything went off smoothly enough. "When you want something very badly," Stanislavsky writes in describing the foundation of the Society of Art and Literature, "it seems very simple and easily attainable." None of them was at first very worried about the financial side of the enterprise. They hoped to raise enough funds from membership fees and donations. Fedotov was appointed director of the dramatic section of the society, Kommissarzhevsky of the operatic and musical section, and Sollogub of the section of graphic arts. The dramatic and opera sections had their own schools. According to its constitution, the Society of Art and Literature was to make it possible for its members to develop their talents and to organize performances of plays, exhibitions, literary and musical evenings, and special celebrations of the jubilees of well-known writers, artists and actors.

Stanislavsky received many friendly warnings about the dangers of so grandiose a scheme but he disregarded them, chiefly, as he himself puts it, "because of that peculiar quality of my nature to carry on stubbornly and almost stupidly with whatever happens to arouse my enthusiasm." The actress Fedotova's pessimism he simply explained as due to her disagreements with her divorced husband, and Sollogub's doubts he dismissed as the unpractical advice of an artist. As it happened, he just then got an unexpected windfall of twenty-five thousand roubles and, as the Society was in need of an advance to secure proper premises, he gave it the money, adding a few more thousands a little later for the decoration of the Society's club premises.

The Society was officially opened towards the end of 1888. Its rooms were beautifully decorated, and it had an excellent auditorium and stage, the auditorium being easily convertible into a dance-hall. Next to the auditorium was a large foyer and a big studio for painters. The opening of the Society was greeted enthusiastically by the Moscow Press, its founders being highly praised for providing a meeting-place for artists, actors, musicians and scholars.

The programme of the first dramatic evening of the Society had been drawn up already in the spring. It was decided to put on Pushkin's *Covetous Knight,* a few scenes from his *Boris Godunov* and Molière's *Georges Dandin.* The producer was to be Fedotov. Fedotov's methods as a producer are fully described by

Stanislavsky in *My Life in Art*. He began by giving first of all, an imaginative outline of the production as a whole. He spent a night with Stanislavsky at the Alexeyev mansion at the Red Gates, where, barefoot and in his nightshirt, he described to his young disciple the scenery and his whole plan of production of Pushkin's tragedy. This first imaginative conception of the production of a play without reference to the text became for a' long time Stanislavsky's own method of producing plays. In this method the producer's imagination very often played havoc with the play itself. Stanislavsky, who possessed an exceedingly vivid scenic imagination, was very good at this sort of thing. If an idea that gave great scope to the producer did not agree with the intentions of the author, then the play was forcibly cast into another mould. The producer in such a case became not only the co-author of the play but the adapter of it. The result was that Stanislavsky often found the text a great hindrance to his own conception of the play's plot and characters. But by judicious cutting the play was eventually strait-jacketed into what the producer thought to be its right shape. Indeed, one of the reasons why Stanislavsky put on so many plays of the German playwright Gerhardt Hauptmann was that at that particular period such plays interfered least with the inventions of his own imagination. It was only during the last period of his theatrical career that Stanislavsky completely abandoned this arbitrary treatment of the playwright and put the main emphasis on the discovery of the ruling idea of the play and gave it complete pre-eminence in the producer's conception of its stage presentation. That was the reason why Stanislavsky finally gave up the idea of the producer as the autocrat of the stage. For if in the production of a play the producer's imagination is to be given pre-eminence, then quite naturally the producer has to impose his own conception of the characters on the actors who willy-nilly have to sacrifice their own creative conceptions and force themselves to play the producer's characters. This conflict became manifest at the very first discussion of the character of the covetous knight between Stanislavsky and Fedotov. It is true that Fedotov's conception of the knight seemed in its general outline to coincide with Stanislavsky's : both saw him as a man who never wavered in his belief in his own rightness and who was majestically indifferent to the opinions the rest of the world entertained of his vice. But the difference was that Fedotov seemed to have taken his idea of the old man from the paintings of the old masters, "the typical face of an old man, lit by the reddish light of a candle, bent over a sword from which he is removing all traces of blood, or pouring over some ancient tome." Stanislavsky, on the other hand, could not rid himself of his operatic idea of an old man with a noble visage, such as St. Brie from *The Huguenots.*

"I was already beginning to see myself," Stanislavsky writes, "as a faithful copy of a well-known Italian baritone, with his well-shaped legs in black tights, wearing wide breeches, lovely shoes, a ruff, and a rapier. Oh, the rapier was the chief attraction of the part for me ! "

The result of these two different conceptions of the part was that Stanislavsky could not make up his mind which of them he ought to copy. He had to copy one of them, for at that time he knew no better. His perplexity increased when he saw Sollogub's sketches of the covetous knight. To his horror what he saw was not a handsome baritone but a miserable beggar : a decrepit old man with aristocratic features, a long, untrimmed imperial, an uncared-for moustache, wearing a dirty old leather cap, a pair of old, worn stockings which were too wide for his thin legs, a thread-bare shirt, a pair of old breeches, and a jacket with wide sleeves resembling a priest's. The whole figure of the old knight was thin and tall, with an exaggerated stoop, bent almost in the shape of a question-mark over his coffer, with gold coins which fell from long, thin, skeleton-like fingers.

Stanislavsky was so disappointed that he decided to throw up his part. Asked what he wanted, he at once explained to the astonished Fedotov and Sollogub his ideal of the operatic baritone, and even showed them the singer's photograph which he had been carrying about with him. "Even now," Stanislavsky writes in explanation of this episode, "I cannot understand how the tawdry notion of the operatic singer could live in me side by side with the sophistication of the French theatre and musical comedy which were chiefly responsible at that time for the development of my taste in the sphere of production. It was obvious that so far as the art of the stage was concerned, I still remained an insipid copyist."

Fedotov and Sollogub, however, gave Stanislavsky such a "talking to" that he remembered it for the rest of his life. They proved to him so conclusively the triviality and vulgarity of his ideas that at first he fell silent and then felt ashamed. He realized that his old ideas were worthless, and that he had nothing to replace them with. "I was not at the time altogether convinced about the rightness of the new ideas," he writes, "but they did persuade me that my old notions were wrong." There followed a long succession of talks and lessons, during which, Stanislavsky remarks, "I felt like a capon which is being fattened on nuts." He had to throw away the photograph of the baritone, but there was still a great deal he had to learn before he could give an external and physical representation of the old miser.

During his exercises before the looking-glass, Stanislavsky had also devoted much attention to the playing of old men. Besides, as was his custom in those early days, he had already fixed his mind on a frail old man whom he intended to copy on the stage. His exercises in front of the mirror convinced him that the physical state of a frail old man resembled the state of a young man who was tired after a long walk : legs, arms and back all stiff ; to get up, you had first of all to bend forward to find the right point of support and raise yourself with the help of your hands because your feet almost refused to function. On getting up you found it difficult to straighten your back all at once, but had to do it gradually. And while your feet were still tired, you walked unsteadily, but the moment your feet began to function again they did not seem to be able to stop. That was the physical action of a tired young man that Stanislavsky thought reproduced more or less faithfully the sensations of old age. But when he demonstrated it to Fedotov, he was told that it was no good at all, that, in fact, it was a mere burlesque of an old man. Stanislavsky began to relax the strain more and more till at last all that was left was "the inertia of an old man's rhythm". Only then did Fedotov seem satisfied. Stanislavsky was puzzled : when he tried to apply the methods he had discovered for the representation of an old man, he was told that he was no good at all, but when he gave up those methods, which Fedotov himself seemed to approve of, he was praised. So it was wrong to look for any methods of acting ? But when he tried to act without any method, he became inaudible and was told to speak up. "However hard I tried," Stanislavsky writes, "I could not discover the key to this secret."

At the subsequent rehearsals of the part of the miser, Stanislavsky still could not achieve any satisfactory result. What annoyed him most was that he could apply the technical methods he had succeeded in mastering so far only in the quiet passages of his part. In the more dramatic places he seemed to lose what he had already found. In those moments, overcome by what he believed to be inspiration, he began to rant.

By the late summer the rehearsals came to an end and Stanislavsky went to Vichy for what was to become his annual "cure" for all sorts of imaginary ailments. There he went on working on his part. It became an *idée fixe* with him and he experienced the worst pains a man could experience—"the pains of creation." This is how Stanislavsky describes these pains : "You feel the *something* that your part lacks ; it is just here, inside you, and all you have to do is to stretch out your hand and grasp it ; but the moment you do so, it vanishes. You approach the strong part of your role with an empty soul, without any spiritual content. All you have to do is to open up, but a kind of wall suddenly springs up all round the strong feeling and prevents you from getting near it. This state of mind resembles the sensation of a man who cannot make up his mind to plunge into icy water."

In his search for a solution of this problem, Stanislavsky tried a rather curious experiment. He decided to get himself locked up in an old medieval castle in the vicinity of Vichy which had huge subterranean dungeons, in the hope that there he would be able to find that mysterious feeling, that general state of mind, that sensation—that elusive *something*, in short, which would explain his part to him and, by enabling him to experience it, perhaps make it possible for him to reproduce it on the stage. Actually, he did not know himself what exactly he was after or what it was that he thought was missing in his conception of his part. But the experiment was a complete failure. He felt creepy and lonely there. It was damp, there were rats, and he could not possibly concentrate on his part. And when he recited the text, which he had begun to loathe, in the dark dungeon, he just felt silly. He was beginning to feel chilled, and his fear of a cold began to take a stronger and stronger hold of him. He got into a panic at the thought that he might catch pneumonia, and there could of course no longer be any question of thinking of his part. He started knocking frantically at the door, but as he had told the caretaker not to let him out on any account, the door remained locked. The only result of this experiment was therefore a severe cold in the head and even greater despair. It was clear to him that to act a tragic part it was not enough to get oneself locked up in a damp, rat-infested cellar. Something else was needed. But what was it ? It seemed that, on the contrary, he had to climb to some eminence, to lift himself up on high. But how he could get there no one seemed to know. "Producers," Stanislavsky writes, "explain to you very ably what they want you to do or express, *what is necessary* for the play ; what they are interested in is the final result. They criticise, they even tell you what is *not* wanted. But how to obtain what they want, they never tell you."

The actor does his best to live his part, to *feel* it, he strains himself to the utmost, he rolls his eyes, his blood rushes to his head till he feels dizzy, his throat tightens till he grows hoarse, but all he achieves is to work himself up into a state where he is quite incapable of feeling anything. That was what happened at the rehearsals of *The Covetous Knight*. What happened at the actual performance was what Stanislavsky calls "pure, unadulterated ham acting." But the performance was a success, and this success he ascribed wholly to the beautiful scenery and the fine costumes designed by Sollogub, and the whole harmonious "tone and atmosphere" of the production, which was due entirely to Fedotov. The audience applauded and, Stanislavsky writes, "I took my calls and bowed, and the audience accepted me because it does not know how to differentiate the work of the actor from the work of the producer. I, too, got my meed of praise, and I sincerely believed that if I was praised it meant that I had made an impression, and that therefore this 'ham acting' was inspiration." As for the producer's criticism, Stanislavsky declares that he dismissed it as jealousy and, of course, if he was jealous of him, there was something to be jealous of. "From this vicious circle of self-delusion," he writes, "there seems to be no way of escape. The actor grows confused and is entirely submerged by the praises and flattery he receives. The actor cannot help believing in what he wants to believe. It is not the bitter truth of the expert but the sweet compliments of his charming female admirers that sound convincing." And this rather sombre reflection leads Stanislavsky to utter this warning to the young actor : "Young actors, beware of your female admirers ! Make love to them, if it amuses you, but do not discuss art with them ! Learn in time to listen to, to understand and love the bitter truth about yourselves ! And get to know those who can tell it to you. It is with them that you should discuss art. Let them criticise you as often as possible ! "

There can be no doubt that Stanislavsky's analysis of the first part in which he appeared in the Society of Art and Literature is justified. He could never play strong tragic parts, though he attempted many. But it is no less true that his first appearance in this tragic part was felt by the spectators to be something that they had never seen before : a departure from convention which, though unsatisfying, was at least fresh and charged with something that promised to open up a new chapter in the history of the Russian stage. As for the production, it was, according to a Russian critic who was present at the performance, remarkable for its artistic truth, especially when compared with the conventionally realistic scenery of the Maly Theatre.

In *Georges Dandin*, Stanislavsky played the comic part of Sotenville. The difficulty of this part was to find a fresh interpretation of a Molière character free from the conventional "uniform" in which such characters were invariably presented on the stage, a "uniform" that Stanislavsky nicknamed "Spanish," because actors of such parts usually appeared on the Russian stage wearing "Spanish" boots and tights and a rapier. It was this "sacred tradition" that Stanislavsky felt had to be challenged and scotched, for Molière was so overlaid by it that he was never seen. Fedotov, who was an authority on French classical drama, could show Stanislavsky exactly how a Molière character had to be played on the stage, but it was one thing to know how a character had to be played and quite another to be able to play him. What seemed so easy to Stanislavsky when he watched Fedotov do it from the auditorium, became the most difficult thing in the world when he tried to do it himself on the stage. "What is so difficult on the stage," Stanislavsky writes, "is to believe sincerely in what is taking place there and to take it all seriously. But without belief and without a serious attitude it is impossible to play a comedy or a satire, and more particularly a French classical comedy by Molière. For everything here depends on the actor's sincere belief in the absurd and improbable situations in which he finds himself and from which there appears to be no way of escape. It is possible to overdo this serious attitude, but then the result is the opposite of what you want. Comedy is so fastidious that it revenges itself on you if you don't treat it the right way. There is all the difference in the world between experiencing something and merely pretending to experience it, the same sort of difference that exists between a natural and organically comic situation and the external grimacings of a clown."

Fedotov seemed actually to believe what was happening on the stage while Stanislavsky, who was merely trying to copy him, merely pretended to believe in it. For in copying Fedotov, Stanislavsky was trying to reproduce Fedotov's embodiment of Sotenville's character and not attempting to give his own embodiment of it. The problem with which Stanislavsky was faced was how to overcome the fundamental difficulty inherent in this particular method of production. For the more talented a producer is, the more liable is he to "show" the actor how a certain part is to be played or even how a certain bit of "stage business" is to be managed. All he expects the actor to do is to reproduce correctly what he has shown him, and, as a rule, all the actor tries to do is to follow blindly the directions of the producer, with the result that the audience only sees a pale copy of the character as conceived by the producer. It is a method particularly favoured by the all too common type of producer-autocrat, and indeed in the period during which Stanislavsky himself was a producer-autocrat he invariably resorted to it. Nemirovich-Danchenko, Stanislavsky's fellow-producer at the Moscow Art Theatre, who was very good at "showing," stuck to this method to the end. The difference between Stanislavsky and all other talented producers is that he was never satisfied to adopt any method without thoroughly analyzing it first, and in this analysis his own experiences on the stage were of the utmost importance to him. The notes in which he put down his doubts and criticisms from the time of his first appearance on the stage at the age of fourteen provided him many years later with valuable material for this analysis. There can, therefore, be no doubt that at the rehearsals of *Georges Dandin* he did feel the incongruity of being expected to present Fedotov-Sotenville on the stage instead of finding a way of presenting Sotenville-Stanislavsky. He might not have realized this dilemma as clearly as he did forty years later, when he discussed it in *My Life in Art,* but unconsciously he undoubtedly felt its influence, though he did not know how to resolve it. He merely did what the majority of actors do at almost every rehearsal : he tried to copy Fedotov, but to his dismay he found that, inveterate copyist as he was, he did not even know how to copy satisfactorily. Fortunately, a pure accident solved his difficulties : something in his make-up gave his face an irresistibly comic expression and that brought him to an inner understanding of the character of Sotenville. It was a miracle ! Something inside him had been growing and ripening until it suddenly opened up. "What can such a moment of great joy be compared to ?" Stanislavsky writes : "Shall I compare it to the return to life after a serious illness or to the safe delivery of a child ? How wonderful it is to be an actor at such moments and how rarely do actors experience them ! In the actor's quests and aspirations they remain a guiding light for ever."

It was thanks to Fedotov and Sollogub that Stanislavsky at last emerged from the blind alley of operatic conventions and absurdities. So far he had found no new way of representing life on the stage artistically, but he realized his mistake of confusing the emotions of an actor—"a sort of hysteria, an imitation on the stage of the screaming of a woman in a fit of passion"—with flashes of real inspiration.

But—accident or not—Stanislavsky's acting in *Georges Dandin* made the Moscow audience realize that a new type of actor had arrived. What they saw was quite different from the acting to which they had been accustomed. What struck them in particular was the naturalness of Stanislavsky's representation of a stupid coxcomb who one moment resembled a puffed up turkey-cock and another a mincingly polite man of the world. Sotenville-Stanislavsky's deportment on the stage, too, was free from every strain, and he manipulated his cane and hat as though he really was a seventeenth century French Marquis.

CHAPTER XI

THE FIRST DRAMATIC production of the Society of Art and Literature took place on December 8th, 1888, and three days later Fedotov put on Pissemsky's play of Russian peasant life, *Bitter Fate*. In this play, Stanislavsky took the leading part of Anany, a tragic part abounding in highly dramatic situations. The main difficulty of such a part for Stanislavsky was his lack of self-control. He had learnt from experience that whenever he had to play a highly dramatic scene he lost control of his body, with the result that it seemed to be either tied up in knots or producing a mass of uncontrollable movements, senseless poses and gestures, nervous tics, and so on. In such a chaotic state he found it impossible to convey the feelings of the character. His problem therefore was to free his body from the grip of his muscles and to subordinate it entirely to feeling.

During the rehearsals of the play Stanislavsky succeeded in freeing his body from muscular spasms by localizing the strain in a single well-defined centre, such as his fingers or toes or diaphragm or, as Stanislavsky hastens to add, "what I believed to be my diaphragm at the time." The result, of course, was that he drove his finger-nails into his hands till they bled or pressed his toes into the floor with all the weight of his body, leaving bloodstains on his socks and shoes. But by creating this localized strain, he freed the rest of his body from tension so that he could stand on the stage without shifting from foot to foot or making any other unnecessary movements. He then went on trying to free himself from the localized strain, but that he did not find so easy, for the moment he released the strain from his clenched fist, it spread all over his body. He had to localize it again in his fist, and thus found himself in a vicious circle from which there seemed to be no way of escape. But when he did succeed once or twice in freeing his body completely from strain, he was congratulated by

65

the producer for the simplicity of his playing and the absence of overacting. Another discovery that he made was that the calmer and more controlled his body was on the stage, the more liable was he to substitute facial expression, intonation and look for gesture. But any over-emphasis in mimicry or intonation again resulted in shouts and grimacing. He then realized that whenever in the quiet scenes of the play he tried to appear calm and indifferent, he invariably felt a strange excitement boiling up inside him. And the more strongly he concealed this excitement, the more powerful it became. The concealment of feeling, therefore, merely led to its intensification. But in a crowd scene where it was impossible to feign indifference, he could not help being carried away by the general excitement and could not keep this grip on himself, so that at the end of the play he could not remember what he had been doing on the stage during such a scene. To his surprise, however, everyone congratulated him on the powerful impression his acting had produced on the audience. What had apparently happened was that by keeping himself under control in the previous scenes he had created the impression that when the climax came he could no longer control himself, that he had, in fact, stumbled on the secret of the gradual growth of emotional tension from piano to forte, while other actors usually overlook this gradual upsurge of emotion and jump straight from piano to forte. That, at any rate, was what his audience felt. At the time Stanislavsky himself was still incapable of finding the exact correlation between the actor's state of mind and the impression created by it on the spectator. And, as in his part of Sotenville, it was his successful make-up that helped him in his part of Anany to get right inside the character and bring it to life on the stage. Having once found the key to this character at rehearsals he then, according to his old habit, merely copied it at the performance, and thus reached that higher stage in the development of the actor which many years later he called in his "system" the "imitative" actor, who stands midway between the mere copyist, or ham actor, and the creative actor.

The play was a great success, and was highly commended in the Moscow Press. For a time it seemed to Stanislavsky that he had discovered the secret of acting, but he soon became disillusioned in the efficacy of what he called the method of "self-control". In the spring of 1889 Fedotov produced two more plays for the Society of Art and Literature : Pushkin's *Stone Guest*, in which Stanislavsky first played Don Carlos and afterwards Don Juan, and Schiller's *Kabale und Liebe*. The "Spanish" boots and rapier in the first play seem to have played havoc with whatever he had learnt in the previous season and once more he was entirely under the powerful influence of the "operatic" tradition. Having taken one step forward, he now took two steps backwards. The truth was that he had been too hasty in undertaking to play parts for which he had not been prepared by experience or training. He had given in to the eternal urge of the inexperienced actor to play the leading parts in a tragedy. In Pushkin's play he again copied the opera baritone, and the more he tried to apply his experience in the part of Anany to Pushkin's hero, the more theatrically unconvincing he became. He was no better in the part of Ferdinand in *Kabale und Liebe*, except that in the scenes with Lilina his genuine feeling for the actress disguised his shortcomings as an actor.

It was at this time, too, that Stanislavsky was beginning to be preoccupied with the larger issues of an actor's position in society. "The actor," he wrote in his *Artistic Notes*, in 1889, "forgets his mission of an interpreter of high human aspirations, and he forgets his former ideals, too—to become the guide and educator of the public. The theatre has ceased to be an academy and has been transformed into a place of cheap entertainment. . . . The only solution for the actor is self-criticism, which is only possible if the actor is able to obtain a definite and precise idea about his work, create an ideal towards which he should aspire, and find in himself sufficient strength to scorn cheap success. To mount the pedestal of fully earned artistic fame, the actor must, in addition to his purely artistic endowments, become an ideal man."

This view grew more and more characteristic of Stanislavsky's conception of the actor's duties towards himself and society, and was one of the most powerful influences which led him to the eventual conception of his "system" not only as a way of attaining perfection on the stage, but also as a way of life.

In the summer of 1889 Stanislavsky married Lilina, and in the autumn he appeared in *Men Above the Law*, an historical play by Pissemsky, in which he played the brutal General Imshin. In this part, too, he was successful. It was a part in which he could apply all the discoveries he had made in the earlier productions of the Society of Art and Literature : self-control, the concealment of inner feeling by a show of outward calm, facial expression and the play of eyes, the fullest possible revelation of pent-up feelings in a climax ; as well as the methods he had discovered for the acting of an old man in Pushkin's *The Covetous Knight*. Since General Imshin was a Russian, he could easily overcome the temptation to revert to his "operatic" ham-acting. In this play he made another discovery which proved very fruitful to him years later when he was evolving his "system". He discovered the fascination of contrast in the acting of a negative character. After watching another actor on the stage from the auditorium and while discussing his part with him later, he suddenly delivered himself of his aphorism : "When playing a villain, try to find where he is good," and suddenly realized that he had uttered a profound truth. This was another acquisition to be stowed away in his "actor's trunk". Stanislavsky, as he himself admits, was never very good at compressing in a single sentence an important truth. But when he tried to prove the correctness of an idea of his to someone else, when, as he says, "philosophy became necessary to me for the sake of proving something," aphorisms seemed to come to him naturally. That was what happened when he tried to prove to his friend that in playing a villain, his acting would become more convincing if he relieved the blackness of his characterization by a splash of white here and there. "When you play a good man, try to find out where he is bad, and when you play a villain, try to find where he is good," he told his friend. And in applying this aphorism to his own part of General Imshin, he made it more human and helped to relieve the general feeling of gloom which this sombre play created among the audience.

It was in this year that Stanislavsky made his only attempt at writing a play. Carried away by his apparent success in playing tragic parts, he wrote a one-act melodrama, *Monaco*, describing the tragic fate which overtakes a Russian gambler who fails to break the bank at Monte Carlo. The play did not pass the censorship, and to judge by a remark he made a year or so later when discussing this play with a friend, he did not seem to be particularly upset by the censor's decision. His friend told him that he, too, had recently finished a play, and he was about to ask him to read it when Stanislavsky rather unkindly cut him short by the question, "What do you want to increase the number of bad plays for ? "

The affairs of the Society of Art and Literature were in the meantime going from bad to worse. At the end of the first year the Society showed a heavy deficit, and the growing disagreements between Fedotov and Kommissarzhevsky soon led to the resignation of Fedotov. Sollogub, too, left the Society. The so-called "family evenings" during which the artists were supposed to go to the Society's studio to paint and the actors to recite also came to an end, the actors saying "We are fed up with playing, even in the theatre," and the artists saying "We are fed up with painting, even at home." What both actors and artists wanted was a club where they could play cards, and as that was prohibited by the statutes of the Society, they left it. The only thing that remained from the original grandiose programme was the dramatic section, which was now under the direct supervision of Stanislavsky, and the operatic and dramatic school, which existed for a short time longer, until, that is, Kommissarzhevsky realized that he could get nothing out of the Society and promptly left it.

In the summer of 1890 the Society moved to cheaper premises, its old premises being occupied by the Hunting Club. The summer after, it had to move again. Stanislavsky made an agreement with the Hunting Club to put on a new play every week at their premises. But even then bad luck stalked the efforts of the Society, for the premises of the Hunting Club burnt down in January, 1891, and for a time Stanislavsky had to produce his plays at the German Club. In November, 1892, the Hunting Club moved to new premises and the Society renewed their productions on its tiny stage. In the autumn of 1894 a new agreement was made between the Hunting Club and the Society, which vested the full artistic responsibility for the Society's productions in Stanislavsky, who undertook to put on two plays every week, on Thursdays and Sundays.

CHAPTER XII

THE MOST IMPORTANT event in Stanislavsky's artistic life in 1890 had little to do with any of the plays the Society of Art and Literature had put on during that year. It was the second visit to Moscow of the company of the Duke of Meiningen under its producer Kronegk. It is rather the fashion among Russian dramatic critics to minimize the importance of the influence of the Meiningen company on Stanislavsky during the first period of his work at the Moscow Art Theatre. References to Stanislavsky as a disciple of Kronegk and to the Moscow Art Theatre as following the naturalistic traditions of the Meiningen Company are usually dismissed as utterly wrong and superficial. But these critics are to a certain extent influenced by the subsequent history of the Moscow Art Theatre and the subsequent abandonment of the Meiningen tradition by Stanislavsky. Ostrovsky, as has been made clear earlier, at once saw through Kronegk's dramatic pretensions. Behind the façade of efficiency, he discerned the utter emptiness of a Kronegk production. But to Stanislavsky in 1890, on the very threshold of his career as an independent producer, Kronegk seemed to possess everything he was looking for. In his eyes at that time Kronegk was undoubtedly the ideal producer whose methods he immediately set about copying. He did not miss a single performance of the company and, as he himself admits, he not only went to see those performances, but also to study them.

What was it that Stanislavsky found so fascinating about Kronegk? In the first place, Kronegk was the most perfect example of the producer-autocrat in Europe at the time. He ruled his company with a rod of iron. While outside the theatre his relations with the actors, even with the most humble members of his company, were extremely friendly, he was completely transformed the moment he sat down at the producer's table. He sat there in silence waiting for the hand of the clock to reach the time appointed for the rehearsal. Then he rang a bell and in a low "ominous" voice uttered just one word : *"Anfangen !"* At once, there was dead silence and the actors, too, seemed to become transformed. The rehearsals began without any delays and went on till Kronegk rang his bell again, after which he made his observations to the actors in a "passionless" voice. Then again the ominous *Anfangen* and the rehearsal was resumed. If an actor happened to be late, everyone waited breathlessly for the producer's verdict, which only came after a dramatic pause, the actor as a punishment being usually deprived of his part and made to take his place at the head of "the last group of extras at the back of the stage". The rehearsal then went on with the actor's understudy taking his part.

All this made a tremendous impression on Stanislavsky. He liked Kronegk's self-control and sangfroid. "I began to imitate Kronegk," he writes, "and with time I became a producer-autocrat myself and many Russian producers began imitating me as I had imitated Kronegk. A whole generation of producer-autocrats arose, but, alas, as they did not possess Kronegk's talent, the producers of this new type merely became theatrical managers who treated the actors as if they were props, as mere pawns to be moved about as they liked on their *mise-en-scènes*."

Stanislavsky is here a little unfair to the Russian producers of the new school. When he himself had outgrown his enthusiasm for the producer-autocrat, the thing that he deplored most was that during that phase of his career he, too, had treated his actors "like mannequins". Ostrovsky was not at all impressed by the way Kronegk treated his actors. Indeed, it was he who accused him of treating them as if they were props. Ostrovsky knew very well the importance of discipline on the stage but, like Stanislavsky in the last period of his work as a producer, it was inner discipline that he sought and not the discipline that is imposed from above. But in 1890 and during the first dozen or so years of the Moscow Art Theatre, it was the Kronegk type of discipline that Stanislavsky admired and insisted on. It was true that at first he did it because it was the best way to deal with amateurs. "It seemed to me at the time," he writes, "that we amateur producers were in the same position as Kronegk and the Duke of Meiningen. We, too, wanted to put on great plays and to reveal the thoughts and feelings of the great playwrights, but as we had no trained actors we had to relegate all the powers to the producer, who alone had to create the performance of the play with the help of scenery, props, interesting *mise-en-scènes* and his own imaginative inventions. That was why the despotism of the Meiningen producer seemed justified to me." But the weakness of this apology for what he himself later acknowledged to have been his own misdeeds as producer-autocrat lies surely in the fact that Kronegk's actors were not untrained. It was Kronegk's despotic methods that led him to disregard any difference between the trained and untrained actor, or rather made him completely deny the need of genius in an actor. What Kronegk did was to convert the actor into a puppet, and it was a matter of indifference to him whether the actor could speak his lines or not so long as he *looked* the part. At that period Stanislavsky, too, seemed to believe that *looking* the part was the best way of getting to live it. In *Georges Dandin* it had been his make-up that had helped him to find the clue to Molière's character. This make-up he had dug up from an historical journal. He had spent a long time looking for it in books and journals of every kind. And, generally, during most of the ten years of the existence of the Society of Art and Literature, Stanislavsky resorted to the art galleries and all sorts of illustrated magazines to find the right make-up for his characters. But even in those days he differed from Kronegk in that he regarded *looking* the part merely as a means to an end, whereas to Kronegk it was an end in itself.

What Stanislavsky never stopped admiring in Kronegk was the fertility of his inventions as a producer, which, he thought, helped to bring out a great deal of the "creative ideas" of the great poets without depending on the help of "exceptionally talented actors". One scene from Schiller's *Maid of Orleans,* particularly impressed him : a little, miserable-looking, perplexed and sickly king sits on a huge throne, his thin legs too short to reach the cushion on the floor ; all round the throne his embarrassed courtiers are trying in vain to uphold his royal prestige ; suddenly the English ambassadors appear—tall, overbearing, determined, and when the unhappy king issues his humiliating order, the courtier to whom it is addressed tries in vain to conform to Court etiquette and bow to the king before leaving to carry it out ; suddenly he stops, straightens himself out and stands for a moment with lowered eyes—then, forgetting all about Court etiquette, he runs out so as not to burst into tears in the presence of the English ambassadors.

This scene seems to have brought tears to the eyes of the audience, and the other scenes in the play showing the humiliation of the King of France were treated in like manner. "The producer," Stanislavsky writes, "has so condensed the atmosphere of the defeated Court that the spectator waits impatiently for the arrival of Joan of Arc, and is so glad when she does arrive that he does not notice the bad playing of the actors. The producer's talent often concealed it."

In this last sentence Stanislavsky puts his finger on the weakest spot of Kronegk's methods as a producer. Carried away by the fertile inventions of his own imagination, such a producer tends to give free play to it and to subordinate everything else, including his actors, to the clever stage tricks he is so good at inventing. A talented actor is a hindrance to such a producer, and that was why Kronegk's company had so few talented actors. Stanislavsky, who possessed an imagination that was even more fertile than Kronegk's, could not help adopting his methods of production, particularly as in the Society of Art and Literature and during the first years of the Moscow Art Theatre he had to deal either with amateurs or with inexperienced actors. The great danger of such a method, however, is that the producer who is good at it—and Stanislavsky was very good at it—is often led to sacrifice the inner meaning of a dramatic masterpiece to his externally effective *mise-en-scènes*, sometimes even suppressing or distorting the playwright's ideas whenever they cut across his own. Another danger of this method is that the producer tends to give preference to the works of minor playwrights in which there is less likelihood of a clash between his own imagination and the imagination of the playwright, and in which he can improve on the playwright's works without fear of criticism. This was, in fact, what happened with Stanislavsky.

It was only many years later that Stanislavsky realized the fundamental falsity of such an approach to the art of the stage. "The producer," he writes in *My Life in Art*, published in 1925, "can do a great deal, but not by any means everything. The chief thing lies in the hands of the actors, who have to be assisted and directed along the right way. The Meiningen producers apparently did not look at it like that, and that was why the producer was forced to work without the help of the actor. . . . He had to transfer the centre of gravity to the production itself, and the necessity of doing everybody's creative work resulted in the producer's despotism."

But it would be a mistake to regard this declaration of Stanislavsky's as anything but an apologia for his past errors. In 1890 he adopted Kronegk's views with enthusiasm and he started out on his career as producer-autocrat without any qualms whatever. Henceforth he modelled himself closely on Kronegk. He, too, like Kronegk, sat at the producer's table with a watch in his hand, waiting for the appointed time of the rehearsal, and when the time came he struck his bell and the rehearsal began. His discipline was ruthless, and he went even further than Kronegk in demanding that in the name of discipline an actor who was one day playing a leading part should raise no objection when ordered to play a walking-on part next day. When he put on Chekhov's *The Bear* in 1895, Nicolai Popov, one of his closest assistants, who played the manservant Luka, objected to Stanislavsky's drastic cuts of his dialogue. The rehearsal took place at Stanislavsky's flat. When Popov arrived, Stanislavsky was not in the room and Lilina, his wife, was busy pouring out tea at the breakfast table.

"Why are you so gloomy?" she asked.

"How can I help being gloomy," replied Popov. "Konstantin has cut out most of my dialogue."

"Well?"

"I shall refuse to play. After all, it's Chekhov!"

At that moment Stanislavsky himself walked into the room.

"Darling," Lilina addressed him agitatedly, "Nicolai Alexandrovich refuses to play Luka!"

"Why?"

"You've cut out most of my lines. It's Chekhov, don't forget!"

"First of all," said Stanislavsky, "there is more of the traditional farce in this play than of the typical Chekhov, and, besides," he added, bringing down his fist on the table with such force that it made the *samovar* jump and the crockery clatter, "*what about discipline?*"

The mention of discipline subdued the rebellious Popov and put an end to his objections to the cuts in his part.

This was not the only time the actors objected to Stanislavsky's iron discipline. But though there were occasional murmurs, some people accusing him of indulging the whims of a rich business man, Stanislavsky forced his actors to accept his discipline because, in the first place, his own devotion to the theatre was so manifest that there could be no question of any personal desire to boss them ; secondly, they could not help falling under the spell of his personality. According to one member of the Society of Art and Literature, he was exceedingly pleasant to get on with both in private life and on the stage. At times, indeed, he was a little too courteous, as though he wished to conceal his natural shyness. Stanislavsky's courtesy, another actor observes, "was of tremendous importance to the general tone which was characteristic of our rehearsals and performances. Not a single harsh word was heard ; there were no shouts or contemptuous remarks." What everybody found so attractive in Stanislavsky in those days was his unusual, almost childlike, sincerity and purity of motive and his bright and cheerful attitude towards life and people. What impressed the actors, too, and helped to preserve his authority over them, was the fact that although he was very friendly and accessible he always kept himself aloof from them. He did not make friends easily. He seemed to lack the desire to open up his heart to people. Outwardly mild and even shy, he would at the right moment point out to the actor (who was, after all, not a paid actor, but a member of the Society of Art and Literature) absolutely fearlessly and without any sign of weakness, his mistakes and shortcomings and make him go over his part again and again until he got what he wanted. Already in the Alexeyev Circle Stanislavsky had introduced the custom of having numerous rehearsals, and he followed this custom at the Society of Art and Literature, and later introduced it to the Moscow Art Theatre.

No doubt his extremely impressive appearance, too, made it easier for Stanislavsky to impose his authority on his actors. He was very tall, with thick dark hair which was already going grey, though he was only in his early thirties, large, expressive grey eyes, and a most charmingly shy smile. He was so well-built that his enormous size did not strike anyone as incongruous except that, as one actor observes, "when he stood next to you he made you look very small beside him." Occasionally, however, his natural shyness led him to express his views with too much self-assurance, which did not always come off, especially when he tried to engage in a literary discussion ; for his revolt against the pedantic classicism of his school left rather a big gap in his literary education.

Another reform Stanislavsky introduced while working with

his amateur group of actors of the Society of Art and Literature concerned the virtual abolition of the prompter. This was certainly unusual for the Russian stage in those days. Stanislavsky, remembering his experience when acting with the Maly Theatre Company in Ryazan, demanded that the actors should be word-perfect in their parts after the first two or three readings of the play. "You must get out of the habit of relying on the prompter," he used to tell his actors. "You have plenty of time to learn your parts". As a result, his prompter, who later became also the prompter of the Moscow Art Theatre, had very little to do during the rehearsals except smoke cigarettes and watch the actors.

CHAPTER XIII

IT WOULD BE IDLE to speculate on the reasons for Stanislavsky's ardent devotion to the stage even in the early 'nineties when his real theatrical career was only just beginning. Towards the end of his life he was rather prone to dismiss his activities at the Society of Art and Literature as smacking too much of a personal desire for limelight. "In those days," he wrote, "the stage was just a shop-window for me." But that is not true. Stanislavsky was always a harsh critic of himself and he was apt to forget that but for his early mistakes he would never have become a great reformer of the stage and an internationally recognized authority on its technique. No—already in the early 'nineties the stage was no longer a "shop-window," nor an amusement, nor a career to him : it was life itself. Even at home he could not live except in an atmosphere of the footboards, and he converted his study into a cross between a theatrical museum and a property-room. His friends and fellow-actors often deplored his lack of taste in furnishing his study. They seemed to agree that it showed a regrettable lack of originality. After his marriage, Stanislavsky occupied a flat in the Alexeyev house at the Red Gates, where he lived from 1863 to 1903. His study was a large but rather dark room, with pseudo-Gothic, narrow windows, set in very thick walls and filled with imitation stained glass with figures of knights in armour. The chairs in his study had very tall backs and were upholstered in imitation Gobelin tapestries. Ancient-looking iron lanterns hung on the walls, and the spaces between the windows were ornamented with what appeared to be military banners. There were also long spears propped up against the walls. An ancient chest with big metal clasps was placed rather incongruously on the thick carpet which covered the floor. Nearby stood a table which resembled a lectern, covered by a bright piece of antique cloth and with a low, pseudo-medieval seat in

77

front of it. The furniture included, besides, two glass-fronted book-cases, also in pseudo-Gothic style, filled with books in leather covers. One corner of the study was partitioned off by a carved wooden screen, and that too, needless to say, was in pseudo-Gothic style.

If all this appeared rather odd to Stanislavsky's friends and stage colleagues, it seemed to agree perfectly with Stanislavsky himself. He had to have the stage always with him. He could not very well live in the theatre, though later on he practically did so. He therefore made his study into the fantastic world which he had so admired as a child. And from time to time the various pieces of furniture found their way on to the stage where they really belonged. The chairs, for instance, were used in Stanislavsky's production of *Uriel Acosta,* in 1895.

Stanislavsky's first independent production of a straight play took place on February 8th, 1891. The play was Leo Tolstoy's *Fruits of Enlightenment,* a production that was compared favourably in the Press with the production of the same play by the Maly Theatre. In the previous year, Stanislavsky had played in three Ostrovsky plays, including *A Girl Without a Dowry,* had repeated his old success as a drunken student in the French light comedy *A Woman's Secret,* and had also been successful in Fedotov's comedy *Rouble,* in which he was again fortunate in finding the clue to his part in the make-up.

Tolstoy's play presented great difficulties to a beginner like Stanislavsky, first of all because it had so many characters. His approach to the play was simple : he showed the actors how to play their parts as he saw them in his imagination, with the result that whenever his feeling was right the play came to life and whenever he went no further than external invention it was dead. "The merit of my work on this play," Stanislavsky writes, "was that I tried to be sincere and looked for truth, while doing my utmost to avoid falsehood, especially theatrical falsehood." His approach to the play was therefore a purely realistic one. He was at the time beginning to hate "the theatre in the theatre," a healthy reaction against his "operatic" enthusiasms. Looking for external truth helped him to find the correct and interesting *mise-en-scènes,* which set him on the right path for finding truth ; truth, in its turn, aroused feeling, and feeling brought creative itnuition into play.

He was, besides, rather lucky in that he got the right kind of performers for the different parts of the play. In this play, too, he discovered for the first time the right way of asserting his authority as producer. What impressed his fellow-actors was his fanatical love of the stage, his capacity for work, and the strictness of his attitude to himself in the first place. The first man he fined, he writes, was himself, and he did it with such conviction that it did not look like a pose. He ruthlessly punished everyone who was late for the rehearsals, everyone who did not know his part or indulged in private conversations during work or left the rehearsal-room without permission, for he knew that any kind of disorder in the theatre could only lead to the chaos which had made him run away from the amateur theatres. He also banned all unnecessary smartness in dress, especially among the women, on the ground that it interfered with their work. Any kind of flirtation was taboo. "Real love—by all means," he used to tell the actors, "for real love raises you up. Shoot yourself for a woman, drown yourself, die if die you must ! But I shall not tolerate any superficial titillation of the emotions, for that merely creates a vulgar atmosphere and pulls you down."

This puritanical attitude to stage morals Stanislavsky preserved all through his life. He declared war to the death on the bohemian life of actors and, especially, amateur actors. Many years later he used to frown on any flirtation between an actor and actress of the Moscow Art Theatre, while if he heard that an actor and an actress had become engaged he would beam with joy, for he held that a happy family life was the best guarantee of an actor's successful work on the stage.

The great success of *The Fruits of Enlightenment,* which was revived several times, not only improved the financial position of what was left of the Society of Art and Literature, but for the first time drew the attention of the theatre-going public in Moscow to a group of actors who, in the words of one of the critics, "might form a theatre that would raise the mental and moral level of Russian society, that is to say, pursue the real aims of dramatic art."

The play also provoked an enthusiastic appreciation from Nemirovich-Danchenko, who six years later was to found the Moscow Art Theatre with Stanislavsky. "I assert," Nemirovich-Danchenko wrote, "that no one has ever seen such an exemplary performance on an amateur stage. Why, if you did not know that they were amateur actors, you would never have believed it !

Tolstoy's comedy was played with a better ensemble and more intelligently than any play is ever played even in the best private theatre in Moscow." As for Stanislavsky as an actor, Nemirovich-Danchenko wrote : "If I had been a dramatic critic, I should have devoted a whole article to his acting. So many subtle and characteristic details did he impart to the role of Zvezdintsev."

Stanislavsky seemed in this play to have found what he calls "an accessory approach to the soul of the actor." This approach was from the outer to the inner, from the body to the soul, from embodiment to experience, from form to content. He had, besides, learnt how to construct a *mise-en-scène* in which "the inner kernel of the play was revealed by itself," though he is careful to add that "the only good new thing in this production was that it lacked all that was old and bad."

It was in this year that Kommissarzhevsky left the Society of Art and Literature, which was now reduced to a mere shadow of its former self and only subsisted on its dramatic section. Owing to the burning down of the premises of the Hunting Club, *The Fruits of Enlightenment* had to be put on at the German Club, where Stanislavsky's second production in 1891, his own adaptation of Dostoevsky's comic masterpiece *The Village of Stepanchikovo*, was performed on November 14th under the title of the hero of the novel, *Foma* (Thomas). Eighteen years later the production of an adaptation of the same novel by the Moscow Art Theatre resulted in the greatest scandal in the history of the theatre and finally widened the rift between Stanislavsky and Nemirovich-Danchenko. In the 1891 production, Stanislavsky played Colonel Rostanev and Lilina, Nastenka. The play was not a success, but in it Stanislavsky for the first time felt really happy in his part, which seemed to come to him naturally.

This was noticed by the critics at the time. Thus, the dramatic critic of the monthly journal *Artist* wrote the following appreciation of Stanislavsky's acting in this part in the issue of December, 1891 : "By far the best performance was given by Mr. Stanislavsky in the part of Colonel Rostanev. The weak-kneed Colonel lived on the stage and was amazingly true to life. Indeed, there were moments when you were ready to believe that it was not an actor but the Colonel himself you saw, sometimes charming in his great goodness, sometimes so completely lacking in self-assertiveness that you could not help feeling disgusted with him. All these transitions from a momentary accession of energy to a new attack of faint-heartedness were conveyed with amazing truthfulness, and at the moment of his attack on Foma for insulting his bride-to-be you could not help feeling that you were in the presence of a wild beast who is ready to crush everything in his way. No actor who did not possess real talent could make people feel like that, however hard he tried, and if we may venture to offer a word of criticism to Mr. Stanislavsky it is for his nervousness which he does not seem able to conceal."

Another critic wrote : "I wish to state emphatically that the Russian public loses a great deal because such an artist as Mr. Stanislavsky is acting on the amateur stage."

"In an actor's repertoire," Stanislavsky himself comments on his experience in *Foma*, "there are few parts which nature herself has for many years been unconsciously preparing him for. The moment he touches such a part it comes to life without any creative pains, without searchings, and almost without any technical work. This happens because the part and the actor's conception of the character have been created organically in him by nature herself. They have turned out to be just as they should be, and they could not be anything else. It is as difficult to analyze them as your own soul."

This complete merging of himself with his part of Rostanev made it unnecessary for Stanislavsky to copy it either directly or indirectly as was his custom with every other part he played at this time. That was why, as he records, in *The Village of Stepanchikovo* it had been vouchsafed to him for the first time to experience the real joys of a genuine creative actor.

During the next two years Stanislavsky took no active part in the productions of the Society of Art and Literature. In 1892 the Society had to interrupt its production till the winter because it could not find a stage, the Hunting Club's new premises being opened only in November. The only play in which Stanislavsky appeared that year was the revival of *The Love Potion*, in which he repeated his successful performance of the versifying barber of ten years earlier. In January, 1893, Stanislavsky's father died, and the family went into mourning, during which even visits to the theatre were considered to be highly improper. However, as it happened the Maly Theatre at the time put on its famous production of Ostrovsky's comedy *Wolves and Sheep,* and unable to resist the temptation, Stanislavsky went secretly one evening to the gallery of the theatre, in which unaccustomed place he was accosted by Nicolai Popov, who had also gone to the gallery by stealth, being on leave from the army. (Soldiers on leave were forbidden to visit theatres by the Russian Army regulations of those days.)

In the autumn of 1894 the agreement between the Hunting Club and the Society of Art and Literature came into force and Stanislavsky, who had undertaken to put on two plays each week during the winter season, produced four new plays, three of them by Ostrovsky. During the same season he went with his amateur company to Tula, where his first meeting with Tolstoy took place at the house of an intimate friend of Tolstoy's which had been put at Stanislavsky's disposal for rehearsals. In the intervals between the rehearsals, during one of the noisy dinners in which the whole company and their host's family took part, Tolstoy made a sudden appearance in his usual get-up of a grey peasant blouse with a wide leather belt. "Not a single photograph or portrait," says Stanislavsky in his account of this meeting, "can convey the impression one received from his living face and figure. How indeed can one reproduce on paper or canvas Tolstoy's eyes, which seemed to bore into your very soul? His eyes were sharp and piercing at one moment and soft and bright at another. When he was looking at a man, Tolstoy grew motionless and concentrated ; he seemed to penetrate right inside him, drawing out everything that was hidden, good as well as bad. At those moments his eyes hid under his beetling brows like the sun behind a cloud. But at other moments Tolstoy's response to a joke was like a child's, he laughed merrily, and his eyes grew gay and playful, reappearing from beneath his thick brows and shining brightly. Whenever anyone said something interesting, Tolstoy was the first to express his delight, he became lively and expansive like a young man and his eyes sparkled with flashes of real genius."

Each of the actors was introduced to Tolstoy in turn, and each one he grasped by the hand and probed with his eyes. "I felt," Stanislavsky declares, "as though his look had gone right through me." The unexpected meeting with Tolstoy threw Stanislavsky into a kind of stupor and he scarcely realized what was happening in and around him. To understand his state of mind, one must realize what Tolstoy meant to a cultured Russian during the last twenty years of his life. "When Tolstoy was alive," Stanislavsky writes, "we used to say, How blessed are we to be living at the same time as Tolstoy ! And when you felt depressed and fed up with life, and people appeared like beasts to you, you consoled yourself with the thought that there, in Yasnaya Polyana, he—Leo Tolstoy—lived ! And once more you wanted to live."

Tolstoy was put opposite Stanislavsky at the table and after examining him curiously for a few moments (Stanislavsky's excessive shyness must have appeared very strange to Tolstoy just then) he bent over and asked him something. But Stanislavsky was quite incapable of concentrating sufficiently to understand his question. Everybody laughed, and that increased his confusion. At last it dawned on him that Tolstoy wanted to know what play they were performing in Tula, but he could not remember its title, though he had been rehearsing it himself only a short while before. Someone told Tolstoy that it was Ostrovsky's comedy *The Last Sacrifice*, and Tolstoy again asked Stanislavsky what the play was about, as he himself had never read it. Again Stanislavsky felt like a schoolboy who has forgotten his lesson and just did not know how to start. In the end their host came to his rescue and told Tolstoy the plot of the play.

Thrown into utter confusion by this final failure to say anything to Tolstoy, the thirty-one-year old Stanislavsky sat there like a schoolboy with lowered eyes, only occasionally daring to glance guiltily at the great man. In the meantime the roast was brought in, and both the grown-ups and the children began teasing the vegetarian Tolstoy by asking him to help himself to some meat. Tolstoy jokingly agreed and, cutting off a tiny bit from the piece he was offered, he put it into his mouth, chewed it for some time, and then with difficulty forced himself to swallow it. Then he put down his knife and fork and said, "I can't eat a corpse ! It's poison ! Give up meat, for only then will you know what it means to have a clear head or be in a good mood ! " He then embarked on a sermon on vegetarianism, which, Stanislavsky observes, though a rather boring theme, he knew how to make extremely interesting. What struck Stanislavsky about Tolstoy that afternoon was the marvellous way in which he remembered every little detail of a story he told them about a sectarian whose religion was based on all sorts of symbols : an apple tree against a red sky meaning one thing, and a dark fir tree against a moonlit sky another, and so on. The conversation then turned to the theatre, and the actors told Tolstoy that the Society of Art and

Literature had been the first to produce his play *The Fruits of Enlightenment*.

Tolstoy, whose play *The Power of Darkness*, written in 1886 and still banned by the censor (the ban was only lifted a year later), asked them to do all they could to "gladden the heart of an old man" and get the ban removed.

"But," they all shouted in one voice, "will you let us put it on ? "

"I don't forbid anyone to perform my plays," was Tolstoy's reply.

"We immediately began to distribute the parts," Stanislavsky writes, "and even hastened to invite Tolstoy to come to our rehearsals." They also, incidentally, asked him which version of the fourth act he would like them to play or how he would like the two versions to be combined so as not to interfere with the action at the dramatic climax of the tragedy.

"Look here," said Tolstoy, "why not write to me how you would like me to combine the versions and let me work it all out in accordance with your directions ? "

The question was addressed to one of Stanislavsky's fellow-actors (Stanislavsky presumably still being too shy to take an active part in the conversation). But the actor was so staggered by the suggestion that he should advise Tolstoy how to alter a play that he quickly hid himself behind the back of another actor. Tolstoy understood their embarrassment and began assuring them that there was nothing unusual or impracticable about his proposal but that, on the contrary, they would do him a great favour, because they were the specialists. But he did not succeed in convincing them.

Two years later Stanislavsky received a note from one of Tolstoy's friends who wrote to tell him that Tolstoy would like to see him. Tolstoy received him in one of the drawing rooms of his Moscow house. It seemed that Tolstoy was dissatisfied not only with the way *The Power of Darkness* was being put on, but also with the play itself.

"Tell me how you would like me to change the fourth act and I will re-write it," said Tolstoy.

Tolstoy had said it so naturally that Stanislavsky plucked up courage and began to explain his own idea of how to alter the play. They sat talking a long time, but what Stanislavsky did not know was that in the next room Tolstoy's wife Sonia was following every word of their conversation and was getting herself more and more worked up about Stanislavsky's impertinence in teaching her husband.

"Just put yourself in her place," Stanislavsky writes. "Do not forget that she was morbidly jealous of anything that had any connection with her famous husband. Just think what she must have felt when she heard some young man criticising her husband's play and telling him how he ought to have written it. To her, who did not know what had happened previously, this must have appeared a piece of unpardonable impudence."

And so, in fact, it did. For very soon the Countess stormed into the room and began giving Stanislavsky a piece of her mind. "I should have caught it even more," Stanislavsky observes, "if their daughter Maria had not run in to quieten her mother." All during this extraordinary scene, Tolstoy sat without moving, just fingering his beard. He never uttered a word in Stanislavsky's defence. When his wife had gone out, he smiled with the utmost affability at Stanislavsky, who quite naturally looked terribly embarrassed.

"Don't take any notice," Tolstoy said, "she's very upset and nervous," and, as if nothing out of the ordinary had happened, he added, "Well, where did we stop?"

CHAPTER XIV

AT THE TIME of his second meeting with Tolstoy in 1896, Stanislavsky had already become known throughout Russia as a producer and actor of great promise. This he owed to the exceptional success of his production of Gutzkow's historical play *Uriel Acosta*, in which for the first time he fully applied the lessons he had learnt from Kronegk and his Meiningen company.

Gutzkow's play has as little to do with life as with history. It is, in fact, pure melodrama. In the first act Uriel Acosta, a Jewish rationalist philosopher who died in Amsterdam in 1647, is excommunicated as a heretic by the Rabbis who suddenly appear in the garden of the rich Jew Menasseh to whose daughter Judith he is betrothed. Judith, as well as Uriel's mother and brothers, implore him to renounce his heretical views. After a great inner struggle between the philosopher and the lover, the latter is triumphant and Uriel decides to renounce his heresies at a public ceremony in the synagogue. But in the middle of the solemn ceremony of renunciation he changes his mind, reaffirms his heretical beliefs, and is nearly torn to pieces by a crowd of fanatical Jews. In the last act Uriel appears at the wedding of Judith to a rich Jew. True to her love, Judith poisons herself and dies in the arms of Uriel, who at once commits suicide.

A play like that simply cries out for a producer of Kronegk's stamp, and Stanislavsky immediately saw its potentialities as "pure theatre". His hatred of the "theatre in the theatre", to which reference has already been made, merely meant his hatred of the stale theatrical traditions of acting which were in vogue on the Moscow stage at that time ; it did not mean a hatred of theatrical situations on the stage. Neither then nor for many years afterwards did it occur to him to differentiate between the inner and the outer contents of a play. Indeed, his genius for seeing everything in terms of "theatre" was for a long time a real obstacle to his appreciation of the profounder aspects of drama. Neither *Uriel Acosta* nor, later, *The Bells* struck him as rather poor plays ; on the contrary, even when, a year after *Uriel Acosta*, he tackled *Othello*, he treated Shakespeare in the same way as Gutzkow—he concentrated on certain situations in the play that possessed the power of arousing his imagination and elaborated them, irrespective of whether or not they had anything to do with the playwright's intentions or whether or not they distorted the playwright's ideas. Now, a play by a minor playwright like Gutzkow obviously gives much greater scope to this method of production than a play by Shakespeare, though Stanislavsky found even *Othello*, thanks to its very poor translation, very amenable to that kind of treatment. The only trouble was that while in Gutzkow's play this treatment was eminently successful, it failed dismally in Shakespeare's tragedy.

The preliminary rehearsals of *Uriel Acosta* began in the Autumn of 1894. They took place in Stanislavsky's study. As the members of the company consisted almost entirely of business men, civil servants, teachers and students who were all busy in the day-time, the rehearsals usually began at about eight o'clock in the evening and went on without interruption till about midnight. Stanislavsky had by then become extremely proficient in "showing" the actors how to deal with their parts. He would also demonstrate single-handed the furious fanaticism of each member of the crowd in the synagogue after the withdrawal of Uriel Acosta's renunciation of his heretical beliefs, screaming, weeping and storming all over the room. However, this demonstration does not seem to have had any practical result, and at the subsequent rehearsals Stanislavsky had to teach every member of the crowd scene not only how to behave during the dramatic climaxes of the play, but also how to wear his costume. The method he adopted for this individual tuition of the extras was to write a different part for each of them, so that at any particular moment everybody engaged his neighbour in a heated conversation. The dialogues of these parts were composed either from the dialogue of the play itself or from sentences which corresponded with it rhythmically. This method made it possible to transform the crowd instantaneously into different talking groups and, when necessary, into one single crowd animated by some elemental feeling.

In *Uriel Acosta* there were two such scenes : the first showing the horror of the guests at Menasseh's house after Uriel's excommunication, and the second when the crowd of fanatical Jews tried to tear Uriel to pieces in the synagogue. In the first scene the guests left the stage muttering, Woe, woe, woe ! amid the hysterical weeping of the women. In the second scene, Uriel rushed back into the synagogue pursued by a crowd of yelling fanatics. After running as far as the footlights, Stanislavsky turned round to face the crowd, which rushed at him with a roar, faces distorted with hatred, and stopped dead within two steps of him, recoiling from him as though he had the plague. When the roaring crowd rushed at Uriel, the people in the first row of the stalls started back for fear that the crowd would jump over the footlights. The whole scene was played with such terrific verve that the audience was led to believe that a real fight had started behind the scenes.

No experiments were permitted in such a crowd scene during the performance. If during the rehearsal some characteristic pose or shout was noticed by him, Stanislavsky would immediately try to fix it once and for all. During the scene in the synagogue, Stanislavsky wanted a bony, twisted hand to appear suddenly above the heads of the fanatics. The only actor, however, whose hand was judged to be sufficiently bony did not take part in the crowd scene. He had therefore to rush back to the dressing-room, put on a different make-up and rush back to the stage, push his angry face through the crowd and at the same time brandish his bare arm above someone's head, twisting his bony hand convulsively, and in this way provide the necessary detail in the crowd scene, carefully fixed during the rehearsals and carried out with mathematical exactitude at the actual performance.

Strangely enough, Stanislavsky found it much more difficult to train the actors than the extras. There were always two or three actors who just could not get out of the habit of imitating the stage mannerisms of professional celebrities. It was then that he invented his method of distracting the attention of the audience from the play of such actors. In the second act of *Uriel Acosta*, for instance, he had to disguise the bad acting of two amateurs in a long scene. To do that, he chose a pretty girl and a handsome man, dressed them in magnificent costumes, and put them on a high platform in the most conspicuous part of the stage. The man was supposed to make love to the girl, who was supposed to be flirting with him. Stanislavsky invented a whole love scene for them so as to distract the attention of the audience from the two main characters on the stage. Only where it was necessary for the audience to hear the dialogue in order to be able to follow the plot did he moderate the ardours of the love-making couple. This trick, so beloved of conjurers, became rather characteristic of Stanislavsky's method of production during the next ten years, and even later, and was often severely criticised by critics who did not realize that Stanislavsky was not trying either to be too original or too conscientious, but was merely doing his best to cover up the shortcomings of his actors.

The decor of this production was also largely influenced by the lessons Stanislavsky had learnt from the Meiningen company. It was Kronegk who taught him to search for the characteristic features not only of a part, but also of the costumes and props (at that time Stanislavsky was still unable to do much with the scenery for lack of a good stage designer). Following his custom of "rummaging in dusty archives", which he was soon to abandon, he found a picture of a lectern in a book which seemed to him sufficiently typical to underline the crushing influence of the church in the middle ages. He immediately had a full-size drawing made of it and had it specially constructed for the scene in the synagogue. During one of his visits to the Moscow galleries he noticed a large glass goblet on a massive metal stem in a Flemish picture, and he at once decided to use just such goblets at the wedding feast in Menasseh's house. Though made of the globe of a gas-light and a wooden stem covered with bronze paint, the spectators were convinced that they were genuine museum pieces. The same principle was applied to the costumes. Unable to afford new costumes for every member of his company, Stanislavsky ordered the usual "Spanish" costumes from a theatrical costumier for his extras, and merely had new hats, wide belts, and large white collars made for them, and the audience was convinced that the costumes were not only new but historically true.

The first night of *Uriel Acosta* on January 9th, 1895, was a real triumph for Stanislavsky as a producer. The play created a tremendous impression not only among the playgoing public, but also among the professional actors of the Maly Theatre, who started visiting the amateurs in their dressing-rooms and asking them about all sorts of "artistic" details in their acting of which they were hardly aware themselves. Six or seven performances of the play were bought up by all sorts of charitable institutions and for weeks there was not an empty seat in the theatre. On February 5th Stanislavsky took his company to Yaroslav, where *Uriel Acosta* was for the first time billed "with the participation of the well-known amateur actor K. S. Stanislavsky". The play was performed in other provincial towns with great success, and it was due entirely to Stanislavsky's production that *Uriel Acosta* did not come off the repertoire of the provincial theatres for many years.

The triumph of *Uriel Acosta* was due chiefly to the crowd scenes. "The play made us famous," Stanislavsky writes, "and we seemed to have taken out a sort of patent on crowd scenes." This, incidentally, gave a new lease of life to the Society of Art and Literature, but it did very little to improve the playing of Stanislavsky himself. He was particularly dissatisfied with his love scenes, where he lapsed into sentimentality and "resorted to the methods of a feeble opera tenor of a feminine type," which was hardly suited to a man of his enormous height. "At the time," he writes, "I did not realize that there existed a manly lyricism, a manly tenderness and dreaminess, and that sentimentality was a bad substitute for genuine feeling. . . . Flabby sentimentality not only in a young man, but also in a young woman, is out of tune with their youthful natures and merely creates a discord." That was why, Stanislavsky maintains, the love scenes were all wasted in his performance. But fortunately there were only a few of them in the play. He was much more successful in depicting the philosophic side of Uriel's character, though there, too, he felt that his "operatic" habits made his acting less effective. His bad memory which was liable to let him down in the dramatic scenes was a further handicap he found it difficult to overcome.

CHAPTER XV

STANISLAVSKY intended to put on his own translation of *L'affaire Clémenceau*, by the younger Dumas, in January of the same year, but he was badly let down by the actor he had cast for the part of the young lover and the play was never performed. Chekhov's one-act comedy *The Bear*, the first Chekhov play to be produced by Stanislavsky, saw its first performance on the tiny stage of the Hunting Club on April 10th. In the same spring season of 1895 Stanislavsky produced two Ostrovsky plays and a light comedy by one of the more popular playwrights of the time. These productions, however, were merely stop-gaps in his repertoire, since he had to carry out his agreement to put on two plays a week for the Hunting Club. The play that now occupied his mind to the exclusion of everything else marked another important turning point in his career : it was Shakespeare's *Othello*.

The rumour that Stanislavsky was thinking of producing *Othello* during the season of 1895-6 spread like wildfire among the members of his company. It became known that he intended to play Othello himself, in spite of the fact that it was not generally considered to be a very suitable part for him. It was therefore concluded that he meant to give quite a different treatment to the Moor of Venice and that his fellow-actors would be·expected to help him to create a proper ensemble for his performance of it. As soon as these rumours were confirmed, his chief assistant, Nicolai Popov, who was a student of Moscow University at the time, plunged into a study of all the available material on Shakespeare's tragedy.

"What are you doing now ? " Stanislavsky asked him one day.

"I am studying the commentaries on *Othello*," replied Popov.

"It's a waste of time," Stanislavsky said, "and, besides, it will probably do more harm than good. You must take a much simpler view of the whole thing : Shakespeare is a great genius and all you have to do is to read him."

It was a rather curious piece of advice, Popov thought, but he did as he was told. It never occurred to him or to Stanislavsky that what they were reading was not really Shakespeare, but a very inadequate translation of him. It is doubtful, however, whether that would have worried Stanislavsky at the time. On the contrary, it is much more likely that Shakespeare's original text would have been a real hindrance to his plan of production. What he wanted was not the text of the play so much as various hints in the text that he could improvise on. The fact that the translation he was using was drained of all poetry was therefore a great help to him, for there was nothing left in it to interfere with the inventions of his own vivid imagination. Did not the first act take place in Venice ? Very well, then, he would go to Venice and draw his inspiration from that city of canals and palaces. A newspaper wit remarked after seeing Stanislavsky's production of *Othello* : "Stanislavsky has been to Venice and brought back a bit of a gondola," and there was a great deal of truth in that criticism.

In the summer of the same year Stanislavsky invited Popov and Arkhipov[1], who had just returned from the provinces where they had been producing plays for the poorer classes, to visit him at his country house of Lyubimovka. He had been working on his plan of *Othello* and he felt the need to talk it over with someone. "At the time," Popov observes in his reminiscences, "Stanislavsky, unlike other men of the theatre, already possessed quite an exceptionally powerful imagination, which to a certain extent was probably due to the fact that he could afford to travel and so absorb a great number of different impressions. A stage direction or a single phrase in a play called forth all sorts of images in his mind and these very often played havoc with the author's text."

Though both Popov and Arkhipov were by now used to "the whims of Stanislavsky's imagination", and were, in fact, beginning to get a little tired of them, his account of the development of the action in *Othello* left them breathless. "Shakespeare's text was pushed into the background", Popov writes, "and what we heard was just Stanislavsky's version of the action of the play."

It was a very lovely moonlit summer night. From the large balcony where they were sitting they could catch a glimpse of the

---

[1] Both Popov and Arkhipov, the latter under the stage name of Arbatov, became well-known producers ; Arkhipov's father was a close friend of Stanislavsky's father.

sluggish stream and the beautifully laid out gardens of Lyubimovka. The frogs were as usual in good voice and the corncrake,
too, could be heard. But this time Stanislavsky was not interested
either in the fine view or in the noises of the night. What he saw
was a Venetian canal and a gliding gondola with Iago and
Roderigo in it. What he heard was the clanking of the chain as
they made fast near Brabantio's house, their subdued voices as
they walked past the bridge, and, suddenly, their shouts in the
dark as they raised the whole neighbourhood with the news
of Desdemona's elopement. And so marvellously vivid was
Stanislavsky's account that his two assistants, too, saw the gondola
cleaving the calm waves of the canal and heard the clanking of
the chain as it was flung on the quayside. The two sinister figures
were at first busy with the chain, then they exchanged a few
whispered remarks, then, suddenly, a shrill whistle followed by
loud shouts, "Brabantio, get up ! Thieves ! Thieves ! "

Stanislavsky went on telling his story in a whisper so as not to
wake anyone in the house, describing the whole of his future
production scene by scene.

Spellbound, the two young men were now themselves in
Venice, on the bank of the canal, they saw Brabantio's servants
opening windows, asking each other frightened questions : then
the whole city suddenly came to life. There was a fight on the
bridge. Swords were drawn, Othello's stern voice was heard.
Then came the meeting of the Senate at night, the excitement at
the news from Cyprus, brought by the two messengers, the sudden
appearance of Brabantio, followed by the majestic figure of
Othello. The old Duke listening attentively to their stories, the
strained silence of the Senators, and the impassive figures of the
soldiers, whose halberds reflected the light of the candles.

Stanislavsky told it all with such gestures and constant changes
of pose as though he were in a hurry to communicate to them
something that he had himself seen as a faithful follower of the
Moor of Venice. He described the feelings of the heroes of the
tragedy, their secret thoughts, and the whole mode of their lives.
The entire action of the play unfolded itself without interruption,
and that in itself, his two friends felt, showed a tremendous
advance in the growth of his talents as a producer. They all
went to bed very late that night, and Popov and Arkhipov
could not help feeling that Stanislavsky's story was much better
than any performance.

Next morning Stanislavsky showed them his own scale model of the scene on Cyprus. He had not managed to visit Cyprus himself, but he did not seem to have found it difficult to construct a whole section of an oriental town. In the centre was a square with tortuous little streets abutting into it on every side. Two- and three-storied houses side by side with hovels, flat roofs with poles and lines of washing stretched between them. Trees in tubs, oriental carpets, cushions, mats.

"But," he was asked, "are we going to have a real theatre this year?"

"Why, no," he replied, looking surprised, "we'll have to carry on at the Hunting Club."

"But the stage there is only about ten feet high, and you have three-storied houses here. And look at this vast square!"

"Oh, well," said Stanislavsky calmly, "I'm afraid this won't be much good then. I'll have to think of something else."

CHAPTER XVI

THIS TIME Stanislavsky was mistaken. Something happened that made it possible for him to produce *Othello* on a really large stage.

What happened was that Stanislavsky's great success in *Uriel Acosta* had attracted the attention of Mikhail Lentovsky, one of Moscow's greatest showmen. It was the same Lentovsky who about ten years earlier had run the Moscow pleasure gardens "The Hermitage," where he put on his successful musical shows which had led Stanislavsky to emulate him in producing the musical comedies in the Alexeyev Circle. It was now Lentovsky's turn to try to get something out of Stanislavsky.

Time had dealt hardly with Lentovsky. His fine black mop of hair and his large black beard were streaked with grey. Gone were the days when he stalked like a lion through the "Hermitage," armed with a huge stick, and at his approach prostitutes fled and lovers recoiled from each other in panic. He had taken to drink and fallen on evil days. Like many another great showman he was bankrupt. He was a frequent visitor at the Hunting Club, where he saw Stanislavsky's productions. In the foyer of the Hunting Club Popov found him one day in tears.

"What's the matter, sir?" he asked the great impresario.

"Oh," replied Lentovsky, "I'm finished."

"But, good Lord, sir, don't we all appreciate and love you? Why, you are still the wizard of our stage!"

But the "wizard of the stage" was disconsolate. "It's time," he replied, "I made way for younger men. Haven't I dreamt of doing for the theatre what Stanislavsky is doing? Why, when I put on an adaptation of one of Zola's novels I got real French laundresses specially from Paris, but no one took any notice. All that happened was that they were snapped up by our rich business-men."

95

It was Lentovsky who had brought the Meiningen company to Moscow, for which he was duly awarded a decoration by the Duke of Meiningen. He looked on Stanislavsky as a successor of Kronegk and he quite naturally hoped to do as well by him as he did by the Meiningen producer. Stanislavsky, on the other hand, was greatly tempted by the prospect of appearing on a real stage with professional actors and he eagerly accepted Lentovsky's offer to produce a number of plays for him at one of the largest theatres in Moscow.

Lentovsky, or, rather, his assistant, an actor by the name of Petrossyan, who acted for him as he himself was an undischarged bankrupt, immediately hired the Solodovnikov Theatre. As the theatre, however, would not be ready for a whole week, Lentovsky, with the promptitude typical of all good showmen, hired a shop, in which he at once proceeded to select the company for Stanislavsky's production of Hauptmann's play *Hannele*, which was to be put on the following spring. Stanislavsky was invited to be present at the interviews with the actors and actresses, and on arriving at the shop he was shocked to find everything in a most filthy condition. The shop was littered with bits of torn paper, old advertisements of haberdashery goods, broken shelves and drawers, a few broken chairs, and all sorts of other junk. Lentovsky and his assistant were sitting on overturned packing cases in a tiny room with a grimy window and a low ceiling, which seemed to be crammed with old cardboard boxes. They were interviewing applicants for the big cast in Hauptmann's play.

"Come on, lift up your skirt! Let's see your legs!" Petrossyan was saying to a young girl as Stanislavsky, stooping so as not to knock his head against the ceiling, entered the room.

The girl looked embarrassed, but she took off her coat, showed her legs to Stanislavsky's future *entrepreneur* and his assistant, and did her best to stand up straight.

"Do you sing?"

"No, I don't. I—I am a dramatic actress."

"She'll do for one of the beggars," Lentovsky decided.

"Or for one of the prostitutes," his assistant tried to do the girl a good turn by offering her a better paid part.

The young actress nodded and went out.

"Next please," Petrossyan shouted.

But here Stanislavsky judged that the time had come for him

to give Lentovsky a lecture on stage ethics. His war on the "bohemianism" of the stage was not limited to loose morals. As he walked through the shop to Lentovsky's "office," he found it full of people who looked to him like the very dregs of humanity: actors and actresses who had come from all over Russia to the annual "fair" at which managers from all over the provinces recruited their casts. Petrossyan's treatment of the girl actress was no exception : it was the generally accepted custom among theatrical managers. But to Stanislavsky the stage was not a way of earning a living. He had already spent on it thousands of roubles he could ill afford. To him the profession of an actor was a calling of the highest possible order, and to see actors treated like scum was not only an affront to his feelings as a man, but also to his conception of the high purpose of the art of the stage. If what he saw was a fair sample of the manners of the professional stage, then he would have nothing to do with it.

"I'm sorry," he addressed Lentovsky in his most charming man-of-the-world manner, "but I'm afraid I can't go on like that. You don't really think that a man can dedicate himself to art and æsthetics in a cowshed, do you ? I'm sure you'll agree that æsthetics impose certain obligations that must be carried out in however limited a degree. Otherwise æsthetics are no longer æsthetics. And the minimum obligation imposed not only by æsthetics but also by the most primitive civilization is cleanliness. Have this dirt swept out, throw out all the rubbish, have the floors scrubbed and the windows cleaned, get the whole place decently warm, get some cheap furniture, a decent table, some pens and an inkstand, so that you can write at a table and not against the wall as you are doing now. When that's done, I shall be glad to apply myself with enthusiasm to the work that interests me so much, but I can't do anything now because all this makes me feel sick, positively sick. And one more thing. You are the head of an organization whose duty it is to instruct, educate and enlighten society and the actors are your closest cultural associates. Don't let us forget it, and let us talk to them not as to prostitutes and slaves, but as to people who are worthy of their high calling. If I haven't offended you, but rather inspired you to carry on with the good work, then let's shake hands and meet again in a day or two. But if my words have offended you, then let's say goodbye for good."

What Lentovsky made of this homily no one will ever know,

but he knew of course of Stanislavsky's reputation as a rich eccentric and he did not doubt that Stanislavsky meant what he said.

"What an old fool I am not to have realized it before," he exclaimed, smiting his forehead and looking embarrassed.

He rose from his packing-case, embraced Stanislavsky in the traditional Russian manner, and they parted. When Stanislavsky turned up again, he found the place spotlessly clean and warm. The rooms downstairs and upstairs were furnished in the best style of a lavish musical comedy setting : the walls were covered with hangings resplendent with the conventional ornamentations of the stage designer, gilt tassels, gilt chairs, silk and velvet tablecloths, property cardboard vases, the same kind of clocks on the tables, carpets, decanters of water and glasses, ashtrays, and tea for the actors. The upper room had been transformed into a regular manager's office. Startled by all this luxury, the actors hastened to take off their overcoats, set themselves to rights, smooth and comb their hair and generally, as Stanislavsky remarks, comport themselves as if they were playing the parts of Spanish grandees on the stage. In short, Lentovsky excelled himself, and though the whole place had a rather weird appearance Stanislavsky was successful in getting what he wanted and, as he says, "it was now possible to speak to people like human beings."

Indeed, so unused were the actors to being talked to like human beings that when Stanislavsky addressed each of them by his or her name and patronymic instead of shouting to them, "Hey, you there ! " as was customary in those days, they became as wax in his hands. Lentovsky was so staggered by this change in the relationship between the actors and their producer that he showered compliments on Stanislavsky for his "knowledge of how to deal with people," but, as Stanislavsky himself remarks, all he did was to treat them just like any other human beings.

After a week Stanislavsky was notified that the Solodovnikov Theatre was now at his disposal, and on his arrival there he again found the place in an indescribable state of filth and disorder. The actors were jostling each other in the corridors while waiting for their cues, and spent their time gossiping and talking scandal. The standard of discipline immediately fell, and Stanislavsky was sorry to have left the shop. To save the situation, another *coup d'état* was obviously necessary, and Stanislavsky left the theatre, leaving a message for Lentovsky in which he reminded him of the ultimatum he had given him in the filthy shop. After a few days Stanislavsky again got a notification to appear at the rehearsals, and this time he found the theatre spotlessly clean with a lavishly furnished room for himself and special foyers for the actors and actresses. It took a long time, however, to eradicate the bad theatrical habits which, as Stanislavsky puts it, "prevent the actors from applying themselves to their work with clean hands and an open heart". He therefore resorted to a trick. The play was opened by a famous provincial actor who had only a small part in it. Stanislavsky arranged with him secretly to come on the stage in his hat and coat and walking stick and begin mouthing his bit of dialogue, as only too frequently happened at rehearsals in many a provincial town. He then very courteously asked his permission for himself, a young amateur producer, to reprimand him, a famous actor, very severely, and order him to take off his hat and coat, to rehearse his part in "full tone" and without relying on the prompter. The actor agreed, and Stanislavsky reprimanded him in the hearing of everybody "courteously but firmly" and "with the full consciousness" that he, Stanislavsky, had a right to exert his authority in such a way. This trick was completely successful, and the discipline of the cast improved at once. The rehearsals now proceeded satisfactorily, but soon Stanislavsky was faced with another and no less troublesome problem. Lentovsky, happy with the way things were going, took to the bottle again. His example was soon followed by another man, and things were beginning to get out of hand again. A third *coup d'état* was obviously needed. Stanislavsky again stopped the rehearsal, apologized to the actors for a wasted evening, and left the theatre. He felt that by leaving without an explanation the effect would be greater just because there was an element of mystery. The same night Stanislavsky sent Lentovsky a sharp note in which he told him bluntly that under such conditions—that is to say, when the manager himself tolerated drunkenness—he, Stanislavsky, refused to carry on. It was a pretty safe thing to do, since Stanislavsky knew perfectly well that Lentovsky had spent all the money he could raise on the production. The result of the note was therefore a foregone conclusion : Lentovsky apologized, promised to turn over a new leaf, and even resorted to medical treatment to cure himself of his addiction to liquor. Stanislavsky accepted his apology and resumed the rehearsals.

The first play Stanislavsky put on for Lentovsky at the Solodovnikov theatre was Pissemsky's historical play *Men Above the Law*, which he had already put on a few times on the stage of the Hunting Club. It was performed with Stanislavsky in his old part of General Imshin, on October 17th, 1895. Stanislavsky took advantage of the large stage he had now at his disposal to introduce a new crowd scene, especially since, after *Uriel Acosta*, he had become rather famous for crowd scenes. As he used his old amateur company only in this production, the technical side of this particular stage "business", which consisted of the storming of a country house by insurgent peasants, did not present any special difficulties. He divided his extras into several groups, each corresponding to the number of men that could get in a cart, and placed them in different dressing-rooms upstairs. Each of these groups then rushed down the stairs, yelling and ringing sleigh-bells, and then on to the stage, brandishing sticks, pitchforks, and so on. Parallel to the footlights at the back of the stage was a fence. After raising a terrible din and backing the imaginary horses, the crowd rushed to storm the fence. Artyom, one of the best actors in the company of the Society of Art and Literature, whom Stanislavsky had first met in 1887 while they were playing together in some private theatricals, and who was to become one of the famous character-actors of the Moscow Art Theatre, was the ring-leader of the mob of peasants and he climbed to the top of the fence and took command of the assaulting rebels. All that scene was carried out with the same verve and enthusiasm as the synagogue crowd scene in *Uriel Acosta*.

That winter Stanislavsky had an occasion to put to the test his critical attitude towards the most hallowed traditions of stage acting, "the theatre in the theatre," which he was growing to hate more and more. He appeared on the stage of the Paradise Theatre, where seven years earlier he had met Lilina, with the celebrated Petersburg actress Polina Strepetova in Pissemsky's play *Bitter Fate*, which he had already produced a few times for the Society of Art and Literature. Strepetova became famous in the part of Lisaveta, the peasant woman in the play who is in love with her master but is forced to marry the peasant Anany, played by Stanislavsky, who eventually murders her child. The great Russian painter Repin had painted Strepetova in that part, and every playgoer in Moscow was agog with excitement at the prospect of seeing how Stanislavsky compared with the famous actress. The comparison appeared to be all in favour of Stanislavsky, who was entirely convincing in his part, while Strepetova, who resorted to the most stale melodramatic effects, was utterly unconvincing. It was a curious example of a famous professional transformed into an amateur when playing opposite an amateur who dispensed with the conventional tricks of the stage.

CHAPTER XVII

THE TWO OTHER plays Stanislavsky produced for Lentovsky at the Solodovnikov Theatre were *Hannele*, put on on April 2nd, 1896, and *Othello*, put on on April 16th, 1896. Each play marked an important milestone in his career as a producer and had its important repercussions on the history of the Moscow Art Theatre.

Though Stanislavsky's preoccupation with Shakespeare came before his interest in Hauptmann, it was the German playwright who undoubtedly took precedence over Shakespeare at this period of his development as a producer. In Shakespeare he had to battle constantly against the text, corrupted though it was by the translation, and he had to force upon it the inventions of his own teeming imagination, a dangerous practice, as was to be proved all too soon. Not so with Hauptmann. *Hannele* as well as *The Sunken Bell*, produced by Stanislavsky during the last year of the existence of the Society of Art and Literature, gave him all the latitude he desired as a producer. They were fairy-tales coated with a thin layer of mysticism and romantic philosophy which were suggested by the plot but not part of it. They therefore helped rather than hindered the inventions of his imagination. Hauptmann's characters, too, were puppets rather than human beings, personified ideas rather than flesh-and-blood characters. The difficulty of the embodiment of a stage character, Stanislavsky's stumbling block at this time of his career, did not exist in Hauptmann's plays. On the other hand, it was just in these plays, and particularly in *Hannele*, that he obtained a firm grasp of the technique of stage action—the ability, that is, to translate everything that happened on the stage into expressive dramatic terms.

In 1896, and much later too, for that matter, Stanislavsky had not yet become a sufficiently mature artist to be able to tackle Shakespeare (it is doubtful whether, relying on bad translations

as he was forced to do, he ever could have tackled him satisfactorily), but he was quite capable of dealing with a playwright
like Hauptmann. And even if occasionally, as in the death scene
in the first act of *Hannele*, he deliberately departed from his text, it
did not matter very much since it merely helped to deepen the
mystical element of the play.

The first act of *Hannele*, which opens on a doss-house full of
beggars and prostitutes, is depicted by the author very natural-
istically ; but with the death of Hannele at the end of the first
act, the play wanders off into the realms of sheer fantasy, and the
inmates of the doss-house, who had treated Hannele so cruelly
before, are transformed into spirits full of love and tenderness
for the heroine, who is herself transformed into a fairy princess
lying asleep in a glass coffin.

This mingling of naturalism and fantasy gave Stanislavsky
an excellent chance of creating an unforgettable sense of suspense
and horror right from the very end of the first act. Hannele
lay in a corner of the room which was in semi-darkness. Suddenly
a long, formless shadow appeared by her bedside. Hannele
gazed intently at this shadow, which rose higher and higher
till a head and shoulders seemed to emerge from the formless
mass. Suddenly a huge pair of wings, transparent like a spider's
web, shot upwards. It was the Angel of Death. He was quite
different from Hauptmann's description in the stage directions
of the play. He inspired terror by his menacing silence and the
faint twitchings of his wings. There was a terrible sense of in-
exorability in the slow way in which he approached Hannele's
bed. As he hovered over it, his wings spread out over the dying
girl, a grey semi-transparent mass covered the bed and the
entire corner of the room. The grey apparition then shuddered
convulsively a few times and suddenly seemed to melt away,
blending with the heap of rags at the top of the bed.

Stanislavsky's chief intention in this scene was to keep the
audience in suspense. He entirely disregarded Hauptmann's
indication of the exact moment of Hannele's death. Asked when
Hannele did die, his reply was "I'm hanged if I know." The
transformation scene which followed the death scene was no less
hair-raising. The scene at first completely baffled Stanislavsky.
Arriving at the theatre for the rehearsal long before it was due to
start (this had already become a rule with him) he found the stage
in darkness except for a shaft of bluish light falling behind some

raised piece of scenery and creating an eerie sense of mystery. Meanwhile the actors were arriving for the rehearsal, and as they walked about the stage and talked in small groups, they would now and then stop in the shaft of light, their long shadows crawling along the floor, the walls and the ceiling. When they moved about in that mysterious light their bodies looked like silhouettes, and as their shadows merged and separated the actors themselves grew as insubstantial as their shadows. Here then was the solution of his problem. Stanislavsky immediately summoned the electrician, marked the spot where the light was coming from, made a careful note of the voltage of the lamp and the shape of the particular piece of scenery that hid it, and then spent the rest of the rehearsal in finding the most effective way for the actors to play that scene. That did not present any great difficulties since the light effect itself suggested the appropriate action. He taught the actors to move about the stage and speak their lines in a nightmarish way : a half-uttered word, then a long pause, the rhythmic swaying of shadows, followed by a sudden outburst of abrupt, high-pitched, slow speech, rising and falling. Another pause, a slow, monotonous swaying of the crowd of ghost-like beggars on the stage, glued to one spot. Shadows slowly moving on the wall and ceiling. Suddenly the front-door was thrust open violently, the latch snapping back into its place with a loud noise, and the shrill, squeaky voice of the beggar-woman who had just entered broke the silence : "It's freezing cold outside ! " The phrase, uttered in a high-pitched, unrealistic sing-song, threw the motionless figures into wild commotion, their shadows merging and separating dizzily. Then everything grew quiet and motionless again, only the shadows continuing to reel drunkenly. Another long and weary pause, followed by soft moaning voices : "Hannele ! Han—ne—le ! " Then a rising and falling whisper— a hopeless sigh : "Hannele's dead ! " That produced another wild commotion among the shadows on the stage, interspersed with a chorus of weeping and moaning voices of young and old women. Then, at the climax of the scene, the clear-cut tenor voice of the mystic messenger announcing the news of Hannele's salvation in a phrase in which the S-sounds were drawn out to form one long continuous hiss, caught up by everybody on the stage as well as by the stage hands and the members of the orchestra ; and amid this "grandiose hissing", accompanied by the dizzy dancing of shadows, the transformed Hannele appeared in a bright spotlight in the centre of the stage, lying asleep in a glass coffin, while the dead body of the earthly Hannele was still lying on the bed in the corner of the stage. With the appearance of the magic glass coffin, the noises died down gradually and everybody on the stage was lost in blissful contemplation of the transformed heroine, only the shadows on the walls and ceiling still continuing their ghost-like swaying. The scene ended with a long pause.

Hannele undoubtedly marked a great advance in Stanislavsky's development as a producer. It was in this play that he had for the first time learnt to make effective use of pauses and orchestration of voices for the creation of "atmosphere," a method that he was to utilize later in his production of Chekhov's plays. The "atmosphere" in *Hannele* was rather theatrical, but it certainly did the trick : the audience was spell-bound by Stanislavsky's so-called "stage miracles". He received a great ovation on the first night and Lentovsky—inveterate showman that he was—presented him with a copy of Gogol's *Government Inspector*, with marginal notes in the playwright's own hand, which Gogol had presented to Mikhail Shchepkin, the great actor presenting it, in his turn, to his pupil Lentovsky. A small silver plate let into the binding of the book bore Lentovsky's inscription to Stanislavsky : "To a worthier artist. M. Lentovsky."

Stanislavsky must have found Lentovsky a great help in the devising of his stage effects for *Hannele*, but the difference in their approach was fundamental : to Stanislavsky stage effects were only a means to an end, and he only made use of them when his actors could not by themselves hold the attention of the audience; while to Lentovsky they were an end in themselves. Thus, during a Sunday performance of *Hannele*, Lentovsky of his own accord introduced a garish stage effect at the end of the death scene in the first act which ruined the whole atmosphere of that scene. As Hannele approached the high staircase on which she was to ascend to heaven and which was lined with angels holding madonna lilies in their hands, the lilies suddenly lit up. When, after the performance, Stanislavsky heard about it, he immediately rushed on to the stage and demanded an explanation. Lentovsky was sitting in a very picturesque pose on a property garden seat, fingering his thick beard with one hand and wiping the perspiration off his forehead with the other. He was supervising the removal of some complicated piece of scenery.

"Why, of course," he interrupted Stanislavsky, "I know all about it. It was I who had electric light bulbs put in the lilies. A Sunday audience, my dear fellow, a Sunday audience ! They must have some extra stage trick."

Noticing, however, that Stanislavsky was not at all mollified by that explanation, Lentovsky promised not to repeat the trick again. On another occasion in the same play, a stage effect that appealed greatly to both Stanislavsky and Lentovsky could not be introduced because the assistant stage manager who was responsible for it would not repeat it. It happened at the end of the transformation scene. After the dramatic crescendo of the hissing had died down, the phrase "They are carrying the coffin of glass" was repeated very simply in a low bass voice, and the effect created by the highly artificial intoning of the phrase by the whole company and the matter-of-fact enunciation of it during the pause was shattering. By the time Stanislavsky and Lentovsky reached the stage to find the "genius" responsible for that amazing stage effect, the assistant stage manager, who, being drunk, was afraid to face Stanislavsky, had disappeared. Nothing would induce him to appear on the stage again in a drunken state, and Lentovsky got hold of a more amenable bass singer in a church choir. He was quite ready to get drunk with Lentovsky, but it proved impossible to get him to repeat the phrase on the stage satisfactorily. The melancholy outcome of it all was that Lentovsky took to drinking again and had to be tactfully kept out of the theatre during his "illness." At home he kept protesting plaintively that he had even taken to drink for the sake of art and that he alone could reproduce that marvellous stage effect.

CHAPTER XVIII

AFTER *Hannele*, Stanislavsky's production of *Othello* fell flat. There were many reasons for that, some of which have already been discussed. But the main reason for the failure of the play was undoubtedly Stanislavsky's own failure in the part of Othello. He was not cut out for great tragic roles, and with a perversity that is so common among actors, it was just such roles he wanted to excel in. He had seen the famous Italian actor, Tommaso Salvini, in this part fourteen years earlier, in 1882, and so tremendous was the impression Salvini's Othello had left on his mind that it remained one of the greatest experiences of his life. In the first scene of the tragedy there did not seem to be anything remarkable at all about Salvini ; even his costume merely brought out the inappropriateness of his figure for the part by emphasizing its corpulence ; as for his make-up, he had not any on to speak of ; there was only the face of the genius which did not seem to require any make-up. But the moment Salvini went up to the dais on which the Duke of Venice sat, he held the whole audience in his power. Every spectator knew who the genius was, the sort of a man he was and what could be expected of him. Stanislavsky, though only nineteen at the time, realized that he was in the presence of a monumental actor who personified some immutable law. The strange thing was that while watching Salvini, he seemed to remember Rossi and a host of great Russian actors. He felt that all of them had something in common, but at the time he did not yet realize that this thing they all shared would one day form the foundation of his own great "system" of acting. He set about finding out all he could about Salvini. Among other things, he discovered that Salvini was greatly excited on the day when he had to give a performance. On that day he did not eat much, kept himself to himself, and refused to see anybody. He arrived at the theatre three hours before the beginning of the performance and spent the time in his dressing-room and on the stage, which he visited several times apparently in an effort to enter into the atmosphere of the play and gradually to get under the skin of the character he was acting "with the help of some kind of preliminary toilet of the soul."

After that Stanislavsky could think of nothing but the part of Othello. But he approached his part, as well as the production of the play, in a way that had very little to do either with Shakespeare or with Salvini. He had been to Venice, and it was the canals, the bridges, and the gondolas that had fired his imagination and set it working along lines that had very little to do with the play. He then went to Paris, and by one of those accidents which were so particularly dangerous to him at the time he met a real Arab in a restaurant and was so impressed by his figure, his deportment and his dress, that he fell into his other dangerous error of copying him, apparently under the impression that the Moor of Venice was an Arab. He went back again to his unprofitable practice of rehearsing before a mirror, which, as he was to discover, merely deadened the intuitive approach to a part by forcing the actor to imitate blindly a stereotyped pose or attitude. And, worst of all, he now had two quite different models to copy : Salvini and the Arab.

In Paris, incidentally, Stanislavsky acquired special padding for the actor he had cast for the part of Roderigo, having first obtained photographs of his legs, for Roderigo in his conception was a very handsome young dandy, for whom he even invented a special hat in the form of a small barrel, ornamented by a huge scarf which covered the wearer's throat and trailed down his back.

On his return to Moscow, Stanislavsky set about casting the play. Here he at once met with difficulties. His wife fell ill and the part of Desdemona had to be given to another amateur actress with whom he could not get on, so that in the end he had to give it to "a very nice young lady" just because she seemed to look the part (another disastrous legacy from the Meiningen company). The casting of Iago was also unfortunate. Apparently under pressure from Lentovsky, Stanislavsky gave the part to Petrossyan, whom he knew quite well to be a very bad actor. The miscasting of Iago, however, led him to a further elaboration of a trick he had already used in *Uriel Acosta* for distracting the attention of the audience from incompetent actors, a trick he was going to use again three years later in *The Seagull*. After the meeting of the Senate and the departure of Othello and Desdemona at the end of the first act, the servants put out the candles and Iago was left alone in the dark (Stanislavsky must have cut out the scene between Roderigo and Iago) except for a faint ray of moonlight coming through some tiny window. He was almost invisible and only his voice could be heard. Here Stanislavsky killed two birds with one stone : he concealed Petrossyan's wooden face and brought out the fine qualities of his voice which, coming from the darkened stage, sounded even more sinister and ominous. The effect of that scene on the audience was quite remarkable : the unexpectedness of it brought its own reward. "No one would have bothered to listen to Petrossyan's soliloquy," Stanislavsky remarked to an actor afterwards, "but now the spectator's interest is aroused—how will this scene end ? "

Two other elaborations of the text by Stanislavsky may be mentioned here as significant of the whole production, particularly as he repeated them in a slightly altered form in his production of *Othello* in 1930. The first relates to the appearance of the two messengers in Act I, Scene 3. The stage directions merely say, "Enter Sailor" and "Enter Messenger". Stanislavsky made the sailor into an old sea-dog who comes in excitedly, bows clumsily to the Duke, and tells his news rapidly in a voice that brings out the imminent danger of war. The second messenger, a frightened negro slave, is hustled roughly to the Duke's throne, falls at his feet, puts one of them on his head, and in this pose says his lines.

The other episode occurs in Act II, Scene 3. Stanislavsky fastened on Iago's order to Roderigo, "Away, I say ! go out, and cry—a mutiny ! " and his following two lines, "Who's that which rings the bell ? Diablo, ho ! The town will rise," to stage a whole scene of the rising of the Cyprus inhabitants (whom he took to be Turks) against their Venetian masters. Iago's deliberately alarming words "The town will rise" were transformed into a stage direction, "The town rises". Stanislavsky therefore erected in the front of the stage something like a Turkish coffeehouse at the corner of two narrow streets going uphill towards the back of the stage, one to the right and the other to the left. In this coffee-house a party of Venetians were making merry, singing and dancing to the accompaniment of the doleful strains of a zither, while the Turks were walking in groups in the street, looking askance at their conquerors and fingering the daggers inside their coats. Iago's plan, therefore, according to Stanislavsky, was not only to stage a quarrel between two Venetian officers, but to make them responsible for a mutiny on the island. And his plan succeeded. Crowds of rebellious Cypriots stole down the two streets towards the coffee-house, armed with bared scimitars, sabres and sticks, intending to attack their conquerors. The Venetian soldiers were drawn up in the foreground of the stage with their backs to the spectators in expectation of the attack. At last the two groups of Turks fell upon the Venetians and a real fight started, in the midst of which Othello rushed in intrepidly, brandishing a huge sword, with which he seemed to cut the contending parties in twain. It was in such a scene, Stanislavsky maintained, that the spectator could fully appreciate Othello's bravery and Iago's Satanic plot. Such treatment, in his opinion, also explained Othello's severe sentence against Cassio, whose action had been responsible for a situation that could have had disastrous consequences. Stanislavsky, however, admitted that his real intention in elaborating Iago's hint at a mutiny into a real uprising was to assist the weak actors of his company.

But by giving free play to his imagination and pushing Shakespeare into the background in his first production of *Othello*, Stanislavsky was probably also trying to make it easier for himself to play a part for which he was not fitted. "For all his imposing exterior," Maria Andreyeva, who had joined the Society of Art and Literature in 1894 and afterwards became a member of the Moscow Art Theatre, observes in her reminiscences of Stanislavsky, "he seemed to lack the inner force which enables an actor to identify himself with the heroic figure he is representing. I can't help feeling that heroism and romanticism were quite alien to his nature. He was most interested in looking for realism and for the typical traits in a character."

While, therefore, his acting in the first half of the play was, as he puts it, "not so bad," he failed completely in the second half. If in *Uriel Acosta* he had failed to bring out the inner struggle between conviction and feeling, between the philosopher and the lover, he proved himself completely incapable of mastering the much more difficult technique needed for a representation of "the mathematical gradualness in the development of the feeling of jealousy, beginning with its hardly perceptible inception and ending with its highest summits of fury and madness."

He had hoped to achieve all that with the help of his intuition alone, but all he actually did was to work himself up into a state of unbearable tension and physical exhaustion. His voice, in particular, gave him a great deal of trouble. Already during the rehearsals he became so hoarse after the second act that he had to rest for several days. It was then that he realized that a tragedy required a special kind of technique if the actor wished to carry on to the end of the play. At first, however, he thought that it was only a question of voice training. He had spent so much time in training his voice for opera that it had become useless in tragedy. He therefore put off the rehearsals and concentrated on adapting his voice to the requirements of drama. He invented his own system of voice production and he achieved results which, without increasing the volume of his voice, certainly made it easier for him to control it. But after each rehearsal he still suffered from palpitations and breathlessness and had to lie down for a rest. The play was becoming a torture to him, but it was too late to take it off now, for a great deal of money had already been spent on its production. Besides, Stanislavsky's vanity was hurt and he himself insisted on carrying on. "No," he thought to himself while resting, exhausted and gasping for breath, after one of the rehearsals, "that's not art ! Salvini is old enough to be my father, and yet he does not go to pieces after a performance, though he may be playing on the huge stage of the Bolshoy Theatre, while I can't go through a rehearsal in a small room. I'm losing weight as though I were suffering from some wasting disease. How am I going to play at a real performance ? And why did I have to choose *Othello* ? No, playing in a tragedy is certainly not as pleasant as I had imagined ! "

More trouble followed. At the dress rehearsal he wounded Iago in the hand and the play had to be interrupted. And yet the audience remained entirely unmoved by his Othello. It was the sight of blood and not his acting that had produced an impression. What so annoyed Stanislavsky was that he had wounded his partner in cold blood and not because his temperament had got the better of him. There was not a trace of temperament in his acting. Not a trace of self-control, either. But the story of the wounding of Iago got into the papers and the public which filled the theatre on the first night came expecting much more than it really got. The performance was a failure. Even the fine scenery did nothing to save it. What the audience had come to see was not the lavish production but Othello, Desdemona and Iago, who were not there at all. The only lesson his first Shakespearean production on a real stage had taught Stanislavsky was that no inexperienced actor ought to try his hand at parts he would be lucky to be able to play at the end of his career. He was once more convinced of the great harm that his stubbornness, self-conceit, and ignorance of the fundamental rules of stagecraft and its technique did to his reputation, and he vowed never to act in a tragedy again. But when a little later the critics compared his Othello favourably with the Othello of a famous actor who was on tour in Moscow, Stanislavsky forgot his vow and started dreaming again of Hamlet, Macbeth, King Lear and other parts which were quite beyond him at the time, and, indeed, at any period of his stage career.

There was, however, another and more important circumstance which helped to revive those dreams. The famous Italian tragic actor, Ernesto Rossi, whom Stanislavsky had worshipped as a boy, was present at one of Stanislavsky's performances of Othello. Next day Stanislavsky received an invitation from Rossi to go and see him at his hotel. He arrived there in trepidation and found the great actor an extremely charming, well-read and highly cultured man. Rossi, who had seen through the whole idea of Stanislavsky's production, including the scene of the Turkish rising in Cyprus and the scene of Iago's soliloquy on a darkened stage, did not seem to be particularly surprised by it. Unlike Stanislavsky, he was against distracting the audience's attention from the actors by lavish scenery, costumes, and stage tricks.

"All these baubles," the great Italian actor told Stanislavsky, "become necessary only where there are no actors. A fine costume is a good cover for a feeble body in which no artistic heart is beating. It is only third-raters who want it, not you. The Iago I saw does not belong to your theatre. Desdemona *e bella*, but it is a little too soon to form any opinion of her. So that there remains only you. God has given you everything for the stage," Rossi went on after a little tantalizing pause. "You have all you need for Othello and indeed for the entire Shakespearean repertoire. Now everything depends on you. What you want is art, and I daresay it will come."

"But," Stanislavsky asked anxiously, "where and how is one to learn art ? Who is one to learn it from ? "

"Well," Rossi replied slowly, "if there is no great master

beside you whom you can trust, there is only one teacher I can recommend you."

"Whom ? Who is it ? " Stanislavsky cried eagerly.

"Yourself," Rossi replied with one of his characteristic gestures.

At the time Stanislavsky did not realise how much this one word uttered by the great Italian actor would mean to him in future when he would take as the fundamental thesis of his "system" that acting cannot be taught, but that every actor must train himself. What worried him now was that Rossi had said nothing about his interpretation of the part of Othello. Only years afterwards did he realise that not only Rossi but he himself had no idea what his interpretation of the character of Othello was. For all he had been concerned about had been to make at least some impression on the spectator and bring the performance somehow or other to an end with a modicum of success and without disgracing himself entirely. Rossi had said that what he wanted was art ; and he meant, no doubt, that he could find no art in his performance of Othello, that he had still far to go before he could play a tragic part and, particularly, before he could hope to emulate his great idol—Salvini.

CHAPTER XIX

ON MAY 14TH, 1896, the coronation of Nicholas II—the last of the Romanovs—took place in Moscow. The ancient Russian capital was invaded by the diplomatic corps and the Alexeyevs put their house at the Red Gates at the disposal of the German Embassy. Stanislavsky himself remained in Moscow, staying with relatives, while his wife and two children, a girl and a boy, went to stay with his younger brother near Kharkov. A letter Stanislavsky wrote to his wife at the beginning of May, throws light on a little crisis that had arisen in his family life as a result of his obsession with the theatre at a time when his wife was too busy with the children to take an active part in his work on the stage[1]. This letter, incidentally, also reveals the rather interesting fact that even at a time when there could be no question of the foundation of the Moscow Art Theatre Stanislavsky was becoming aware of his destiny as a great reformer of the theatre and, consequently, more than ever filled with anxiety about his future stage work. Having tried his hand at producing plays on the stage of a big theatre, his work at the Society of Art and Literature no longer satisfied him. He was embarrassed and annoyed when some of his friends would talk to him about the necessity of founding a special kind of theatre, a theatre that would maintain the high ideals of art and culture and at the same time be accessible to a public larger than the small group of rich members of the Hunting Club. His stock answer was that it was too soon to talk about creating a theatre of their own and that they still had to do a lot of work before such a hazardous enterprise could be launched. But the truth was that he was not sure of his own

---

[1] In a letter to Chekhov about five years later on December 27th, 1901, his wife, Olga Knipper, adds this characteristic note :

"He (Stanislavsky) keeps comforting me and assures me that it is a good thing that I am on the stage and that you and I are living apart. He says that before his wife went on the stage as a professional actress their life was dull, uninteresting and impossible. He is such a big baby ! "

ability to organize such a theatre, first, because he could not very well manage the administrative and the artistic sides by himself, and, secondly, because he knew perfectly well that what he lacked most was a literary education, that his knowledge of world drama was very slight, and that unless he had a man at his side on whose literary knowledge and taste he could rely, the theatre he dreamt of would have to remain a dream. The season at the Solodovnikov Theatre had, besides, left him physically exhausted and a prey to doubts about his own future as an actor and producer. All this made him seriously consider the question whether he should not leave the stage for good.

In this state of domestic unsettlement and artistic doubts he turned for advice to Nadezhda Medvedeva, a famous actress of the Maly Theatre.

"I spent the whole afternoon with Medvedeva," he wrote to his wife. "Had lunch and tea with her and, of course, spoke of the theatre all the time. Medvedeva was in an unusually good mood. She kept asking me whether you were jealous of my preoccupation with the theatre and whether that was not the real cause of your illness. I was surprised that she should have guessed it ! But it seems there was the same sort of trouble between her and her husband. I am sorry, darling, but I could not help telling her that I believed your illness was at least partly due to your not seeing enough of me. Medvedeva understands the difficulties of my position as an actor and a husband, and she realizes how difficult it is to combine these two duties. She said that the love of a woman was one thing, and the love of the theatre—another. They were two quite different feelings, and one did not destroy the other. I think she is right and that you ought to have a talk with her when you come back. I can't help feeling that she will understand you as a woman and me as an actor. All the time," Stanislavsky added rather significantly, "she kept for some reason talking about my *duty*[1] to do something for the theatre and saying that *my name ought to pass into* history. She has been talking about it for a long time at the Maly Theatre, especially after *Hannele*. Lensky[2] *thinks so too*. I don't know why she told me that, but I couldn't help feeling that she must have guessed my growing lack of enthusiasm for the stage."

[1] These italics are by Stanislavsky (D.M.)
[2] Alexander Lensky (1847-1908), a famous actor of the Maly Theatre whom Stanislavsky greatly admired.

Stanislavsky's fame as a producer was by this time so firmly established that Lydia Yavorskaya, an actress who enjoyed the doubtful reputation of stopping at nothing for self-advertisement (she even accused Chekhov, who was a friend of hers, of lampooning her in one of his stories because she had rejected his advances), approached Stanislavsky to produce Edmond Rostand's new play, *La Princesse Lointaine*, which she was putting on in Moscow just then. To get rid of her, he promised to let her have some of the scenery from *Othello*. Unfortunately, the man who was in charge of the scenery was away, and the translator of the play wrote to Stanislavsky asking him to get the scenery for him and inviting him to the rehearsals of the play.

"Here I remembered," Stanislavsky writes to his wife, "not so much my intention of getting out of the theatre gradually as your advice to have nothing to do in stage matters with such ladies as Yavorskaya who could involve me in some unsavoury public scandal. After making all sorts of excuses, I succeeded in putting them off. But the whole thing was very unfortunate, and I shouldn't be surprised if I had got another stage enemy now. It is strange how this sort of thing invariably happens to me when I have to refuse someone's request. At the most decisive moment when I ought to say 'no' quickly, I miss my chance, make a pause during which I do my best to find as polite an excuse as possible, look awfully embarrassed, and the person who is asking the favour takes advantage of that momentary hesitation of mine, starts thanking me for agreeing to do what he wants me to do, and I cannot think of anything to say, and get more and more embarrassed. In the end I seem to be floundering in a fog and start talking a lot of nonsense, with the result that the impression is created that I am just being difficult and giving myself airs— a most hideous impression. Anyway, I refused for the third time and now I expect they will leave me alone. This morning, thank goodness, the scenery was sent off to them, and I sincerely hope that I shan't be bothered by them any more."

Stanislavsky, however, was mistaken. In another letter to his wife, written a few days later, he tells her of another "attack" by Yavorskaya. On the morning of May 5th, he had had another conference with a member of the Society of Art and Literature about the creation of a permanent theatre ("I hope," he writes to his wife, "you don't mind my wasting time in building castles in the air on a holiday"), and in the evening he went to the first night of Rostand's play. "I have seen a lot in my lifetime," he writes to his wife, "but such an abomination I never saw." In the theatre Yavorskaya tried to entice him behind the scenes, but, he writes, "I remembered your advice and got out of it most brazenly". After the performance he met Suvorin, the editor of the Petersburg reactionary daily *Novoyne Vremya* (The New Times), who ran a private theatre of his own in which Yavorskaya played. Suvorin dragged him off to the bar where they sat for hours talking about the theatre. "Hearing that Suvorin was still in the theatre," he writes, "Yavorskaya and her friends rushed in with candles in their hands and tried to drag.us to her room (she is staying at the theatre). But here, too, I remained firm and with a coolness that is alien to me I flatly refused, but they dragged off the old man. Congratulate me on my success," Stanislavsky ends his letter to his wife. "I arrived back home about midnight."

These letters were written only two years before Stanislavsky's historic meeting with Nemirovich-Danchenko at which the decision to found the Moscow Art Theatre was taken. All Stanislavsky's plans for the creation of a theatre of his own had foundered, and in the autumn of 1896 his intention to leave the theatre for good must have been given up, for he resumed his regular productions of plays on the tiny stage of the Hunting Club. Of the two Ostrovsky plays produced during that season, the revival of *A Girl Without a Dowry*, in which he had appeared in the part of Paratov at its first production by another member of the Society of Art and Literature in 1890, deserves to be mentioned, if only for the fact that Stanislavsky had at that time apparently become a firm adherent of the view all too frequently held by producers that he had a right to impose any interpretation he liked on a play so long as such an interpretation gave greater scope to his talents as producer. Taking the hint from Medvedeva, who was present at one of the rehearsals, he altered the whole ruling idea of the play so drastically that Ostrovsky himself would not have recognized it. Larissa, the heroine of the play, became "a half-gipsy brought up in Bohemia" and her mother an "ex-courtesan" in spite of the fact that Ostrovsky had made it abundantly clear that they belonged to a noble, though impoverished, family, and that the mother, in particular, was a highly respectable and rigidly conventional woman. But it was the character of the hero of the play that Stanislavsky distorted beyond recognition. He made Paratov into an ex-guardsman, who for some reason was still wearing military uniform. Ostrovsky's stage direction simply says : "Enter Paratov in a black, single-breasted, elegantly cut coat, a white cap, high lacquered boots and a travelling bag over his shoulder." This travelling bag Stanislavsky converted into "a carelessly worn military overcoat", and in addition he gave Paratov a whip to carry about with him, like some villain of melodrama, and Paratov, it seems, knew how to use it "on men, too". The hankering after melodramatic touches was certainly very strong in Stanislavsky at this period. Thus he made Larissa "give herself to Paratov" during a sail on the river in which, according to Ostrovsky's text, two wealthy men and a band take part in addition to Larissa and Paratov, and in spite of the fact that the conversation of the two wealthy men after the trip on the river merely suggests that all Paratov and Larissa did was to engage in very animated talk, during which, as one of them surmises, Paratov "must have been pitching her another of his tales," and the other one remarks that "his promises to her must have been pretty definite, for she would otherwise hardly have believed a man who had deceived her already" by a previous promise of marriage. No wonder Stanislavsky found Ostrovsky's text in this play very troublesome.

It was the problems of stage production that interested and fascinated Stanislavsky at this time and for many years afterwards. Plays of rich lyrical content like *A Girl Without a Dowry* and, only two years later, *The Seagull*, were utterly beyond his grasp. He therefore tended to misconstrue the author's ideas completely and, in attempting to "dramatise" the situations, distorted them. Hence his preference for plays of purely melodramatic situations, such as *The Bells*, his next production for the Society of Art and Literature, by the two French playwrights Emile Erckmann and Alexandre Chatrian, in which he played Sir Henry Irving's famous part of the mayor Mathias. This so-called "literary melodrama" gave him an excellent chance of displaying his genius as producer by a fantastic scene in the last act, where, unlike *Hannele* in which the light effects predominated, sound effects played a predominant part.

The scene showed an attic with a sloping ceiling, two large windows at the back, covered by Venetian blinds through which a glimpse of the dark night outside could be caught. Between the windows in the middle of the room stood a huge bed, and the rest of the furniture—a table, chairs, a chest of drawers and so on

—as well as the stove, were placed along the footlights with their backs to the audience (Stanislavsky's first attempt to treat the proscenium as the fourth wall). When the curtain rose, the stage was dark and from the room below, where the wedding of the mayor's daughter was being celebrated, merry songs, music, laughter and drunken shouts could be heard. Then on the staircase behind the sloping ceiling people were heard talking to the mayor who was indisposed and retiring to bed early. (During the wedding festivities the sound of the sleigh-bells of the Polish Jew, whom he had murdered and robbed many years before, had driven the mayor to distraction and to drown it he started singing at the top of his voice and whirling round in a mad dance which frightened the wedding guests.) The company followed the mayor into his bedroom and, after bidding him good-night, went downstairs again. The mayor, looking pale and weary, rushed to the glass door to lock it. Then he sat down exhausted, while from below there came again the sounds of merry-making amid which he once more seemed to hear the ominous ringing of the sleigh-bells. The distracted and conscience-stricken mayor hastened to undress and go to bed so as to fall asleep and hear them no longer. He extinguished the candle, but in the darkness a whole symphony of all kinds of terrifying noises started again : a hallucination in which the merry songs and the wedding music imperceptibly merged into a funeral march. The joyous voices and cries of the young people became drowned in the sombre funereal voices of elderly drunkards, and the noise of the clinking glasses at times sounded like the tolling of church bells. And the ringing of the sleigh-bells, sometimes faintly, sometimes loudly and threateningly, kept coming more and more persistently through the cacophony of noises from downstairs. Every time the mayor heard the bells, he started groaning and shouting something in a smothered voice. He was probably tossing in his bed, because the bed creaked and something fell with a thud on to the floor—a chair he must have accidentally overturned with his hand. But suddenly bluish-grey shafts of light began to appear somewhere near the bed ; the light kept fading and coming on again imperceptibly. Gradually, to the accompaniment of this auditory hallucination, the figure of some man came into sight. His head with its loosely hanging hair drooped. His hands were manacled, and as he moved them the clanking of a prisoner's chains could be heard.

Behind his back was a post with some kind of an inscription. It looked like a pillory with a prisoner chained to it. The light was increasing and getting greener and greyer. It spread along the back wall, forming a sinister background for some black creatures, phantom silhouettes, along the footlights, with their backs to the audience. In the centre where the table had stood, on a high dais, sat a large fat man wearing a black robe and a hat that reminded one of the hat of a judge. On either side of him sat several similar figures in smaller hats. On the right, where the chest of drawers had been and just behind the dais, stood a serpent-like figure in a black robe, and on the left, where the stove had been, stood another figure in a black robe and a small hat, leaning against the judge's desk and covering his eyes mournfully with his hand—the counsel for defence. The cross-examination of the accused was carried on in a whisper and in a continually changing rhythm, as in a nightmare. The prisoner's head drooped lower and lower. He refused to answer the questions put to him. But suddenly another long, thin figure made its appearance from behind the corner of the room where the clothes were hanging. It rose higher and higher along the wall, crept over the ceiling, and then descended over the prisoner and gazed straight at him. That was the mesmerist. Now the prisoner was forced to raise his head, and the spectators recognized the haggard and exhausted face of the mayor. Under the influence of the mesmerist, he began making his confession, weeping, and continually stopping in the middle of a word. In answer to the question of the prosecuting counsel, who leaned sinuously towards him, what had he done with the body of the Polish Jew he had killed and robbed, the accused again lapsed into silence, refusing to say anything. Then a veritable gale of nightmarish sounds burst upon him. The stage gradually darkened, and behind the glass door leading on to the staircase a crimson light blazed up. The mayor mistook the light for the lime-kiln and rushed madly towards it in order to push the body of the Jew through the narrow opening of the furnace and thus destroy every trace of his crime. He burnt it, but with it he had also burnt his own soul. Again the stage was plunged into darkness. From behind the windows and through the chinks of the blinds the red beams of the rising sun penetrated into the room, and from below the merry laughter of the revellers could still be heard. They were coming up the stairs to waken their host. There was a knock at the door. No reply. Another knock followed by an outburst of laughter. The surprised guests smashed in the glass of the door and, entering, found the mayor dead.

The transformation of the bedroom into a courtroom took place almost imperceptibly, and the impression the scene produced on the audience was so terrifying that almost at every performance many women left the auditorium and some people even fainted. Stanislavsky, the inventor of this trick, felt very proud, though on the stage he could hardly restrain himself from laughing as he watched his amateur actors, among whom were some highly placed persons, crawling on their bellies in the darkness, each anxious to reach his appointed place on the stage before the lights went on. He used to shut his eyes and think, "So that's what the stage is like ! Here I am bursting with laughter, and there they are fainting with terror."

In recalling this production of his twenty-five years later, Stanislavsky makes this characteristic confession : "I love to invent all sorts of devilries on the stage. I rejoice when I can invent a trick which deceives the audience. The stage can still do a lot in the sphere of the fantastic. It has not done half of what can be done. I must confess that one of the reasons for my choosing this play—and I produced it not as it was written but as my imagination prompted me—was this trick in the last act which I thought interesting on the stage. And I was not mistaken. It was successful. The audience applauded. Whom ? Why, me. The producer or the actor ? At the time I liked to believe it was the playing of the actor that the audience was applauding. For that meant that I was a tragic actor, the part having been made famous by such great actors as Henry Irving, Ludwig Barnay, Paul Mounet, and others. Now, looking back, I cannot help thinking that I did not act so badly. My interest both in the play and in my part was steadily growing, but this interest was not created by the psychology of the character, nor by the life of the human spirit of my part, but by the external plot of the play. The audience were kept in suspense simply because they wanted to find out who had committed the crime. There were no doubt a number of dramatic climaxes in the play, such as the fainting of the mayor at the end of the first act (at the appearance of the ghost of the murdered Polish Jew), his mad dance at the end of the second act, and, of course, in the transformation scene of the last act. But who was responsible for the

creation of these moments of high drama ? The producer or the
actor ? The producer. So it was to the producer and not to the
actor that all praise was due."

The famous German actor Ludwig Barnay, incidentally, saw
Stanislavsky's production of *The Bells*. "Your skill in the sphere
of play-production is so great," he wrote to Stanislavsky on
December 4th, 1896, "that it puts you among the artists of the
first rank. Your production of *The Bells* filled me with delight.
The acting of yourself and your colleagues in the leading parts
of the play, the crowd scenes in the second act, and the feeling
of truth that pervaded everything on the stage were so convincing
that, taken together, they resulted in a first-rate performance."

Stanislavsky was more modest. "Though I have not gone
forward in this production," he writes, "I haven't gone backwards, either. I have merely grown more confirmed in the good
stage habits I have already acquired."

CHAPTER XX

HAVING BURNT HIS fingers in Shakespearean tragedy, Stanislavsky decided to try his hand at comedy, for, as he puts it, "without Spanish boots and medieval swords I found life an awful bore." He decided to start the new season of 1897 with a production of *Much Ado About Nothing*, with himself in the part of Benedick.

There was another reason for his choice of this Shakespearean comedy. During his visit to Italy he spent a few days in Turin. Walking one day in the park with his wife, he came across a faithful replica of a medieval castle. There was a moat filled with water, a drawbridge, huge gates which opened with a creaking sound, and on passing through the gates they found themselves in a feudal city. Narrow streets, jutting-out houses, a square, a genuine medieval cathedral, curious little courtyards with fountains, and, of course, the huge castle itself with stone stair-cases leading to the battlements, and soldiers armed with halberds and pikes mounting guard at the gates. No detail of medieval life had been overlooked : the inhabitants were all dressed in period costumes ; the butchers and greengrocers stood outside their shops in the narrow lanes; the blacksmiths were busy forging swords and other weapons ; a street minstrel was singing a serenade under a window ; an Italian version of Doll Tearsheet stood outside an inn, inviting travellers for a rest and a meal, and inside the inn a whole sheep was being roasted on a spit in a huge fireplace. The castle was empty as (Stanislavsky and his wife were gravely informed) the Duke and his family were away on a visit. But they were shown round. They saw the barracks where the soldiers of the Duke lived and the little kitchen where their food was prepared for them ; the big kitchen of the Duke himself with the huge carcase of a bull suspended beneath the ceiling on a spit ; the dining-room with the two high seats of the Duke and his duchess and the long trestle tables ; the inner courtyard with hunting hawks chained to an upper balcony ; the throne room with the portraits of the Duke's ancestors on the walls ; the bedroom with a huge painting of the Madonna and Child ; the door, which led out of it into a narrow little corridor, and at the end of it a stone staircase, leading to a small tower with a round room, in which stood a huge four-poster bed, the bare stone walls decorated with flowers, bunting, rolls of coloured paper, a cloak and a rapier—the room of the Duke's page ; the Duke's private chapel and the priest's cell. Taking it all in, Stanislavsky understood why in Shakespeare's plays the priest appeared so quickly when he was sent for : he lived practically next door to the Duke's chamber. And one had only to walk through a corridor in order to be married in the Duke's private chapel. The castle positively reeked of the middle ages.

Ten years earlier, when working on the part of the covetous knight in Pushkin's play, Stanislavsky had had himself locked up in the damp cellar of a medieval castle near Vichy in order, as he thought, to experience the feelings of an old miser sitting in the cellar of his castle and counting his golden coins. That experiment was a ghastly failure. And yet now Stanislavsky could not resist taking a similar tempting short cut to the re-creation of feeling on the stage. He decided to live in this feudal city for some time in order to saturate himself with impressions of medieval life. However, his intention could not be carried out because strangers were forbidden to spend even one night in the castle. But deeply stirred by what he had seen, he felt he had to have a play in which he could use the picturesque material he had gathered during his visit to the Turin castle. He was not searching for material for the production of a play, but for a play in which he could use the material he had already collected. He began looking through Shakespeare and, on re-reading *Much Ado About Nothing*, it seemed to him that it was the sort of play in which he could "squeeze in" the plan of production he had already formed in his head. One thing he forgot to consider, namely, whether a man of his huge physique was fitted to represent the part of a frolicsome, lightfooted and gay man like Benedick. It was only during rehearsals that this incongruity between himself and Benedick struck him. Someone had remarked that one could make two Benedicks out of him, but never one. He thought the observation was just and he tried a compromise : he decided to represent Benedick as a coarse soldier who hated women and thought only of military glory. He attempted, in short, to conceal his own unfitness for the part by foisting upon it an interpretation that was completely at variance with the character created by Shakespeare. In the case of Benedick this solution was not successful, and Stanislavsky had to fall back on his "operatic" tricks : after all, it was the "Spanish boots" that he was longing for.

From the point of view of production the play was a success. It "squeezed itself" into the medieval castle beautifully. On the stage Stanislavsky felt as if he were at home. Everything was clear to him. He knew where the room in Leonato's house was, where Don John, Borachio and Conrade hatched their plots. He knew where Claudio was married. He knew where Benedick went to challenge Claudio to the duel. He knew where Dogberry, Verges and the Watch met. Everything was happening just next door, as in the Turin castle. At the time he thought that it was the duty of the producer to study and live the life of the characters in the play so as to be able to show it to the spectators and make them, too, live and experience that life as if they were at home. It was only years later that he realized that the only function of realism and even naturalism on the stage was to assist the actor to find the door leading to his subconsciousness, and that if he did not succeed in bringing to life the physical aspects of the character his mind would never believe in what he was doing on the stage. For the time being he merely realized the importance of visiting museums, travelling, collecting books that provided him with materials for his productions as well as engravings and paintings and anything, in fact, that depicted the external life of stage characters and enabled him to glean some understanding of their inner life. If before he had satisfied his collector's instincts rather indiscriminately, he now concentrated on collecting books and all sorts of other things that had a direct bearing on the theatre and play production.

The production of *Much Ado About Nothing* was also useful to him because it made him realize more than ever the importance of discovering the most typical traits of a stage character, for it was these that protected the actor from the wrong methods of acting. At the time he thought that the only way to inner feeling was through outer characteristics. As he was to find out afterwards, that was not the best approach to the creative art of the stage. For one thing it was not so easy to discover the outer characteristics of a person that were typical of him alone. When he did not succeed in finding them, he was completely at a loss. But the search for the best way of discovering the typical traits of a stage character made Stanislavsky abandon the old stage conventions and traditions and turn to life itself for his models. It was not individual people he now copied. What interested him was the characteristic traits of certain people out of which he began to "compose", sometimes consciously and sometimes unconsciously, a unique stage personality.

Having failed as Benedick, Stanislavsky must have asked himself what other Shakespearean comic figure he could play without encountering the same difficulties of embodiment. For Stanislavsky's physique was not really the serious obstacle to the successful re-creation of Benedick he had thought it was. The fact was that Benedick was much too subtle a character for Stanislavsky to tackle at that particular time. Certainly too subtle a character for the method of getting to his inner life through his outer characteristics. That was the real reason why Stanislavsky had tried the much cruder method of representing him as a coarse woman-hater. What he wanted, then, was a character less subtle, a character more amenable to external representational methods, a character in whose skin he would feel more comfortable. The choice was not really difficult : Malvolio ! And so it was that Stanislavsky chose *Twelfth Night* as his next production for the winter season of 1897.

The preliminary work on *Twelfth Night*, however, revealed another serious shortcoming of the productions of the Society of Art and Literature which, after the "stage miracles" of the Solodovnikov Theatre, Stanislavsky could no longer put up with : the absence of a really talented stage-designer. His first experience with Sollogub's excellent stage designs for Pushkin's *Covetous Knight* and Molière's *Georges Dandin* convinced him that a stage-designer's task was not only to create the decor of a play, but to help the actor to grasp the playwright's real intentions ; that the stage-designer, in fact, was almost as important an artist of the theatre as the producer himself. Such a view, however, was considered more than revolutionary in those days and, after Sollogub, Stanislavsky had to make do with all sorts of hack artists who had not the slightest conception of how to create a scenic illusion on the tiny stage of the Hunting Club.

For the scenery of *Twelfth Night*, Stanislavsky availed himself of the services of the scene designer of the Moscow Imperial theatres, a very painstaking artist of the "chocolate-box" school of art. His scenery had neither depth nor perspective. When an actor had to sit down at the back of the stage, he became two or three times as big as the houses or trees near him. Because of the difficulties of changing the scenery on so small a stage, which demanded long intervals between each act, he decided to content himself with only one scene—an open-air landscape in front of a painted back-cloth of a castle. The lack of proportion of this scenery became particularly noticeable when Stanislavsky had to bend double every time he came out through the low door of a clumsily constructed little house representing the "dark room" in which Malvolio was locked up. The scene-designer repainted the scenery many times, but he just could not get what Stanislavsky wanted.

"This isn't an Imperial artist but an Imperial cobbler!" Stanislavsky exclaimed one day after watching patiently the scene-designer's uninspired work.

For his next production of *The Sunken Bell*, another of Hauptmann's fairy-plays, he decided to find an entirely different sort of scene-designer. He was recommended to try Victor Simov, a young artist who had done some excellent work for Mamontov's operatic stage. Their first meeting took place in the early autumn of 1897[1]. Both men at once "took" to one another. Simov was immediately charmed by Stanislavsky's smile and the generous gesture with which he stretched out his large hand to shake hands with Simov's mother, his wife and himself. Stanislavsky's hair was already going grey, but his eyebrows and moustache were still black. Stanislavsky examined Simov's work and made up his mind to engage him there and then. At their next meeting at Stanislavsky's study in the house at the Red Gates, they discussed the future production at great length, Stanislavsky showing Simov his own scale models of the proposed settings, which he did not like because of their lack of a "real fairy-tale atmosphere." He then embarked on a spell-binding narration of the plot of *The Sunken Bell* which made Simov forget the pseudo-medieval atmosphere of the study and really feel himself to be at the bottom of the mysterious chasm in the mountains where the

[1] In his reminiscences, Simov gives the year of his first meeting with Stanislavsky as 1896. But he is obviously mistaken since at their second meeting a few days later, Stanislavsky gave him a ticket for the first night of *Twelfth Night* which took place on December 17th, 1897.

action of the play takes place. At the beginning of their talk a
tray was brought in with a large teapot, covered by a brown
woollen tea-cosy, two glasses in metal glass-holders, a sugar basin
and a jar of jam. At first Simov could not take his eyes off
Stanislavsky's large hand which moved with such unconscious
ease from the teapot to the glasses and from the glasses to the small
napkins. But soon he was so carried away by Stanislavsky's
vivid narrative that when he came to he found that his tea was
cold, the napkin had slipped off his knees and was lying on the
floor, and just after Heinrich's fatal fall into the chasm, he
became suddenly aware of the jam on the tiny saucer beside his
glass and asked himself with amazement where he was and what
the jam was doing there. It was his hospitable host himself who
bent down to retrieve his napkin, having suddenly transformed
himself from the bell-founder Heinrich to Konstantin Alexeyev.

A little earlier that year Stanislavsky performed another
"operation" on himself : he finally got rid of his "Spanish boots".
Like the great event of that summer—his meeting with Nemirovich-Danchenko on June 22nd, which led to the foundation of
the Moscow Art Theatre—this happened almost by accident.
The rehearsals of the Society of Art and Literature, which took
place in Stanislavsky's small flat, were becoming more and more
of a nuisance. The actors filled the rooms with tobacco smoke,
the maid grumbled because she had to stay up late to serve tea,
Stanislavsky's wife, whose health was none too good, could not
get her proper rest. "The whim of a rich man", as Stanislavsky's
ill-wishers described his passion for the stage, was beginning to
interfere seriously with what the "rich man" valued so greatly—
his family life. It was obvious that the first rehearsals of the new
theatre would have to take place somewhere else. It was then
that one of Stanislavsky's old friends, Nicolai Arkhipov, who had
been a member of the Alexeyev Circle and assisted him in the
Society of Art and Literature both as actor and producer, came
to the rescue. He proposed to convert a barn in the grounds of
his country house near Pushkino, a holiday resort within easy
reach of Moscow, into a little "theatre" where the rehearsals
of the new theatre could be conducted. To celebrate the opening
of this "theatrical" barn it was decided to put on two farces :
a skit on the "Spanish" traditions of the Moscow stage under the
title *Honour and Revenge*, which Stanislavsky had put on for the
Society of Art and Literature on March 18th, 1890, and *Hercules*,

a farce he had put on in the Alexeyev Circle on April 28th, 1883, in which he played the title role of Hercules, a famous circus "strong man" who arrives in a little provincial town where he reveals his identity after a number of comic incidents.

It was in the first of these farces, reduced by Stanislavsky to a grotesque parody of what he had once admired and found so difficult to forget, that he worked his passion for "Spanish boots" out of his system. The action of this farce takes place in a Spanish town at night, and its characters are all without exception Spanish "hidalgos" who, curiously enough, bear French-sounding names. As the curtain parts a night-watchman is seen walking on the stage. He lights a street-lamp and walks off. Then two Spanish hidalgos come walking from opposite directions and meet under the street lamp. One of them asks the other where he is going and receives an impertinent reply. They draw and fight. In the heat of the fight the elderly hidalgo inquires very gallantly of the wounded young blood where he should send his body.

"To Countess Blanche—de Vieille—Castelle."

"Why, you're not the Vicomte de Pengoelle ? "

"Yes, sir. Would you—I rather—"

"Vicomte Armand, I am your father ! "

Stanislavsky played the father who kills his own son in the duel. At the end of the play the stage is strewn with the dead bodies of the other members of the ancient family who arrive to avenge the death of Pengoelle. Stanislavsky used all sorts of tricks to heighten the grotesque effect of the farce. He made one huge "hidalgo" fight a little man and get the worst of it. Another one suddenly started crowing like a cock from the top window of a house and squealing at the top of his voice : "He sees you—he forgives you ! " Five other "hidalgos" suddenly stopped fighting, seized each other by the hand and began dancing in a ring, rolling their eyes and limping.

At the rehearsals of this farce (and, as usual, he had many of them), Stanislavsky never wearied in his efforts to achieve the most perfect stage illusion. He would make an actor walk the two or three paces he had to take on the tiny stage twenty or more times until he was absolutely satisfied. And the miracle he achieved was that instead of seeing a big man walking on a little stage, the spectator saw a man of normal size walking along a huge street.

One more notable achievement of this farce was that Stanislavsky seems to have brought the acting of the ensemble in it to
the height of perfection which was to make the Moscow Art
Theatre famous only a few years later.

The other farce performed on the same evening of July 16th,
1897, is notable for the fact that Stanislavsky's acting in the title
part of Hercules was considered by some spectators to have been
one of the finest feats of stage acting he had ever done. Stanislavsky had cut out the rather weak dialogue of the farce, transformed the "strong man" into a phlegmatic and toothy stage
Englishman, and reduced his speech to two English words "yes"
and "indeed", which he kept repeating with an extraordinary
variety of inflexions. His mimicry and gestures were so expressive that they evoked peals of laughter from the audience. The
difference between the Stanislavsky of the Alexeyev Circle and the
Stanislavsky of the last year of the Society of Art and Literature
was indeed most striking. When he had appeared in the same
part fourteen years ago he noted down in his journal : "I was not
bad in the part of Hercules, though I never really overcame my
mistake of overstraining my voice. I shouted and gesticulated
too much." Now he was a complete master both of mimicry and
voice and, what was more, he knew how to hold the attention
of his audience by transforming his broad clowning into so characteristic a piece of pure stage art that the farcical figure sprang to
life.

CHAPTER XXI

THE AUTUMN OF 1897 Stanislavsky spent on the rehearsals of *Twelfth Night* and his preliminary work on the production of *The Sunken Bell*. Shakespeare and Hauptmann again, with the German playwright leading by several lengths in this race for the stakes of theatrical success and popularity. In *Twelfth Night*, Stanislavsky's self-restraint in the part of Malvolio, his costume, gestures and mimicry as well as the on the whole convincing atmosphere and the effective composition of the production created a favourable impression, but the play was not a success for the reasons already mentioned in connection with the other Shakespearean productions of the Society of Art and Literature. The faults committed by the scene-designer were no doubt glaring, but the fact that the same play, revived two years later by Stanislavsky at the Moscow Art Theatre, ran for only eight performances seems to show that the bad scenery of its first production had little to do with its failure. It was in Hauptmann's *The Sunken Bell* that Stanislavsky won his last resounding success as producer at the Society of Art and Literature.

In this production Stanislavsky was certainly fortunate in his scene-designer. Indeed, it would be absurd to deny Simov's great share in the ultimate success of the play. The scale model of the proposed setting of the first act of the play which Stanislavsky himself had designed did not please either the producer or the stage designer. The small stage of the Hunting Club made it difficult to convey the eerie atmosphere of a deep cleft in the mountains with the rising pile of high peaks on either side and at the back of it. Simov's solution was to give up the idea of giving a "full size" representation of the scene and to concentrate only on the lower part of the landscape, leaving the rest to the imagination of the audience. He put a huge boulder askew in the foreground of the stage, a boulder covered with lichen and moss, with smaller stones of every size thrown haphazardly beside it. He built a large number of platforms, placed irregularly all over the stage and creating a three-dimensional illusion of great depth, piled with rocks and affording a glimpse of a bubbling brook, spanned by a fallen tree, and increasing the chaotic impression of a natural landfall. On such a scene the rock with the cave in which the sorceress lived looked very natural ; and so did the well out of which appeared the watersprite, a huge greyish-green toad with a human face whom Stanislavsky cleverly camouflaged by never showing him to the audience below the waist. The back of the stage was filled with a mass of uprooted trees whose network of branches seemed to conceal a distant prospect of wild mountainous country with a faint glimmer of the water of a lake overgrown with sedge.

When Simov paid his second visit to Stanislavsky to show him this scale model of the setting, he could not help feeling a little nervous. Stanislavsky patiently watched him fumbling with the strings. He smiled encouragingly and, as was his habit, bit the back of his hand. When the model was at last produced, he examined it carefully against the light and at last made a remark that finally settled the question of their future collaboration :

"Where did you get such a knowledge of the stage ? To feel it like that is a great achievement."

It was just such a setting Stanislavsky wanted for the un-hampered play of his imagination. Among the chaotic pile of rocks, he saw the winding path leading to the lair of the sorceress and he immediately began to describe her bent figure appearing from behind the dirty hide which covered the entrance to her cave, and, leaning on a thick, gnarled stick, hobbling to the heap of boulders and then going down to the well of the watersprite.

"You see," he exclaimed excitedly, "there out of the well rises the fat-bellied, bandy-legged monster with his green skin of a toad and his webbed feet and—beside him the graceful figure of the fair-haired Rautendelein ! "

Screwing up his eyes, Stanislavsky already seemed to take in the comic and moving contrast of these two figures.

And from behind the fallen trees in the background he could already see the strange figure of the woodsprite, half-goat, with huge horns and a scraggy neck, his body covered with tufts of dark brown wool, skipping over the roots and branches with his goat's hoofs.

Another flight of imagination : a deserted valley—sunset—
darkness falls—a mist rises—the moon appears—and in the silvery
haze the fairies come out and dance, waving long muslin scarves
on concealed sticks. But how was he to suggest a whole multi-
tude of fairies on such a tiny stage ? He would have to invent some
trick to deceive the spectator. He would have to think out a
special intonation with which the fairies would call to Rautendelein in drawn out voices, repeated more and more faintly behind
the scenes. That ought to create the impression of countless
numbers of fairies. And he might apply the same trick in another
way in a different scene. A pretty head of a young girl appearing
suddenly from behind a rock, then another face appearing from
some cleft, then further just a wisp of hair, and so on. And
again he would create the illusion of a great number of fairies,
who would call to each other softly in their fresh girlish voices :
"Balder's dead—Balder's dead ! " and it would sound like a
strangely mysterious and sad melody sung by the wind.

Stanislavsky next began looking for a place in the scale model of
Simov's set from which he—Heinrich—would be able to
roll down the mountainside into the gorge. The stage was so
small and so low that even if he jumped from the ceiling, he would
not hurt himself. If his fall should take place in front of the stage,
it would look clumsy and ridiculous ; if it should take place at the
back of the stage, it would lack conviction, for then he would fall
into the lake from which he would emerge bone-dry. Stanislavsky took some time to solve this problem. Finally, he hit on
the idea of constructing a chute, down which he would slide
head foremost, just like a man who slips and falls headlong down
a steep slope, and to add to the illusion a heap of property stones
would be sent after him down the chute, the sound effect of falling
stones being reproduced behind the stage. His outstretched
body would then lie beside the huge boulder and would appear
small in comparison.

Having thought of this trick, Stanislavsky looked up question-
ingly at Simov, who approved of it at once as a brilliant idea with
which he could find no fault at all. (The carefully camouflaged
chute was usually examined before every performance by Stanislavsky, who took particular care to see that there were no splinters
in it. He never took any unnecessary chances that might spoil
his performance.)

Hauptmann's play, a "philosophic" fairy-tale, in which

Heinrich himself is a sort of superhuman Wagnerian hero who perishes because the truth he wants to give to humanity (the mystic bell) is only accessible to the gods and is deadly to men, was just the sort of thing that exercised a strong appeal on Stanislavsky at the time. A fantastic allegory does not require a deep insight into the human heart, and it was the human heart that offered such insuperable difficulties to Stanislavsky in his efforts to represent it on the stage. The embodiment of a part was still a mystery to him, and just then he did not even attempt to look for the key to it. Neither he nor his amateur actors were yet able to hold an audience by their mere presence on the footboards. But he had already become very proficient in all sorts of stage tricks which kept the attention of the audience glued to the stage, including the use of light and sound effects and an understanding of the dramatic significance of pauses. And now, thanks to Simov's sets, Hauptmann's play gave him the further opportunity of mastering the art of using three-dimensional objects on the stage and with their help lending a greater expressiveness to a part by the use of plastic poses, movements and actions. Give the actor a "period" chair, and he will invent countless numbers of poses and movements round it ; give him a stone, and he could either sit dreaming on it, or lie in despair on it, or stand on it so that his whole pose could show his aspirations for the stars. The actor, Stanislavsky discovered, could *live* with three-dimensional objects, which could also *live* with him.

There was, moreover, another and no less important aspect to this stage expedient (and, after all, it was nothing but an expedient, for it merely provided the actor with a way of disguising his inexperience in the art of character embodiment). To walk on the stage, Stanislavsky had learnt by now, was one of the most difficult accomplishments for an actor to acquire. It took him hours as a producer to teach an actor to take two or three steps on the stage. Many years later, indeed, Stanislavsky asserted that in all his long experience he had only met two or three actors who knew how to walk on the stage. In *The Sunken Bell*, therefore, he made his actors dispense with walking altogether. Instead they climbed or sat on stones, jumped from rock to rock, balanced themselves or crawled along the trunks of fallen trees, disappeared through trap-doors and popped out of them again. All that— and this was really what Stanislavsky was after—made them give up not only the traditional ways of acting which by then had become so stereotyped that they did not express anything but the actor's own impotence, but also taught them new gestures and movements that were more natural and more convincing, too. And by moulding the stage floor he made the actor almost against his will resort to new gestures and movements and new expressive methods of acting.

"It is only fair to say," Stanislavsky writes, "that this time I have taken a step forward as a producer."

As an actor, however, Stanislavsky admits (and this is, surely, a very significant admission) that he had failed. His interpretation of Heinrich suffered from a cloying sentimentality that was poles apart from the lyricism and romanticism of his part and which merely fell back upon the time-hallowed traditions of acting.

"But," he writes, "my admirers merely again confirmed me in my mistake. It is true that many of my friends whose opinions I valued were sadly and significantly silent. But that made me respond to flattery all the more strongly, for I was afraid to lose faith in myself. And once more I stupidly explained away this silence as due to envy and intrigue. But inside me I could not help feeling the nagging pain of dissatisfaction."

In self-justification Stanislavsky goes on to make the important point that it was not vanity or success that made him so self-confident, but rather his fear that if he gave way to his doubts and lost faith in himself he would not have the courage to walk on the footboards and face an audience. He had either to stifle those doubts or give up the stage. Curiously enough, he did neither. The flattery of his admirers merely acted on him as a spur to carry on with his work on the stage, while his doubts led him slowly but inevitably to deepen his self-analysis and to search for those hidden laws of acting which he felt the art of the actor must possess.

The Sunken Bell, first performed on January 27th, 1898, was a great popular success, and it owed its success, to some extent at any rate, to something Stanislavsky does not mention, but for which he was as much responsible as for the entire production of the play, namely, the marvellous ensemble of the actors whose playing blended so well together that it was impossible to pick out a single actor who was either better or worse than his partners. The play was the last production that Stanislavsky put on for the Society of Art and Literature. He was about to set out on a new and perilous adventure, an adventure that just then seemed as likely to fail as to succeed. About six months earlier, on June 21st, 1897, a visiting card had been left at his house. He was away in the country, but the moment he saw it on his return he knew that his dearest wish was about to come true : he would at last get the theatre he wanted.

The visiting card had this message scribbled on it :

"Have you received my letter ? I am told you are expected back in Moscow tomorrow, on Wednesday. I shall be at the Slav Bazaar[1] at one o'clock. Could we meet there ? If not, let me know at this address where and when we could meet."

The visiting card was from Nemirovich-Danchenko. They had never met before.

[1] A famous restaurant in Moscow.

Part Two

THE MOSCOW ART THEATRE

CHAPTER XXII

IF THE FOUNDATION of the Moscow Art Theatre appears today to have been a date of the utmost significance in the history of the Russian as well as of the world theatre, it was certainly not regarded as such in 1898. Stanislavsky was at the time a man of thirty-five and he had already appeared in 75 different parts (in the Moscow Art Theatre he appeared in only a further 28 new parts) and yet his fame as an actor or even as a producer was far from established. Most of the critics still refused to take him seriously, and he had taken a particular dislike to one young dramatic critic, Nicolai Efros, who was very outspoken about the many faults of his acting. Thirteen years later, while spending a holiday with Efros and his wife in Brittany (Efros had by then become one of the most enthusiastic supporters of the Moscow Art Theatre), Stanislavsky said : "I regarded Efros at that time as my personal enemy. In those days my actor's petty vanity could not bear criticism. I only liked the praise I heard from my friends and acquaintances. I considered myself almost a genius, and suddenly a young man whom I had known as a schoolboy and as a student had the audacity to attack me ! I was sure that he was inspired by personal animosity towards me and that all he thought about was to cause me unpleasantness. I am ashamed to confess it, but there was a moment when I felt like taking a pistol and going to demand an explanation from him."

There can be no doubt that Stanislavsky resented the attacks on him very much, particularly as there was a good deal of truth in them. The critics could not be expected to know anything about the painful process of self-criticism that was going on continually in Stanislavsky's mind. But that process, which was itself a symptom of the growing-pains of genius and which distinguished Stanislavsky from all the other gifted amateurs of his day, was not a protection against the vanity of the artist. At heart he knew that one day his claims to genius would be justified. Medvedeva's remark that his name would pass into history did not surprise him, though he would not have dared to repeat her words to anyone but his wife. Was there not that curious coincidence about the date of his birth, which was exactly one hundred years after the death of Fyodor Volkov, the founder of the Russian theatre? And was it not also the year of the death of Mikhail Shchepkin, the great reformer of the Russian stage? Fate itself in its mysterious way seemed to point to him as the successor of these two great historic figures of the Russian stage, which, after all, was still very young. It was only in 1756 that by an edict of the Empress Yelisaveta the first theatre was founded in Petersburg. The Moscow Maly (Little) Theatre, the theatre which, as he said himself, exercised a greater influence on his spiritual development than any other school, was founded only about forty years before his birth, and till 1882 it still enjoyed the monopoly of dramatic performances in Moscow. His Alexeyev Circle was merely one of many similar "circles" of private amateur theatricals in Moscow which sought to circumvent the monopoly in drama of the Imperial theatres in Moscow and Petersburg. The first of these dramatic "circles" was formed in Moscow as far back as 1850 with the express purpose of putting on "plays forbidden by the censor" and, generally, of giving the Moscow playgoer a chance of seeing plays that would never be performed on the stage of the Maly Theatre. Later on a "Shakespeare Circle" was founded in Moscow, which produced *Henry IV* for the first time on the Russian stage. In 1865 Alexander Ostrovsky and Nicolai Rubinstein, the founder of the Moscow Conservatoire, formed the "Artistic Circle," which also put on a number of plays never performed on the Imperial stage, but, like the Society of Art and Literature, its programme included other activities. And perhaps most significant of all in view of the fact that the Moscow Art Theatre was at first founded as a People's Art Theatre, was the foundation in 1872 by a group of distinguished Moscow citizens of a People's Theatre with a "classical repertoire" which carried on till 1877.

As for the new principles of acting and play production Stanislavsky was to introduce, most of them had already been formulated by Shchepkin, followed by Ostrovsky, long before the foundation of the Moscow Art Theatre. When Shchepkin became a professional actor (he was born a serf in 1788 and appeared on the stage for the first time in "serf theatres" run by rich Russian landowners), he found the Russian stage entirely under the influence of the pseudo-classical French theatre. An actor in those days was not expected to speak his lines in a natural voice. He had to declaim them, accompanying each word by some theatrical gesture. Stage lovers, especially, were expected to say their lines with great passion, and the words "love" and "treachery" had to be shouted in as loud a voice as the actor could manage. And when an actor had to leave the stage after some important soliloquy, he was expected to raise his right hand dramatically and go out like that. Shchepkin tells of an actor who, remembering to raise his hand only after walking half across the stage, immediately decided to "correct his mistake", raised his hand solemnly, and strode off in the approved manner.

So generally accepted were these "classical "traditions of acting on the Russian stage that Shchepkin himself never thought of questioning them till one day he happened to be present at a performance of a play given by Prince Meshchersky at his country house (it was in the summer of 1810), and to his surprise saw that the prince himself was not *acting* on the stage but just behaving as he would in real life. The curious thing was that, strange as Prince Meshchersky's acting seemed to him at first, he was more and more carried away by it till in the end he felt so moved that he burst into tears. "I fell under the spell of real life," Shchepkin wrote in his memoirs, "and it did not release its hold on me till the end of the performance. I saw no one on the stage except the prince. My eyes seemed to have become glued to him. His suffering struck a living chord in my soul ; every word of his delighted me by its naturalness and at the same time tormented me."

To Shchepkin this simplicity and sincerity on the footboards was a revelation that produced a radical change in his own approach to the art of the stage. He realized that it was a great mistake for an actor to violate his own nature and renounce his own personality. An actor, he claimed, anticipating Stanislavsky by more than fifty years, must always remain himself. He must never invent his stage characters, but create them as living people with the help of his own experience of life. Everyone who claimed to be an artist as well as an actor, Shchepkin maintained, must speak his "own words", must utter his "own sounds", which must come straight from his heart. He became the propagator of a "simple" diction. One day he was rehearsing Molière's *Sganarelle*. As he had already rehearsed the title part of the play hundreds of times before, he felt bored, and instead of "acting" he just spoke in his usual voice. Suddenly he became aware of the fact that he enunciated some of his lines so simply that if he had had to say them in real life, he would have said them in exactly the same way. All this led Shchepkin to work out a system of acting based on stage realism. He demanded that the actor should stop imitating the external habits, voice and mannerisms of whatever class his character belonged to. An actor, he taught, must penetrate into the "soul" of his part, he must get "under the skin" of the character, and not just copy life outwardly. At the same time, however, the actor must be very careful not to rely on his intuition alone : on the stage he must strive to represent "a living man, a man alive not only in body, but also in mind and heart." An actor, according to Shchepkin, ought to understand the fundamental problem of his part (Stanislavsky in his "system" called it the "through-action") and possess the right technique for its embodiment.

It was Shchepkin who raised the Maly Theatre to the position of one of the foremost theatres in the country not only by his own acting, but also by training a large number of actors and actresses who became famous on its stage. After Shchepkin's death Ostrovsky continued his work, and as a playwright who was in constant touch with the actors of the Maly Theatre, which to all intents and purposes became the Ostrovsky Theatre as it had earlier been "Shchepkin's Playhouse", he, too, was responsible for training a new generation of great players. But at the end of Ostrovsky's life the Maly Theatre was beginning to lose its pre-eminence among the Imperial theatres and entered on a period of rapid decline. The ensemble for which Ostrovsky had been responsible had gone. For a time the theatre maintained its prestige because it still possessed a number of great players, but even then Ostrovsky claimed that it could be said "without exaggeration" that it existed only "in a nominal sense."

To raise the prestige of the Imperial stage Ostrovsky kept presenting memoranda to the authorities who were in charge of it. In his memorandum on the decline of the dramatic stage in Moscow, he drew a rather significant distinction between a theatre run for the entertainment of the rich who could afford to pay for the expensive seats of the Maly Theatre, and one for the less well-to-do classes who could afford only cheap seats but who went to the theatre "to feel and understand" and who therefore demanded "an excellent company." He pointed out that the monopoly enjoyed by the Imperial theatres made it impossible for the playwright to write plays for the less well-to-do but more exacting audiences. The bureaucrats who ran the Imperial theatres did not care what play they put on so long as their box-office returns showed a good profit for the year. To them a translation of a trashy and banal French comedy was a much more lucrative proposition than a serious play by a Russian author. The authorities of the Maly Theatre, in particular, had no desire to put on serious plays because, the theatre being small, they could always be sure of a full house provided they put on some light entertainment for their rich patrons. Moreover, the system of "benefits" which was then in vogue left the choice of the play to the actor or actress whose turn it was to have a benefit night and who naturally preferred some light and amusing comedy because it would be certain to fill the house. Thus the Russian playwright had the choice of either adapting light French comedies or writing similar comedies himself. Indeed, the "popular" playwrights did nothing else. As for the serious playwright who had the cause of Russian dramatic art at heart, he was reduced to the position of a humble petitioner who had to bow and scrape before the civil servant in charge of the theatre, who resented any talk about the sad state of Russian drama for the simple reason that he did not care a rap whether Russian drama existed or not. Besides, an original play involved the theatre in all sorts of expenditure on costumes and scenery, while the adaptations of the French comedies were all so alike that the same costumes and scenery could easily be used for all of them. Another cause of the decline of the Maly Theatre listed by Ostrovsky was also connected with the anxiety of the directors to show a good profit for the year. When one of the leading actors died, they never tried to engage a good actor to take his place, for that would have meant paying him a good salary. Instead they filled the vacancy by employing an incompetent actor who would be satisfied with a small salary. As a result of this cheese-paring policy, the fine company of the Maly Theatre began to dwindle and, Ostrovsky writes, "little by little the tradition of the stage was destroyed, the whole tone of the performance was lowered, and the former unity and integrity of the ensemble was gone."

Lacking any knowledge of the stage and being unable to

distinguish between a good and a bad actor, the authorities of the Maly Theatre could not be expected to do anything about the training of young actors, nor indeed had they any idea of how to produce or rehearse a play. Their notion of stage discipline was crude in the extreme, and, Ostrovsky writes, "without genuine artistic discipline the art of the stage ceases to be an art and becomes an empty pastime." Stage discipline Ostrovsky defined (and here, too, he anticipated Stanislavsky) as a system of stage management in which (1) the combined art of the performers was directed towards the achievement of the fullest possible effect ; (2) the part every actor took in the play was directly dependent upon the extent to which his participation was necessary for the creation of one organic whole ; and (3) every actor was carefully watched to make sure he did not give either more or less than this part demanded in relation to the whole. "Discipline," Ostrovsky added, and here he anticipated the views Stanislavsky held towards the end of his life, "is achieved only by an expert production and by a wisely exercised control over the performance of the actor." An actor, he insisted, must never be bullied or shouted at. "If the theatre is a temple of art," Ostrovsky wrote using the identical definition Stanislavsky used, "then it deserves the respect of everyone who works in it and every negligence in the service of art becomes a profanation and an insult, for it shows a craven lack of understanding of his duties by the actor. I do not exaggerate the importance of discipline," Ostrovsky concluded, "for discipline merely means an honest attitude towards one's work and it is impossible to be too honest where one's work on the stage is concerned."

There was not a vestige of that kind of discipline in the Maly Theatre, for the discipline there was imposed from above by a bureaucrat and was not the natural result of the authority exercised by an expert of the stage whom the actors could respect and whose advice they would be glad to accept. The absence of such an artistic as opposed to a purely bureaucratic discipline was, according to Ostrovsky, directly responsible for the lowering of the standards of acting among the actors of the Imperial theatres who even began to regard their negligent attitude to their art as something that was in itself meritorious and that distinguished the "star" from the common player. The result of such a lowering of general standards was that the actors soon began to regard a play merely as a vehicle for self-display.

In concluding his memorandum on the reasons for the decline of the Maly Theatre, Ostrovsky outlined a scheme for the establishment of what he called a "national theatre" which in all essential points corresponded to the plan Stanislavsky and Nemirovich-Danchenko worked out at their first meeting at the Slav Bazaar about twenty years later. He foresaw that such a theatre would not make any profits at first, but he was certain that it would slowly but surely create its own public. He insisted that such a theatre ought to be supported until it had trained its own competent company of actors and established "a strong artistic repertoire". But what seemed to him to be the most essential guarantee of the ultimate success of such a theatre was that it should possess a producer who was an expert of the stage and had good taste, and whose authority the actors would accept without questioning. "Theatrical speculators are no authorities on the theatre," he wrote, "and while they may be able to draw up a good repertoire, they will never stick to it. They will never be able to get an audience of their own and will merely keep complaining to the authorities and trying to get all sorts of exemptions and privileges from them (as has already happened in Moscow with the People's Theatre), and they will resort to all sorts of blandishments to get the people to come and see their plays and end up by dragging live elephants on the stage."

Ostrovsky's proposals for the reform of the stage, which were only published after Stanislavsky's death,· were completely ignored by the authorities. After the abolition of the monopoly of the Imperial theatres in 1882, Ostrovsky tried to run a theatre of his own, but it failed because he could not compete with the "stage profiteers" who opened a large number of theatres in Moscow. One of these, F. Korsh, survived till the October Revolution of 1918.

In the interval between Ostrovsky's death on June 14th, 1886, and the foundation of the Moscow Art Theatre in 1898, the Maly Theatre continued on its downward path. It made no attempt to improve its rehearsals, which were conducted in a most extraordinary way. They usually began at 11 o'clock in the morning. At precisely a quarter to eleven the uniformed and bemedalled commissionaire of the Maly Theatre could be seen lugging a big chair to the centre of the stage and placing it in front of the prompter's box. The producer then made his appearance, walking slowly and solemnly to his chair and sitting down.

This was the signal for the prompter to take his seat beside him. The rehearsal began. The producer hardly ever opened his mouth. Only from time to time would he turn to the commissionaire and say, "What's that infernal noise behind the scenes ? " or ask a young actor, who had only a walking-on part, "How did you get among the boyars ? Off with you to the beggars ! " For the parts of the boyars in a Russian historical play were usually reserved for the leading actors and the presence of a young actor among them was considered an affront to their dignity. The play was in fact rehearsed by the leading actors, who discussed the *mise-en-scènes*, went over their parts together, and corrected each other's acting in language that was not always dignified. One of the producers of the Maly Theatre was known to be so attached to his chair of office that even when the theatre was closed for the summer holidays he used to arrive regularly twice a week, wait for his chair to be solemnly placed in front of the prompter's box facing the auditorium, then walk slowly along the footlights, sit down in his chair, and spend two hours in silent contemplation of the empty rows of stalls.

The scenery of the Maly Theatre consisted of a standard "garden" or "wood", one and the same drawing-room with the usual soft furnishings, or a more ambitious "ballroom" with painted columns. "In the middle of the stage," Stanislavsky writes, "you usually saw a wide expanse of dirty floor with a few chairs corresponding to the number of performers. In the gaps between the wings the spectator could catch a glimpse of the crowd of stage-hands, extras, make-up men and dressers walking about or staring at the stage. If a door was wanted, it was placed between the wings and no one seemed to care about the gaping hole above it. Whenever required, a street with a distant perspective and a huge deserted square with fountains, monuments, etc., was painted on a backcloth, the actors near it being taller than the houses. The dirty floor of the stage was left in all its unsightly bareness, allowing the actors absolute freedom to stand before the prompter's box, which exercises so great an attraction on the servants of Melpomene. The resplendent Empire or rococo pavilion, painted in the conventional manner, held complete sway over the stage. The canvas doors vibrated every time they were opened or closed, and they usually opened and closed by themselves every time an actor came on the stage."

As for costumes, each actor was supposed to have his own

wardrobe, made according to his taste and pocket. It never occurred to the actors to ask the advice of the producer or stage-designer, and their only concern was to avoid having costumes of the same colour. In the wardrobe room the choice was limited to a certain number of "styles", chiefly "Faust", "Huguenots", or "Molière", which were considered suitable for any "period" play.

The curse of officialdom was indeed to be seen everywhere in the Maly Theatre. The greenroom, for instance, was a very solemn affair. Chairs were placed along its walls. A grand-father clock in the corner ticked away solemnly, chiming the quarters and the hours. In the intervals the leading actors and actresses occupied their particular chairs, smoking and exchang-ing views on current topics and plays. Occasionally a young actor would enter, go up to the old ladies, bow, kiss their hands and then withdraw respectfully. One of the actresses had once had her hand kissed by a royal personage and she would never allow anyone to kiss it again. The young actors had therefore to go through the motions of kissing her hand. One of the greatest actresses of that time, Olga Sadovskaya, whose husband and children were also famous actors (they had all been trained by Ostrovsky) was never known to sit down in the greenroom. She used to stand at the door of her dressing-room, smoking and contemplating in silence the solemnities of the greenroom. She was still playing in 1907, when the Moscow Art Theatre was already world-famous, without changing her manner of always addressing herself to the audience. Nicolai Popov, Stanislavsky's assistant in the days of the Society of Art and Literature, who was producing for the Maly Theatre that year, explained to her that it was not natural to sit facing the audience and that she ought to look at her partner when saying her lines. At the rehearsals the old lady did as she was told by the producer, but on the first night she stopped the assistant stage-manager just as he was about to signal for the curtain to go up, turned her chair to face the audience and shouted to Popov, who was standing in the wings, "This isn't the Moscow Art Theatre, my dear sir!" She then gave the assistant stage-manager a radiant smile and told him to raise the curtain. Stanislavsky used to say: "Only Olga Sadovskaya has a right to do as she does: in the presence of genius the laws of the stage are silent!"

In view of such a state of affairs in one of Moscow's leading theatres it is not surprising that Stanislavsky's methods of rehearsing a play and, particularly, his insistence on a large number of rehearsals, a practice he had followed ever since the days of the Alexeyev Circle, should be considered eccentric, if not downright revolutionary. At the first theatrical conference which took place in Moscow in March, 1897, the question of the training of actors produced a most vehement debate. A large number of well-known actors objected to the idea that an actor should be trained or indeed carry out the orders of a producer. They believed that a born actor should not be interfered with by any-one and should be allowed to rely entirely on his inspiration. These adherents of the "inspiration school", as Stanislavsky called them, were led at the Moscow conference by no less a person than the famous Petersburg actress Polina Strepetova, opposite whom Stanislavsky had once played in Pissemsky's tragedy *Bitter Fate*. Her hero was Pavel Mochalov (1800-1848), Russia's greatest romantic actor, whose first appearance on the stage, in the part of Hamlet, at the age of 17 had made him famous and who was supposed to be a shining example of the "elemental" actor. "Down with the dramatic schools !" Strepetova shouted at the conference. "Down with training ! Back to Mochalov !" She was loudly applauded by a large number of the delegates, but she was opposed by Alexander Lensky, the famous actor of the Maly Theatre, whom Stanislavsky greatly revered and admired. Lensky considered the dramatic school as essential to the future of dramatic art in Russia and, in his address to the conference, he laid particular stress on the importance of a competent producer who should be an artist and "not only a person with a label 'Producer' stuck on his forehead." Lensky advocated a four-point programme for raising the level of the Russian stage : (1) a repertoire of serious plays and the abolition of the practice of daily performances of new plays ; (2) the establishment of per-manent companies ; (3) the lowering of prices of admission ; and (4) producers.

This was practically the programme Stanislavsky and Nemiro-vich-Danchenko hoped to carry out when they founded the Moscow Art Theatre. Lensky did not possess Stanislavsky's fanatic driving power and his attempts to reform the Maly Theatre by conducting its dramatic school and acting as producer came to nothing. Besides, the evils of the professional stage were too deep-seated to be amenable to reform. A clean cut had to be made ; a total separation from the worn-out traditions of the theatre, from the selfishness and intrigues that pervaded the stage, the lack of the most elementary human decencies in the treatment of the less fortunate and less gifted actors, the spirit of self-aggrandizement and self-advertisement. To do all that a different type of man was needed : a man who was an expert on stage technique and at the same time had nothing whatever to do with the professional stage ; a man who was mulishly obstinate in pursuing a certain course of action and at the same time possessed the gift of relentless self-criticism and self-analysis which made him acknowledge his mistakes without the slightest hesitation and set out on a new course with the same zeal and enthusiasm ; a man who was deeply critical of himself and at the same time ruthlessly overbearing when convinced that he was doing the right thing ; a man, too, of independent means whose interest in the theatre was entirely free from any financial considerations. Such a man was Stanislavsky, and the curious thing is that the negative sides of his character, which he himself deplored, were as useful to him in his work on the stage as the positive ones. Even his reputation as a rich and rather eccentric amateur, which had stood in the way of his recognition as a new force in the theatre, proved useful to him in the end by underlining the difference between him and the professional actors. If he hesitated to challenge the professional stage by the foundation of a theatre of his own, he did so for a very good reason : he knew very well that the fate of such a theatre would in the last resort depend on its repertoire, and he had a fully justified mistrust of his own literary judgment. His "classical" upbringing had left a great gap in his education and it seemed to have completely ruined his sense of literary values. He knew from experience that he did not possess the ability to distinguish between a great dramatic work and a play that merely gave him an opportunity of dazzling an audience by a pyrotechnic display of his original methods of production. It is certainly remarkable that Stanislavsky should have kept himself so entirely aloof from the society of literary men. In his own reminiscences of those days he does not mention any meeting with a writer of note except Tolstoy, whom he had met for the first time by chance and in whose presence he had behaved like a schoolboy. It must not be forgotten that it was Nemirovich-Danchenko who had first approached Stanislavsky. Indeed, it is doubtful whether the Moscow Art Theatre would have been founded at all if its foundation had depended on Stanislavsky's taking the initial step of approaching Nemirovich-Danchenko, who was at the time one of the most popular "highbrow" novelists and playwrights in Russia with a wide circle of friends and acquaintances among the literary confraternity in Moscow and Petersburg, and one of the few writers who discerned Chekhov's great dramatic genius.

Born in 1859, Nemirovich-Danchenko began his literary career very early. By the end of the nineties he was already the author of a number of best-sellers and successful plays, many of which had been produced on the stage of the Maly Theatre. His interest in the theatre went back to his student days when he took part in amateur dramatic performances in the provinces and in Moscow. In 1890 he took over the dramatic classes of the Moscow Philharmonic School and threw himself with great zest into the work of training a new generation of actors who should be free from the stale and outworn traditions of the stage. As a writer of the "psychological" school he laid particular stress on bringing out the "psychological" undertones in the acting of his pupils, and his first great success in that particular line was the production at his school of Ibsen's *A Doll's House* in 1896. In 1897 he submitted to the authorities a series of proposals for the reform of the Moscow Imperial theatres. Not expecting anything to come of it, he at the same time wrote a letter to Stanislavsky in which he expressed the wish to meet him in order to discuss a matter of great concern to both of them. Neither in his letter nor in his message on the visiting card did Nemirovich-Danchenko even mention the possibility of founding a new theatre.

To Stanislavsky the letter and visiting-card from Nemirovich-Danchenko must have come as a complete surprise. It seemed to him, though, that they had long been looking for each other and that it was only natural for Nemirovich-Danchenko and not for him to have taken the first step. Now that they had found each other, everything was going to be different ; for one thing he could count on having at his side a literary authority whom he could trust to choose the right plays for their repertoire. For the theatre he dreamed of had to be *literary* as well as artistic. Indeed, for the moment "literary" became the magic word which Stanislavsky and Nemirovich-Danchenko were never tired of repeating.

"So you'll be able to put on Schiller's *Kabale und Liebe* and all that sort of thing now ? " Nicolai Popov, who happened to meet

Stanislavsky a few days after the foundation of the Moscow Art Theatre, asked innocently.

"Good Lord, no," said Stanislavsky, with a frown. "We shan't have any of that melodramatic stuff in our theatre. We've got quite different plans ! "

The Theatre with a capital "T" he had been dreaming of was now also to be Literary with a capital "L." It was also, incidentally, to be a People's Theatre with specially reduced prices for the poorer classes, challenging the professional stage, with its cheap French comedies. The attempt to run a People's Theatre with a classical repertoire had, no doubt, been made before and had to be given up, but that was in the days of the monopoly of the Imperial theatres. It was the marriage of the stage and literature that kept the Moscow Art Theatre going during the first ten years of its hazardous career. It was that which made Chekhov's fame as a playwright possible. It was that which brought Gorky into the theatre. And however inevitable the subsequent rupture between Stanislavsky and Nemirovich-Danchenko was, it remains a fact that but for the close co-operation between the man of the theatre and the man of letters the Moscow Art Theatre would never have survived.

CHAPTER XXIII

STANISLAVSKY and Nemirovich-Danchenko met at the Slav Bazaar at two o'clock in the afternoon on June 22nd, 1897, and sat discussing their scheme for a new and revolutionary theatre till eight o'clock the following morning. And one frequently forgotten fact should be noted here : these were not two young enthusiasts spending eighteen hours together in concocting some hare-brained plan to astonish and shock the theatrical world. Nemirovich-Danchenko was already a man of forty who had practically come to the end of his successful literary career. Stanislavsky was a man of thirty-five who had a responsible job in an old family business and who had a varied and astonishingly original stage career behind him. Both of them knew perfectly well what they wanted and they realized the risks they were running in challenging the old-established traditions of the theatre. But they were also convinced that they knew the causes that had brought about the failure of similar enterprises in the past and that they would be able to avoid them. These causes were : (1) the absence of artistic discipline among the actors themselves, many of whom were men of not inconsiderable talent. At a recent performance of Schiller's *Don Carlos* by a private theatre, for instance, no less than seven actors demanded to be given the title part, and when one of them at last consented to take a secondary part he did not think it necessary to turn up at the rehearsals and never bothered to learn it ; (2) with the exception of the first two plays of the season, no adequate rehearsal was considered necessary, and even the first two plays were rehearsed only a fortnight before the beginning of the season, the other plays being given two or three rehearsals at most ; (3) performances usually began half an hour or even three-quarters of an hour after the advertised time and the intervals between the acts were quite unnecessarily protracted, with the result that at the end of the performance the audience was usually tired out ; (4) lack of originality in the production of the plays and their trite interpretation ; and (5) absence of a decent repertoire.

The last two reasons for the failure of new theatrical ventures at once brought Stanislavsky and Nemirovich-Danchenko up against the problem of dividing their duties to avoid any possible misunderstandings that might have a serious effect on the smooth running of the new theatre. Stanislavsky gladly conceded to Nemirovich-Danchenko the deciding voice in the selection of the repertoire, but insisted that he himself should enjoy the same unlimited authority in the production of the plays. There seems to have been some reluctance on Nemirovich-Danchenko's part to accept Stanislavsky's demand. But, as Stanislavsky declares, "once I got carried away by something, I took the bit between my teeth and rushed straight to my goal uninfluenced either by argument or reason." It was therefore decided (they put it in writing and signed it) that Nemirovich-Danchenko enjoyed a right of veto in literary matters, while Stanislavsky enjoyed a similar right in matters of production. This both of them observed faithfully during the first critical years of the existence of the Moscow Art Theatre. It was enough for one of them to utter the magic word *veto* for all arguments to come to an end, the entire responsibility for the choice of the play or its production being borne by the man who had used his drastic powers to overrule the other.

There was no disagreement about who should be put in charge of the administration of the theatre, Stanislavsky being only too anxious not to burden himself with administrative duties.

"An international conference," Stanislavsky writes, "does not discuss questions affecting the welfare of States with such thoroughness as we discussed the fundamental principles of our future enterprise, our artistic ideals, questions of pure art, stage ethics and technique, plans of organization, our future repertoire and our mutual relationship."

At first they decided to create a "People's Theatre" on the lines advocated by Ostrovsky, but in view of the fact that the repertoire of such a theatre would have been greatly restricted by the severe stage censorship of the time, they somewhat limited its scope by charging "popular" prices for 375 seats out of a total of 815 seats, and introducing special matinees at reduced prices for students, etc. The actual name of the theatre was not decided till much later, when Nemirovich-Danchenko suddenly burst into Stanislavsky's dressing-room at a rehearsal and proposed to call the theatre "The People's Art Theatre". The "popular" character of the theatre, however, had to be given up after the first two seasons for financial reasons, and the theatre was henceforth known as The Moscow Art Theatre.

The company of the new theatre was formed from the amateur actors of the Society of Art and Literature and Nemirovich-Danchenko's best students. The former included Stanislavsky's wife, Lilina ; Andreyeva, who joined the Society of Art and Literature in 1894 and whom Stanislavsky admired as a "gothic" actress, an actress, that is, who was capable of playing the leading parts of a classical repertoire ; Samarova, wife of the Dr. Markov whose acting at the tiny Secretaryov theatre Stanislavsky had so admired as a boy that he had afterwards taken over his stage name ; Artyom, a fine character-actor Stanislavsky first met in 1887 in one of Moscow's amateur dramatic circles ; Luzhsky, one of the students of the short-lived dramatic school of the Society of Art and Literature who first appeared on the stage with Stanislavsky in 1890, becoming one of Stanislavsky's chief assistants afterwards and producing several plays for the Society; and Burdzhalov, who first appeared on the stage with Stanislavsky in 1894. Nemirovich-Danchenko's students included Olga Knipper, Chekhov's future wife, Savitskaya, Roxanova, Meierhold, and Moskvin—all of them very young and most of them destined to become famous either as actors or as producers. In addition, Stanislavsky and Nemirovich-Danchenko decided to invite a few good provincial actors to strengthen their team. It was this introduction of professional actors, who had probably already become infected with most of the prevailing vices of the Russian stage, that provided the liveliest discussion between the two future directors of the Moscow Art Theatre.

"What about Mr. A ? " Stanislavsky asked. "Do you consider him a talented actor ? "

"Absolutely ! "

"But would you invite him to join our company ? "

"No."

"Why not ? "

"Because he regards the stage merely as a career and is too anxious to please the public and the stage managers by pandering to cheap theatrical tastes."

"And what is your opinion of Miss B. ? "

"She's a good actress but I'm afraid she won't do for our theatre."

"Why not ? "

"Because she doesn't love art in herself, but herself in art."

"And Miss C. ? "

"No good. An incurable egoist."

"What about Mr. D. ? "

"He is worth considering."

"Why ? "

"Because he believes in ideals and is ready to fight for them. He is not satisfied with things as they are. He is a man of ideas."

"I agree with you," Stanislavsky said, "and with your permission I'm going to include him in our list of candidates."

Next they turned to a discussion of stage ethics. They agreed that before expecting their actors to behave like civilized human beings they must create such conditions in the theatre as would conform to the demands of civilized life. They therefore decided that every actor should have his own dressing-room, small though it might be, which should be decorated and furnished according to the taste of its occupier. It should have a writing desk with all the necessary accessories which could be converted at night into a make-up table, a small library, a cupboard for clothes and costumes, a wash-basin, a cosy armchair, a sofa for a rest after the rehearsals and before the performance, and large windows which would let in the sunshine which the actor has ordinarily so little time to enjoy. The dressing-rooms were to be kept spotlessly clean, which would entail the engagement of a large domestic staff. The dressing-rooms of the actors should be on different floors from those of the actresses (that must have been Stanislavsky's idea), with separate greenrooms for the actors and actresses where they could receive visitors. The greenrooms should have pianos, libraries, a large table for newspapers and journals, and chessboards with chessmen. (Cards and other gambling games were to be strictly prohibited !) No one was to be permitted to enter the greenrooms in an overcoat, hat, or goloshes. Women, in addition, were to be forbidden to wear their hats in the theatre.

All this was strictly speaking a question of æsthetics which the two founders of the Moscow Art Theatre very properly considered to be inseparable from ethics. As for stage ethics in the more limited sense of the word, a series of aphorisms they wrote down expressed the attitude they were determined the actors should adopt towards their parts. These were : (1) there are no small parts, there are only small actors (a well-known saying of Shchepkin's); (2) today Hamlet, tomorrow an extra, but even as an extra the actor must be an artist ; (3) the playwright, the actor, the scene-designer, the dresser, and the stage-hand all serve one purpose, namely, to express the playwright's main idea in writing his play ; (4) the theatre begins with the cloakroom ; (5) every violation of the creative life of the theatre is a crime ; and (6) arriving late at the theatre, laziness, capriciousness, hysteria, ignorance of parts, the necessity of repeating the same thing twice are all equally harmful and must be rooted out.

The importance of these "aphorisms" became all too evident as soon as the rehearsals began in the converted barn in Pushkino on July 14th, 1898. One day two actresses had a violent quarrel which had nothing to do with their work but which seriously interfered with the rehearsals. To Stanislavsky this was a personal tragedy : the whole future of his theatre was at stake ; his most cherished dream was to be shattered by human spite and stupidity even before it was realized. He rushed out of the barn, sat down on the stump of a fir-tree, and burst out crying like a child, clenching his handkerchief in his hand and forgetting to wipe the tears which were rolling down his cheeks.

"To ruin everything—everything—because of some private quarrel," he whimpered. "Such great and wonderful work to be ruined because of some silly little female vanity ! "

It was the first and last time that the actors saw Stanislavsky cry, and the effect of it was such that not only did the two actresses make up their quarrel, but personal quarrels during a rehearsal never occurred again. That, however, did not prevent all sorts of breaches of good manners. Stanislavsky and Nemirovich-Danchenko decided to leave the punishment of those who were guilty of them to the decision of the whole company. In one case an actor who was found guilty of unethical behaviour was asked to resign and in another the culprit was fined and reprimanded in public by several of his colleagues in turn. This seems to have been enough to scotch any further outbreaks of bad manners.

The rehearsals in Pushkino began with an address to the company by Stanislavsky. He reminded them that it was exactly ten years before that he had founded the Society of Art and Literature together with Kommissarzhevsky and the late Fedotov. The Society had been successful in gaining a certain amount of popularity because of the team-work of its members. The founders of the new theatre, Stanislavsky went on, did not expect any material advantages from it ; all they hoped for was that it would "bring light into the darkness and add a touch of poetry to our prosaic lives." He begged them, therefore, to be careful with the thing that had been placed in their hands, "so that," he added, as though in anticipation of what he himself would be doing so soon, "we shall not have to cry like little children when their cherished toys are broken. If," he went on, "we do not approach this work with clean hands, we shall soil and vulgarize it, and we shall have to disperse all over Russia, some to resume our personal occupations and others to profane our art for a crust of bread on the provincial stage. And remember, if we do disperse, we shall have dishonoured ourselves and we shall be rightly laughed to scorn, for the business we have undertaken is for the good of all and not only for our own honour and glory. Be careful then," he concluded, "not to crush this beautiful flower, or else it will fade and its petals will fall off."

This call to team-work and selfless devotion to the cause of the new theatre might have fallen on deaf ears if Stanislavsky had not been determined that his words should be taken seriously.

The repertoire of the new theatre was to be based (according to a statement made by Nemirovich-Danchenko in his report to the joint meeting of the Permanent Commission on Technical Education of the Russian Technical Society on January 15th, 1898) on the principle that "everything that bears the stamp of falsehood and perverted taste" should be avoided, while "everything that is pervaded by a healthy feeling for the living truth" should be welcomed. Nemirovich-Danchenko's public address on the aims of the new theatre was given for the express purpose of appealing to that wider public of the less well-to-do classes of the population which he and Stanislavsky at first hoped to attract. (They also hoped to raise funds by such appeals, a hope that does not seem to have materialized.) Nemirovich-Danchenko did not, therefore, think it necessary to enter more fully into the question of the theatre's future repertoire except in such vague terms as the ones quoted, and references to Russian and European classical drama leavened with modern plays—"altogether a vast and fresh repertoire of plays suitable for stage representation." Actually, what he was particularly keen on was that the repertoire should consist mainly of "modern" plays. A good second-rater himself, he possessed the distinguishing characteristic of all second-raters of not being able to see further than his nose in his persistent pursuit of "modernity" at all costs. He was very good at putting his own interpretation on any play and in the process "improving" it out of all recognition, so that when Stanislavsky afterwards came to read it, he discovered that what Nemirovich-Danchenko had told him about the play was his own invention and had nothing whatever to do with its author. It was he, as much as Stanislavsky, who, despite Chekhov's persistent protests, could see nothing in Chekhov's plays but a bleak comment on the declining fortunes of the Russian land-owning class. Having read the manuscript of *The Cherry Orchard*, he was so disappointed in his inability to find anything new in it that in his letter to Chekhov he could not help suppressing a sigh for that "pearl" of his early dramatic work—*Ivanov*. The classical drama, therefore, occupied a very insignificant part in his choice of plays for the Moscow Art Theatre. Indeed, the preliminary announcement of the repertoire of the new theatre, signed by Nemirovich-Danchenko as "director of the repertoire" and by Stanislavsky as "Chief Producer", gave pride of place to Count Alexey Tolstoy's rather pedestrian historical play *Czar Fyodor Ioannovich*, which had only just then been passed by the censor and which was described rather extravagantly in the announcement as "one of the greatest masterpieces of Russian drama". The other plays included in this initial announcement were Gerhardt Hauptmann's two plays, *The Sunken Bell* and *Hannele* (both revivals of the productions of the Society of Art and Literature, the second of which was shortly to be banned on the intercession of the Holy Synod), *Uriel Acosta* and *Men Above the Law* (two more revivals), *The Merchant of Venice* and *Antigone* (the only two classical plays), and *The Seagull*.

In a letter to Stanislavsky on June 21st, 1898, Nemirovich-Danchenko goes into the question of the repertoire at great length. The letter, incidentally, was written in reply to a letter by Stanislavsky, who had carefully considered Nemirovich-Danchenko's suggestions and, while disclaiming any desire to oppose them, pointed out that *The Merchant of Venice* and *Antigone* were "interesting and solid" and would lend the theatre a character of its own, which it might lose if they put on such "modern" plays as *Greta's Happiness* by an obscure contemporary playwright he had never heard of (the play was the biggest flop of the first season, being taken off after the third performance).

Nemirovich-Danchenko began his letter by expressing his firm opposition to a purely classical repertoire. "A theatre that devotes itself exclusively to a classical repertoire and does not reflect modern life at all," he wrote with some justice, "runs the risk of soon becoming academic and dead. The theatre is not an illustrated book which can be taken off a shelf whenever you want it. By its very nature it must serve the spiritual needs of the modern playgoer, who, no doubt, responds to what may be called 'eternal beauty' but is even more interested in getting an answer to his own personal problems and troubles. If our contemporary repertoire of plays were as rich and varied in colour and form as the classical one we might have dispensed with classical plays altogether. For new plays attract the playgoer just because they look for new answers to the problems of life. A good theatre must therefore present either such classical plays as reflect the noblest modern ideas or such modern plays as express our contemporary life in an artistic form. We can't possibly stick to the first kind of play because we have neither the means to do it nor the company with which to perform it ; neither can we stick to the other kind of play because we do not possess a rich contemporary repertoire. We must, therefore, sail between Scylla and Charybdis, especially in Moscow where both types of play are so wretchedly produced, and especially during the first few years when we ourselves have still to prove our mettle."

Having made this differentiation, Nemirovich-Danchenko proceeded to place *Czar Fyodor* and *Antigone* side by side among the "classical plays with a modern message", dismissed *The Merchant of Venice* as having nothing to say to the modern playgoer and *Twelfth Night, Much Ado* and *Tartuffe* as "mere artistic trifles". "These plays by Shakespeare," he explained, "are only necessary because there is more skill and talent in them than in similar trifles audiences like to amuse themselves with. They may be necessary because they develop the public's taste for good art, but they are trifles nevertheless and it would be a pity to devote to them all one's creative energy and imagination. Even the most serious of these—*Tartuffe*—is so full of exaggerations that it is merely the cleverest and most serious of these trifles.

"You yourself agreed with me," Nemirovich-Danchenko attempted to turn the tables on Stanislavsky, "that in *Much Ado* and *Twelfth Night* you do not consider it necessary to curb your imagination and that you permit yourself 'any liberty you like' with them. And quite right too ! "

It is not surprising that after that Nemirovich-Danchenko committed himself to the view that the plays of Hauptmann and "the less serious ones" of Ibsen "are much more important than the trifles of great playwrights like Shakespeare and Molière." As for *The Seagull*, Nemirovich-Danchenko very significantly regarded it as valuable only because "we feel the pulse of our contemporary Russian life in it."

"I value my 'union' with you so highly," Nemirovich-Danchenko concluded this significant letter, "because I can see that you possess the qualities of an artist *par excellence*, which I do not possess. I am far-sighted enough so far as the subject-matter of plays and their significance for the modern playgoer are concerned, but as far as form goes I am inclined to be conventional, though I do appreciate originality deeply. Here I lack both your imagination and your great artistic skill. And that's why I think the best work we could do together would be in plays which I esteem highly for their subject-matter and which will give your creative imagination the fullest freedom it needs. Such, above all, is *Czar Fyodor*."

And the irony of it is that Nemirovich-Danchenko was right. Had his judgment not been so commonplace, he would most probably have found it impossible to work with Stanislavsky, as, indeed, Stanislavsky himself found it impossible to work with him when (as Nemirovich-Danchenko himself confessed) he had begun to overtake him "with giant strides". For the time being, however, the combination worked well enough.

In Pushkino, the actors and actresses had been accommodated in summer cottages, and the tidying up of the rehearsal theatre and the different duties connected with it were undertaken by the members of the company in rotation. Stanislavsky volunteered to be the first "housemaid" and showed himself completely unfit for the job : he stuffed the *samovar* with burning charcoal but forgot to fill it with water, with the result that it came unstuck and the company was left without tea. Nor was he very brilliant at sweeping the floor, or sweeping up the dirt into the dustpan, or wiping the chairs, and so on. However, he immediately put the rehearsals on a strictly business-like footing. He introduced a journal into which the day's programme was noted down, that is to say, what play was being rehearsed, which actor missed a rehearsal and with what excuse, who was late and how late, what incidents harmful to discipline had occurred, and what had been ordered or done for the continued progress of the work. The rehearsals began at precisely 11 o'clock in the morning and went on till five o'clock in the afternoon. Then the actors were given three hours in which to have dinner, go for a bathe (it was a very hot summer), or take a rest. At eight they were all back and the rehearsals went on till eleven. In this way Stanislavsky succeeded in rehearsing two plays a day. While the rehearsals were going on, either he or Nemirovich-Danchenko (who only arrived in Pushkino on July 25th, having gone to the Crimea to finish a novel) went over their parts with individual members of the cast in a nearby wood or in the keeper's lodge.

Stanislavsky himself lived in Lyubimovka with his family. It was only a few miles away, and he arrived punctually every morning at 11 o'clock and remained there till late at night. His free time he spent discussing the sets with Simov in Simov's little hut. On August 12th he went off to Andreyevka, his younger brother's estate near Kharkov, where he stayed till September 20th, writing the production notes of *The Seagull*. At the beginning of October the actors returned to Moscow where the rehearsals at first went on at the Hunting Club and from October 7th at the Hermitage Theatre in Karetny Ryad (Coachmaker's Row), which was to be the home of the Moscow Art Theatre for the next four seasons.

Of the nine plays which the new theatre put on during its first season of 1898-99, only two—*Czar Fyodor* and *The Seagull*—were successful, and but for them the whole grandiose venture would have failed. The two plays which had been so successful when Stanislavsky produced them for the Society of Art and Literature—*The Sunken Bell* and *Men Above the Law*—survived only 17 and 9 performances respectively; *The Merchant of Venice*, which Stanislavsky had already started rehearsing for the Society of Art and Literature, ran for only 10 performances; *Greta's Happiness*, as already noted, saw only three performances; *Antigone*, which was only put on in the new year as a matinée play for schools (neither Stanislavsky nor Nemirovich-Danchenko could do anything with it) was performed fourteen times, and *Hedda Gabler*, put on on February 19th, was taken off after the eleventh performance. Between the first night of *Czar Fyodor* on

October 14th and the first night of *The Seagull*, on December 17th, the theatre had no less than five failures.

"At that moment," Stanislavsky writes, "our whole artistic future was at stake. Our programme was revolutionary. We protested against the old methods of acting, against theatricality, against false pathos, declamation, overacting, the bad conventions of production and scenery, the 'star' system which destroyed the ensemble, and the low level of the repertoire. We declared war on every convention of the theatre under whatever form it might appear : in acting, scenery, costumes, interpretation of the play, and so on. We simply had to be successful. We had become the target of our Moscow wits. The Press and a number of influential persons in town prophesied our failure. We were contemptuously dismissed as 'amateurs.' People said that our company had no real actors, and that we only relied on gorgeous costumes and scenery, and finally, that the whole undertaking 'was the whim of an eccentric business-man. What they could not forgive us was that we had only announced a repertoire of ten[1] plays, while other theatres gave a new play each week and even then found it difficult to fill their houses—and suddenly these amateurs had the audacity to dream of getting through a whole season with only ten plays ! "

And, of course, the trouble was that the scoffers and ill-wishers were almost proved right. The one hundred and twenty rehearsals given to seven plays of the season were practically wasted. The hundred rehearsals of the two other plays (seventy-four rehearsals of *Czar Fyodor* and twenty-six rehearsals of *The Seagull*, of which Stanislavsky took nine, Nemirovich-Danchenko fifteen, and Luzhsky two) saved the theatre from an ignominious end.

---

[1] Actually only 9 plays. (D.M.)

CHAPTER XXIV

THE LARGE NUMBER of rehearsals of *Czar Fyodor* shows the great care Stanislavsky gave to the reproduction of the spirit of the sixteenth century in this play. He was, no doubt, again merely following in Kronegk's footsteps, but that did not matter very much since Alexey Tolstoy's play was essentially a pageant rather than a play of great human passions. Besides, he could be much more independent in his treatment of this play because its spirit was so entirely different from the Spanish or Italian traditions to which he was accustomed. His experience with the medieval castle in Turin, which had been of such great help to him in his production of *Much Ado*, made him wish to soak himself in the spirit of sixteenth-century Russia. There was the Kremlin next door to him, to be sure, but he was too familiar with it for it to be of any use to him. Simov proposed that they should organize an expedition to Rostov, which possessed an ancient Kremlin with a famous White Tower which had recently been restored and which provided him with everything he needed for the sets of *Czar Fyodor*, a museum of ancient costumes, printed cloths, rugs, etc. Stanislavsky had already undertaken a successful expedition to different market towns to get the material for the costumes of *Czar Fyodor*. The visit to Rostov and some other ancient Russian cities and monasteries, described by Stanislavsky in *My Life in Art*, was organized in great style, Stanislavsky, his wife, Simov and several actors of the newly formed theatrical company travelling in a special railway carriage which was put in a siding every time they felt like relaxing and enjoying the countryside. In Rostov Stanislavsky was certainly luckier than in Turin, for he easily obtained permission to spend the night in Ivan the Terrible's palace in order "to absorb the atmosphere" of the place. Sitting in the great Czar's dimly lit bedroom at night, Stanislavsky and his friends suddenly heard heavy footsteps on the stone flags outside. The low door slowly opened and a tall figure in monastic garb with a lighted candle in its hand stooped to go through and then rose again to its full height. Its appearance was so unexpected and so eerie that Stanislavsky seemed to feel himself transported to the grim days of Ivan the Terrible's reign. The monk, needless to say, was only a disguised member of Stanislavsky's party, but when the actor, wearing the genuine clothes of the period, walked slowly along the long corridor and over the ancient arched gateway, his candle throwing "ominous shadows", Stanislavsky thought for a moment that the ghost of Ivan the Terrible himself was taking a walk through the palace.

Next day they heard the ringing of the famous Rostov cathedral bells and then they continued their journey, stopping to inspect ancient monasteries and cities and going down the Volga on a steamer to buy old oriental Tartar materials, robes and boots. On the last day on the river they had a kind of fancy-dress ball, the actors and some of the passengers putting on the old costumes they had bought, and Stanislavsky and Simov taking advantage of the occasion to get an idea of the best way of wearing them on the stage.

On their return, Stanislavsky found that they still did not possess the right material for the Czar's costumes. He was anxious to get away from the crude stage imitations of the regal robes and find "a simple, rich trimming with the genuine feel of antiquity about it." So he undertook another expedition to the Nizhny-Novgorod fair where he was lucky to find what he was looking for : it was a piece of the exact material he wanted sticking out of a heap of . rubbish belonging to some remote monastery which had fallen on evil days and was trying to dispose of some of its property. He bought the lot for a thousand roubles, and brought back to Moscow a whole museum of costumes, wooden bowls, bits of carved wood for furniture, oriental rugs, and so on.

In designing the sets with Simov and the costumes with his wife Lilina, who had undertaken the tasks of wardrobe-mistress for this occasion, Stanislavsky enunciated two principles which with time were to take him further and further away from the practices of the Meiningen company. He decided that there was no need for a faithful reproduction of furniture, utensils, etc., on the stage and that what he needed was merely a number of vivid "spots", which would attract the attention of the audience to the exclusion of everything else. Similarly it was not necessary for the sets to be absolutely faithful historically. The important thing was that the audience should believe in the authenticity of the scene. For instance, in discussing with Simov the scene in Prince Shuysky's garden (in which, incidentally, Stanislavsky introduced for the first time the distant croaking of frogs), he thought that the audience ought to catch a distant view of the Kremlin.

"Without the steeple of Ivan the Great? " queried Simov. Stanislavsky frowned.

"Why without it? It would be like Venus without arms."

"But the church did not exist at the time of Czar Fyodor, and, besides, people are so used to Venus without arms that if they saw her with arms they would not believe it was Venus."

"The Kremlin without the Ivan the Great? " Stanislavsky wondered. "Strange! I'll tell you what: let's hide it behind some bushes! "

The compromise was adopted. An interesting problem Simov tried to solve in that particular scene was how to find some way of making the spectator forget that he was in a theatre and forcing him to imagine himself in Shuysky's garden. That was one of those cardinal problems of stage art that Stanislavsky himself was trying to solve, and, as in the first act of *The Sunken Bell*, it was again Simov who hit on an original solution: he moved the trees nearer to the footlights and placed a line of young birches right across them, so that it seemed that the garden grew out of the proscenium. Simov covered the scale model of the set with a piece of cardboard and only removed it after Stanislavsky had knelt in front of it. The effect was instantaneous: Stanislavsky gazed at the scene a long time, biting the back of his hand and unable to take his eyes off the magically transformed garden. He was as pleased as a child with it; it was a method of dealing with the "fourth wall" that became a favourite of his in many of his subsequent productions.

On the whole Stanislavsky found the production of *Czar Fyodor* easy enough: the pattern was already familiar to him. It was a play which he later placed among a number of other similar plays produced during the first years of the existence of the Moscow Art Theatre as belonging to its "social-historical" period and as being merely "the first, transitory stage in our development". What he was chiefly concerned with was to get away from the *boyar* traditions of the Russian stage. It was a particularly obnoxious, tiresome and infectious theatrical cliché. He had to find new methods of acting these *boyar* plays that would do away once and for all with the old ones. These new methods he had already learnt from the Meiningen Company and they consisted of an entirely naturalistic presentation of historical details and an utter disregard for what Stanislavsky was later to call "the birth of feeling". Luckily, *Czar Fyodor* was an ideal play for such a naturalistic solution of the problems of stage representation, since it was not particularly rich in inner content. The "external image" therefore became all-important, and most of the rehearsals were spent in trying on all sorts of costumes, boots, padding, beards, moustaches, wigs, hats, and so on, in the hope of finding the right face or voice, and of getting the right physical feel of the character in the play. It was all a matter of chance, but it taught the actors how to reproduce the typical external features of a character, a not unimportant part of the actor's art.

Stanislavsky himself wrote the *mise-en-scènes* and showed the actors how to play their parts. He afterwards justified this method as the only possible one in the circumstances, since he had to deal with inexperienced actors. But the truth was that at the time he knew of no other method. "I could not teach others," he writes, "but merely could act myself, and that, too, by instinct, for I had brought with me to the theatre a bagful of all sorts of methods which were thrown together higgledy-piggledy, without any system or order, and all I could do was put my hand into it and take out whatever I happened to light on."

The result was that, having at its disposal a talented scene-designer like Simov, the theatre merely copied his costumes and scenery, whose effects were reinforced by Stanislavsky's own inventions and tricks, most of which were designed to hide the shortcomings of the actors. The realism of the production was further increased by the fact that, dealing with inexperienced actors, Stanislavsky had to limit himself to the most elementary creative problems, which he tried to solve by falling back on his experience of everyday life. Unable to tackle the truth of inner feeling, he mistook external, material truth for genuine art, for the victory of the new over the old, and, to quote Stanislavsky, "having once hit on the methods of external realism, we followed the line of least resistance".

There was, however, at least so far as Stanislavsky was concerned, a redeeming feature even in these blatantly naturalistic tendencies : it was Stanislavsky's genuine desire to achieve artistic truth upon the stage. "This artistic truth," he writes, "was at the time merely external ; it was the truth of objects, furniture, costumes, stage properties, light and sound effects, the reproduction of the typical features of a stage character and his external, physical life ; but the very fact that we succeeded in bringing real, though only external, artistic truth on the stage, which at that time only knew artistic falsehood, opened up some perspectives for the future."

CHAPTER XXV

BUT ALL THESE reflections are mainly retrospective in character ;
at the time he was producing *Czar Fyodor* Stanislavsky did not
doubt that he was on the right track. He was obsessed by the
divine dissatisfaction of genius which drove him to the discovery
of new truths and the rejection of what had seemed to him to be
the truth only a few years earlier. At the time of the foundation
of the Moscow Art Theatre Stanislavsky had reached the stage
in his development as an artist where he was perfectly competent
to deal with a play that was devoid of inner feeling and that gave
him a chance of applying the methods of stage presentation he
had already used with signal success in his last productions both
at the Solodovnikov Theatre and at the Society of Art and
Literature. Such, in particular, were the crowd scenes in *Czar
Fyodor* and, generally, the fine pageantry of scenery and costume
and all the other purely theatrical elements of the play. It was
quite a different matter with *The Seagull*.

Beside *Czar Fyodor*, *The Seagull* appeared drab and meaningless
to Stanislavsky. "Are you sure it can be performed at all ? "
he asked Nemirovich-Danchenko. "I just can't make head or
tail of it ! " Nemirovich-Danchenko spent two days trying to
explain to Stanislavsky what he found so fascinating about
Chekhov's play, but as his explanations were mainly of a literary
nature and as he himself had only a vague idea of the dramatic
structure of the play except that it seemed to abolish all the
preconceived notions of what a play should be like, they made no
impression whatever. There was, besides, the fact that Stanislavsky himself was at the time rather hostile to Chekhov. He
first met Chekhov on February 18th, 1889, at a fancy dress ball
organized by the Society of Art and Literature, but neither then
nor at any of their subsequent meetings did Stanislavsky "take"
to Chekhov. "He seemed to me," Stanislavsky writes in his

reminiscences of Chekhov, "to be proud, supercilious and not without guile," a curious statement which may have been due to the fact that Chekhov must have found Stanislavsky's amazing ignorance of literature an irresistible temptation for his rather circuitous way of gently pulling a man's leg. Stanislavsky himself ascribed it to Chekhov's habit of throwing back his head and fixing his gaze somewhere above the man he was talking to (considering Stanislavsky's height, Chekhov must have had a crick in the neck every time he talked to him), and his annoying way of constantly adjusting his pince-nez. "All this," he writes, "made Chekhov look supercilious to me, although it was really caused by his shyness, of which I was not aware at the time."

At another meeting (on January 4th, 1897) Chekhov's quizzical manner really got on Stanislavsky's nerves. It happened at a special literary and musical evening in aid of the Literary Fund which took place at Korsh's Theatre. Stanislavsky was billed to read Lermontov's poem *On the Death of a Poet*. As he was never good at reading poetry and as, in addition, it was his first appearance on such an occasion, he was more than usually nervous. By that time he had become a public figure. The success of his season of plays at the Solodovnikov Theatre in association with Lentovsky had roused his actor's vanity which was just then more than forgivable. "Not entirely unintentionally," Stanislavsky recalls, "I left my overcoat in the corridor next to the stalls and not behind the scenes as I should have done, for I intended to put it on right before the eyes of the public whom I had hoped to surprise."

However, Stanislavsky's recitation of the poem was not quite the success he had anticipated and he was anxious to get away as inconspicuously as possible. It was just at that "critical moment" that he found his way barred by Chekhov, who went up to him and, wishing no doubt to soothe the wounded vanity of the actor, set about it in his usual roundabout fashion.

"I hear," said Chekhov, craning his neck, "that you play my *Bear* wonderfully. Look here, why not put it on again? I'll come and have a look at it. I may even write a notice about it in the papers."

That, of course, was a leg-pull all right and, perhaps, even a "supercilious" hint.

Stanislavsky said nothing.

"And I'll collect some royalties, too," said Chekhov, after a pause.

Stanislavsky still did not speak.

"Tuppence ha'penny," said Chekhov.

By now Stanislavsky was furious. The fellow might have had the common decency to say something complimentary about his recitation even if he did not mean it, but this open derision (he did not realise that all Chekhov was trying to do was to cheer him up) was an outrage, particularly as it came from an author whose last play with the curious title of *The Seagull* had been such an awful flop in Petersburg only about two months ago. As Stanislavsky rushed away in a huff both of them would have been the most astonished people in the world if they had been told that only two years later their fate and fame would become inextricably bound up.

Not that Stanislavsky had any reason to change his mind about Chekhov or his ability as a playwright when on August 12th, 1898, he left for his brother's estate with a copy of *The Seagull* in his pocket. The play seemed to him "monotonous" and not "scenic". He had found it "strange" because, as he tried later to explain, "my literary ideals at that time continued to be rather primitive. To my shame," he writes, "I did not understand the play. It was only while working on it that I imperceptibly got into it and unconsciously grew fond of it. Such is the quality of Chekhov's plays. Having once fallen under their spell, one wants to go on savouring their bouquet." But that was written a long time afterwards. In August and September, 1898, all he was concerned about was to interpret the play in terms of action, a procedure that proved to be a stroke of genius, considering that in those days he had only a hazy notion of the inner action of the play. "I shut myself up in my study," Stanislavsky writes, "and wrote a detailed *mise-en-scène* as I felt it and as I saw and heard it with my inner eye and ear. At those moments I did not care for the feelings of the actor ! I sincerely believed it was possible to tell people to live and feel as I liked them to ; I wrote down directions for everybody and those directions had to be carried out. I put down everything in my production notes : how and where, in what way a part had to be interpreted and the playwright's stage directions carried out, what kind of inflexions the actor had to use, how he had to move about and act, and where and how he had to cross the stage. I added all sorts of sketches for every *mise-en-scène*—exits, entries, crossings from one place on the stage to another, and so on and so forth. I described the scenery, costumes, make-up, deportment, gaits, the habits of the characters, etc. This tremendously difficult work on *The Seagull* I had to finish in about three or four weeks, and that was why I spent all my time in one of the turrets of the house, from which there opened up a most depressing and melancholy view of the endless and monotonous steppe."

In trying to explain the play to Stanislavsky, Nemirovich-Danchenko had laid great stress on its "atmosphere", its "mood". "Stanislavsky and I," he wrote to Chekhov, "spent two days over the play, and we have, I think, succeeded in getting a great deal that will help us to bring out its mood (which is so important in your play)." Stanislavsky himself found the play "monotonous", and he had only to look out of the turret window of his study to get the "mood" Nemirovich-Danchenko had been talking so much about. "Depressing", "melancholy", and "endlessly monotonous"—that was the mood Stanislavsky so recklessly imposed not only on *The Seagull*, but on all the other Chekhov plays, a mood that seemed to correspond entirely with the prevailing mood of the educated classes in Russia at that time and that became accepted in England and in America as the typical mood of a Chekhov play and even earned it the epithet of "Chekhovian"! "What always amazed Chekhov," Stanislavsky wrote in 1914, in his reminiscences of the great writer, "and what, to the end of his life, he could never reconcile himself to, was that his *Three Sisters* and subsequently *The Cherry Orchard* were tragic dramas of Russian life. He was sincerely convinced that *The Cherry Orchard*, in particular, was a gay comedy, almost a farce. I cannot remember any other occasion on which he defended his views with greater heat than at one of our meetings where for the first time he heard me express such an opinion of *The Cherry Orchard*." But what was even more amazing was that it never occurred to Stanislavsky that Chekhov could have been right about his own plays. Stanislavsky always brushed away Chekhov's objections to his interpretation with the good-humoured tolerance of a man of experience dealing with the unaccountable tantrums of a man of genius.

Having, therefore, got the "mood" of *The Seagull*, Stanislavsky set about reinforcing it with appropriate stage action. He made use of every stage device he had learnt in the past, donned his mantle of conjuror, and did his best to squeeze every ounce of magic out of a play which was rich in magic, anyhow, not in order to enchant the spectator by the inner unfolding of the hidden dramas in the lives of the characters, but in order to dazzle him by a whole series of external realistic devices which brought out the mood of the play as he chose to interpret it. There was his well-tried device of plunging the stage into darkness to conceal the inexperience of his actors ; there was the device of disregarding the "fourth wall" by making the characters in the first act sit with their backs to the audience on a bench placed right across the whole length of the footlights ; there was his device of using every light and sound effect he could think of to hold the attention of the audience ; and there was the device of "constructing" the floor of the stage by cluttering it up with all sorts of three-dimensional objects, such as seats, bushes, trees, bridges, tables, and so on, so as to provide the actors with something *to do* while saying their lines and in this way perhaps discover the most characteristic traits of the people they represented. He also made the utmost use of inflexion, orchestration of voices, poses, gestures and pauses. Finally, being now the acknowledged authority on crowd scenes, he deliberately introduced a most elaborate crowd scene at the end of Act III.

The opening scene of the first act illustrates this method of providing an imaginative interpretation of the play which has very little to do with the text.

"The play," the first sentence of Stanislavsky's production notes of *The Seagull* runs, "starts in darkness ; an (August) evening. The dim light of a lantern set on top of a post ; distant sounds of a drunkard's song ; distant howling of a dog ; the croaking of frogs, the cry of a corncrake, the slow tolling of a distant church-bell. All this helps the audience to get the feel of the sad and monotonous life of the characters. Flashes of lightning, faint rumbling of thunder in the distance. After the raising of the curtain a pause of ten seconds. After the pause Yakov knocks, hammering in a nail (on the stage) ; having knocked the nail in, he busies himself on the stage, humming a tune."

Compare this with Chekhov's simple stage direction : "The sun has just set. Yakov and other workmen are busy on the stage behind the lowered curtain ; sounds of hammering and coughing."

Stanislavsky had not only deliberately thickened the atmosphere to emphasize "the sad, monotonous life of the characters" (which, after all, is neither so sad nor so monotonous as he chose to make it—there is nothing particularly sad in the opening of the first act, and whatever view one chooses to take of it, it is certainly not monotonous), but also almost unbalanced the entire action of the opening scene by inventing the distant roll of thunder, the drunkard's song, the howling of the dog, and the slow tolling of the church-bell. It was, no doubt, just because Stanislavsky thought (as he had told Nemirovich-Danchenko) that "the characters of the play are incapable of supplying the actors with good stage material," which to him just then meant merely external action, that he undertook to supply it himself. But even then the play left him completely cold. In a letter to his wife from Kharkov in September of that year, he wrote : "I have just read Trigorin's part—I like it much better than that of Dorn. At least there is something in it, and there is nothing else there, but they seem to expect goodness knows what. I don't like that. I am going to see two or three acts of *The Pit of Vice*, an interesting play."

But having seen the "interesting play," he tells his wife in his next letter that "it has produced a most appallingly hideous impression—the author seems to be an absolute ninny. All this," he goes on, apparently unable to see the difference between the cheap melodrama he had seen and Chekhov's masterpiece, "is not serious. It is certainly not worthwhile devoting one's life to this sort of thing. Can it be that I am doing the same ? This thought worries me very much. I thought the stage was a serious occupation, but it seems to be nothing but nonsense. I am beginning to wonder whether not only my life but the life of other people is being wasted. Again I could not help thinking that I ought perhaps to be doing something different."

The feeling of dissatisfaction and diffidence, always characteristic of him, must have been particularly strong when he was working on *The Seagull* to have prompted him to write such a letter. But it was just that feeling, strengthened by his extreme susceptibility and hyper-sensitiveness, which led him to become the producer-autocrat he did become at that time and which later made him blame himself for having "crippled" the actors by imposing his will on them.

A producer, preoccupied as Stanislavsky was just then by the external details of a production, cannot, in fact, avoid becoming an autocrat. And Stanislavsky, according to the testimony of Leonid Leonidov, one of the outstanding actors of the Moscow Art Theatre, "was so carried away by the unimportant details that he very often forgot the main thing—thought and words." The trouble was that Stanislavsky's "primitive literary conceptions" prevented him from discovering the inner meaning of a play, and as his idea of a character was evolved purely from the external traits he arbitrarily foisted upon it, he simply had to disregard the actor's own individual conception of his part and demand that he should follow blindly his own directions. Any disagreement between him and an actor about the interpretation of a part produced an explosive outburst of anger, which in itself was sufficient proof of Stanislavsky's lack of confidence in his methods. Thus the paradoxical situation arose that while the producer-administrator, whom Stanislavsky condemned as incompetent (which he was), did not interfere with the creative initiative of the actor, a producer-autocrat like Stanislavsky, who was both an expert on stage technique and an artist of great sensibility, suppressed the creative initiative of the actors and transformed them into "mannequins" who spoke and acted just as he thought fit. It was just this that the adherents of the so-called "inspiration school of acting" dreaded so much, for ultimately it meant the supplanting of the living actor by the puppet. But there was this important difference between the usual type of producer-autocrat and Stanislavsky : while the producer-autocrat (as happened on the Russian stage after the Revolution) broke out into a rash of "isms" and proceeded ruthlessly to sacrifice the art of the theatre and drama to his own megalomaniac whims, Stanislavsky remained a producer-autocrat for only as long as his inner development as an artist was still in a rudimentary stage ; the moment he reversed his method of going from the outer to the inner, he also abandoned his external methods of production and began to evolve his "system" of acting which is quite incompatible with the conception of the producer-autocrat.

CHAPTER XXVI

AT THE BEGINNING of October, Stanislavsky was back in Moscow, where he found a "whole exhibition of boots for *Czar Fyodor*" waiting for him, which pleased him very much. The papers had published the news of his return, and the moment he arrived home he received a telegram from the theatre, inviting him to a rehearsal of Alexey Tolstoy's play which had been arranged especially for him. "At first," he wrote to his wife in Lyubimovka, "I refused to go, but later I felt that I'd better go and see what was happening so as to stop worrying."

At last he had a theatre of his own, a stage, dressing-rooms, a company of professional actors (engaged for one year at an average salary of 900 roubles with the right to renew their contracts for two more years at a somewhat higher salary), and now he would be able to transform the theatre from a cheap place of entertainment into a temple of art. But when he arrived at the theatre he found the sort of vulgar amusement hall he had just been abolishing in his thoughts. The Hermitage Theatre was in a terrible state : it was filthy, badly built, cold, reeking of cheap beer (it had been a kind of music-hall with a pleasure garden attached and in bad weather its patrons consumed their drinks inside the building), its walls were covered with cheap advertisements, its curtain was the last word in vulgarity, its attendants wore ghastly uniforms. It was horrible. Fortunately he arrived after the rehearsal had already begun and Moskvin's acting of Czar Fyodor was so magnificent (though Stanislavsky had been warned that he was not in good form that day) that he forgot all about his disagreeable impression of the theatre. "I could not help crying," he wrote to his wife, "and I even had to blow my nose loudly a few times. A stout fellow ! The crowd scenes (still, I'm afraid, rather ragged) are all ready. I think that another two rehearsals and my work on *Czar Fyodor* will be finished."

But first of all the theatre had to be made presentable in spite of the fact that they had not the money to do it properly. The first thing Stanislavsky did was to order the walls to be whitewashed. Then he had the flamboyant curtain removed and a plain grey cloth curtain, which parted in the middle, hung in its place ; he had linen covers put on the cheap seats, got decent rugs for the corridors adjoining the auditorium, had the windows cleaned, their frames painted and nice gauze curtains hung over them, and screened all the unsightly corners with laurel trees and flowers. The place looked much cosier, but it was in a frightful state of disrepair all the same. Trying to knock a nail into the wall of his dressing-room, Stanislavsky knocked out a brick and the icy air from the street streamed through the hole. Another time he found his costume frozen to the wall and had to rip it off and put it on just as it was. The heating facilities of the theatre had broken down because all the chimneys had fallen in and everybody in the theatre had to freeze until they were put right. The electric wiring, too, was so bad that the whole theatre had to be re-wired and the rehearsals conducted by candlelight. There was also trouble with the scenery, which proved to be too big for the stage. They had only one week to get everything in working order, but by the time opening night arrived everything was ready.

The curtain was to go up for the first performance of the Moscow Art Theatre at half-past seven on Wednesday, October 14th. All that day Stanislavsky's nerves were on edge. Nemirovich-Danchenko very sensibly decided to give the actors a day's rest, and Stanislavsky had nothing to do. That increased his excitement : there was nothing more he could do—everything now was in the hands of the actors. "We all realized," Stanislavsky writes, "that our whole future was at stake : either we succeed in passing through the gates of art or they will be slammed in our faces and I shall have to spend the rest of my life in my dull office." A few minutes before the beginning of the performance he felt that he just could not sit in his dressing-room without doing something to encourage the actors. Suppressing his panicky fear of the future and trying to look cheerful, calm and confident, he went on the stage intending to address the actors just as a commander-in-chief might address his troops before a decisive battle. But he was too excited to speak : he was short of breath and his voice broke again and again. Then the orchestra behind the scenes (another innovation of the new theatre, which abolished the orchestra pit) struck up the overture which was specially composed for the play and drowned his words. Suddenly his feet began to move in rhythm, he started humming the tune and dancing, faster and faster, his face deathly white and his eyes panic-stricken, breathing hard, flinging up his arms convulsively, and shouting words of encouragement to the actors to fill them with his own pent-up vitality. Stanislavsky's *danse macabre*, as it was to be known afterwards, was sternly interrupted by the stage manager, who ordered him back to his dressing-room. Deeply hurt, Stanislavsky obeyed the order (his sense of discipline was always a shining example to the actors), rushed back to his dressing-room and locked himself in. "Fancy," he thought furiously, "driving me off the stage, who have given so much work and energy to make this performance possible ! " However, he soon realized, as he explained many years later, that his tears were merely the tears of an actor. "We actors," he wrote, "are sentimental folk and we love to play the part of injured innocence not only on the stage, but also in real life."

Czar Fyodor was a great success. Indeed, it is doubtful whether the theatre could have chosen a better play for its opening night. Moscow had never seen anything like it on the stage. Even Kronegk's productions paled into insignificance beside it. The picturesque costumes of the ancient Russian nobility ; the servants, in the scene of Prince Shuysky's feast, moving about with dishes laden with geese, sucking pigs, huge joints of beef, vegetables and fruits ; barrels of wine rolled on to the stage ; the large wooden bowls and plates Stanislavsky had brought back from his expeditions ; the tipsy guests being regaled with goblets of wine by the beautiful Princess Mstislavskaya ; the hubbub of voices as the guests engaged in argument or gave way to merriment ; the life at court with its ancient etiquette, and, last but not least, the magnificently produced crowd scenes, especially the scene where Prince Shuysky is led to his execution, in which Stanislavsky introduced a fight between Shuysky's adherents among the common people and the Czar's private guard (a more elaborate piece of stage production than the crowd scenes in Act I, Sc. 2, and Act II, Sc. 2, of *Othello*, but very reminiscent of them) —all that was so unusual in those days that the first-night audience was enthralled. The Press, too, was enthusiastic, though here and there voices could still be heard muttering about the "Don Quixotes of Karetny Ryad".

It seemed, therefore, that Stanislavsky's external methods of production, and particularly the great care he took in filling the stage with "genuine antiques", had been fully justified, though he soon convinced himself that even in this production too naturalistic an approach was not always necessary. He had, for instance, lent the theatre an old piece of embroidered silk material he valued greatly as a cover for a bench. He issued strict instructions, however, that after every performance it must be carefully shaken, folded and put away. As sooner or later it was sure to be damaged, Simov substituted for it a piece of painted canvas. Stanislavsky did not notice the difference till one day Simov said in his hearing during a rehearsal that the old cover had not been dusted properly and showed signs of wear and tear. "Call the property man!" roared Stanislavsky. The property man brought the imitation cover made by Simov, which even from a short distance looked "genuine." Stanislavsky gave his consent to the change and the antiquarian rarity was sent back to his study.

But the success of *Czar Fyodor* was not enough to establish the reputation of the theatre, let alone assure its financial position. The failure of the five subsequent productions confronted the theatre with a real crisis. Their entire hope now rested on the revival of *Hannele*, but the Moscow archbishop suddenly took it into his head to ban the play. What was there left? *The Seagull*? The very idea that Chekhov's play might save the new theatre seemed utterly absurd to Stanislavsky. And, besides, even with *The Seagull* there were last-minute complications. Trouble arose with one of the professional actors who was originally given the part of Trigorin, Stanislavsky being cast, in spite of his own preference for Trigorin's part, for the part of Dorn. And the actress playing Masha was also found to be inadequate. A reshuffle of the parts became necessary, Stanislavsky taking the part of Trigorin, and Lilina, Stanislavsky's wife, stepping into the breach to play Masha. Then at the dress rehearsal, which, according to Stanislavsky, passed off very weakly, a new difficulty arose. Chekhov's sister came to the theatre to demand that *The Seagull* should be taken off, as she had just received bad news from Yalta about Chekhov's health and she was afraid that a second failure of his play might have grave consequences, particularly as Chekhov had been displeased with the realistic incidents introduced by Stanislavsky into the play when he was present at some of the rehearsals while stopping in Moscow on the way to the Crimea. Stanislavsky and Nemirovich-Danchenko were wondering whether it would not be better to take the play off after all. But the position of the theatre was so desperate that it was impossible to give up a play on which so much time and money had already been spent.

The theatre was far from full when the curtain, which was subsequently to have the emblem of a seagull with spread wings embroidered on it, parted on the first act of Chekhov's play on December 17th, 1898. Stanislavsky himself could not afterwards recall how the first act was played. All he remembered was that every actor and actress smelt strongly of Valerian drops, a favourite Russian sedative. He also remembered that he felt frightened as he was sitting on the dark stage with his back to the audience during Nina's long monologue and that he had to hold on to his leg, which was shaking convulsively. When, amid the dead silence of the audience, the curtain closed at last, it seemed to him and to the other actors on the stage that they were faced with another and, perhaps, final failure. Instinctively they huddled closer together, listening intently for any sound from the auditorium. But the uncanny silence continued. In the wings the stage-hands were craning their necks as they, too, tried to catch the sound of clapping or booing. An actor suddenly gave a whimper. Olga Knipper, who played Arkadina, had to force herself not to burst out crying hysterically. They began walking off the stage in a kind of stupor and without uttering a word. Suddenly a roar of applause burst from the audience. It was incredible. Never had they heard such ecstatic clapping before. The curtain parted again, but the actors had been through such agonizing moments of sheer despair that it did not occur to them to turn round to the audience to take a bow. They stood there frozen into immobility, their faces pale and drawn, hardly conscious of what was happening. One of them even remained sitting on the stage. However, their bewilderment did not last long. There were five curtain calls after the first act. After the third act not a single person left the auditorium. They all stood up and their calls were transformed into a noisy and seemingly endless ovation. The dramatic critic, Nicolai Efros, hitherto an uncompromising detractor of Stanislavsky's work, was the first to rush to the stage, jump on a seat, and start applauding demonstratively. Behind the scenes, as Stanislavsky put it, it was a real Russian "Easter Sunday". Everybody was exchanging kisses with everybody else, including the large number of spectators who had invaded the stage. One actor was lying on the floor in hysterics. Stanislavsky again performed a wild dance, but this time it was a dance of triumph in which the other actors joined. A miracle had happened. A new theatre was born.

CHAPTER XXVII

WHILE NOT UNANIMOUS in its praise, the Moscow Press hailed the production of *The Seagull* as an event of the utmost importance to the Russian stage and, particularly, to the future of the new theatre. The points it singled out for special commendation are interesting as showing what it was that had made such a tremendous impression on the first-night audience. In the first place the "mood" of the play seemed to correspond exactly with the despondent mood of the Russian educated classes before the rumblings of the coming storm were heard only a few years later. Secondly, what struck the audience and the critics so forcibly was the amazing freshness of the production, the original *mise-en-scènes* and the marvellous ensemble of the company. "Everything was delineated with such a delicacy of feeling and presented with such an extraordinary unanimity," the critic of the monthly *Russian Thought* wrote, "that one could not help being forced to the conclusion that such a play could only be emotionally felt by a heart highly sensitive to the maladies and sufferings with which a certain set of people is afflicted in our society."

But, as has already been pointed out, the "mood", the *mise-en-scènes* and the ensemble were entirely the work of Stanislavsky, who remained completely in the dark as to the meaning of the play and, indeed, did not know what it was all about. In addition, he utterly failed to understand the character of Trigorin, whom he played as "a dandy in white trousers and shoes *bain de mer*". He had consequently entirely misunderstood the character of Nina and in doing so distorted the ruling idea of the play. He was too much a man of his own time to be able to see Chekhov's masterpiece in the larger perspective of a great work of art. In this he shared the faults of his contemporaries. The success of *The Seagull* at this vital juncture in the fortunes of the Moscow Art Theatre was ultimately due entirely to his external methods of production—the croaking of the frogs, the cry of the corncrake, the chirping of the crickets, the tolling of the church-bell, the ominous reddish light hovering over the darkness of the first act, and the meticulously faithful reproductions of the smallest details of the domestic life on Sorin's estate, which were at the time quite unheard of on the Russian stage. It was true that Chekhov's plays led Stanislavsky through "the line of intuition and feeling" to "inner realism", but that happened later. In *The Seagull* it was not the playwright but the producer who triumphed. Stanislavsky had pulled it off.

Shorn of the producer's devices, the play, when it was shown to Chekhov at the Paradise Theatre without the scenery, in May, 1899, not only fell flat, but provoked the mild Chekhov to utter the threat that he would not permit the company to play the vital fourth act because, as he declared emphatically, it did not belong to his play at all. He objected in particular to Stanislavsky's interpretation of the part of Trigorin. "Trigorin," Chekhov wrote to Gorky, "walked about and talked as though he were paralyzed ; he has 'no will of his own', so the actor interpreted that in such a way that it made me sick to look at him." So disappointed was Chekhov with the acting of *The Seagull* that he actually started negotiations with the Maly Theatre, the most powerful rival of the Moscow Art Theatre, for the production of *Uncle Vanya*. In spite of the great artistic success of *The Seagull* (it never was a material success, having run altogether for 57 performances during its first season, for 13 performances in the 1899-1900 season and only 9 performances in the 1900-1901 season, after which it was taken off the repertoire of the Moscow Art Theatre), Chekhov would not trust Stanislavsky. Their relations had never been very friendly. Both were shy and reserved men. In the presence of great writers Stanislavsky always felt constrained, and Chekhov liked people to be natural with him. When the negotiations between Chekhov and the Maly Theatre fell through because the directors of the Imperial theatre demanded a thorough revision of the play, objecting in particular to the scene where Uncle Vanya fires at Professor Serebryakov on the ground that it was inadmissible that a professor of a University (that is, a high civil servant) should be fired at on the stage, Chekhov still hesitated to give the play to the Moscow Art Theatre. It was only after Nemirovich-Danchenko had asked him persistently for it and after he had been assured that Stanislavsky would place himself entirely in the hands of Nemirovich-Danchenko in rehearsing his part in the play, that he was finally prevailed on to give his consent. ("Alexeyev," Nemirovich-Danchenko wrote soothingly to Chekhov, "went over the part with me as if he were a student of a dramatic school.") Nor would Chekhov trust Stanislavsky with producing the three parts of the heroines in *The Three Sisters*, and again Nemirovich-Danchenko had to pour oil on the troubled waters and assure the playwright that Stanislavsky would carry out his own directions faithfully. Only in *The Cherry Orchard* did Stanislavsky feel safe enough with Chekhov to put his foot down and do the play without any interference from Nemirovich-Danchenko, but, as has already been noted, his misinterpretation of the play as "a tragic drama of Russian life" provoked a violent protest from Chekhov. By that time, however, Stanislavsky had made Chekhov famous on the Russian stage and it was not so easy to over-rule him. Besides, Chekhov had always been extremely reticent about his own plays, refusing to enter into any discussion about their interpretation ("Why don't you read my play ? You'll find everything there ! " was his stock answer to the questions put to him by the actors), and by the time he had finished *The Cherry Orchard* he was a dying man.

It would be a mistake, however, to underestimate Stanislavsky's part in popularizing Chekhov's plays and in finding a new approach to their stage representation. To him the chief enchantment of a Chekhov play lay in bringing out what was hidden between the lines of the dialogue by pauses or "irradiation" of their inner feelings in the eyes of the actors. That, and that alone, he found, brought to life the inanimate objects on the stage, the sounds and scenery, the characters created by the actors, and the very mood of the whole performance. Lacking a critical appreciation of Chekhov's plays, he relied entirely on "creative intuition and artistic feeling". To discover the inner meaning of a Chekhov play, Stanislavsky maintained, one had first to set about digging up its buried treasure of inner feeling. The Moscow Art Theatre succeeded in doing that because it had discovered a new approach to Chekhov, and that discovery Stanislavsky considered his chief contribution to dramatic art.

Experience had taught him, Stanislavsky declared, that Chekhov's plays did not reveal their poetic significance all at once. At first, indeed, one found his plays rather disappointing.

Their plots seemed to him (curiously enough, considering how very complex they really are) very simple. They contained many good parts, but no "star" parts. Mostly, as a matter of fact, the parts were small. He found that to begin with he could only remember a few words or scenes of a Chekhov play, and yet, strangely enough, the more he tried to remember, the more he wanted to know about the play ; and the more he read it, the more aware did he become of the rich deposits it contained. Chekhov seemed to Stanislavsky to possess such an inexhaustible store of spiritual treasures because he always bore in mind the fundamental problems of humanity. He discovered besides—and this is really one of the most important of his discoveries—that Chekhov's plays were not inactive, as was generally assumed, but were, on the contrary, replete with both external and internal action. "In the very inaction of his characters," he shrewdly observes, "there is hidden a most complicated inner action. Chekhov," he goes on, "has proved better than anyone that stage action must be understood in its inner meaning, and that a dramatic work in the theatre can be based and built only on such inner action, which has been cleansed of everything that is pseudo-scenic. While external action merely amuses the spectator, diverts him and tickles his nerves, inner action takes complete possession of our souls."

In a Chekhov play, Stanislavsky maintains, inner action must always occupy the foremost place. Chekhov, moreover, is a great idealist, a believer in a brighter future for the human race, and he quite imperceptibly forces the spectator to identify himself with this belief. In delineating external life in his plays, too, Chekhov knows perhaps better than any other playwright how to make the best possible use of the inanimate objects on the stage, the scenery and the light effects, and how to instil life into them. "Twilight, sunset, sunrise, a storm, rain, the songs of the awakening birds, the trampling of horses over a bridge, the rattle of a carriage as it drives off, the striking of a clock, the chirping of a cricket," Stanislavsky writes, "are necessary to Chekhov not for the sake of their external effects but for the revelation of the life of the human spirit. For it is impossible to separate us and everything that takes place in us from the world of inanimate things, light and sound among which we live and on which human psychology depends so much."

Chekhov, Stanislavsky further maintains, is also able "with

the art of a real master" to kill external and internal lies on the stage by "beautiful, artistic, and sincere truth." Chekhov is very careful to avoid trite and artificial feelings to which people are so used that they no longer notice them. Chekhov seeks his truth in the most intimate moods and in the inmost recesses of the human soul. That kind of truth possesses the power to thrill the spectator by its unexpectedness, its mysterious connexion with the forgotten past and the inexplicable presentiment of the future, as well as with the special logic of the sort of life which does not seem to make any sense and which apparently mocks at, amuses, or even bewilders people. All these moods, presentiments, hints, and half-realized, shadowy feelings cannot be expressed in words, for they emanate from the hidden depths of men's hearts and minds where they come into contact with men's profoundest emotions, such as religious feelings, social conscience, the higher conceptions of truth and justice, and the quest for an understanding of the mysteries of life. These uncharted tracts of man's emotional life are full of highly explosive matter, and as soon as some fleeting impression or memory penetrates into these hidden depths of the human soul, it acts like a spark "and sets our souls alight with living feelings." Stanislavsky, therefore, maintains that before an actor is able to play Chekhov he must give himself up entirely to the feeling of truth that is so characteristic of Chekhov the playwright, fall under the spell of his charm, believe everything—and then follow the inner line of his conception of his part to the secret doors of his own artistic superconsciousness (or subconsciousness, as Stanislavsky varied this term later). For it is in those mysterious workshops of the mind that the "Chekhov mood" is engendered—"the vessel in which all the invisible treasures of Chekhov's soul are kept, treasures that are very often imperceptible to the actor's senses."

Stanislavsky was always prone to indulge in quasi-metaphysical speculations when his artistic perception got the better of his common sense. So far as the plays of Chekhov were concerned, these "obstinate questionings of sense and outward things" were closely allied to his fondness for Hauptmann's no less vague and mysterious probings of human destiny which Stanislavsky, however, knew how to transform into "the glory and the freshness of a dream". To a sensitive artist like him, deprived of the key to Chekhov's plays, it was only natural to grope for a solution to a mystery that he was beginning to find so fascinating and so tantalizingly amenable to his still imperfect method of stage presentation. It was here that he came into conflict with Nemir-ovich-Danchenko's much cruder and even vaguer "literary" inter-pretation of Chekhov's plays. ("Only a literary man with taste would know how to present your plays," Nemirovich-Danchenko wrote to Chekhov, "a man who knows how to appreciate your work and who is at the same time an expert producer himself. Such a man I can truthfully claim to be.") But during the first years of the existence of the Moscow Art Theatre these "arguments and even quarrels", to use Stanislavsky's expression, were not dangerous, since both of them were eager to learn from one an-other. Right from the start they found that the division of their respective fields of activity into "literary" and "artistic" was un-real because it was impossible to separate the form of a play from its content, or its literary, psychological, or social side from the actual work of its mounting and presentation. Stanislavsky, too, realized that by himself he was still incapable of dealing with a Chekhov play and that he needed the literary authority of Nemirovich-Danchenko as well as Simov's fine flair for designing the right kind of scenery for such a play, the sort of scenery that stimulated his imagination, and helped him to find the approach to inner feelings through outward and characteristic detail. For as an actor he felt that this outward truth and the intimate recollections it evoked helped him to reproduce the right kind of feeling. It was then that he stopped acting in a Chekhov play and began living his part. It was then that, as Stanislavsky put it, "the words and actions of the part were transformed into the actor's own words and actions. A creative miracle happened—the most important and necessary sacrament of the soul for the sake of which it is worth making every possible sacrifice in our art."

It must have been some time in 1898 that Stanislavsky again met Tolstoy, and again, as at their first meeting in Tula in 1893, he felt like a schoolboy and dared not utter a word in the presence of the great man. Tolstoy was then writing his two famous articles against war and military service, and he met Stanislavsky and an acquaintance of his by accident near his Moscow home. He looked so stern, his eyes completely hidden behind his beetling eyebrows, that Stanislavsky let his friend carry on a conversation with him while he himself lagged respectfully behind. Tolstoy was fulminating against the legal killing of people, exposing the military and their ways all the more convincingly since he himself had taken part in many campaigns. Suddenly round a corner of a street there appeared two guardsmen in their long greatcoats, shining helmets, jingling spurs, and rattling sabres. Their young, tall and handsome figures, their cheerful faces, and their fine military carriage made Tolstoy stop short, open-mouthed and with his arms frozen in an unfinished gesture. His face beamed. "Fine fellows ! " he said with a deep sigh, and began talking excitedly about the importance of correct military bearing.

CHAPTER XXVIII

THE YEAR 1899 began inauspiciously for Stanislavsky. His production of *Hedda Gabler*, first performed on February 19th, was a failure and had to be taken off after the 11th performance. He must have put in a great deal of work on Ibsen's famous play, for his acting of Loevborg was generally considered to be above criticism. Indeed, many years later Nicolai Efros singled out his performance as one of the most outstanding representations of an Ibsen character he had ever seen. "Stanislavsky," he wrote, "succeeded in conveying the impression of genius in his characterization of Loevborg, a thing which hardly ever happens on the stage. And he made the spectator feel it and not only take it for granted. His Loevborg was both a profligate genius and a genius in profligacy."

The failure of *Hedda Gabler*, following upon the still greater failure of *Greta's Happiness* in the previous December and followed by the even more unexpected failure of Hauptmann's naturalistic play *The Driver Henschel* in October, aroused his superstitious feelings to such a pitch that he infected the whole theatre with them. Everybody in the theatre, including Nemirovich-Danchenko, began to dread a play which had an *H* in its title. The same year saw the failure of Stanislavsky's revival of *Twelfth Night*, which was perhaps not so very surprising, and Stanislavsky's personal failure in the title part of Alexey Tolstoy's *Death of Ivan the Terrible*.

The choice of Alexey Tolstoy's historical play to open the second season of the Moscow Art Theatre on October 29th, 1899, was a logical consequence of the success of *Czar Fyodor* the previous season. But this time Stanislavsky allowed himself much more freedom in the interpretation of the play, with the result that, as had happened so many times before, a conflict was created between his conception of it and the dialogue of the author. Even while discussing the sets for the play with Simov, this conflict between the producer and the playwright became so apparent that Simov could not help asking himself whether a producer had a right to allow his imagination to play havoc with a play. Was not that rather like a transposition of a classical piece by Liszt? If a producer or an actor were to be allowed such freedom of interpretation would that not amount to a complete distortion of the author's work? Where was the borderline beyond which a producer's imagination ought not to venture? And what would have happened if Stanislavsky had begun interfering with Alexey Tolstoy in the writing of his play? Would not the author have protested most vigorously against such an intrusion into his own province even by a producer of genius? A scene-designer must obviously take his orders from the producer, but what about the author?

These questions which worried Simov while he was working with Stanislavsky on the sets of the *Death of Ivan the Terrible* are questions which crop up constantly in the theatre. And it may be interesting to note that while Stanislavsky was still a producer-autocrat, he never hesitated to superimpose his own conception of a character or even a play upon the given text, with almost always disastrous results. And though as a rule he never meddled with his author's text, he did not hesitate to alter radically the play-wright's stage directions and occasionally even cut out a line or two which conflicted too violently with his own ideas of what the play should be like. This, in fact, seems to be the invariable practice of the producer-autocrat who regards himself as the only authority on the stage and seems to disregard entirely the existence of the dramatist as an artist in his own right. To such a producer the dramatist, even the acknowledged dramatist of genius, is practically always a nuisance. In the Moscow Art Theatre this tendency was at first very noticeable, and Stanislavsky's failure in the part of Ivan the Terrible was mainly due to his conflict with his author. In a letter to Chekhov, Nemirovich-Danchenko praised Stanislavsky's production of the play, but found that Stanislavsky was not successful in the title part. "No one liked him," he wrote, "and that has produced a painful crisis. The actor feels that the audience is not with him, but he just has to go on playing. His part causes him a great deal of nervous strain, but the audience does not accept his conception of it. I am afraid I can't judge whether he is right or not. I have got so used to his conception of the part that I can't help liking him in it, but I seem to be the only one who does." And there was the further complication that, as Nemirovich-Danchenko observed, "it is not so much his part that tires an actor as his lack of success in it. Alexeyev gets so worn out that neither on the day he plays Ivan the Terrible nor on the following day is he fit to do any work. That is why," Nemirovich-Danchenko explained, "he has not been able to take part in the rehearsals of *Uncle Vanya*. We have got all the scenes without Astrov going so well that I have had to cancel today's rehearsal : we can't do anything without Astrov."

The first night of *Uncle Vanya* had indeed to be put off for almost a fortnight, and when at last it was performed on October 26th, 1899, they were all appalled that the play was not received with the same ecstatic enthusiasm as *The Seagull*. "We were so worked up in our expectations of a tumultuous reception," Nemirovich-Danchenko wrote to Chekhov, "that the fact that they were not realized spoilt our mood." And Stanislavsky records that after the first night the whole company went to a restaurant and "cried bitter tears" over "the failure" of the play. In the long run, however, *Uncle Vanya* turned out to be a much greater success than *The Seagull*. The very fact that the audience on the first night was not hysterical showed that the effect of the play had been much deeper than the more showy and noisy effect of the ill-starred *Seagull*. In *Uncle Vanya*, the most Chekhovian of Chekhov's plays, Stanislavsky was not only successful in getting the right atmosphere of intimacy that was to become so characteristic a feature of his Chekhov productions, but also in achieving his first real triumph in what he had originally taken to be a secondary part. "I did not like the part of Astrov at first," Stanislavsky writes, "and would not agree to play it because I always wanted to play Uncle Vanya. But Nemirovich-Danchenko succeeded in overcoming my stubbornness and making me like Astrov."

But it was much more than stubbornness that made Stanislavsky insist on playing the part of Uncle Vanya. The clash between Chekhov and Stanislavsky after the performance of *The Seagull* which had been arranged for Chekhov's benefit was much sharper than it would appear to have been from the subsequent accounts of it by Stanislavsky himself. It was a clash that arose out of the different conceptions of the final test of a production : to a producer it is to earn the enthusiastic applause of his audience, and the only measuring-rod he applies to the success or failure of a play is the reaction of the audience to it. Stanislavsky, therefore, would have been fully justified in pointing out that *his* production of *The Seagull* had resulted in such a triumph for Chekhov that it completely obliterated the ignominious failure of the play at the Alexandrinsky Theatre and fully atoned for Chekhov's humiliating flight from Petersburg after its failure. But it seemed that what mattered to Chekhov was not the great success of the play but that it had been distorted beyond recognition by the producer. He was particularly savage in his criticisms of Roxanova who took Nina's part, demanding that she should never be allowed to act in his plays again. He could not very well prevent Stanislavsky from acting in his plays, but there seemed to be little doubt that he would not let him act the title part of *Uncle Vanya.* He sent Stanislavsky a complete edition of his published works, which seemed more like a prescription from Chekhov the doctor than a present from Chekhov the writer. In acknowledging the receipt of the books in the first letter he ever wrote to Chekhov, Stanislavsky rather stiffly thanked him for them and assured him that he had already "swallowed" almost half of them and hoped to do the same to the other half during his projected Volga holiday. He asked Chekhov to thank his sister for all the trouble she must have taken in sending him the books and to convey his own and his wife's best regards to her and to Chekhov's mother. He signed the letter very formally as "Respectfully yours and always at your service, K. Alexeyev."

It was Nemirovich-Danchenko who patched things up between Chekhov and Stanislavsky. In a letter to Chekhov in May, 1899, he informed him that "Alexeyev and Vishnevsky have agreed to exchange their parts. I always thought," he added soothingly, "that Vishnevsky was much more suitable for the part of Uncle Vanya, but I had to take Alexeyev's wishes into account though it was against my conscience." And in another letter he again assured Chekhov that "I always thought Vishnevsky should play Uncle Vanya, but I kept postponing my decision. Alexeyev," he added, "will be an excellent Astrov." And already in his first letter to Chekov after the performance of *Uncle Vanya,* Nemirovich-Danchenko was happy to report that "Alexeyev excelled everybody as Astrov. He was a great success."

But even Nemirovich-Danchenko did not dream how great a success Stanislavsky would be in the part of Astrov in the subsequent performances of *Uncle Vanya*. Leonidov, who joined the company of the Moscow Art Theatre two years after the first production of Chekhov's play, left this description of his impression of *Uncle Vanya* and, particularly, of Stanislavsky in the part of Astrov :

"The performance of *Uncle Vanya* made an unforgettable impression on me. What was there actually in this performance ? What was the secret of the tremendous influence it had on the spectators ? I have seen many good performances and many great actors, but never have I experienced anything like it before. I realized what it was : here one believed everything ; here was no trace of theatricality ; it almost seemed that there were no actors on the stage and no previously contrived *mise-en-scènes*. Everything was so simple, just as in real life, but beneath this simplicity one became aware of the seething cauldron of human passions. Sometimes I could not help feeling rather ill-at-ease : it was as though I, a complete stranger, was witnessing the intimate life of people I did not know.

"Such was the entire performance and such was Stanislavsky. And what was so striking about the whole performance and about Stanislavsky himself was that there was no evidence of the greatest enemy of the art of the stage—vulgarity, which the majority of actors do not seem able to shake off."

And here is another description of Stanislavsky's playing in *Uncle Vanya*, this time by Olga Knipper, who acted Helen opposite Stanislavsky's Astrov :

"I can see Stanislavsky even now," Olga Knipper wrote forty years after the first production of *Uncle Vanya*, "in the big grey cloak and cape he wore in the first act. I can see and hear him say in a voice full of emotion, 'When I hear the rustling of the young trees I have planted with my own hands, I realize that the climate is to a certain extent in my power and that if in another thousand years man is happy, I shall have contributed a little to his happiness.' When I looked at the hands of Astrov-Stanislavsky, I could not help believing that those hands had really been planting trees, and when I looked into his eyes I was convinced that he hated the humdrum life of a philistine and that he was able to look far ahead. 'I am in love with life, but our provincial philistine Russian life I find intolerable and I despise it from the bottom of my heart,' he says to Sonia. It is Astrov who is saying this, but you hear the voice of Stanislavsky and you become aware how determined he is that his thoughts and experience, all the tremendous work he has given to the art to which he has dedicated the whole of his life, should not be lost to the coming generation of actors.

"Stanislavsky used to say that he was surprised at his success in the part of Astrov," Olga Knipper continued. " 'Why,' he told me, 'I hardly do anything there and the public praises me ! ' And I simply could not believe that he did not realize what a wonderfully poetic and courageous personality his Astrov was, and that he conveyed it all with such an amazingly light touch. . . . In the last act when he walked up to the map of Africa and, looking at it, said 'Oh, I expect it must be frightfully hot in that Africa—simply terrific heat ! '—how much of his own bitter experience of life he used to put into that sentence. And he said those words with a kind of bravado and even with a kind of challenge. When the sound of the bells of his departing carriage was heard, a pang went through one's heart at the thought of the dull, dreary and hard life which was in store for that talented and courageous man in the remote provincial district where he would spend the rest of his life. And one did not want to part with that unforgettable character Stanislavsky had created.

"When I played the scene in the third act with him," Olga Knipper concluded, "I walked on the stage as though I were walking on air. When I felt his loving look on me, a look which was so full of banter, and when I heard his tender, ironic words, 'You're a sly-y one ! ' I always felt annoyed with the 'intellectual' Helen for refusing to go away with him to the woods he had planted."

Stanislavsky, incidentally, took a great deal of trouble with the sound of the bells in the last act. The effect he finally achieved was much subtler than the same effect in *The Bells* a few years earlier. While seeking an entirely realistic solution, he at the same time contrived that the sounds of the departing carriage should also express the vanishing dreams and hopes of the characters in the play.

In his performance of Astrov Stanislavsky intuitively stumbled on one of the most characteristic traits of Chekhov's heroes—their courage, a trait that is mostly missed by producer and performer in England. He also acted it in a state of high emotional tension which, however, he knew how to keep under control and, by doing so, enrich it, making Astrov into an exciting and memorable dramatic figure, magnificently alive and convincing. In this part he apparently achieved for the first time on the stage that complete fusion of the actor with his part which he was later to term "I-part" in his "system", or, alternatively, "I am".

Uncle Vanya, despite its somewhat lukewarm reception by the first-night audience, was soon the most successful play in Moscow. The tenth performance of the play was graced by the presence of the Moscow Governor-General and his wife, the Grand Duke Sergey Alexandrovich and the Grand Duchess Yelisaveta Fyodorovna. With them was no less a person than Konstantin Pobedonostsev, the reactionary lay head of the Holy Synod. Thus State and Church seemed at last to have become aware of the existence of the Moscow Art Theatre. Next day, November 27th, Stanislavsky and Nemirovich-Danchenko went to pay a visit to the Grand Duke. "They told me," wrote Nemirovich-Danchenko to Chekhov, "that for the last two days in the palace, at dinner, supper and tea, they had talked of nothing but *Uncle Vanya*. One of the Grand Duke's *aides-de-camp* said to me, 'What is this Uncle Vanya? The Grand Duke and Duchess talk of nothing else.' " As for Pobedonostsev, the Grand Duke told Stanislavsky and Nemirovich-Danchenko that the President of the Holy Synod had not been to a theatre for many years and had gone to see *Uncle Vanya* reluctantly, but that he had been so carried away and had felt so crushed by what he had seen that he could not help wondering whether the actors who gave so much to the stage had anything left over for their families. "Every man," Nemirovich-Danchenko observed drily, "draws his own conclusions."

On January 24th, 1900, Tolstoy himself appeared at a performance of *Uncle Vanya*. He remarked that there were undoubtedly brilliant places in the play, but that he missed any really tragic situations. Nemirovich-Danchenko tried to explain to him what the "central point" of the play was, but all Tolstoy said was : "Good Lord, a guitar and a cricket—all this is so nice that I don't see why I should look for anything else."

It was in the autumn of 1899 that Stanislavsky invented a special method of adapting the stage of the Moscow Art Theatre for the dramatization of short stories. For that purpose he suggested a small raised stage (with the curtain only partly drawn). The scenes were to be changed with "cinematographic" swiftness, four scenes following each other without an interval. Nothing much seems to have come of the idea except one performance devoted to dramatized versions of a number of short stories by Chekhov produced by Stanislavsky in 1905, one year after the writer's death.

CHAPTER XXIX

AT THE END OF ITS second season the Moscow Art Theatre was already firmly established. "Our affairs are in excellent shape," Nemirovich-Danchenko wrote to Chekhov, and though he might have been exaggerating a little to win Chekhov's goodwill, which was still rather uncertain, it was obvious even to the ill-wishers of the theatre that it had come to stay. It was different, and it proved its ability to survive its failures by a number of productions of outstanding imaginative power. Among these, Chekhov's plays occupied a foremost place. Stanislavsky was now convinced that in Chekhov his theatre had found a dramatist who would give it a character of its own. He saw that, when applied to a Chekhov play, his methods of production resulted in that unpredictable thing—success. What they wanted now was obvious : another Chekhov play, a *new* play this time, for both *The Seagull* and *Uncle Vanya* had been performed many times on the provincial stage before their production by the Moscow Art Theatre. Nemirovich-Danchenko had already raised the subject of a new play with Chekhov. "I don't know anything about your new play yet," he wrote to Chekhov in February. "Will there be a play or not ? We have got to have it. We've just got to. The sooner the better, of course, but we must have it by the autumn at the latest. Please, let us have it by the autumn." But Chekhov was hedging. He had not seen their production of *Uncle Vanya*, and until he saw it he could not make up his mind whether he wanted them to do his new play : his disappointment with their production of *The Seagull* had been too great, and the notices he had read of their production of *Uncle Vanya* were not so favourable as to remove his doubts. Nemirovich-Danchenko wanted to know what notices he had read. The play, as a matter of fact, had had a number of very good notices, including one by Nicolai Efros. There were, no doubt, some critical notices, too, but—and Nemirovich-Danchenko did his best to explain that the people who criticised the play unfavourably were either wilfully exaggerating "the impotence of the movement in art which finds life humdrum and depressing," or had a personal grudge against him, like the husband of the lady who had sent him her translation of Pinero's comedy *The Notorious Mrs. Ebbsmith*, which he, as a matter of fact, had wanted to put on, but which he had had to reject because of all sorts of insuperable difficulties. That lady had been a friend of his for ten years, but on receiving her manuscript back she wrote to him a letter in which she addressed him as "Dear Sir," and told him that his conduct towards her had been "unforgivable". Unforgivable, mind you, just because *Uncle Vanya* was such a great success !

But it was no use : Chekhov quite obviously did not want to commit himself. All they got out of him was that *if* he had been feeling well, he would most certainly have come to Moscow to see *Uncle Vanya*, but as his health was rather bad just then—

"If," said Stanislavsky, "Mahomet does not go to the mountain, then the mountain must go to Mahomet," and the "mountain"—the actors with their families, scenery, props and all ("a new migration of peoples", as Stanislavsky called it)—left Moscow for the Crimea in April. They planned to give four plays in Sebastopol and Yalta—the two Chekhov plays, *Hedda Gabler* (re-named *Edda Gabler* to avoid using the unlucky *H*), and Hauptmann's naturalistic play *The Lonely*, with which they had closed their second season and which had been well received.

In Sebastopol it was very cold. An icy wind was blowing from the sea. The sky was overcast. It was snowing. The actors, who had been expecting sunny skies and warm spring weather, were freezing in their hotels. The theatre on the front, which was only open during the summer season, had been boarded up since the winter, and a gale was tearing off the old handbills from its walls. However, next day it cleared up, the sun shone, and the hoardings were removed from the doors of the theatre. When Stanislavsky entered it, he found it cold and musty as a cellar. It would have taken a whole week to air it properly and they had to start their performances in a couple of days. What worried them was that there was not a single seat in the theatre in which Chekhov would be sure not to catch a cold. Fortunately,

Chekhov did not arrive before a comfortable, warm seat had been prepared for him. The whole company went to the harbour to meet him. He was the last to appear on deck and he looked very ill and wretched. Stanislavsky felt like crying when he saw him. The amateur photographers among the actors snapped him as he came down the gangway, and he afterwards put a similar scene into *The Three Sisters*. Rather tactlessly, Stanislavsky thought, the first question the actors fired at him was about his health.

"I'm all right," Chekhov replied. "Never felt better."

The theatre opened on Easter Monday with Chekhov's *Uncle Vanya*. At eight o'clock a handbell announced the beginning of the performance. The first act was received rather coldly, but the audience got carried away more and more and the play ended amid a veritable storm of applause. They yelled for the author, and Chekhov had reluctantly to come out on the stage and take a bow. He hated it, but he had to do it at almost every performance of his plays in Sebastopol and Yalta. This time he was very satisfied both with the production and with the acting of *Uncle Vanya*. During one of the intervals he even made a point of going to see Stanislavsky in his dressing-room to congratulate him on his performance. The breach between them was being healed.

Chekhov, though, did make one critical remark about the way Stanislavsky played Astrov in the last act.

"Look here," he said, cryptically, "he whistles. Whistles. Understand? Uncle Vanya is crying, but Astrov is whistling."

He refused to say anything more. For a long time Stanislavsky racked his brains in a vain endeavour to find out what Chekhov meant by this cryptic remark. "Why should Astrov be whistling?" he asked himself. "Melancholy—hopelessness—and, suddenly, gay whistling!"

But Chekhov's remark "came to life," as Stanislavsky puts it, at one of the subsequent performances of the play. "One evening," Stanislavsky writes, "I made up my mind to try it out and see what happened, and the moment I did it I felt that Chekhov was right. Uncle Vanya is dejected and broken-hearted, but Astrov is whistling. Why? Because he has lost faith in people and life so completely that his mistrust has been turned to cynicism. Nothing people do can surprise him any more. Fortunately, he loves nature and serves her faithfully : he plants trees and the woods preserve the moisture which is so necessary for the rivers."

Stanislavsky's reminiscences of Chekhov reveal a curious inability to understand the great writer. It was an inability that seems to have been psychologically inevitable. To him Chekhov was a man of genius who did all sorts of amusing and perverse things, but who was quite incapable of doing anything practical. It was a sort of popular, almost musical-comedy idea of a genius who, in his child-like innocence, had no notion what his great masterpieces were about and whose quizzical attitude towards them had to be treated with the sort of good-humour with which an enlightened man would treat the antics of a problem child. Occasionally, indeed, such a genius would make some cryptic remark that, just because it appeared to be so cryptic, had to be treated with the utmost respect, while his unaccountable and very uncryptic statements about the nature of his plays could be safely disregarded as they were so obviously perverse and absurd. It never occurred to Stanislavsky that Chekhov's remarks were "cryptic" only because, as he himself had so recently confessed in a letter to his wife, he did not know what Chekhov's plays were about. On the other hand, Chekhov was loath to enlarge on them because that would merely have involved him in a long argument about the essentials of his art, which was hardly the sort of thing he could expect an actor to understand, while a few vivid words giving a graphic description of one of the characters in his plays might very well convey something to him. Stanislavsky, therefore, tends to exaggerate what seemed to him the odd and humorously perverse sides of Chekhov's character. It seemed absurd to him that a great writer like Chekhov should take his profession of a doctor seriously. He probably did not know (very few people did know) that while he lived on his small estate near Moscow, Chekhov had a very large medical practice among the peasants, or that this "unpractical" writer had founded hospitals and schools on his own slender means. He, therefore, relates with undisguised relish the following incident of Chekhov's treatment of Artyom, an actor Chekhov was very fond of and for whom he wrote the characters of Chebutykin in *The Three Sisters* and Firs in *The Cherry Orchard*, as a highly amusing joke.

"Next morning Artyom, who got too excited on the first night, took to his bed and did not turn up at the rehearsal," Stanislavsky writes. "Chekhov, who was very fond of curing people, was overjoyed to hear that he had a patient. He at once went with Tikhomirov (an actor of the Moscow Art Theatre) to pay a visit to Artyom. We, on the other hand, took very good care to find out what treatment Chekhov was going to prescribe for his patient. It is interesting that while on the way to his patient's hotel, Chekhov went back home to fetch his percussion hammer and his stethoscope. 'Look here,' he said to Tikhomirov anxiously, 'I just can't go like that. I must have my instruments.' He spent a long time examining Artyom, listening to his chest and tapping it. Then he began telling him that it was silly to coddle oneself. In the end he gave him a peppermint. 'Look here, you'd better have this.' That was the end of the treatment, for next day Artyom was well again."

The story seems to have amused Stanislavsky, a chronic valetudinarian himself, so much that in *My Life in Art* he supplies another version of it. "Chekhov," he writes, "went to see his favourite actor Artyom and prescribed Valerian drops for him, that is to say, the same medicine he makes Dr. Dorn, one of the characters of his *Seagull*, prescribe in jest for all his patients."

Stanislavsky was particularly amused by Chekhov's attempts to meddle in his own sphere of stage effects. Chekhov was very fond of going behind the scenes and watching the stagehands put up the scenery or the actors put on their make-up. (Chekhov's knowledge of the stage went back to his schooldays when he used to do a lot of voluntary work, including amateur acting, in the theatre of his native town of Taganrog.) In Sebastopol, however, it was too cold and draughty for him to stay behind the scenes long. He therefore used to sit for hours in the sun in front of the theatre. One day Stanislavsky watched him trying to teach the stage carpenter how to reproduce the chirping of a cricket.

"Listen," said Chekhov, "this is how a cricket chirps : tick-tick, then it is silent for a few seconds, and then again : tick-tick !"

In Moscow about a year later Chekhov criticised the sound of the alarm bell in the third act of *The Three Sisters* and expressed a wish to put it right himself. Stanislavsky, of course, immediately agreed to give him a free hand and put a number of stage-hands at his disposal. "Chekhov arrived at the theatre for the rehearsal in a cab laden with saucepans, brass bowls, and all sorts of tin cans," Stanislavsky writes. "He himself placed the stage-hands at a certain distance from each other, each holding one of the domestic utensils in his hands, and told them excitedly how each of them had to bang his particular instrument, looking very confused and embarrassed as he issued his instructions. Then he rushed to the auditorium a few times to listen to his own sound effects, but nothing seemed to satisfy him. At the performance Chekhov waited breathlessly for his alarm bell. The din, when it came at last, was frightful, a most horrifying cacophony of sounds, every man behind the stage banging away with such fervour that it was impossible to hear the actors. The people in the box next to Chekhov's began cursing the din, then the play, and, finally, its author. Chekhov withdrew further and further into his box until, unable to bear it any longer, he went behind the scenes and sat down quietly in my dressing-room. 'Why, what's the matter?' I asked. 'Aren't you watching the play at all?' 'Look here,' Chekhov replied, 'they're abusing me dreadfully out there. It's damned unpleasant.' And so," Stanislavsky concludes, "he spent the rest of the evening in my dressing-room."

Chekhov left Sebastopol before the performance of *The Seagull*. He had already seen it, he remarked shortly. The play, however, was warmly received, and after it Stanislavsky was waylaid by a crowd of boys from the local grammar-school who were determined to carry him to his hotel. As Stanislavsky was a very big man, all they managed to do was to lift one of his legs while he hopped about helplessly on the other. He tried arguing with them, but they kept yelling "Hurrah!" at the top of their voices and he could not make himself heard. He had come out of the theatre with an umbrella, as it was pouring with rain, but in the scrimmage a gust of wind had snatched his umbrella away, and he had to let the young men half-carry, half-drag him to his hotel, Lilina running after them, afraid that they might do him some injury. Near the entrance of the hotel, the young students let him go. As he reached the front steps, however, they made another concerted dash at him, evidently intending to carry him up the steps, but they only succeeded in throwing him down on the wet pavement. Fortunately, the hotel commissionaire came to his rescue, and while he was brushing down Stanislavsky's coat, the students were debating the cause of their failure to carry him shoulder high all the way from the theatre to the hotel.

In Yalta, where they again put on the same four plays, Stanislavsky met Gorky for the first time and tried to persuade him to write a play for the Moscow Art Theatre. "Every morning,"

Stanislavsky writes, "we all went to the harbour. I usually attached myself to Gorky and during our walk threw out all sorts of suggestions for a play. One day Gorky told me the subject of the play he proposed to write for us. A dosshouse, a huge stuffy room, bunks, a long boring winter. Their horrible life turns the inmates into beasts, they lose patience, they give up hope, get on each other's nerves, and spend all their time philoso-phizing. Everyone does his best to show that he is still a human being. An ex-waiter is particularly proud of his cheap paper shirt front—the only thing that remains of the evening dress he once wore. To annoy the ex-waiter, someone steals his shirt-front and tears it in two. The ex-waiter finds his torn shirt-front, is in despair because with his shirt-front the last link with his former life is snapped, and the whole place is all at once turned into a bear-garden. The fighting and quarrelling go on till late at night, till peace is suddenly restored by the news that the police are coming to inspect the place. After hiding away everything of a compromising nature, they all lie down on their bunks and pretend to be asleep. The police arrive. Some-one is led away to the police-station. The tramps fall asleep on their bunks. Only one old man climbs slowly down from the stove, takes out a wax candle-end from his satchel, lights it, and starts praying. Then the head of a Tartar appears from some bunk. 'Pray for me' the Tartar murmurs."

That was Gorky's first sketch of the first act of *Lower Depths*. At the time he had only a vague idea of the other acts of the play which two years later was to earn the Moscow Art Theatre another great triumph.

Visiting Chekhov at his Yalta home almost every day and meet-ing a large number of literary people there, Stanislavsky found their conversation much more profitable than any lecture on literature he had ever heard. "These discussions," he writes, "revealed many literary mysteries to me which I found very useful as a producer afterwards."

The visit to the Crimea had served its purpose. Both Chekhov and Gorky promised to write a play each for the Moscow Art Theatre.

CHAPTER XXX

BACK IN MOSCOW, Stanislavsky spent the months of May and June in the usual preparatory work for the next season, which was to open in October with Ostrovsky's fairy-play *The Snow Maiden.* They had no idea what Chekhov's play was to be about, but they were sure of getting it : they had not only satisfied Chekhov, who, according to Stanislavsky, went about telling his literary friends, "They're doing wonderful work ! You must write a play for them," but had been able to show him that financially, too, he would not be a loser. Already in March they had paid him over 3,500 roubles in royalties for *The Seagull* and *Uncle Vanya* and, as Nemirovich-Danchenko cautiously hinted, if he was not satisfied they were quite willing to pay him more than ten per cent of their total receipts. Stanislavsky was busy writing the *mise-en-scènes* for *The Snow Maiden* and *An Enemy of the People,* the two plays he was producing himself, and with helping Nemirovich-Danchenko, who was producing the other Ibsen play of the coming season, *When We Dead Awaken.* He was, besides, already conducting negotiations with his friend, Savva Morozov, the millionaire industrialist, for the construction of a new theatre and the conversion of the People's Art Theatre into a limited company, to be officially known as the Moscow Art Theatre, since it proved impossible to keep up with the theatre's original policy of popular prices. What was his day like ? In a letter to his wife, who was in Lyubimovka with the children, he describes it like this : "What did I do yesterday ? In the morning rehearsals, then the dentist, then a business dinner with Morozov and Nemirovich-Danchenko, then spent some time ordering costumes with Grigoryeva (the wardrobe mistress), then saw off Andreyeva and her husband (two members of the company who were going off on their summer holidays) and sent Andreyeva a bouquet for the journey, then walked with Morozov, and so to bed."

In another letter a few days later he complains of a splitting headache because he had only gone to bed at 5 a.m. "Went to the end-of-season dinner given by our actors. Tried to be as cheerful and as natural as possible and the result was that they all got drunk and started opening up their hearts to me which made me feel sad and lonely."

Himself a teetotaller, Stanislavsky was horrified every time he saw an actor the worse for drink. "An actor," he kept repeating, "must never get drunk ! It's horrible ! " As his treatment of Lentovsky showed, he was ruthless when it came to keeping drunken actors out of the theatre. His horror of drink goes back to the early days of his enthusiasm for the stage. Kashdamanov and he had seen a famous actor give one of the most magnificent performances of his career. They were so deeply moved that they felt they simply could not go home without first exchanging their impressions of it. They went to a restaurant and during their talk the great man himself came in. They rushed up to him to express their great admiration for his fine playing, and he very graciously invited them to have dinner with him in a private room. But it seemed that all he wanted was that they should pay for his drinks, which he kept consuming in quite astonishing quantities. In the end they had to see him to his hotel, as he was too drunk to get there by himself. The contrast between the actor's inspiring art and his behaviour off the stage so shocked Stanislavsky that he could never forget it.

In July Stanislavsky went away for his annual cure. As he was thoroughly sick of Vichy by now, he went for the first time to the Caucasus. He found Yessentuki, the famous Caucasian spa, a very depressing place at first ("There was only one man who laughed here today," he wrote to his wife, "and that man was I ! "), but he was glad at any rate to be away from a telephone. Even in Yessentuki he could not escape from his Moscow female admirers. One of them, whom he had the misfortune to meet at the house where he was staying, kept telling him that she was not at all surprised that a man like him, who put so much into his work on the stage, should have to go for a cure every summer, for she was quite sure that he was a nervous wreck, and that his wife was a nervous wreck, and that his children, too, were nervous wrecks. Stanislavsky felt that if he went on listening to her much longer he would most certainly become a nervous wreck, so in the evening he went for a stroll in the park. "I went to watch the children on the Giant Stride," he wrote to his wife, "and the first thing I saw was a little urchin putting his foot into the sling and a big lubberly fellow giving him a mighty push before he had time to put his other foot in and sending him flying with his head against the post. I ran up, took the sobbing little boy to the stream where I spent a long time applying a wet handkerchief to his head and trying to prove to the big boy that he was behaving stupidly. In short, I spent a very profitable evening attending to the wounded and spreading enlightenment in the Far East. Don't forget to tell it to the children. I'm sure they'll find it very edifying."

He soon got used to Yessentuki and found it not at all as depressing as he had thought. "As usual with the Russians," he wrote, "the really interesting things are hidden away. Here, too, the decent houses are hidden behind trees, and all you see is the hideous street." He now entered on the usual routine of his cure : regular medical examinations, most thorough discussions with the doctor about the state of his internal organs (he had persuaded himself just then that he was suffering from pernicious anæmia), baths, waters, rest, meals. He soon got into the company of the local actors and had to refuse their persistent demands to appear on the stage or at least rehearse one scene for them. One day he had a most extraordinary meeting. He was having tea at a restaurant when he noticed two ladies at another table who were regarding him rather strangely. He seemed to remember having seen one of them somewhere. Who could she be? Her face certainly looked familiar. Then he heard a man addressing her by her Christian name. Sonia! Of course, it was the ballerina he had been so madly in love with—his first "flame"—years ago in Moscow, the girl he had "abducted" from the theatre after the ballet. "Our eyes met," Stanislavsky wrote to Lilina, "and I did not know what to do, whether I should go up to her or not, for she might not have acknowledged my bow. I did go up and she returned my greeting : a familiar voice and smile. We exchanged a few general remarks and I went away. Somehow, I did not feel like talking trivialities to her." He only saw her once again and then they just exchanged distant bows.

Stanislavsky left the Caucasus in August for the Crimea, where his wife and children had already gone for their holidays. He was back in Moscow in a few weeks. The new season began on September 24th, 1900, with the production of Ostrovsky's fairy-play *The Snow Maiden*. This season was remarkable for three Stanislavsky productions, each different in conception and execution and each revealing his maturity as an artist in a different way. *The Snow Maiden*, which Stanislavsky describes as "a fairy-tale, a dream, and a national saga", afforded him the opportunity of displaying his genius mainly as a producer ; *An Enemy of the People*, first performed on October 24th, gave him his greatest part as an actor ; *The Three Sisters*, first performed on January 31st, 1901, further enhanced his reputation as a typically "Chekhovian" actor and producer.

Stanislavsky's work on *The Snow Maiden* shows a distinct advance on any of his previous essays in the fantastic genre. The fantastic had always exercised the strongest possible attraction on him because it gave his imagination the fullest scope for contriving all sorts of wonderful stage effects unhampered by the necessity of making the characters in the play convincing and credible as human beings. Indeed, his chief aim in these plays was to make their characters credible as personified ideas with as few human attributes about them as possible. Mainly concerned with the external problems of stage expressiveness, the production of a fantastic play was "a real holiday" to Stanislavsky at that time. "The fantastic," he writes in discussing his production of *The Snow Maiden*, "was one of my oldest passions. I was ready to put on a play just for the sake of it. To me it was something like a glass of sparkling champagne. It made me feel happy if I could invent something that could never have happened in life but that was nevertheless true, something that exists in all of us—in our imagination and in our superstitious beliefs." But even in a fantastic play Stanislavsky was now looking for something that was typical both of the characters and the scenery, and he made those who worked with him, too, always look for something that was fresh, vivid and original. Even fairyland had to be endowed with artistic truth ; the whole production of the play had to have its roots firmly planted in the earth.

The first question Stanislavsky therefore asked himself before he started work on *The Snow Maiden* was in which part of Russia he ought to place the action of the play. All Ostrovsky's stage direction says is that "the action takes place in the country of the Berendeys in pre-historic times." That was too vague for Stanislavsky : his imagination had to have something more definite to work on. After a great deal of discussion, it was finally decided the Berendey's kingdom lay somewhere between Vologda and the White Sea. The next step was clear. As with *Czar Fyodor*, he had to send out an expedition to get all the local colour he might need for his production. The expedition, consisting of Simov, Simov's assistant and Stanislavsky's younger brother Boris, was duly dispatched, and it brought back all the material Stanislavsky wanted : photographs, sketches, all sorts of country dresses (carefully disinfected before being submitted to a most meticulous examination), specimens of local handicrafts, and so on.

Work on the play began in earnest after the company's return from their visit to Chekhov. Simov moved to Lyubimovka where he did the sketches for the costumes, which Lilina again undertook to make, and discussed his set with Stanislavsky, who left for Moscow every day for the preliminary rehearsals of the play (it had altogether 103 rehearsals). For the first two months Stanislavsky did nothing but go through the text of the play with the actors, line by line, every movement and inflexion being submitted to a careful scrutiny till he was absolutely satisfied, and even then he would as often as not change his mind.

"Wrong ! " Stanislavsky rapped the table sharply with his pencil. "I don't feel it ! You're overdoing it ! Simpler ! Much simpler ! For God's sake get rid of your theatrical clichés ! That's not the way to beg for something ! Who would dream of asking for anything like that ? No—no ! Wrong again ! "

The younger actors got more and more nervous ; the actresses bit their lips so as not to burst out crying ; the old actors shrugged, or rubbed their hands nervously. The scene was rehearsed all over again, and again the sharp rapping of the pencil on the table followed by a stream of critical remarks.

"But," an actor objected in a despairing voice, "yesterday I did that piece exactly like this and you said it was all right ! "

A short pause. Everyone was eager to hear what Stanislavsky would say.

"What if you did ? " cried Stanislavsky. "Yesterday you did it one way and today you must do it another ! "

The actor had no option : the producer's word was law.

Many years were to pass before Stanislavsky realized his mistake in treating the actor as a puppet, and many more years before he recalled those days of his dictatorship on the stage with a shudder and a feeling of shame and disgust.

The most characteristic feature of Stanislavsky's production of *The Snow Maiden* was the way he used highly realistic touches to lend greater credibility to the fantastic elements in the play. To make the grotesque figure of Jack Frost acceptable to the spectator he brought him on the stage accompanied by a most faithfully realistic grizzly bear. To make the fantastic transformation scene in the first act more plausible, he introduced the realistic detail of the Berendey inhabitants sinking in drifts of snow (a deep box filled with salt placed along the whole length of the footlights) as they walked heavy-booted back to their villages after burning the straw effigy of the Winter Goddess. Again, in the second act the mythical figures of King Berendey and his courtiers were all busy doing the most ordinary jobs. The King himself was standing on a piece of scaffolding and daintily painting a flower on a column, while his chief minister was sitting on the floor in his robes of state and painting a wooden panel with a huge housepainter's brush. Two icon-painters, old men with long white beards, were suspended in cradles under the ceiling and were painting intricate patterns on it. This juxtaposition of the realistic and the fanciful, each enhancing the effect of the other, was used by Stanislavsky again and again throughout the play.

It was, however, in the transformation scene in the first act that Stanislavsky revealed the great advance he had made as a producer during the last three or four years. In *The Bells* and in *Hannele*, too, the transformation scenes were carried out in darkness (a rather stale theatrical trick), Stanislavsky relying mainly on his light-effects to thrill and harrow the spectator ; in *The Snow Maiden*, on the other hand, the transformation took place in full view of the audience, the trees and bushes which covered the steep slope of the mountain in the background (another example of Stanislavsky's "constructional" use of the stage floor) coming to life with the approach of Jack Frost and transforming themselves into grotesque wood-demons. The audience had had ample time to accept these camouflaged actors for what they pretended to be and when, to the accompaniment of a cacophony of the weirdest sounds, they suddenly began to move about, the impression produced on the audience was all the greater because of the shock of seeing a familiar enough object come to life in a totally unfamiliar and fantastic guise.

"A fantastic scene like that," Stanislavsky writes, "only comes off if the spectator is taken by surprise by the stage trick. And this time, too, it was quite impossible to guess that the trees and bushes, which were on the stage from the very beginning of the act, were really a number of camouflaged people."

The play was not a success and was taken off after twenty-one performances. Stanislavsky ascribed its failure to the fact that the change of scenery after the third act took too long and that consequently he had to use the setting of Act III also for Act IV. The result was that the *mise-en-scènes* got hopelessly mixed up and he had to cut the text of the play drastically. But it is much more likely that the failure of the play was due to his overloading it with too much detail. Olga Sadovskaya, who was with difficulty persuaded to see a performance of *The Snow Maiden*, hit the nail on the head when, in reply to a question how she had liked the play, she said : "There was a cradle hanging there under the very ceiling and a painter was lying in the cradle and painting the ceiling of the palace. The moment I saw that man under the ceiling, I could not look at anything else or think of anything else—I was so terrified that he might fall out and kill himself." Stanislavsky invested each detail with so much significance that the audience very often could not see the wood for the trees : Ostrovsky's play got lost in Stanislavsky's maze of imaginative *mise-en-scènes*.

The cradle, or rather the two cradles, Stanislavsky had suspended under the ceiling of King Berendey's palace played rather an important role in the development of Stanislavsky's system many years later. For it led Stanislavsky to realize the importance of what he was to call the "affective" or "emotional" memory of the actor as an "element" that was most likely to awaken his inspiration through the subconscious processes of his mind.

When he first rehearsed this scene, Stanislavsky found that the two painters in the cradles under the ceiling seemed to stimulate the work of his imagination. When the two men got bored and insisted on being taken down, he felt "like Samson after his long hair had been cut off," and however hard he tried, he could not carry on with the rehearsal. At last the two extras took pity on him and allowed themselves to be hoisted up under the ceiling again, when his imagination came to life once more. Stanislavsky could not explain this curious phenomenon until many years later, when he paid a visit to the Vladimir Cathedral in Kiev. The cathedral was empty : only from one of the chapels came the quiet singing of a prayer. It was then that he remembered that long before the production of *The Snow Maiden*, when the cathedral was still under construction, he had come to see it. Then, too, it had been empty. From its dome, shafts of golden sunlight fell on the metal settings of the icons. Suddenly the silence of the cathedral was broken by the quiet singing of the icon painters who were suspended in cradles beneath the dome and were painting it slowly, as though they were anointing it with oil. They, too, had long white beards. So that was where he had got his scene for King Berendey's palace in *The Snow Maiden* !

"It was only then," Stanislavsky writes, "that I realized what the source of my creative devices was and how they happened to find their way on to the stage."

CHAPTER XXXI

IBSEN WAS NEVER a favourite of Stanislavsky's. Most of his plays produced by the Moscow Art Theatre he lumps together under the general heading of the theatre's "line of symbolism and impressionism". He is anxious to explain that the actors of the Moscow Art Theatre were never really able to cope with them because "to perform symbolic plays the actor has to become firmly fused with his part and the play, absorb its spiritual content, crystallize it, polish this crystal and find a vivid, clear and artistic form for it which will synthesize its many-sided and complex nature." The actors of his theatre, he maintains, were too little experienced to carry out such a task. Their inner technique was insufficiently developed. He could never agree with the experts who claimed that the whole tendency of the Moscow Art Theatre was too realistic for its actors to make a success of symbolic plays. The real reason why the actors were unsuccessful with Ibsen, he claims, was that they were not realistic enough so far as the inner life of the play was concerned. "Symbolism, impressionism, and other 'isms' in art," he writes, "belong to the sphere of the subconscious and begin where the ultra-natural ends. It is only when the spiritual and physical life of the actor on the stage is unfolding itself *naturally* and normally in accordance with the laws of nature that the subconscious comes out of its hiding-places. If the slightest constraint is put on nature, the subconscious immediately hides itself away in the most inaccessible places of a man's soul, fleeing from crude muscular anarchy."

In those early days of the Moscow Art Theatre the actors were not yet able to achieve a natural and normal state of mind on the stage at will. They did not know how to create within themselves the favourable conditions for the work of their subconsciousness. They liked to argue too much, they thought themselves too clever, and kept themselves deliberately on the plane of consciousness. Their "symbols" were too rational : they could not sharpen the inner realism of these plays to a point where their symbolic significance emerged. Only accidentally, for reasons which were obscure to them, did "inspiration" descend upon them. He himself, for instance, had been lucky enough to reach, at the dress rehearsal of *Hedda Gabler*, a deep and thorough understanding of the tragic moments in the part of Loevborg when, after the loss of his manuscript, he is plunged into a despair which ends in his suicide. But such lucky chances occurred only by accident, and accident, Stanislavsky adds, "cannot of course serve as a basis for art."

All the more astonishing, therefore, was Stanislavsky's great success in the part of Dr. Stockmann in Ibsen's *An Enemy of the People*. But the word "success" hardly describes the wonderful transformation that came over him even at the first reading of the play. Here it was not a question of understanding what the playwright was driving at, a thing that always baffled him in Chekhov. He became instantly *obsessed* with the play. The part of Stockmann touched some hidden chord in his soul, and by that miracle of art which defies all definition he instantly felt that he *was* Stockmann. Neither he nor anybody else could find a satisfactory explanation of this unusual event in his stage career, unusual because even his most successful parts never came easily to him. Leonidov, who had seen him in the part of Stockmann two years before joining the company of the Moscow Art Theatre, is the only one to attempt to advance some reason for it which sounds plausible. "Stockmann's loneliness," Leonidov writes, "was of the same nature as Stanislavsky's loneliness. Stanislavsky had enjoyed little support in his life and he had experienced a great deal of derision, but he never gave way and, like Stockmann, he fought courageously against everything that he thought false in the theatre. It was indeed impossible to separate Stanislavsky from Stockmann. It almost seemed that that would have been equivalent to tearing the skin off a living man."

This explanation fits in with Stanislavsky's own statement that the concluding phrase of the play—"The most powerful man in the world is he who remains alone"—slipped off his tongue so naturally that it seemed to him as though he himself had put those words into the play. And when Stanislavsky-Stockmann shouted to the crowd in the fourth act of the play : "You are mistaken ! You are beasts ! Yes, you are beasts ! " he might have been addressing his own detractors and critics.

Other actors of the Moscow Art Theatre, too, were amazed at the completeness of this fusion of Stanislavsky and Stockmann. "He was so imbued with the life of Ibsen's character," one of them writes, "that he became quite a different man. Those who happened to be near him on the stage were absolutely convinced that they were in the presence of a new person."

It is highly significant that, having obtained through "intuition and feeling" this miraculous fusion of his own personality with that of Ibsen's character, Stanislavsky no longer felt any need for external aids, not even from the scenery which hitherto had formed the pivotal point of a Stanislavsky production. Many years later Stanislavsky remarked that to a great actor external aids were unnecessary, and that even if he were to appear on a bare stage he would be able to hold the attention of the audience without difficulty. But Stanislavsky was not a great actor, as indeed he himself stated many times. He was not a Salvini or an Irving. It was only in *An Enemy of the People* and, as he claims, in his adaptation of Dostoesky's *The Village of Stepanchikovo*, that this complete fusion of himself and his part came about naturally so that he never felt the need of scenery nor was worried by the bare floor of the stage. Nor did he waste any time in reshaping the play to suit his own purpose by giving full rein to the imaginative elaborations of its plot, as he invariably did with Shakespeare or Chekhov. This, by the way, rather upset Simov. "All that I remember of Ibsen's play," he writes, "is that it was rather a feeble show so far as the stage-designer's art was concerned. The artistic performance of the leading part and the conception of the play itself apparently exercised so powerful an influence on the producer that he could dispense with any additional stage effects. Indeed, any stage tricks or original inventions (as I gathered from Stanislavsky's remarks) were quite superfluous, as they would have distracted the attention of the spectators from the performance itself and would have diminished the effect the play had on them."

Another important clue to the workings of the subconscious mind which Stanislavsky got from his performance of Dr. Stockmann concerned two such important elements of the actor's technique as deportment and gesture. The progress of Stanislavsky's own acting technique from the mere copying of the

mannerisms of his favourite actors to his attempts to train himself before a looking-glass, which merely fixed a number of
specific gestures and facial expressions to the detriment of inner
feeling, and finally to copying living people, has already been
discussed. In his part of Dr. Stockmann this "copying" took a
much subtler form. As a producer, Stanislavsky at this stage of
his career taught his actors the method of reaching to the inner
nature of their parts through the external idiosyncrasies of any
person they knew in life who seemed to approach most closely
their mental picture of the character they had to represent. He
even went so far as to encourage them to make up as the person
they had in mind for the model of their parts. Stanislavsky himself took the composer Rimsky-Korsakov as his model for the
make-up of Dr. Stockmann. In this part, Stanislavsky found
that his stage deportment and gestures seemed to come to him by
themselves. But it only seemed so. When he came to analyse
his acting, he discovered that while he assumed that Stockmann's
gestures, gait and deportment had come to him intuitively, they
had really emerged ready-made from his subconscious mind
where he had stored up a great number of impressions of people
he had met in life and then unconsciously picked out those that
were most characteristic and typical of Dr. Stockmann. Thus
Dr. Stockmann's short-sightedness, his hurried gait, his manner
of walking with the upper part of his body thrust forward, and
particularly the expressive use he made of his fingers—forefinger
and middle finger thrust out and the two other fingers folded
with thumb on top—were all taken from life. "A few years after
the creation of Stockmann," Stanislavsky writes, "I happened to
meet a scholar in Berlin I had met before in a Vienna sanatorium,
and I realized that I had got my fingers in Stockmann's part from
him. Quite likely they came to me unconsciously from that
living model. And my manner of shifting about from foot to
foot *à la* Stockmann I got from a well-known Russian musician
and critic." As for his way of "sawing the air," when engaged in
a heated argument, with his thumb stretched out and forefinger and middle finger as well as third finger and little finger
held close together and the two sets of fingers held apart like
the blades of a pair of scissors, he got it from Maxim Gorky, who
always drove home his point that way. Stanislavsky claimed that
the moment he assumed those external mannerisms off the stage,
the sensations and emotions he felt when playing Stockmann came

to him automatically or, vice versa, his own feelings were transformed into Stockmann's feelings. Moreover, he seemed to be convinced that Gorky's manner of arguing helped him to understand Stockmann's character. The actors always repeated these assertions of their producer with a sceptical smile, and some of them even regarded them as being part of the eccentricity of a great artist. But they were wrong. They had not realized that by that time Stanislavsky had worked out a highly satisfactory method of analyzing his own sensations on and off the stage and was slowly accumulating the material he needed for the formulation of the general laws of acting.

One of the most moving scenes in *An Enemy of the People* occurred towards the end of the fourth act. "Stanislavsky played the scene of the public meeting with such tremendous force," Kachalov's wife, Nina Litovtseva, an actress and later on one of the producers of the Moscow Art Theatre, writes, "that even if the extras who had been instructed how to take part in this crowd scene had been told to remain indifferent, they would not have been able to do so. I shall never forget how deeply moved the two boys, Stockmann's sons, were during that scene, how tears streamed down their faces and how they kissed their father's hands. That had not been part of the original planning of the act, and the boys seemed to have done it all spontaneously because they wanted to do something to comfort their father who was in such despair and who suffered so greatly at that moment. And he hugged the younger boy so tightly to him that it seemed as though he wished to protect him from the fury of the mob. That was one of the most remarkable crowd scenes I ever saw."

It is interesting that during this highly dramatic scene Stanislavsky used scarcely any gestures at all. During his speech he never lifted an arm and he concentrated all his latent energy in his hand, so that, as one actor expressed it, one could see it pouring from his fingers like an electric current.

How brittle an actor's emotional tension can be is shown by a small incident related by Simov. "When Stockmann began his address," he writes, "his audience sat in front of him with their backs to the auditorium which, as it were, formed a continuation of the lecture room. Stanislavsky seemed to be disconcerted by the fact that from his place at the back of the stage he could not see the prompter's box. He knew his speech by heart and did not want any prompting, but he was so used to seeing the prompter's face that without it he did not feel at ease on the stage. What was to be done ? The producer solved the difficulty in a very original manner. He asked the prompter to become a Norwegian woman for one act and to sit on the stage opposite him so that he could see her face all the time. Dressed in a Norwegian costume and hat, the prompter took her place in the first row and holding a notebook in her hand pretended to take down some sentences of Dr. Stockmann's speech. She never actually had to prompt Stanislavsky."

Stanislavsky's habit of keeping a journal of his experiences on the stage, to which many references have already been made, had become almost a routine by the time the Moscow Art Theatre was founded. Every afternoon at five o'clock, when the rehearsals came to an end and the actors went home, Stanislavsky went back to his dressing-room, sat down at his desk and made careful notes of everything that had occurred that day. During the intervals of the performance in the evening, he again noted down whatever had struck him as significant while the play was in progress. After five o'clock Stanislavsky usually remained in the theatre. His dinner was brought in immediately after the rehearsals. It consisted usually of a meat and vegetable course and a sweet. As a rule, he had a bottle of Yessentuki mineral water during his meal. After dinner Stanislavsky took off his coat and lay down for a rest on the sofa. He usually covered himself with his old black overcoat and slept till a quarter past six. He then got up, sat down in his armchair and called for "Jacob", his old and trusted make-up man, Jacob Gremislavsky. His make-up had already been prepared and carefully checked in the morning and was lying in readiness on his dressing-table covered by a clean towel. His costumes, too, were all ready for him to put on. The make-up began with the putting on of the wig. Stanislavsky never put any vaseline on his face, but began directly with the grease-paint. As a rule, he was made up by Gremislavsky, but he used always to check his make-up by comparing it with the plan he had carefully drawn up in his notebook, in which every wrinkle, shape of face, etc., were marked. Occasionally he would draw this plan on a special sheet of paper and pin it on the wall by his mirror. In the same notebook, Stanislavsky kept the list of all the small articles that went with each of his costumes, such as ties, watch, spectacles, pencil and so on. During the first years of the Moscow Art Theatre he would check his costumes personally to see that they were all there and that everything was in order.

His make-up was always prepared from his own descriptions. For the part of Astrov, for example, he wanted chestnut hair, thrown back, but with just the suggestion of a parting. A small beard. For the part of Stockmann he kept his own hair, but wore a fair beard slightly streaked with grey.

However satisfactory his make-up, Stanislavsky invariably said to Gremislavsky, "I say, Jacob, do try and see if you can't find something better." As a rule, Gremislavsky prepared two or three different make-ups, though it was usually the first one that was finally accepted.

During the thirty or forty minutes he spent on his make-up, Stanislavsky was never known to talk to anyone. Once the question of the make-up was settled, he never changed anything and always saw to it that every little part was carefully stowed away in the different empty pill-boxes he kept for that purpose.

Having finished with his make-up, Stanislavsky began to dress. At first he used to buy all his costumes himself. Thus the costumes of Trigorin, Astrov and Stockmann were taken from his own wardrobe. By the first bell Stanislavsky had finished dressing and by the second he was already sitting in his chair in the wings and waiting for his cue.

Stanislavsky's excitement on first nights usually took the form of complete silence. No one, not even his make-up man or dresser, dared to go up to him unless called.

In the theatre Stanislavsky was very economical, as well he might be, considering that for the first ten years the Moscow Art Theatre ran at a loss. But his love of economy took rather extreme forms. For instance, he refused to have a clean shirt for each performance. Sometimes he would ask for his old shirt and, on being told that it had been sent to the laundry, he would lose his temper. "Who asked you to send it?" he would shout. "Don't you know that they ruin shirts at the laundry?" He would always take off his make-up with one side of the towel and wipe his face clean with the other, keeping it to take off his make-up next time and using only one side of the new towel. When he noticed a button on the stage, he would pick it up and tell the wardrobe-mistress to find out who had lost it and have it replaced.

During the intervals he was never known to visit the

greenroom, not even during the run of *Uncle Vanya* and *The Three Sisters* when his wife and another actress had refreshments served there for the actors. A piece of cake had to be sent to his dressing-room. After the performance he would usually remain on the stage for ten or fifteen minutes to see to all sorts of things and only then would he go back to his dressing-room, take off his costume, put on his old overcoat, and after that start taking off his make-up. By the time he had taken it off and made some more notes on the night's performance only the caretakers remained in the theatre. Having put away his notebook, he would send his dresser out for a cab. He was always the last to leave the theatre.

CHAPTER XXXII

"After the success of *The Seagull* and *Uncle Vanya*," Stanislavsky writes, "our theatre simply had to have a new Chekhov play. After that our fate was in the hands of Chekhov : if we got a new play we would have a new season ; if not, our theatre would lose its special atmosphere."

This time they were sure of getting the new play, but Chekhov seemed to be taking an unconscionably long time over it. "Either the play would not write itself," Stanislavsky observes, "or it had been written and Chekhov did not want to send it off till he was absolutely satisfied with it—at any rate, he kept delaying, fobbing us off with the excuse that there were plenty of excellent plays in the world to choose from. His excuses drove us to despair and we kept bombarding him with letters, begging him to send us his play as soon as possible."

At last Chekhov sent them the first and second acts of *The Three Sisters*. "We read them with avidity," Stanislavsky writes, "but as invariably happens with real dramatic masterpieces, we seemed unable to discover the great beauties of the work at the first reading." It was, besides, quite impossible to start rehearsing the play with only two acts. On November 6th, Chekhov himself arrived in Moscow with the last two acts of the play. It was during the discussion that followed the reading of the play by the company that the first serious clash with Chekhov over the interpretation of his plays occurred.

This is how Stanislavsky describes the reading and his subsequent disagreement with Chekhov :

A large table was placed in the foyer of the theatre and we all sat down round it with Chekhov and the producers in the centre. There were present : the entire company, the employees of the theatre, and a few stage-hands and dressers. There was a feeling of excitement in the air. The author looked agitated and ill at ease in the chairman's place. He kept jumping up and pacing the room, especially when the conversation seemed to take a wrong or even unpleasant turn for him. In exchanging our opinions about the play, some of us called it a drama and others a tragedy without realizing that such labels merely threw Chekhov into bewilderment. One of the speakers, with a strong oriental accent, began his speech very pompously : "While disagreeing with the author on principle, I—" That was too much for Chekhov, who took the first opportunity to leave the theatre inconspicuously. When we noticed that he had gone, we did not understand what had happened and at first we thought that he must have been taken ill.

After the meeting Stanislavsky rushed to Chekhov's house and found him "not only upset, but absolutely furious." Stanislavsky, who had never seen Chekhov in such a rage, thought that it must have been the unfortunate "on principle" that had made him lose his patience with them. On second thoughts, however, it occurred to him that there must have been another more important reason. "The author," he explains rather naïvely, "was apparently convinced that he had written a gay comedy, while at the reading of the play everybody had taken it as a drama and wept as they listened. That made Chekhov think that his play had not been understood and had failed."

As usual, Stanislavsky exaggerates a little. Chekhov could not possibly have told him that he had written a gay comedy (that happened later, with *The Cherry Orchard*). He himself called *The Three Sisters* a "drama". But there could be no doubt that Chekhov was convinced that his play had been misunderstood or that he was right in feeling that it would consequently be a failure. Indeed, so little did Stanislavsky and Nemirovich-Danchenko (who supervised the "literary" part of the production) understand the play or Chekhov's methods as a dramatist that it only just scraped through the rehearsals.

"We used to arrive at the rehearsals," Stanislavsky writes, "work hard on the play, lose heart, go home, and next day the same thing happened all over again. Something was lacking, but what that magic *something* was we did not know." At last one of them (Stanislavsky does not say who, but as likely as not it was himself) declared that they were just wasting their time and that they might as well try to act the play as though it were a "light comedy". They tried it, but at the quickened tempo of a light comedy it was impossible to make out what was happening on the stage. It was only when the confidence of the actors in their producer was on the point of being lost that the "magic something" materialized itself in the true Stanislavsky manner, that is to say, what Stanislavsky took to be the right *mood* was suddenly created in some purely accidental and "external" way, which gave him the chance of applying the method he was so fond of at the time, of going from the outer to the inner.

"We were all sitting in different corners of the stage, silent and depressed," Stanislavsky writes. "Two or three electric lamps were burning dimly. The stage was in semi-darkness. I felt that our position was hopeless. My heart was beating fast. Someone began scratching the bench on which he was sitting with his nails and the sound of it was like the scratching of a mouse. For some reason it made me think of a family hearth ; I felt a warm glow all over me ; I sensed truth and life, and my intuition began to work. It is of course also possible that the sound of the scratching mouse combined with the darkness and the helplessness of my position had been of some significance in my life before and that I had forgotten about it. Who can say what the ways of the subconscious mind are ? Be that as it may, I suddenly *felt* the scene we were rehearsing. I felt at home on the stage. The Chekhov characters came to life. Apparently they were not all wallowing in their depression, but were longing for gaiety and laughter. I sensed the truth of such an attitude towards the Chekhov characters, and that filled me with courage and I realized intuitively what had to be done."

However, it seemed that the sound of the scratching mouse and Stanislavsky's rather astonishing *volte face* about the Chekhov characters made little difference so far as Chekhov himself was concerned. Chekhov could not stand the thought of another failure similar to the failure of *The Seagull* at the Alexandrinsky Theatre in Petersburg and he decided to clear off in good time. No doubt the worry about the fate of *The Three Sisters* had a rather bad effect on his health, too. At any rate, when he left for Nice at the end of December he gave his bad health as an excuse. "But," Stanislavsky writes, "I can't help thinking that there was another reason, namely his worry about the success of the play. This is confirmed by the fact that he did not leave his address with us to let him know the result of the first performance of his play."

And well may Chekhov have felt worried. The first night of *The Three Sisters* was a flop, though not by any means such a flop as the first night of *The Seagull* in Petersburg. "The success of the play," Stanislavsky declares rather guardedly, "was rather indefinite." After the first act there was a great deal of applause and the actors had to take about twelve calls. After the second act they had only one call ; after the third "only a few people clapped rather hesitantly," and after the fourth there was only one call. Still, they had to do something about Chekhov, and they decided that, considering the state of his health, a white lie was entirely justified. So the following telegram in rather curious French was dispatched to him by Nemirovich-Danchenko, addressed *"Poste Restante, Naples*[1] : *Premier acte énormes rappels dix fois. Seconde acte parut long. Troisième grand succès. Après le fin rappels ont tournés en veritable ovation. Public a démandé te télégraphier. Les artistes ont excessivement bien joué. Surtout les dames. Salut de tout théatre."* The play, in fact, only ran a few times during its first Moscow season.

It took the theatre over three years to get the play on its feet, after which, unlike *The Seagull*, it was never taken out of the repertoire and its success steadily increased with the passing years. So did Stanislavsky's personal success in the part of Vershinin, though he himself never felt satisfied "because," he writes, "I could never achieve that creative state of mind in which a complete fusion between the actor and his part takes place."

Stanislavsky was always a severe critic of himself and, besides, after his deeply satisfying experience in the part of Dr. Stockmann, a part like that of Vershinin, which only came to him after a great deal of nerve-wracking work, could not possibly gratify him entirely. Olga Knipper, who played Masha in *The Three Sisters*, has left quite a different account of Stanislavsky in the part of Vershinin. "In Stanislavsky's Vershinin, the only dreamer in *The Three Sisters*," she writes, "there was great nobility, restraint and purity. His dreams of a brighter future helped him to carry on and put up with the wretched conditions of his time and his own

---

[1] Chekhov first went to Nice, but before the first night of *The Three Sisters* he planned to go to North Africa without leaving his address. As, however, the sea was very stormy, he went to Italy instead and asked for his letters to be sent *poste restante*, Naples.

In Nice he saw Nemirovich-Danchenko, but found his interpretation of the play no less objectionable than Stanislavsky's. "When I met Nemirovich-Danchenko here and discussed the play with him," he wrote to Olga Knipper on January 14th, 1901, "I was fed up and I could not help feeling that it would most certainly be a flop and that I would never again write for the Moscow Art Theatre."

personal failures and misfortunes. I can still hear his voice and his little laugh in the first act—'Yes, yes—the lovesick Major—that's so.' Or—'There is a dreary bridge on the way there, and under that bridge the water flows noisily. A lonely man can't help feeling melancholy.' Or—'It is just such flowers that I seem to have missed in my life.' Or—'In another two hundred, three hundred, or maybe a thousand years—it does not matter how long —a new and happy life will dawn. We shan't have any part in it, of course, but it is just for that sort of life that we live and work now, that we suffer and do our best to bring it about—and that is the only purpose of our existence, and if you like, it is our only happiness.' And I, Masha, was pleased to hear his voice, which I loved already. I felt so happy when I looked at his eyes which seemed to gaze somewhere far away, or heard his quiet laugh as he talked, a laugh that seemed to express some deep emotional feeling. Vershinin-Stanislavsky knew how to make those speeches about a happy future and those dreams about starting life afresh sound not like the vapourings of a man who likes to hear himself talk, but of one who means what he says sincerely, who believes in them because they give a meaning to his life and make it possible for him to rise above the petty misfortunes of his own life which he bears so patiently and meekly. How pure this Vershinin's love for Masha was ! 'I'm in a queer mood today : I just want to go on living !' Vershinin-Stanislavsky says, and he laughs quietly as he hums a snatch of a love-song followed by that undefinable 'tum-tee-tum'—and the faces of Vershinin and Masha are radiant with love. They understand the meaning of that 'tum-tee-tum.' And when a little later Vershinin's voice is heard from behind the scenes again humming the same little tune, Masha knows what she has to do. She echoes his little tune and away she goes to him with a heart overflowing with love. And how easy I—Masha—found it to confess my love for a man like Vershinin to my sisters : at first I thought him strange, then I was sorry for him, and then I fell in love with him—I loved him for what he was, with his voice, his words, his misfortunes, and his two little girls.

"I cannot recall the scene of my parting from this Vershinin without tears," Olga Knipper goes on. "When I left my dressing-room for this parting, I did not feel the ground under my feet. It was as though I were being carried along by some unknown power. And how apt it is that Chekhov gave Masha only one word—'goodbye'. I treasure the memory of this Vershinin in my heart and I am eternally grateful to him for making it possible for me to experience on the stage such a love as Masha's love for Vershinin."

There can be no doubt about the genuineness of this tribute from Knipper, one of the most outstanding actresses of the Moscow Art Theatre, but it must be remembered that it refers to the Vershinin of Stanislavsky's last years on the stage rather than to his earlier appearances in this part. He played Vershinin about 300 times in 27 years, not counting his appearances in it abroad, and it was actually the last part in which he appeared on the stage during the celebrations of the thirtieth anniversary of the foundation of the Moscow Art Theatre.

CHAPTER XXXIII

SOON AFTER Chekhov had left Moscow for Nice, Stanislavsky had another meeting with Count Tolstoy. This time it was the Countess who, forgetting her angry outburst against Stanislavsky a few years earlier, approached him with the request to take part in a charity concert she was organizing with her husband's benevolent support. She was particularly anxious for a play-reading by members of The Moscow Art Theatre Company and, being a rather astute business woman, she suggested that Chekhov's still unperformed new play would prove a great draw for the aristocratic public she had in mind. She took good care that her illustrious husband should be present at her interview with Stanislavsky. Tolstoy himself does not seem to have uttered a word during the whole of this interview, but his presence was sufficient to deprive Stanislavsky of all powers of resistance. "I must confess," Stanislavsky wrote to Chekhov, "that I felt so shy in Tolstoy's presence that I did not have the courage to refuse the Countess's request. I merely said that without your consent I had not the right to permit the reading of extracts from a play that had not yet been performed on the stage. Now," he went on, "you are my only hope : don't give your consent ! "

Having thus shifted the onus of refusing Countess Tolstoy's request on to Chekhov, Stanislavsky went on to suggest that Chekhov should give her something else (the last thing Chekhov wanted to do) because such a reading in a large hall before "a fashionable, *décolletée* audience" by two or three actors was bound to have an undesirable effect on the play. "So for God's sake," he implored Chekhov, "don't give your consent or try and find some other solution. I am awfully sorry—got shy ! The Countess is expecting to get a letter or even a telegram from you soon."

Chekhov's reply to this appeal from Stanislavsky has not been preserved, but it is evident from Stanislavsky's next letter, written in January, 1901, that Chekhov was more than annoyed at being saddled with so uncongenial a task as refusing a request from the Tolstoys. Fortunately, that was not necessary. As Stanislavsky explained, the charitable concert was not going to take place after all. "I am sorry you were troubled," he writes, "but I merely wrote that letter to you because I wanted to find a more convenient way of refusing the Countess."

Stanislavsky's correspondence with Gorky also began at this time. Gorky had visited the Moscow Art Theatre during a rehearsal in May, 1900, with Leopold Sulerzhitsky, who was to become Stanislavsky's closest friend (the only real friend he had after Kashdamanov). He had also been to see a performance of *An Enemy of the People* at the end of October. He was now writing from Nizhny-Novgorod, his native city, where he was kept under police supervision, to ask Stanislavsky to get Morozov to send him money to buy winter clothes for a thousand poor children for whom he was organizing a New Year's party. Stanislavsky got him the money, and in his second letter Gorky, after thanking Stanislavsky for his help, made an observation about the general tendency of the Moscow Art Theatre which was destined to play a significant part in the development of Stanislavsky's ideas many years later. "What you all, and especially your theatre, have not been given is enough gladness," Gorky wrote. "I'd like to let in a ray of sunshine on your stage," he went on, "happy sunshine—Russian sunshine, not too bright, but all-embracing and all-loving."

And this was what Gorky had to say about Stanislavsky himself : "I think you are a marvel ! You're a talented fellow and no mistake, and your heart, too, is like a mirror. How clearly you snatch from life her smiles, the sad and kind smiles on her stern face ! "

While the question of building a new theatre still remained undecided, the founders of the Moscow Art Theatre felt sufficiently established at the end of this season to open a school of dramatic art. Only those applicants were to be accepted whose "stage individuality was interesting from the point of view of the theatre." To give the students time to show whether they possessed this "stage individuality", they were required to spend one winter at least in the theatre as "contributors", that is to say, to take part as extras in crowd scenes or take walking-on parts

under the supervision of the producer ; they were also expected
to be present at all the rehearsals, take an interest in the work of
the theatre, familiarize themselves with its demands, and so on.
In spring these probationers had to pass an examination, and,
if successful, they were admitted to the school.

But before the foundation of its school, which existed for thirteen years, the Moscow Art Theatre went on its first tour to Petersburg to replenish its dwindling funds. The deficit of the theatre,
Stanislavsky explains in describing this first tour of the theatre
which was to become an annual event, increased every month in
spite of its artistic success and something had to be done to save
it from collapse till it could get firmly on its feet. As the new
season usually started at the end of the autumn and went on till
February or March of the following year, Stanislavsky decided to
take the whole company to Petersburg for about a month during
which the last season's most popular plays were to be presented
to a different audience. Stanislavsky was rather doubtful about
the success of this experiment since as a rule what pleased a
Moscow audience was sure to displease a Petersburg one. But
it seemed that this rule did not apply to the Moscow Art Theatre :
before the beginning of its Petersburg season all the tickets were
sold out in spite of the rather lukewarm reception the theatre had
received in the Press. Curiously enough, it was Chekhov who
was the chief attraction of this first season of the Moscow Art
Theatre in Petersburg : *Uncle Vanya* and *The Three Sisters* were
performed nine times each to packed and enthusiastic houses,
while *An Enemy of the People* was performed only four times,
Hedda Gabler twice, and the two Hauptmann plays, *The Lonely*
and *The Driver Henschel*, twice respectively. In a telegram to
Chekhov on March 6th, Nemirovich-Danchenko could truthfully
announce "the tremendous success" of *Uncle Vanya* as well as the
fact that the Petersburg dramatic critics were unanimous in their
opinion that Stanislavsky as Astrov gave by far the best performance in the play. Next day he wired Chekhov that, in spite of the
unanimous praise, the notices in the papers were on the whole
"vulgar and superficial" and that Hauptmann's *The Lonely*
was a failure. Wiring Chekhov again on March 15th, Nemirovich-Danchenko told him of the success of *The Three Sisters*,
adding that "the Petersburg public is much more cultured and
sympathetic than the Moscow one," a rather oblique admission
of the misleading telegram he had sent him after the Moscow

first night of the play. "The success of the theatre in Petersburg," he informed Chekhov, "is quite unprecedented." And as a warning to Chekhov not to take the notices he read in the Petersburg papers seriously, he concluded his telegram with the assurance that "the bark of the newspapers is worse than their bite." And as final proof of the success of his two plays, he sent a telegram to Chekhov with the news that his royalties from the performances would amount to over 3,000 roubles, that is, almost as much as Chekhov had received for a whole year from the Moscow performance of *The Seagull* and *Uncle Vanya*. They did not think it wise to try a Petersburg audience with *The Seagull* again.

CHAPTER XXXIV

ON HIS RETURN TO Moscow, Stanislavsky spent six weeks on the rehearsals of Ibsen's *The Wild Duck* and Hauptmann's *Michael Kramer*, the two plays which were to open the next season of the Moscow Art Theatre. Gorky's promised play did not arrive. "I'm in terrible trouble," he wrote to them. "All these characters in my play are not giving me a moment's rest. They crowd round me, push me about, refuse to be put in their proper places, are constantly quarrelling with one another. My goodness, how they talk ! They just go on talking and talking and, you know, they talk so well that I simply haven't got the heart to stop them ! " The play—*The Lower Depths*—was not finished in time, and Gorky had to give the theatre his first play—*The Artisans*—and even that arrived too late. However, the Petersburg success considerably improved the relations between Stanislavsky and Nemirovich-Danchenko and there were no scenes during the rehearsals of the Ibsen and Hauptmann plays. "My relations with Alexeyev," Nemirovich-Danchenko wrote to Chekhov at the end of June, 1901, "are now better than ever and they remind the company of the days of the foundation of the theatre"—a rather ominous confession. "This," he added rather smugly, "always happens when I take everything into my hands energetically."

In June, Stanislavsky went off to the Caucasus for his annual cure, and as usual he was bored at first and spent his time writing "business letters", including a letter to Shalyapin. But towards the end of his stay in Yessentuki things seem to have improved considerably. He had met two well-known actresses and spent his time sightseeing and picnicking. One of them, Yablochkina, he found "very sweet" and with her he went for moonlight walks, had rides on *troikas*, talked a lot and, Stanislavsky added in his letter to his wife, "very daringly". In August, Stanislavsky was back in Moscow. The rehearsals of *The Wild Duck* were not going well. "At first," he wrote to his wife in Lyubimovka, "yesterday's rehearsal made a bad impression on me, but it improved later on, though the play as a whole is heavy and boring (I'm telling you this as a great secret). I am rather apprehensive about its fate." At the next rehearsal of Ibsen's play he felt a little more hopeful about it. He was feeling much more energetic and in "good producing form". He had a temperature, though, and was gargling and taking quinine.

The rehearsals of *Michael Kramer*, which had been postponed a few times, were also getting under way. Stanislavsky, who played the title part in the play, had great difficulty in finding the right make-up for it. He collected the whole company and, putting on different make-ups one after another, kept asking them their opinion. The company, presented with so wonderful an opportunity of getting their own back on their producer, took full advantage of it. Every time Stanislavsky appeared from his dressing-room in a new make-up, cries were raised : "No good ! Worse than ever ! " Stanislavsky rushed back to his dressing-room in despair, put on another make-up, which was again found unsatisfactory. It never occurred to him that anyone could be pulling his leg on a matter as important as the right make-up for his part. The play was only moderately successful.

He was also rehearsing *The Three Sisters*, having decided to give the play another trial in Moscow after its great success in Petersburg.

The dress rehearsal of *The Wild Duck* went off all right, but, Stanislavsky wrote to his wife, "on the whole I can't help feeling that the play will be boring." The play, with which the season was opened on September 19th, was, as Stanislavsky had anticipated, a failure, but by that time he had fallen ill with pneumonia, which kept him in bed for about six weeks. Contrary to all expectations, *The Three Sisters* saved the situation : it played to full houses that season. None of the new plays was a success. Gorky's play arrived too late and was only put on during the company's second tour in Petersburg and that only after Nemirovich-Danchenko had assured the authorities that the season-ticket holders alone would be admitted to its performances. Its first night was on March 25th, 1902, and the distant rumblings of the approaching revolution had made the authorities panicky and policemen in plain clothes filled the theatre to prevent gate-crashing by students.

In 1902, the Moscow Art Theatre moved to its new quarters. Morozov, who rebuilt the old Omon Theatre in Kamergersky Lane at his own expense and made an up-to-date modern theatre of it, insisted that it should be organized as a limited company with a working capital of 50,000 roubles, most of which was advanced by Morozov himself. The shareholders included most of the actors of the theatre as well as Morozov, Simov and Chekhov. The management of the new theatre consisted of Stanislavsky, Nemirovich-Danchenko, Morozov and Luzhsky. Stanislavsky now became the chief producer and had to produce four of the six plays of the season. Luzhsky was put in charge of the cast and had to produce one play each season. Nemirovich-Danchenko was given the title of "artistic director" and made the chief link between the theatre and the literary world, and "adviser" for all the productions of the theatre ; he himself was to produce only one play each season. Morozov, much against Nemirovich-Danchenko's will, was put in control of the affairs of the theatre as Chairman of the Board of Management. A special clause in the constitution of the new theatre laid it down that "the repertoire of the theatre must confine itself to plays which have a social interest, and those plays which have no such interest are not to be included in the repertoire of the theatre even though they might be sure of financial success."

According to Stanislavsky, Morozov's motto when building the new theatre was : everything for the actor and for art ; for then, he claimed, the spectator, too, would feel happy in the theatre. "In other words," Stanislavsky writes, "Morozov did exactly the opposite of what is usually done at the building of a theatre, when three-fourths of the available capital is spent on the auditorium, the foyer, and the special bar-rooms for the audience, and only one-fourth on the actors, art, and the stage. Morozov, on the contrary, did not spare any money for the stage and its equipment and for the dressing-rooms of the actors, while the part assigned to the audience he decorated in the simplest possible style according to the designs of the architect, Franz Schechtel, who planned the theatre free of charge (it was Schechtel who suggested that the flying seagull should become the emblem of the theatre). Not a single bright or gold spot was admitted into the colour scheme, so that the spectator's eyes should not be tired unnecessarily and the whole effect of bright colours should be kept exclusively for the scenery."

The new theatre was built in a few months, Morozov supervising the work personally. "He lived," Stanislavsky writes, "in a little room near the office amid the din and clatter and the clouds of dust raised by the builders." Morozov paid special attention to the building and equipment of the stage, which was of the revolving type, so that not only the floor but the whole basement, with its trap-doors and all sorts of improved stage contrivances for the erection of mountains or the representation of valleys and streams, revolved with the floor. Morozov, who was himself a good amateur electrician, also provided the latest lighting equipment for the stage.

CHAPTER XXXV

THE FIRST SEASON of the new theatre opened on November 19th, 1902, with Tolstoy's play *The Power of Darkness*. Stanislavsky's first approach to the play was along the line of "intuition and feeling", but, as he himself declares, "something went wrong and I found myself producing the play on the line of ordinary, every-day life," or in other words, in accordance with the purely naturalistic tendencies of the theatre at the time.

The rehearsals of the play began in spring. Stanislavsky had made his own adaptation of the two versions of the fourth act but, afraid to approach Tolstoy directly for his approval of the changes he had made, since the play had already got him into trouble with Tolstoy's wife, he wrote to Chekhov to ask him to send the play to Tolstoy. "It would be a good idea," he wrote rather cautiously, "to show my alteration (no—that's a dangerous word—my adaptation) to Count Tolstoy. If he agrees, it would be nice if he would just write 'I agree. L. Tolstoy.' I am sorry to trouble you, but I don't know whom to approach. Perhaps Dr. Altschuler[1] might choose a convenient moment to discuss this matter, which is so important to us, with the Count."

By that time (May, 1902) Stanislavsky's correspondence with Chekhov had become very cordial. Stanislavsky's part in Chekhov's vindication on the Petersburg stage must have done a great deal to remove the feeling of mistrust with which Chekhov had regarded Stanislavsky. Indeed, there can be no doubt that it was Chekhov himself who took the first step in patching up their misunderstandings, for already, in January, 1902, he had written Stanislavsky "a wonderfully sincere and cordial letter," which deeply moved Stanislavsky and, as he wrote to Chekhov, "even brought tears to my wife's eyes." Chekhov set about effecting his reconciliation with Stanislavsky in the right way :

[1] The doctor who attended Chekhov and Tolstoy.

he had long ago discerned the streak of vanity in Stanislavsky's character which it took Stanislavsky himself so long to get rid of, and he had asked him for his autographed photograph for the library of his native town of Taganrog, which he kept constantly supplied with books and autographed photographs of famous men. "I feel embarrassed and flattered," Stanislavsky wrote to Chekhov, "that the Taganrog library should want my photograph. Please, don't think that I'm being insincere. I really don't know what to do in such a case. Suppose I send you an ordinary unframed cabinet photograph, won't they say 'What a stingy blighter he is ! Too mean to send us a large portrait in a nice frame !' And if I send them a large photograph in a frame, they might say 'Isn't he glad to have got into a museum ! ' What am I to do ? I should be so grateful to you if you would add a line to one of your letters to your wife (Chekhov and Olga Knipper, one of the leading actresses of the Moscow Art Theatre, had got married on May 25th, 1901) to say what sort of a photograph I ought to send : a cabinet one or a little larger one ? And please don't forget to convey my thanks. to those who have done me this honour."

No doubt Chekhov supplied the necessary information.. The ice was broken ; but it was not until later in the year that their relationship became more intimate. This was brought about by the illness of Chekhov's wife. Olga Knipper fell very seriously ill during the theatre's second Petersburg season in 1902, and Stanislavsky, together with Chekhov, watched over her day and night. Before that, Stanislavsky declares in his reminiscences of Chekhov, "I could never feel quite at ease in Chekhov's company. I could never forget that I was in the presence of a famous man, and I always tried to appear cleverer than I was. This attitude of mine probably embarrassed Chekhov, who liked people to be natural with him. And it was only during the long days I spent with him in his wife's sick-room that I succeeded for the first time in putting our relationship on a natural footing."

The trouble with Stanislavsky was that, unlike Chekhov, he was brought up in a wealthy patriarchal family where all the children stood in awe of their father. There was, besides, the additional difficulty of his strained relations with his mother, who had always shown a preference for her eldest son and, if not a dislike, then an unconcealed coldness for her second son, who had been such a sickly child and had caused her so much concern by his unsocial behaviour in the drawing-room. It was only after Stanislavsky had become famous that his mother began to show how proud she was of him, though even then their relationship had never really become simple and cordial. This feeling of uneasiness and awe in the presence of his parents Stanislavsky projected into his relations with people who, as it were, occupied a position of prominence similar to that occupied by his parents. He could not help feeling and behaving like a boy in the presence of Tolstoy or Chekhov. And his first impulse after overcoming his shyness was also a purely boyish one : he began to brag about things that really did not matter. This involved him in a very painful scene with Chekhov. They had become so friendly that Chekhov's natural reserve with strangers disappeared and he asked Stanislavsky, who had been bragging to him about his proficiency with a hypodermic syringe, to give him an injection of arsenic. Stanislavsky agreed with enthusiasm and set about preparing the hypodermic for the injection. Chekhov watched him with professional interest, smiling approvingly, obviously impressed by Stanislavsky's efficiency and forgetting that he was dealing with an actor who could easily impress an audience with whatever he happened to do at the moment. When the preparations were finished, Chekhov obligingly lay down on the bed with his face to the wall and Stanislavsky began pushing the needle through the skin of his back. Unfortunately Stanislavsky, as he naïvely puts it, was only used to giving injections with "new and sharp needles", and here he just "happened" to lay his hand on an old needle that had been used many times before. The situation was symbolic : the great producer tried his best to pierce through the skin of the great playwright and found to his dismay that he could not do it. As nothing on earth would induce Stanislavsky to confess his incompetence, he went on jabbing the needle into Chekhov's back. "I must have hurt him badly," Stanislavsky writes, "but he did not even wince. He only gave one little cough and that cough, I remember, finished me. I lost my nerve completely and tried desperately to think of some excuse to get me out of that painful situation." But he was too flustered to think of anything, so he just went through the process of giving the injection as though he had been doing it on the stage. He placed the hypodermic obliquely against Chekhov's body, exerting a little pressure to create the illusion of the prick of a needle. Then he simply pressed it down, ejecting the fluid all over Chekhov's back and shirt. When the operation was over and Stanislavsky was sheepishly putting away the hypodermic, Chekhov turned round and gave Stanislavsky a very charming smile.

"Thank you," said Chekhov, "that was lovely ! "

But though they had arranged beforehand that Stanislavsky should always in future give Chekhov the injections, the matter was never mentioned by them again. Something about Stanislavsky prevented Chekhov from discussing this mishap with him in a natural way, as he would have done with anybody else : their relations may have become friendly, but they never became friends. When, a few months later, Stanislavsky and his family left for the Czech spa of Franzensbad, Chekhov and his wife stayed for some time at Lyubimovka. Stanislavsky did all he could to make their stay as comfortable as possible. Chekhov spent only a short time there, as the damp climate disagreed with him ; but he enjoyed his stay. "I never had a better time," he wrote. He was a keen fisherman, and he did a lot of fishing. He also made friends with Stanislavsky's relatives in the neighbourhood, particularly with one of his cousins, Sergey Smirnov, at whose house he met the rather plain but very jolly English governess Lily ("a very queer person : neither man nor woman," as Stanislavsky's daughter describes her), whom he used later as his model for Charlotte, the governess in *The Cherry Orchard*. After Chekhov's departure for the Crimea, Olga Knipper stayed on at Lyubimovka for another month.

At the beginning of September Stanislavsky and his family were back in Moscow. There a rather disquieting rumour reached him. "Don't be angry with me," he wrote to Chekhov, "but I simply can't help writing to you about what is agitating and worrying me all the time. My wife and I have a feeling that you are no longer satisfied with us and are thinking of breaking with our theatre. I've even been told that you no longer want to be one of our shareholders. The thought that you might be leaving us deprives me of every desire to go on working for the stage. I cannot believe that any pecuniary considerations can possibly play any part in preventing the closest possible collaboration between one of our best Russian writers and an artistic organization which has been created and become consolidated by his works."

Stanislavsky demanded an explanation from Chekhov, for

he felt that his break with the Moscow Art Theatre would discredit it. "There must be some important reason," he wrote, "for the begetter of the theatre, who is mainly responsible for its success, to leave it. Money or the larger or smaller number of shares cannot be the cause of it. I know that I am discussing this question a little too frankly perhaps," Stanislavsky continued, "but I cannot help it, as it has upset me too much. I know that I would not dare to send off this letter if I read it through, so I have decided to send it off without reading it. I am sure you will understand how I feel about it and you won't be angry with me for wanting to keep up our friendly relations and avoid any misunderstandings. Please write just two words : 'I remain,' and you will make me wish to go on with my work. Forgive me for this impulsive appeal to you. Perhaps I ought to have acted differently, but I can't reconcile myself to your leaving us."

It is not clear what made Stanislavsky send this despairing appeal to Chekhov. It must have arisen out of a letter Chekhov had written to Morozov expressing his inability to pay his share[1]. In his reply to Stanislavsky Chekhov denied any intention of severing his relations with the Moscow Art Theatre. "I have never dreamt of doing anything of the kind," he wrote, "and I shouldn't have thought of it even in jest." And to his wife Chekhov wrote, "I refused to become a shareholder because I should never have been able to repay my debt to Morozov, and I don't want to be only a nominal shareholder. You are an actress and, as you are paid much less than you deserve, you can be a shareholder on credit, but I can't."

Stanislavsky's agitation can only be explained by a deep-seated feeling of guilt he had towards Chekhov. He just could not make him out, which was rather strange, seeing that he claimed to understand Chekhov's plays much better than Chekhov did himself. The incongruity of this apparently never struck Stanislavsky, but at the back of his mind he must have been worried by it. Why should Chekhov persist in his quixotic interpretation of his plays when his own interpretation of them seemed to make them so successful on the stage ? He was never sure of Chekhov. He had completely misjudged his genius as a playwright at the

---

[1] At first Chekhov was very eager to become a shareholder of the Moscow Art Theatre. In a letter to his wife on February 2nd, 1902, he wrote : "I am writing to tell Morozov that I agree to become a shareholder and that I am ready to subscribe 10,000 roubles, half to be paid on January 1st, and the rest on July 1st, 1903. See, how generous I am ? "

very start and now that the Moscow Art Theatre had become so closely associated with the name of Chekhov, the whole thing still remained a mystery to him. All he knew was that without Chekhov the theatre, which was dearer to him than his own life, would be lost. They had no new Chekhov play for the coming season. When Stanislavsky wrote his last letter to Chekhov, the rehearsals of Tolstoy's play had already come to an end. Following the now established practice of a thorough study of the locality in which the action of the play takes place, the whole company of the theatre, headed by Stanislavsky, spent a fortnight studying the life of the peasants of the villages in the vicinity of Yasnaya Polyana, Tolstoy's country house. Simov made sketches of the cottages, barns and yards, while the wardrobe mistress copied the clothes worn by the peasants and Stanislavsky and the actors "studied" the local customs and dialect. The "expedition" brought back with them a veritable museum of clothes, shirts, sheepskins, crockery, etc., so that it was hardly surprising that Tolstoy's play was lost sight of in all these naturalistic details of the life of the peasantry. In addition, they brought with them an old peasant and his wife who were to watch over the faithful reproduction of these details of village life. The rather amusing consequence of what had by now become a hoary tradition of a Stanislavsky production was that the old peasant woman put the whole company to shame by the "realism" of her own "acting". She, too, like Stanislavsky and Nemirovich-Danchenko, seemed to regard the author as an interloper, and when Stanislavsky tried to give her one of the minor parts in the play, she excelled Tolstoy himself in the realism of her speech, dispensing with his dialogue and interspersing her own with so many pithy but unprintable expressions that Stanislavsky had to hand her part back regretfully to the actress who was to have played it originally. And yet "when," Stanislavsky writes, "she handed Anissya the powder with which to poison her husband and thrust her crooked hand into her bosom, fumbling between her withered breasts for the packet with the poison, and then, very calm and business-like, began to explain to Anissya how she should proceed gradually and imperceptibly to kill her husband, without showing the slightest understanding of the dreadful nature of the murder, a cold shiver passed down our spines."

This demonstration finally convinced Stanislavsky that, as he put it, "realism on the stage becomes naturalism only when it is justified by the actor from within. Only when it is thus justified, realism either becomes wholly unnecessary or you simply do not notice it because external facts have become saturated with their inner meaning."

Unfortunately, the realism of the external settings of the play was not sufficiently justified from within, so that both the play and its parts were smothered by the faithfully reproduced details of external life. The same thing happened to Stanislavsky's part of Mitrich. He was, as one actress put it, a little "too clever" : his own make-up showed up glaringly the shortcomings of his present methods of production. He had stuck warts on his face, covered his cheeks with a stubbly growth of hair and hidden his mouth in his moustache so that he looked like a grotesque caricature of a peasant. Samarova, an actress who was a close friend of his, could not help remarking apropos of this make-up : "Our Konstantin has covered himself with lumps, he coughs and wheezes, but nothing comes of it." And, in fact, Stanislavsky had in the end to give his part to another actor.

CHAPTER XXXVI

By the time the rehearsals of Gorky's *Lower Depths* were due to begin in the early summer of 1902, Stanislavsky's method of a first-hand study of the "local colour" of a play had become more or less stereotyped. It failed singularly in *The Power of Darkness*, but came off triumphantly in *The Lower Depths*. Stanislavsky's new "expedition" led him only a few streets away from the Moscow Art Theatre to Khitrov Place, the "market" where manual labourers were hired and where tramps, beggars and thieves spent their nights in cheap lodging houses. Neither Nemirovich-Danchenko's "literary" analysis of the play nor Gorky's circumstantial accounts of the life of the people he had used as models for his characters were of any use to Stanislavsky. He wanted something to fire his imagination. He wanted to be among those outcasts of society himself and to see with his own eyes how they lived and what sort of people they were. The visit to their haunts in Khitrov Place became famous because of a dramatic incident which nearly cost Simov his life.

The "expedition" to Khitrov Place was led by Vladimir Gilyarovsky, a Russian writer who specialized in descriptions of low life. He took them to a dosshouse one part of which was occupied by beggars and the other by tramps, including former civil servants, actors and army officers. One army officer, known as "the gentleman", was distinguished by his grand manners and his knowledge of English and French. He was always drunk and walked about mostly in his underclothes. Most of the tramps in this dosshouse were employed by a theatrical agency for copying out the scripts of plays for the Moscow theatres, including the Moscow Art Theatre.

According to a long established custom, the visitors were expected to stand drinks to the inmates of the dosshouse. The drinks were usually provided by the landlady, who had a plentiful supply of cheap corn-brandy which she sold in champagne bottles—the champagne bottles being more difficult to break. The arrival of the visitors from the Moscow Art Theatre was greeted by the tramps with a great show of *bonhomie* and a general air of good fellowship, and the cheers increased in volume when the drinks were fetched and the bottles began to go round. The tramps were soon joined by the beggars from next door and by a number of thieves who crowded in the doorway, appraising professionally the well-dressed "toffs", including the elegantly got up Nemirovich-Danchenko and Luzhsky who sported an expensive diamond ring. Stanislavsky at once singled out "the gentleman", who addressed the visitors as fellow artists who have descended from their theatrical Olympus to the nether regions whose inhabitants, too, serve the great cause of art. "You," he waved an eloquent arm in a torn shirt-sleeve at Stanislavsky, "like gods and we like the powers of the underworld, for you and we alike are men of the theatre." After this grandiloquent oration, "the gentleman" impressed the whole company by roaring out "All right ! " in English, raised his glass with a superb gesture, describing an appreciative semi-circle with it and emptying it at a gulp. He then clicked his heels with an imaginary jingle of spurs and bowed lightly to Stanislavsky.

Stanislavsky immediately attached himself to "the gentleman" : he seemed to him to be an eminently romantic figure of the underworld who could serve him as a model for Satin's part in *The Lower Depths*. They stood talking at the table—two tall figures, both with the exquisite manners of born aristocrats and both treating each other as equals, Stanislavsky wearing an excellent overcoat and a soft hat, "the gentleman" in a torn shirt and a disreputable pair of filthy pants. His beard and moustache, though, were carefully trimmed (Stanislavsky incorporated them into his make-up afterwards), and he appeared to be particularly proud of the beautifully manicured nail of the little finger of his left hand.

Meanwhile Simov had sat down at the table and was busy sketching the room with the bunks and its inmates, who had crowded round him and were making critical remarks about his work. "The gentleman", who kept helping himself to the corn-brandy, was regaling Stanislavsky with a highly imaginative account of the story of his life, interspersed with philosophic observations on the true meaning of freedom. "You must come here if you want to know what life is like," he was saying. "It is only here that you will understand the meaning of the word freedom. Only by sinking to the state of the savage, can you do what you like and live the life of a free man. Why," he shouted, "this is real luxury ! *C'est superbe !* "

Stanislavsky was deeply impressed. "One of the tramps in particular," he wrote in his description of the scene, "charmed me by his fine appearance, his education, his aristocratic manners, his exquisite hands and his fine profile. He spoke almost all European languages excellently, for he had been an officer of the Horse Guards. Having gambled away his fortune, he found himself among the outcasts of society in Khitrov Place, from which, however, he emerged for a time to lead the life of a civilized man again. He married, rejoined his old regiment and was once more wearing his splendid uniform. One day it occurred to him that he would like to visit Khitrov Place to show off his uniform to his old cronies. He soon forgot all about it, but after some time the same thought occurred to him again and again till, finding himself on official business in Moscow, he could no longer resist the temptation, took a walk through Khitrov Place and stayed there for good."

Stanislavsky, who was a romantic by nature and still had a strong hankering after novelette situations, which was one of the reasons he found Chekhov's plays so difficult to understand, had swallowed everything "the gentleman" had told him. Indeed, he found his story so fascinating that he did not notice the appearance of a drunken tramp whose great physical strength had earned him the nickname of "Ivan the Horse". Seizing a bottle of brandy, Ivan the Horse put it to his mouth and, throwing back his head, was about to swallow its contents when he discovered that it was empty. This infuriated him so much that he began to push his way roughly through the crowd round Simov, intending to get hold of the full bottle of vodka he saw on the table. The tramps resented his intrusion and a fight started. Someone hit Ivan the Horse across the face. With a savage roar Ivan the Horse raised the empty champagne bottle and was about to hurl it at Simov's head. It was at that critical moment that Gilyarovsky let out a "five-storied" oath which astonished and delighted everybody, including the tramps who were for a moment stunned with sheer "surprise and æsthetic appreciation", as Stanislavsky put it. Stanislavsky's own account of this incident in *My Life in Art*, by the way, completely misses the vital part Ivan the Horse played in it. Stanislavsky, engrossed in conversation with "the gentleman", evidently believed that the fight had started because of a disagreement between Simov and a tramp about the artistic value of a highly edifying picture, cut out of an illustrated magazine, which depicted an elderly father pointing an accusing finger at a bill of exchange forged by his prodigal son who appeared to be utterly crushed with shame. This mis-interpretation of the famous incident in the dosshouse is typical of Stanislavsky who could only think in the terms of the stage. To him Ivan the Horse was an irrelevance, since action on the stage loses its dramatic force if it is not strictly logical, while in life dramatic action need not always be logical. Anyway, "the gentleman" was quick enough to take advantage of the sudden lull in the fighting to seize the champagne bottle from Ivan the Horse, thus saving Simov's life.

The "expedition" to Khitrov Place served its purpose in that it had aroused Stanislavsky's imagination and creative feeling more than Gorky's talks about his play and Nemirovich-Danchenko's "literary" analysis of it. "At last," Stanislavsky writes, "I had something out of which I could mould the living material of the characters on the stage. Everything had now a realistic basis. Everything was now in its right place. When I wrote my *mise-en-scènes* now I was guided by something I had actually seen and not by mere suppositions and inventions. The chief result of the expedition, however, was that it had made me aware of the inner meaning of the play. 'Freedom at all costs!' The freedom for the sake of which people descended to the lowest depths of life without realizing that they merely became slaves there."

The "stunning effect" produced by the visit to Khitrov Place on Stanislavsky, made him, according to Simov, wish to make the audience experience "the crying injustice" of what he had seen and cause it "to shudder at the senseless sufferings" of these outcasts of society. It had thus supplied him with a strong social incentive for the play, which was to a great extent responsible for its success. Strangely enough, the only part in the play that was weak at first was Stanislavsky's own part of Satin. Again he had copied a living model too closely from life with the result that he was carried away by the "romantic" figure of "the gentleman" and lapsed into his old theatrical habits. There was, besides, the further difficulty that he had to convey to the audience "the social mood of that particular time" and his author's political tendencies as expressed in Satin's long sermons and monologues. He found it impossible to achieve consciously in the part of Satin what he had achieved unconsciously in the part of Dr. Stockmann. For in the part of Satin he "acted" the tendency itself, keeping constantly in mind the play's social and political significance, while in the part of Dr. Stockmann he did not think either of politics or of tendencies, the part being created intuitively, by itself.

The conclusion Stanislavsky drew from this was that "in plays of a social and political significance it is particularly important that the actor himself should live with the thoughts and feelings of his part, for then the tendency of the play will be conveyed by itself. The direct way of tackling the tendency itself, on the other hand, simply leads to overacting."

The first night of *The Lower Depths*, on December 18th, 1902, was another great triumph for Stanislavsky and the Moscow Art Theatre. "The audience," Stanislavsky writes, "kept calling for the producers and the actors and, finally, for the author himself. It was funny to see Gorky appearing on the stage for the first time, smiling with embarrassment and forgetting to take his cigarette out of his mouth before bowing to the audience !"

The play ran for sixty-one performances during its first season alone.

Writing to Chekhov on December 19th, Stanislavsky confessed that the failure of a second play by Gorky would have ruined everything. "Now, as you know already," he continued, "victory is on our side and, what is even more important, Gorky is satisfied. The first night was real hell for the actors and, but for the fine reception of the first act, I doubt if we would have had sufficient strength to bring the play to an end. . . . I am dissatisfied with my own playing, although people praise me. Gorky was present at two performances and was a great success."

The last play of the season, Ibsen's *The Pillars of Society*, which was produced by Nemirovich-Danchenko and in which Stanislavsky played the part of Bernick, was a failure. It was first performed on February 24th, 1903, but already in his letter to Chekhov on December 19th, Stanislavsky was writing : "We are faced with a very difficult time now : instead of the enjoyment of beginning the rehearsals with a play by Chekhov, I have to carry out the onerous duty of rehearsing Ibsen. Pity Knipper and

Stanislavsky most, for they have to carry out the most difficult part of the work." And on February 21st, three days before the first night of *The Pillars of Society*, he wrote in another letter to Chekhov : "We are now engaged on the dress rehearsal of *The Pillars of Society*. If we spent one fourth of the efforts we have spent on this disgusting play on your *Cherry Orchard*, the theatre would collapse from applause and we would have the pleasant prospect of performing your play for several years. But now when we think of the uncertainty of *The Pillars of Society*, we keep repeating your favourite phrase : Who on earth wants it ? ! ! ! "

Stanislavsky was to repeat Chekhov's favourite phrase even more emphatically when writing to him about the next production of the Moscow Art Theatre—*Julius Cæsar*, for Shakespeare's play, which was also produced by Nemirovich-Danchenko, fared even worse than Ibsen's so far as Stanislavsky was concerned, though for quite different reasons.

In April, 1903, Nemirovich-Danchenko informed Stanislavsky that he was going to open the next season with *Julius Cæsar*. There seems to have been a strong disagreement between the two producers about the theatre's repertoire for the coming season. In a letter to Chekhov on December 28th, Nemirovich-Danchenko asked the playwright for his advice about what plays they should put on. Chekhov had completely ignored his request in March of the same year to send a list of plays of his own choice for the theatre's coming season. And, indeed, it is very likely that his resignation as a shareholder of the Moscow Art Theatre in September was caused as much by his reluctance to be involved in the constant disagreements between the two producers about the new repertoire as by his inability to pay his share of 5,000 roubles. In December Nemirovich-Danchenko, who was merely asking for Chekhov's advice, included in his own suggested list of plays *Julius Cæsar*, *Macbeth*, and Goethe's *Faust*. Stanislavsky was evidently against having any of these plays and, failing to agree, they both began writing desperate letters to Chekhov to hurry up with *The Cherry Orchard*. In February, Stanislavsky cautiously expressed the hope that he would let them have his play by March 20th. In the same month Nemirovich-Danchenko was urging Chekhov "to use all the methods of psychology" he knew "to buck up" and write his play "with that wonderfully poetic taste" of his. In March he declared that "without your play we shan't have any new season. Please," he implored Chekhov, "exert yourself a little more and finish your play. Are you writing it at all? Don't read the papers. I find that reading the Press destroys one's desire for work."

But Chekhov, who was very ill (a fact of which both Stanislavsky and Nemirovich-Danchenko seemed to be curiously unaware), could not hurry up. Nor could Stanislavsky and Nemirovich-Danchenko come to any agreement about the next season's plays. In fact, their disagreements seem to have assumed the character of open quarrels. "The more I quarrel with Alexeyev," Nemirovich-Danchenko wrote to Chekhov in February, "the more we draw together, for what unites us is a healthy love for our work." Which, as subsequent events showed, was only true up to a point : Stanislavsky possessed too loyal a character ever to forget the fact that but for Nemirovich-Danchenko the Moscow Art Theatre would never have been founded and that but for him it would never have had its first resounding success with *The Seagull*. But the two of them never became friends. They never addressed each other in familiar terms. And very soon they were to part company as producers. What Nemirovich-Danchenko must have resented most was that their original agreement, which gave him the deciding voice in the choice of plays, had been completely ignored when the new company with Morozov at its head had been formed. "If *The Pillars of Society* turns out to be successful beyond expectation," he wrote to Chekhov in February, "I shall insist on *Julius Cæsar*." But Ibsen's play was far from successful and Stanislavsky's objection to Shakespeare, whose plays seemed to be beyond his grasp, were as strong as ever. But by April a decision had to be made. Nemirovich-Danchenko put his foot down and, faced with the necessity of starting the rehearsals of the new season's plays immediately, Stanislavsky gave in. Once the decision was taken, the usual procedure was followed. An "expedition", headed by Nemirovich-Danchenko, who was to produce the play, and Simov, was dispatched to Italy (they left on May 31st), and during their absence, Stanislavsky organized the actors, by now welded into a homogeneous team, into several groups, each concentrating on a different aspect of the production : the study of the text, "archæological" research, the purchase of the dress material for the costumes, the props and Roman weapons, and so on.

Stanislavsky also began the preliminary rehearsals of the play.

At the first rehearsal he made a statement which rather surprised the actors, but which was very typical of his current attitude and explains his objections to Shakespeare. He told the actors that they must play Shakespeare "in Chekhov tones". He did not specify what he meant by it, nor did the actors take any particular notice of his statement, for none of them intended to play Shakespeare "in Chekhov tones". But what Stanislavsky meant becomes evident when one examines his few *mise-en-scènes* for the play, written in June, 1903. His production notes for the first act are merely a repetition of his former methods of producing a Shakespearean play, the crowd scenes, in particular, being simply a variation of his crowd scenes in *Othello* : there is a Jewish merchant ; a Gaul with a donkey ; flower girls sitting with their backs to the audience ; a Syrian dancing girl performing a "stomach dance" to the accompaniment of a flute in front of a barber's shop, the barber being busy pulling out the superfluous hair from the chests, arms and chins of his customers, who shrieked with pain ; a Roman matron with her two sons and her slaves ; a most realistic representation of a thunder storm, and so on. The "Chekhov tones", however, come to the fore in the scene in Brutus's orchard : toys left lying on the ground by the children of Brutus, who is deeply moved as he catches sight of them during one of the pauses in his soliloquy while he is looking at the distant Rome ; a parrot swaying on a branch ; the head of a stork appearing from behind a bush and squawking while one of the conspirators is trying to catch it ; falling stars— a whole display of meteors rushing across the sky ; and (an echo from his production of *The Seagull*) the croaking of frogs in the distance and the cries of corncrakes and nocturnal birds to emphasize the stillness of the night. This is how he further elaborated the "Chekhov tones" : "the noise of a babbling brook and, if possible, the splashing of a fountain on the stage ; in the distance the barking and howling of dogs, and from time to time the roaring of tigers and other animals in the circuses ; distant shouts of sentries in different voices, approaching and retreating (gramophone) ; the knocking of nightwatchmen (comes through excellently on a gramophone) ; cries of southern frogs like high-pitched bells (accidentally got this sound on a record). Other nocturnal noises."

This over-elaborate use of light and sound effects to bring out the mood of a certain scene had certainly been one of the main causes of the great success of *The Seagull*, but Nemirovich-Danchenko refused to accept them, or at any rate adapted them to suit his own purposes, which were to put on a version of his own "psychological" interpretation not of Shakespeare's play, but of his own notions of what ancient Rome was like at the time of the collapse of the republic. By that time Nemirovich-Danchenko had already evolved his theory of the "creative producer", that is to say, a producer who merely uses the playwright as a peg on which to hang his own ideas of what his play ought really to be like. Such a producer must, above all, be different from every other producer. It was no longer the repetition of the usual Shakespearean stage clichés that Nemirovich-Danchenko was afraid of ; what appalled him was Shakespeare's idiosyncrasies as a playwright : his use of soliloquies, his "heroic" conception of character, his blank verse. What he did, therefore, was to make his actors purposely lower their voices in their soliloquies so that they could hardly be heard and put the entire emphasis of his production on those moments in the play which Shakespeare either did not mention at all or merely hinted at, with the result that some of the most "psychologically" significant moments in the play were acted in dumbshow. As he could not very well dispense with Shakespeare's text altogether and write his own text instead (for that would certainly be Shakespeare no longer), he did his best to push it into the background. And, as the "creative" producer's prerogative was not only to suppress his author, but also to exact complete obedience from his actors, he found no difficulty at all in grafting his idea of "Rome at the time of Julius Cæsar" (Stanislavsky's description of Nemirovich-Danchenko's production) on to Shakespeare's tragedy.

Leonidov, who had only recently joined the Moscow Art Theatre (he played Cassius in *Julius Cæsar*), characterizes Nemirovich-Danchenko's production of the play in these words : "The producer did a tremendous amount of work before even beginning his rehearsals with the actors. In his production he put down not only what Julius Cæsar, Brutus or Antony did or when they spoke, but what the twenty-eighth legionary shouted in the last scene of the battle and to whom he addressed himself. To achieve the greatest possible historical faithfulness, Nemirovich-Danchenko and Simov went to Rome so as to plan all the details of the action on the stage on the actual site of the Forum. Such a method made the actors into passive performers. The actor was given a ready-made interpretation, his text was cut for him, he was told which word to emphasize, he had the *mise-en-scènes* thrust upon him, he was given his costume, carefully checked over by the stage-designer and the history expert, he was taught how to wear his toga, and he was made up. All he was expected to do was to carry out his orders. To argue with the producer was strictly forbidden. To find one's own interpretation of one's part was not permitted. On the other hand, however, the play was produced in time, and we paid a certain tribute to naturalism. Our producer, indeed, seemed to be very enthusiastic about it. The Meiningen company had left its trace on the Moscow Art Theatre : a whole number of scenes and moments in the play showed its influence. There were a great many interpolations, and highly interesting ones, too, but they did not help the spectator to get a better grasp of the play. On the contrary, they distracted him by obtruding themselves too much on his attention. Take this sort of scene, for instance : straight in front of the spectator is a very narrow street, going uphill ; all sorts of shops : one shopkeeper selling arms, someone else selling his slave-girl, someone buying arms and the slave-girl. But what Shakespeare wanted to show in this scene was merely the inception of the conspiracy against Cæsar. A thunderstorm on the stage. That is required by the play. But in our theatre they made such a thunderstorm, such a downpour of rain, such realistic claps of thunder that it was quite impossible to make oneself heard on the stage and I, who played Cassius, had to yell at the top of my voice all the time, for which I was properly taken to task by the critics. Today," Leonidov concludes, "we should never tolerate such a production."

Apart from the "psychology" on which Nemirovich-Danchenko so prided himself, the production of *Julius Cæsar* was merely an imitation of Stanislavsky's own methods, but, strangely enough, instead of reconciling Stanislavsky to the production, it merely convinced him, now that he could watch it as an onlooker rather than as a producer, that his methods had in their turn become theatrical clichés. But he reached that conclusion only after the play had been put on. In April there was still no suspicion in his mind that he had outgrown the wonders of his own inventions. Stanislavsky was hard at work on the preliminary rehearsals of *Julius Cæsar*. Every morning he left Lyubimovka for Moscow and, as he found his work at the factory and at the theatre very tiring, he stayed in Moscow for days on end. In his letters to his wife he complained of headaches and insomnia. "The last two nights," he wrote, "I slept badly. Last night a mouse would not let me go to sleep. I knocked and shouted, but it was no use. At last I started miaowing and scratching the sheet like a cat. At once everything grew quiet and I fell asleep. Don't you think I ought to take out a patent for my new invention against mice and rats ? "

CHAPTER XXXVII

In JULY, AFTER the return of Nemirovich-Danchenko and Simov with the trophies of their expedition, Stanislavsky went for his annual cure to Yessentuki. His little son was ill and he kept worrying about him. "I'm doing my best," he wrote to his wife, "to stop being a pessimist : it is poisoning my life and the lives of other people."

It was a very hot summer and the heat added to his discomfort. Fortunately, Gorky and a few of his friends turned up after a walking tour in the Caucasus, and for a week he spent most of his time with the famous writer. "Gorky and his friends," he wrote to Chekhov, "cheered me up a lot, but they did not stay long. Gorky arrived in fine fettle but he left a very sick man. He caught a cold after a thermal bath on the day he left Yessentuki. While I was speaking to him before the train moved out of the station, I noticed that he went pale suddenly and slumped in his seat. He had fainted. Luckily, there was a doctor I knew on the train and I had time to warn him about Gorky's illness. As the train began to move, Gorky sat clasping his head in his hands and looking white as a sheet. I have sent off a telegram to find out how he is, but so far I have had no reply. I have nothing much to tell you about myself : I get up in the morning, drink the waters, have breakfast, sunbathe, go for a walk, take an alkaline bath, take the train to Kislovodsk and talk a lot of nonsense to Forcatti (the manager of the local theatre) and Davydov (a famous actor), and so every day. The season fever has already started with me. I want to finish quickly with *Julius Cæsar* and start on a new play by Chekhov. I have already made a gramophone record of the shepherd's pipe."[1]

In his letters to his wife Stanislavsky described a characteristic

---

[1] For the production of *The Cherry Orchard*. Chekhov replied : "Your Lyubimovka shepherd plays well. It's exactly what I want."

incident with Gorky. "We went to eat *shashlyk*,[1]" he wrote, "but the moment we sat down we heard heart-rending cries. A little boy was being thrashed in the kitchen. We rushed there to save him. Gorky snatched the child from his mother's hands and told her off properly. There was rather a rowdy scene."

Stanislavsky, who was only forty at the time, though his prematurely grey hair made him look older, was already beginning to feel old. Writing to his wife about a young girl he had met, he remarked, "The part of a father is much more in my line than the part of a lover." Towards the end of his stay even the weather had changed and it was raining almost every day, but he was soon back in Moscow where the rehearsals of *Julius Cæsar* began in earnest.

Stanislavsky played Brutus in *Julius Cæsar* and, according to the strict rules of the producer-autocrat he himself had laid down, he had to follow Nemirovich-Danchenko's interpretation of the part. "My whole tone and tempo for the second act," Nemirovich-Danchenko told Stanislavsky, "and especially for Brutus, is quite different from yours, and I must insist that you should follow my directions implicitly : I have spent a very long time in working on that scene." It was a case of a Daniel come to judgment. But that Stanislavsky would perhaps not have minded so much. After all, he had put himself entirely under Nemirovich-Danchenko's authority when rehearsing *Uncle Vanya*. There was a much more powerful personal reason which made the part of Brutus particularly distasteful to him and in this way, no doubt, sharpened his critical perceptions not only about his own abilities as an actor, but also about his stale methods of production, and perhaps even sowed the first seeds of dissatisfaction with the whole conception of producer-autocrat. The reason was that in the part of Brutus he had to shave off his moustache.

Stanislavsky's moustache had always been a great worry to Gremislavsky, his make-up man. "I must say," Gremislavsky writes, "that the most difficult part of his make-up was that, however much we begged him, he would not part with his moustache, and he had a very large and thick moustache which I had to spread out all over his face and cover up with putty when making him up. In *Julius Cæsar* I tried to cover it up entirely, but nothing came of it. At last Stanislavsky agreed to have it shaved off, but only after I had assured him that I would make

---

[1] Caucasian dish : slices of mutton roasted on spits.

him a moustache that was absolutely indistinguishable from his own and which he could wear whenever he wanted."

But his moustache meant more to Stanislavsky than Gremislavsky suspected. Writing to his wife in September, 1903, Stanislavsky asked her what he was to do about shaving off his moustache. "I shall have to shave it off by next Sunday for certain, but I dare not do it without you, for it is your moustache and not mine. Write to me please whether you won't mind my having it shaved off without you."

But personal vanity and intimate memories, important and excusable though they be, were not the only thing that made him feel the loss of his moustache so deeply. There was a much more important reason that made him loath to part with it. Ever since his adolescence the moustache had acted as a screen between him and the world ; it gave him the confidence in himself that he lacked so badly when associating with people ; without it he felt unprotected and naked. That, too, must have greatly increased his difficulties with his part of Brutus and considerably sharpened his sense of dissatisfaction with himself. And the result was that on the first night of *Julius Cæsar*, on October 10th, 1903, Stanislavsky suffered his first great failure on the stage.

"The success of the play," Nemirovich-Danchenko wrote to Chekhov, "was uneven. In some places, to judge from the applause, it had a splendid reception, but in others the reception was much less enthusiastic. Some actors, and I am sorry to say Stanislavsky in particular, were not liked at all."

At the end of October, Stanislavsky, in a letter to Chekhov, spoke of "the hateful *Julius Cæsar*". In November, in another letter to Chekhov, he wrote : "There is only one good thing about *Julius Cæsar*, namely, it leaves me time to write these notes to you, which gives me a lot of pleasure though I expect you will hardly find them amusing." In another letter to Chekhov he was more specific. "You ask me," he wrote, "why I don't like *Julius Cæsar*. The reply is really very simple : I don't like it because I am not successful in it." And again some days later : "My only trouble is *Julius Cæsar*. I wish I could chuck everything and think only of *The Cherry Orchard*, but as soon as I feel in the right mood for it, I have to play Brutus in his heavy, hot toga, bare legs, cold armour and—those long speeches ! I go on playing, but I can't help asking myself who on earth wants it."

At last in October Stanislavsky received from Chekhov the manuscript of *The Cherry Orchard*, read it at once, and was "so excited" that he was hardly able "to collect his thoughts". He at once sent off a telegram to Chekhov in which he declared the play to be "the best of all the beautiful things" he had ever written, congratulated him as "a writer of genius", and thanked him for the great pleasure he had been given and would still be given in reading the play.

Stanislavsky's excitement worried Chekhov. He still did not trust him. "I received a telegram from Alexeyev today," he wrote to his wife on October 21st, "in which he calls my play the work of a writer of genius. That is equivalent to overpraising it and depriving it of half the success it might have under favourable circumstances." But Chekhov's disquiet increased when he received Stanislavsky's letter written on the day he had sent off the telegram.

"In my opinion," Stanislavsky wrote, "*The Cherry Orchard* is your best play. I am even more fond of it than of your sweet *Seagull*. It is definitely not a comedy or a farce, as you wrote, but a tragedy, whatever solution you may have found in the last act. The impression it made on me was tremendous, and you achieved it all in half-tones, in delicate water-colours. It has more poetry and lyricism and is more scenic than any other of your plays. All the parts, even that of the tramp, are brilliant. If I were to choose between the parts I liked most, I should be in difficulties, so much does each part appeal to me. I am afraid, though, that it is much too subtle for our audiences. It will take a long time before they will be able to appreciate all its subtleties. Alas, how much nonsense I shall have to read and hear about it ! All the same its success I am sure will be enormous, and it grips me powerfully. It is so compact that it is impossible to cut a single word out of it. Perhaps I am partial, but I can't find a single fault in it. One fault it does possess, though. It requires great and sensitive actors to reveal all its beauties. At the first reading I was struck by the fact that I was immediately entranced by it and that it came to life at once. That did not happen to me either with *The Seagull* or with *The Three Sisters*. I am used to receiving rather confused impressions from the first reading of your plays. That was why I feared so much that I would not find the play as entrancing at the second reading. But, dear me, I wept like a woman. I tried to pull myself together, but couldn't. I can hear you say, 'But, look here, this play is a farce ! ' No, for the ordinary man it is a tragedy. I feel a special kind of tenderness and love for this play. I have heard hardly a single critical remark about it, though actors like to criticise. This time everybody seemed somehow to have followed my lead at once. And if someone does try to criticise something in it, I just smile and do not even take the trouble to argue. Someone remarked that the best act is the fourth and the least successful—the second. I find such an opinion absurd, but I don't argue. I just begin recalling one scene after another, and the critic is flummoxed. The fourth act is so good because the second act is so splendid, and *vice versa*. I have declared this play to be beyond criticism. Anyone who does not understand it, is a fool. That is my sincere opinion. I shall be delighted to act in it and, if it were possible, I should have gladly acted every part, including that of dear Charlotte. Thank you, dear Anton Pavlovich, for the great pleasure your play has already given me and for the even greater pleasure it will give me in future. How I wish I could chuck everything, throw off the burdensome yoke of Brutus and live all day with *The Cherry Orchard*. The horrible Brutus is getting me down. I hate him even more after your sweet *Cherry Orchard*. I press your hand warmly, and please don't think I am a neurotic old woman. Your loving and devoted Alexeyev."

What is the real meaning of this overwrought letter ? It can hardly be considered a serious piece of criticism, and Chekhov certainly did not consider it as such. Its highly emotional tone can only be explained by two things : first, Stanislavsky's utter disgust with *Julius Cæsar* as produced by Nemirovich-Danchenko, and, secondly, his determination to produce *The Cherry Orchard* without any interference from anybody. This time it was he who put his foot down. Nemirovich-Danchenko was far from impressed by *The Cherry Orchard*. It was he who found the fourth act the best and the second the weakest. "I am very worried by certain crudities in the play which I dislike," he wrote to Chekhov on October 18th. "Again, there are too many tears. From the social point of view the subject is not new but it is revealed in a new, poetic, and original light." And on October 27th he wrote to Chekhov : "Perhaps I am not so excited about the play as Alexeyev seems to be. He keeps on saying that you have never written anything more talented or more powerful. But if I do not agree with him, I don't want to dispute his statements, for it is undoubtedly a very talented and powerful play."

Chekhov himself must have made clear to Nemirovich-Danchenko his anxiety about allowing Stanislavsky a free hand with *The Cherry Orchard*, but this time he did not find his old friend so eager to act as mentor to his fellow-producer. "As the producer," he wrote to Chekhov on November 7th, "Alexeyev must be allowed more freedom in *The Cherry Orchard*. First of all, he has produced no play for over a year and he must therefore have accumulated a great store of energy and imaginative invention ; secondly, he understands you excellently ; and, thirdly, he has left his whimsies a long way behind."

Chekhov was a sick man (how sick neither Nemirovich-Danchenko nor Stanislavsky ever suspected), and he gave way. On the first night the play was, in fact, only "moderately successful", according to Stanislavsky, who adds that "we blamed ourselves for our inability to reveal from the very first what was most important, beautiful and valuable in the play."

As with every other Chekhov part, it took Stanislavsky a long time before he brought the part of Gayev in *The Cherry Orchard* to a high pitch of perfection. In the end it became one of his most famous parts. Olga Knipper, who played Mrs. Ranevsky in *The Cherry Orchard* and whose impressions of Stanislavsky in the parts of Astrov and Vershinin have already been given, left this impression of him in the part of Gayev :—

"I loved him tenderly in *The Cherry Orchard*. The whole performance acquired a much greater significance when he played in it. I always tried to catch the extraordinary ease with which he would slip from one mood to another—it was such a great help to me in my part of Mrs. Ranevsky. His famous speech before the bookcase. 'It was only when I finished it,' he soon tells Sonia, 'that I realized how silly it was.' And, to be sure, he finished the speech with his favourite billiard terms, looking highly embarrassed, as though he himself realized how silly it was. And his famous 'Beg your pardon ? ' and the whole of his bulky figure, looking so absurd and yet so elegant, too, and his good-humoured face, smiling tenderly when addressing Anya, and looking so fastidious and indignant when listening to Lopakhin's tirades on the best way to save the cherry orchard, and his expression of disgust and nausea whenever Yasha came near him :

'Go away, my dear fellow, you smell of chicken.' I find it quite impossible to forget his arrival in the third act after the sale of 'the cherry orchard,' when, after handing Firs the anchovies and the Kerch herrings, he says, brushing away a tear, 'I haven't had anything to eat today—I've been through hell !' And his forlorn figure in the last act, his taking leave of the old house in which he had spent his whole life, and his words : 'I'm a bank clerk now—a financier—cannon off the red,' which he always spoke with a smile, trying his best to cheer up, and his last tears, 'My sister ! Oh, my sister !' and his exit.

"When we played *The Cherry Orchard* for the first time after Stanislavsky's death, I could hear his voice and intonations so clearly that it gave me almost a physical pain ; through my tear-filled eyes I seemed to see his figure, his smile, the movements of his hands—he stood before me all through the performance like a ghost. The sensation I experienced was both painful and joyful, and Stanislavsky as Gayev remains indelibly imprinted on my memory and I can see him before me as large as life."

The first performance of *The Cherry Orchard*, during which Chekhov was given a rousing ovation, took place on January 17th, 1904. By that time Stanislavsky and his family had left the house at the Red Gates and moved to a flat in Karetny Ryad, opposite the Hermitage Theatre where the Moscow Art Theatre had spent its first four seasons. Stanislavsky occupied the first and second floors of the house. To reach his flat one had to go up a very wide staircase which led straight into a spacious entrance hall. From the hall one entered a large, rectangular room—the dining-room. Next to it, on the left, were two more rooms, the large drawing-room with its well-polished parquet floor and tropical plants in flower pots looking out on the Karetny Ryad, and the children's room. There were two or three more rooms on the first floor, and a narrow staircase led to the attic with the old-fashioned low ceilings where Stanislavsky had his study and bedroom. The whole flat was furnished with great simplicity. There was nothing in the whole place that was characteristic of a great actor. Many of Stanislavsky's friends remarked on the very plain middle-class surroundings amongst which he lived. But he hardly ever noticed them : his imagination was always full of whatever play he happened to be working on at the moment. Contrary to the general idea of him, Stanislavsky was far from rich. His income from his family factory was sufficient to assure him a comfortable living, and if he had any money to spare, he usually put it away, as he did his salary from the Moscow Art Theatre, so as to be able to spend it, when the right occasion arose, on some new theatrical venture.

According to the testimony of his closest friends, Stanislavsky was never very talkative either among his friends or in his family circle. It was only when the conversation turned on the subject of the theatre that he would come out of his shell and start talking animatedly and listening attentively. He would use the same phrases over and over again, repeating them like an actor repeating his lines in a play, but he would always speak with great conviction. There was a striking difference between Stanislavsky the man and Stanislavsky the actor. On the stage the spectator was struck by the infinite variety of his inflexions, expressing the most complex emotional feelings, each character he played being endowed by him with a different voice, a different rhythm of movements, and quite different facial expressions. But in ordinary life he seemed shy of revealing the extraordinary powers he possessed of disclosing every shade of feeling and mood. He usually spoke in a very low voice, and his inflexions were, if anything, rather monotonous, which tempted many people to mimic his voice and manner of speech, especially when repeating his words. His manners were perfect and he was always exquisitely groomed. When displeased by something or somebody or when his curiosity was powerfully aroused, he was in the habit of biting the back of his hand and at the same time scrutinizing the person he was talking to with almost child-like intensity.

In the spring of 1904 Lilina was indisposed and could not accompany Stanislavsky to Petersburg where the Moscow Art Theatre was performing *Julius Cæsar* and *The Cherry Orchard*. On April 2nd, after the first night of *The Cherry Orchard*, Stanislavsky sent Chekhov a telegram to tell him that the play had been a bigger success than in Moscow. He warned him, however, not to pay any attention to the notices in the papers as "the newspaper scribblers understand very little."

In a letter to his wife, Stanislavsky gives this description of his day in Petersburg : "I get up, that is, I wake up at half past ten, and before I have time to get out of bed some of our actors usually come in for a business talk. I get rid of them at last, dress and go out to have my tea. It is then that a regular invasion starts : letters, business visitors, or Knipper coming in for a talk. Thus time passes till two or three o'clock. At last I manage to escape, go out for a walk or a shave, or to do some shopping. Then come the visits that must be paid, and I pay them in my leisure time so as not to get stuck in Petersburg after the end of the season. We have, besides, five or six meetings to discuss the question of enlarging the number of our shareholders. So time passes till dinner. I usually dine at four, then I take a nap, and after that I am off to the theatre. After the performance we all have supper here. At first it was rather a modest occasion : Olga Knipper, Rayevskaya and myself. Now the' Kachalovs and the others join us, too. We don't usually go to bed till two a.m."

On his free nights Stanislavsky usually visited the other Petersburg theatres. He saw the famous Petersburg actress, Maria Savina, the "dictator" of the Alexandrinsky Imperial Theatre, in *A Month in the Country* and was "pleasantly impressed".

"Savina," he wrote to his wife, "has charmed us all by her kindness."

A week or so later he made a personal call on the fifty-year-old celebrity, who made a valiant attempt to vamp him, little realizing what a waste of time it was. "Savina," he wrote to his wife, "was indisposed and she received me in her dressing gown. I saw at once that the whole thing had been carefully planned. She flirted and paid me lots of compliments, but all in vain— nothing doing ! I spent a long time with her, though, listening to her stories about the theatre."

The whole of June Stanislavsky spent in Lyubimovka. In his last letter to Chekhov, on July 4th (Chekhov was already in Baden-weiler, where he died on July 15th), Stanislavsky complained of feeling ill most of the time and ascribed it to the after-effects of the season. The Russo-Japanese war had just broken out and there was the danger that some of the actors of the Moscow Art Theatre might be called up. Stanislavsky's mother fell seriously ill and Stanislavsky had to accompany her to Contrexeville. He received the news of Chekhov's death on the way to France. "I can't get Chekhov out of my head," he wrote to his wife. "Kiss Knipper and tell her how sad I felt to have to go abroad at such a time. Our whole future appears to me now in the blackest colours : it may not have been noticed, but Chekhov's authority preserved our theatre from many things."

Stanislavsky, in fact, had now reached a dead end. His work

at the Moscow Art Theatre had been merely a continuation of his work at the Society of Art and Literature. Only in Chekhov's plays had his methods of production been different. Chekhov's plays required no special expeditions ; their seemingly diffuse and indeterminate form prevented his methods from becoming stereotyped : the more he played in them, the deeper their meaning became to him. But now that Chekhov was dead, his own work, too, seemed to be at an end. "I am constantly pursued by one thought—Chekhov," he wrote to his wife from the South of France on July 27th. "I never expected to become so attached to him or that his death would leave such a gap in my life." And in his next letter : "I can't get poor Chekhov out of my head. I am re-reading his stories and I love and esteem him more and more. I have just been told that Goltsev[1] has arranged his funeral. It is we who should have done it. We must start thinking of putting up a memorial to Chekhov at the expense of our theatre." And on July 11th, before his short trip to Paris to study the electric equipment of the theatres there, he wrote to his wife : "Odd ! Before I should have been glad of such an opportunity, but now—I suppose I must be getting old. The thought of our theatre makes me sad. It won't last long now. I can't imagine life without it, though. Perhaps the war will give the necessary impetus to our society and we shall be able to keep our crusading powers. It is a pity that whatever is good should fade away and perish so quickly." And on July 15th : "I am reading Chekhov, thinking a lot of him, and writing my notes. I could not help crying when I read the description of the funeral in the papers, and I was very worried about Knipper, especially after you had confirmed that she looked ill. I am terrified for her and for the future of our theatre. I hardly expect she will be in a condition to play, not in Chekhov's plays, anyway. Now I realize the truth of the saying that troubles never come singly. Our theatre, too, will now have to go through very hard times. Oh, how desolate everything is, particularly during the last few days when it has been raining continuously. Even Lyubimovka seems sweet to me now and the people there angels."

But his pessimism about the future of the Moscow Art Theatre did not prevent him from taking a keen interest in theatrical affairs. The period of search into the laws of acting was just starting, though not for another two years would his work on

---

[1] Editor of *Russian Thought*, to which Chekhov contributed regularly.

his "system" actually begin. He realized more than ever now that in the past he had been relying entirely on blind chance when producing a play or acting a part. He let his imagination run riot and merely waited for the scratching of a mouse or some other mysterious cause to set it working. But no art, and least of all the art of the stage, could afford to wait on chance. Every other art, in fact, conformed to certain laws ; only the art of the stage, it seemed, was at the mercy of "inspiration", which was so wayward and uncertain, as he himself had found out long ago when playing in Pissemsky's tragedy with so famous an actress as Polina Strepetova, the high priestess of the "inspiration school" of acting. But what were those laws of the stage ? He did not know. Nobody knew. The great actors were too busy with their art to have thought it necessary to formulate those laws, and the random observations they had left behind were of no use for the task he had in mind. The "notes" he was constantly writing now, however, showed that he was carrying on with his ruthless analysis of himself both as an actor and as a producer. He may have become disillusioned with his own methods of production, but he never became disillusioned with the theatre, for that would have been equivalent to becoming disillusioned with life itself.

In his last letter from Contrexeville to his wife he mentioned with annoyance the fact that he had missed seeing the French mystery play *Joan of Arc*, "something on the lines of Oberammergau," and in a hastily scribbled note on the day of his departure from Contrexeville, he expressed his satisfaction with his wife's suggestion of putting up a memorial to Chekhov in Lyubimovka.

On his return from abroad, he spent a few weeks with his family in the Crimea. He was back in Moscow by the middle of September. In October his mother died. In spite of the apparent coldness of their relations, Stanislavsky was deeply attached to his mother ; but on the day of her funeral the company was rehearsing *Ivanov* (produced by Nemirovich-Danchenko) in which Stanislavsky played the part of Prince Shabelsky, and so strong was his sense of duty that he was present at the rehearsal as usual.

He had now entered the period of search and for the rest of his life he was the seeker *par excellence*. A few months before his death he told one of his assistant producers : "If you must make mistakes, let them be big ones," and this phrase admirably sums up his own career in art. Even after he had formulated his system in his last book, *The Actor's Work on Himself*, which was only published after his death, he immediately began turning it up-side down by inventing an entirely new method for the actor's approach to his art ; and even·then he pointed out that it was not the final goal of his search, but probably only one of its phases which would be followed by new and more perfect discoveries in the art of the stage.

Part Three

SEARCH AND FULFILMENT

CHAPTER XXXVIII

IT WAS VALERY BRYUSSOV, one of the most outstanding Russian poets and the leader of the symbolist movement in Russia, who fired the first broadside at Stanislavsky's naturalistic methods of production. In his famous article, "Unnecessary Truth", published in *The World of Art,* the organ of the Russian symbolist movement, at the time of the first Petersburg season of the Moscow Art Theatre, Bryussov poured scorn on Stanislavksy's attempts to give a faithful reproduction of the environment of a Chekhov play, his studied efforts to disregard "the fourth wall", and the naturalistic details he was so fond of at the time, such as, for instance, the blowing of curtains in front of an open window. "It is time the theatre put an end to imitating reality," Bryussov urged, "for the art of the stage is by its very nature unrealistic." He went on to expound the theories of his own movement as based on the thesis that "creative feelings form the only reality on earth and, according to the poet, all outward things are only a dream, a fleeting dream." Bryussov concluded his article by appealing to the Moscow Art Theatre to give up "copying life" and indeed to sever all connections with life because the real object of art was not reality but "the artist's emotional life, the artist's soul".

This call for a highly stylized and purely symbolic method of production as well as for the "release" of the actor from his dependence on the author formed the constant subject of discussion in the symbolist and other "advanced" periodicals in Russia, at times assuming a mystic or religious tinge of a totally abstract nature, and at other times culminating in demands for the abolition of the picture stage and for a return either to the ancient Greek and Roman amphitheatre or to the Elizabethan apron stage.

Stanislavsky could not remain unaffected by all this clamour for a radical reform of the art of the stage and the drama. Even before he realized that he had come to a dead end himself, the new trends in the world of art had affected the Moscow Art Theatre very closely, for in 1902 a number of its actors, headed by Vsevolod Meierhold, the future leader of the symbolist movement on the Russian stage, left the theatre, hired their own theatre in Kherson and formed themselves into a "Company of the New Drama". Meierhold had only to wait two years to see Stanislavsky practically wrecked on the shoals of his own realistic stage methods and in desperation turning to Maeterlinck, the mystic and symbolist. Stanislavsky put on two of Maeterlinck's plays, *The Blind* and *The Uninvited,* during the season of 1904-1905, and it was while he was producing the first play that a trifling incident made a deep impression on him. He was wondering how to devise the statue of the dead pastor who was the spiritual leader of the crowd of helpless blind men in the play. He approached a certain left-wing sculptor who, after examining the scale models of his sets and listening for some time to his explanations, very brusquely (the rudeness of *avant-garde* thinkers is, of course, proverbial) told him that what he really wanted was a stuffed dummy. With that parting shot the sculptor went away without even saying goodbye. Stanislavsky, though hurt by the sculptor's bad manners, could not help reflecting that there was a great deal of truth in what he said. The old ways of the Moscow Art Theatre were most certainly being undermined and the new roads seemed to be closed to it. Something had to be done to save the theatre from perishing in the welter of its own stage *clichés*. Stanislavsky was already beginning to feel "an inward emptiness" every time he walked on the stage. And so once again he set out on a search for the new just for the sake of novelty. He began visiting art galleries and studying the pictures of the expressionistic painters, trying to find the key to their particular "mood" and some kind of physical adaptation which might express it more or less faithfully. But every time he tried to reproduce those twisted and contorted lines before a mirror, he merely succeeded in achieving a caricature of the artist's creations, "teasing" their outward lines but missing their inner content. "No," he told himself, "such a task is beyond the capacity of man to accomplish, because the human forms in expressionistic paintings are too immaterial and abstract. They are too far removed from the actual well-fed body of modern man whose lines have unfortunately been fixed once and for all and are unchangeable." But perhaps it was not the artist but the human body itself that was at fault? Why should actors be doomed to remain the slaves of their bodies and be forced to convey only what was crudely realistic? After all, ballet dancers like Taglioni and Pavlova seemed to have discovered the secret of overcoming the limitations of their bodies. And what about acrobats who fly like birds from one trapeze to another? Why should not actors become as proficient with their bodies as ballet dancers and acrobats? One had to go on searching. One had to train oneself to achieve a similar mastery over one's body.

And at the age of forty-two Stanislavsky again started training himself in front of the mirror at night as he had done in the days of the Alexeyev Circle and the Society of Art and Literature. Simultaneously, he applied himself once more to voice training, only to discover again that, lacking the necessary resonance of voice, he had to resort to the usual tricks of vocalization and recitation that were so common on the stage. How could one express lofty thoughts, world sorrow, the feelings of the mystery of existence or of the eternal, in which the new drama seemed to specialize, in such a voice? It was only in moments of genuine inspiration that the actor's voice somehow or other found the necessary resonance, nobility, and simplicity. Where did it come from? That seemed to Stanislavsky one of the great mysteries of nature. What it amounted to was that the actor had to *feel* his part, for then everything happened by itself. So he did his best to *feel* and be inspired, but all he achieved was an unnaturally taut body which was liable to go into convulsions at any moment. As for his attempt to penetrate into the inner meaning of words, it merely made him look like a mentally defective.

Having despaired of finding a solution to all these perplexing problems, Stanislavsky, who was never averse to learning from anyone, turned to Meierhold. The difference between him and Meierhold, he felt at the time, was that he was merely seeking the new while Meierhold had apparently already discovered it but was prevented from achieving it, partly because his company of actors was not sufficiently experienced, and partly because he could not afford the money for his experiments. He, therefore, decided to come to Meierhold's aid, and in this way what became known as the Studio in Povarskaya Street came into being.

But there was also another practical reason for the foundation of this experimental studio. Already in the winter of 1903, about a year and a half before its foundation, Stanislavsky had suddenly appeared during one of the performances of *Julius Cæsar* in the dressing room of the students of the school of acting of the Moscow Art Theatre and asked one of them, a student by the name of Boris Pronin, who was to become the stage manager of the studio and eventually one of the producers of the Moscow Art Theatre, to go to his dressing room after the performance. Pronin was rather worried as he expected to be reprimanded for an involuntary laugh in the Senate scene, and it was with a feeling of trepidation that he knocked at the door of Stanislavsky's dressing room. "Come in," Stanislavsky shouted in a very cheerful voice, and, feeling more at ease, Pronin opened the door and got the shock of his life : Stanislavsky was standing naked before him and calmly smoking a cigarette. That was apparently how he rested after the difficult part of Brutus. According to Pronin, there was such a childish simplicity in the naked giant he saw before him that he immediately recovered from his shock. Stanislavsky could wear any costume, or none, with "real Hellenic dignity".

Stanislavsky invited Pronin to accompany him to his home in Karetny Ryad as he had some important business to discuss with him. In Stanislavsky's flat a cold supper was laid in the dining room, and Stanislavsky offered Pronin a glass of wine, which rather surprised the young man as he remembered Stanislavsky's telling him again and again that actors ought never to drink. Stanislavsky himself drank a glass of sour milk. The business he wanted to discuss with Pronin concerned the organization of a number of provincial companies. He had been worried by the fact that the Moscow Art Theatre could not offer any jobs to the majority of the students of its school, who had to find themselves jobs on the provincial stage where they very soon forgot all they had been taught. He therefore thought of creating three separate companies, each of which was to prepare a repertoire of ten plays, rehearse them in Moscow or somewhere within easy reach of Moscow, and then perform them in rotation in three large provincial cities.

"We shall spread our ideas in the provinces," Stanislavsky said, "and the public there will refuse to go to inartistic performances put on hurriedly."

During the next three seasons Stanislavsky discussed his project again and again with Pronin. His chief difficulty was to find the right man to manage the financial side of so vast a scheme. At last, on March 4th, 1905, he turned to Sergey Popov, a former member of the Society of Art and Literature and a well-known Moscow business man, who agreed to become the business manager of the Studio.

Popov soon found a little private theatre over a chemist's shop on the corner of Povarskaya Street and had the whole place re-built and redecorated. The new company, headed by Meierhold, had its first meeting in the Moscow Art Theatre on May 5th. It consisted of young actors and students of Moscow and Petersburg dramatic schools. They were addressed by Stanislavsky, who told them that the new drama had to be approached in a new way. The old methods of acting, however great the talents of certain individual actors, were out of place in it. The Moscow Art Theatre itself was not by any means the last word in stage art. The new theatre would have to continue its work in the provinces and at the same time go much further. The social forces in the country were awakening (the 1905 revolution was gathering momentum just then) and he did not think the theatre ought to be the servant of pure art alone : it must respond to the social de-mands of the times and must endeavour to be the teacher of society. In conclusion, Stanislavsky impressed on the young actors of the new company the absolute necessity for strict discip-line. They must renounce all personal ambitions and carry out the orders of their producers. They must remember that if a part given to a certain actor were found to be unsuitable for him, he must not take it as a personal slight if it were taken away from him. (Stanislavsky himself was to learn from personal experience twelve years later how bitter such a slight could be.) For personal ambitions must never be allowed to interfere with the ensemble or the success of a performance or their whole enterprise.

The company began its rehearsals on June 6th in a large stone barn near Pushkino which, like the first barn in Arkhipov's grounds in Pushkino, was specially converted into a small theatre. Its repertoire included six plays from the repertoire of the Moscow Art Theatre and four new plays which were to be used for experi-mental purposes. These were : *La morte de Tintagiles,* Maeter-linck's powerful little drama written to be performed by marion-ettes, produced by Meierhold, who was so soon to start converting living actors into animated puppets, Hauptmann's dramatic jeu d'esprit *Schluck und Iau,* Ibsen's *The Comedy of Love,* and a play by a modern Polish playwright. The company was also supposed to rehearse *Twelfth Night* and *Hannele,* the latter play being still under the ban of the Moscow Archbishop. Actually, however, the studio concentrated entirely on the rehearsals of the first three plays, though during the summer it did make a half-hearted attempt at rehearsing *Twelfth Night.*

Stanislavsky did not interfere with the rehearsals as he was anxious to give Meierhold a free hand, hoping that the young people under him would themselves discover new ways of dramatic expression and pull him after them. While the rehearsals were going on in Pushkino, Popov carried on with the reconstruction of the theatre, and round the Studio itself all sorts of auxiliary sections were formed, as in the old days of the Society of Art and Literature, such as an art section, a literary section, headed by Valery Bryussov himself, and a musical section which organized an expedition to the wilds of Russia in search of native musical talent and new musical instruments.

Stanislavsky left for his usual cure in the Caucasus, this time taking his family with him. He received long reports from Meierhold and others who kept him in touch with the work of the Studio. Meierhold, in particular, explained to him the new principles of production and acting he was introducing, which made Stanislavsky wonder whether those clever and original ideas of his could ever be applied in practice. He hoped that they could, for then he could present the new plays for the first time in Moscow and with the money obtained from their performances subsidize the provincial tours of his new company. Unfortunately, he made the mistake of entrusting the entire work of production to Meierhold, who was too obsessed by the *new* drama to bother about doing anything with the plays from the Moscow Art Theatre's repertoire. For it was an essential part of the *credo* of the new studio and its producer that realism was dead and that the time had now come for what Stanislavsky was soon to call "irrealism". Life had to be presented not as it actually was, but as it was dimly perceived in dreams and visions and in moments of great exaltation of the spirit. It was that tantalizingly nebulous state of man's soul that had to be expressed in stage terms just as the painters of the new movements expressed it on their canvases, or the modern composers in their music, or the *new* poets in their verse. The main strength of this new stage art seemed to Stanislavksy to lie chiefly in all sorts of new combinations, in a new blending of colours, lines and musical notes, and in a new harmony of word-sounds which were supposed to create certain moods and unconsciously fire the imagination of the spectator and make him take part in the creative work of the playwright and producer.

Thus, in his rehearsals of Maeterlinck's play, Meierhold first of all got rid of what he called "the usual naturalistic sound wave". He made his actors "draw" straight lines and angles by their intonations, refusing to permit any roundness of sound or any *glissandos*. Agitation, alarm, fear, grief, joy—every emotion was conveyed by means of "a cold, bright sound like the sound of drops falling to the bottom of a deep well". No suppressed or tremolo notes in the voice were allowed. Great stress was laid on finding what Meierhold called "the inner rhythm", and pauses were always treated as the continuance of the dialogue. This rhythm had to be kept up all the time to prevent the actor from being carried away by his own emotions.

Meierhold conducted his rehearsals against the background of an ordinary canvas sheet. He paid particular attention to plastic poses. Movements he considered merely as an accompaniment to the spoken words. They had either to add something to the dialogue or intensify the impression produced by it by forecasting what was going to happen. For instance, in *La morte de Tintagiles* Boulanger's musical weeping was preceded by a forceful gesture of raised arms and bent-back hands. The weeping was "musical" and so unreal that it sounded more like some musical instrument than a voice.

After reading Meierhold's letters Stanislavsky came to the conclusion that fundamentally the two of them were in agreement and that what they sought was merely what had already been discovered by other arts but was so far inapplicable to the art of the stage. Stanislavsky could not help feeling, however, that Meierhold's discoveries might be merely the result of self-deception and that his methods were most probably not based on inner experience, but were merely outward imitations of the new forms of art. He himself could see no way of applying to the stage those dimly perceived emotions evoked by the expressionistic paintings or by the music and verse of the followers of the new movements. He did not know how to embody on the stage those shadowy feelings which were hidden in the words of the symbolist writers. But he comforted himself by the thought that perhaps the new movements would produce new actors who would be able to overcome their bodily impediments and thus achieve an unheard of intensification of the spiritual values of the art of the stage. Perhaps, he told himself, the new generation of actors would find those things normal which baffled the older generation of actors. There might be many fallacies in Meierhold's experiments and his work might even be wasted, but it was as useful to know what one ought not to do as what one ought to do.

By the middle of August Stanislavsky was back in Moscow. It was cold and there was an autumnal nip in the air. The autumn was a season Stanislavsky not only disliked, but feared. "Autumn is death," he used to say. However, he was rather cheered by the work so far carried out by the studio in Pushkino. A dress rehearsal was arranged and it was attended by Stanislavsky, Nemirovich-Danchenko, most of the actors of the Moscow Art Theatre (who rather frowned on this new enterprise of Stanislavsky's), Gorky and a host of other people. Only a few scenes from the first three new plays, scenes which were most characteristic of Meierhold's methods, were shown. The scenes from *La morte de Tintagiles* produced the greatest impression on the audience. Stanislavsky beamed with pleasure. Gorky, who at first was rather aloof and unapproachable, grew very sociable and friendly.

"Yesterday's rehearsal," Stanislavsky wrote to Popov, who could not be present because of illness, "gave me a great deal of joy. It was a great success. The whole of the company of the Moscow Art Theatre was there and Gorky, too, was there. *Schluck und Iau* made an excellent impression. *La morte de Tintagiles* created a sensation. *The Comedy of Love* was weak, but I think I know why and I shall be able to give them some good advice. The main thing is that what I saw yesterday convinced me that we have got a company or rather some good material for one. This question worried me the whole summer, but yesterday my mind was set at rest. Yesterday even the pessimists began to believe in the success of the Studio and agreed that it had scored its first victory."

Six weeks later, however, Stanislavsky was not so sure. He had been working with the Studio for several weeks and he had come to realize that his first favourable impression was mistaken.

"It isn't that ! " he told Popov after a rehearsal of *La morte de*

Tintagiles. "It's an excellent production, but in its present form it is not wanted."

"But what is wanted in your opinion ? " asked Popov.

"They should have had a plain, light-coloured curtain at the back and the actors should have played in dark costumes against that background," said Stanislavsky, who was disgusted by the amateurish way in which the figures of the actors lost their outlines against the scenery and in the greenish-blue light one of the artists had specially devised for the scene.

"But you should have thought of it before," Popov retorted. "Think of the money we have wasted."

But Stanislavsky's objections to the background were only an excuse : he was already disillusioned with the whole thing. He realized that all the young and inexperienced actors could do was to show the result of their experiments in a few short scenes and that when they had to present a play in its entirety and to convey its subtleties in a symbolic form, they merely displayed their childish incompetence and helplessness. In Meierhold's hands the actors became the clay out of which he moulded his striking groupings and *mise-en-scènes*. All he had done was to demonstrate his principles, ideas and experiments ; he did not succeed in embodying them in a satisfactory artistic form, perhaps, Stanislavsky reflected generously, because his actors lacked the necessary stage technique. His ideas were therefore merely transformed into an abstract theory, a scientific formula.

Stanislavsky once more came to the conclusion that there was a wide gulf between a producer's dreams and their realization. But already the fundamental difference between him and Meierhold had emerged : to Meierhold the actor was a means to an end, while to Stanislavsky the actor had now become an end in himself. The theatre, he was now convinced, existed first of all for the actor. Without the actor it could not exist at all. The producer was only important in so far as he was able to assist the creative work of the actor. Here Stanislavsky came round to the conception of Alexander Ostrovsky, who had always insisted that the producer must be the actor's instructor and assistant. In a theatre where the producer occupied the foremost place, Ostrovsky held, the actor was merely a marionette with the sole difference that the audience never actually saw the strings which made him go through his movements on the stage. That was exactly the impression Stanislavsky received after studying

Meierhold's methods at the Studio in Povarskaya Street. The break with his own past and with the Meiningen traditions of the Moscow Art Theatre was now complete ; and it is surely a curious fact that it should have been Meierhold's "new" abstract methods of stage production that finally brought about this break. Its completeness can be judged from the fact that Stanislavsky had also turned away from the art of the stage-designer as an essential part of the presentation of a play. He was now against all external means of production and all the tricks devised by the producer, a position from which he was going to retreat later on, but which shows how deeply dissatisfied he was with his *own* past. All he was concerned about at the moment was the discovery of the laws of acting. He knew that such laws must exist, and with the fanaticism that was so characteristic of him when obsessed by an idea, he was no less sure that when he discovered them he would be able to devise an infallible system of acting that would enable every actor to become perfect in his art. From that position, too, he was going to retreat, but not until after a long period of trial and error had convinced him that it was dangerous to force human nature, and particularly the subconscious creative processes of artists.

The Studio in Povarskaya Street had, therefore, served a very useful purpose in setting him on the road of new great discoveries, but as an experiment it had failed. His original idea was to establish a number of travelling companies with a repertoire of plays that had already been successful at the Moscow Art Theatre. Meierhold, on the other hand, did not seem to be interested in that part of his plan at all. The political revolution in the country exerted its influence on the producers and the actors in the Studio, too. Murmurs were heard that Stanislavsky was no longer any use, that it was time he was sent packing and a company created that would devote itself entirely to the "new" art of the stage. In the meantime the authorities had closed down all the theatres in Moscow because of the political disturbances, and by the time the theatres were reopened Stanislavsky had made up his mind (as he told Popov) that "the Moscow public has no time for a new theatre," and closed the Studio. The whole experiment cost him over 50,000 roubles.

CHAPTER XXXIX

THE FAILURE OF the Studio in Povarskaya Street confronted Stanislavsky with an inner crisis he did not know how to resolve. What he wanted was a period of rest from the questions which agitated his mind so violently. For the time being he decided to produce a classical play. His choice fell on Griboyedov's comic masterpiece, *The Misfortune of Being Clever*. Stanislavsky was never interested in social problems, not, at any rate, sufficiently to be able to handle them adequately on the stage, and what he eventually produced was not a biting social satire, but a love story. It was not, as several Russian critics pointed out, *The Misfortune of Being Clever*, but *The Misfortune of Being in Love*. While the rehearsals of Griboyedov's comedy were going on, the Moscow Art Theatre was performing its only new play of the 1905-1906 season, Gorky's *The Children of the Sun*, and, as Gorky was hated by the reactionaries and especially by the gang of political terrorists known as "The Black Hundred", rumours went round that an attack would be made on the Moscow Art Theatre on the first night of the play on October 24th, 1905. In consequence, the first night audience was very jittery, and when in the last act a crowd of extras "stormed" the fence of the house of the leading characters and one of the actresses fired a pistol at the crowd and her supposed husband, played by Kachalov, fell, the audience, mistaking the extras for the terrorists (an unconscious compliment to Stanislavsky's proficiency in his old naturalistic methods), and thinking that Kachalov was their first victim, panicked, some rushing to the exits and others to the footlights. The curtain was drawn and Nemirovich-Danchenko appeared before it and assured the audience that the whole thing was a regrettable misunderstanding. But when the play was resumed at the point where it was interrupted, people in the audience were still unconvinced and shouted, "Kachalov

275

get up ! " Kachalov got up and then lay down again. At that moment a critic rushed up to the stage and began shouting : "We've had enough of horrors ! We can see them in the streets ! We don't want to see them on the stage ! " Again pandemonium broke out and the curtain had to be drawn. But the majority of the audience began to protest and the play went on to the end in a house that was far from full.

In December firing broke out in the streets. A curfew was imposed. During one of the rehearsals of *The Misfortune of Being Clever*, in which Stanislavsky played the heroine's father, Famussov, a clash occurred between the police and the revolutionaries outside the theatre. Stanislavsky went on rehearsing. He was told of the fighting in the street and that it would soon be impossible to reach home in safety. "Just a few more minutes," Stanislavsky said. "Let's finish the scene." But he was forced to stop in the end and was escorted home by the commissionaire of the theatre, who had to take him by a roundabout way to escape being hit by a stray bullet. He then realized that circumstances had come to his aid and that now was the chance to take the period of rest he wanted. Since it was impossible to carry on in Moscow, the theatre should stop its performances and go on its first tour abroad. As they did not possess the means to defray the costs of such a tour, they applied for a loan of 25,000 roubles from the Moscow Literary and Artistic Circle, founded in 1899 as a successor to the Society of Art and Literature. It had sufficient funds, which it raised in fines from members who wished to go on playing cards after the permitted hours, and it gladly agreed to advance the loan to the Moscow Art Theatre.

It was at the Literary and Artistic Circle, incidentally, that Stanislavsky read a paper on Play Censorship in April, 1905, in which he protested against the constant police interference in the affairs of the Russian theatres even after a play had been passed by the censorship, and demanded the enactment of a special law to protect the theatre "from being strangled by the arbitrary action of the authorities."

The Moscow Art Theatre left for its first foreign tour on January 24th, 1906. Its repertoire consisted of five plays : *Czar Fyodor, Uncle Vanya, The Three Sisters, The Lower Depths,* and *An Enemy of the People.* During its tour it gave a total of sixty-two performances in Berlin, Dresden, Leipzig, Prague, Vienna, Frankfurt-on-Main, Hanover, Karlsbad, Wiesbaden and

Warsaw. The attitude of the German public was not very friendly at first. The relations between Germany and Russia were rather strained at the time and the general attitude towards Russians after the disaster of the Russo-Japanese war was openly contemptuous. Feeling that it was his duty to uphold the prestige of his country, Stanislavsky did his best to impress the Germans by the discipline and efficiency of his company and stage-hands.

The Moscow Art Theatre opened its Berlin season in the *Berliner Theater* with *Czar Fyodor*. The play had an enthusiastic reception and the Press notices, too, were highly favourable, though some papers could not refrain from a sarcastic reference to the political situation. "The Russians," they wrote, "have won their first victory since their defeat by the Japanese." The second performance (the play was Gorky's *Lower Depths*, which had already scored a success at Max Rheinhardt's *Kleines Theater*) was also highly successful, but the theatre on these and subsequent performances was never full, and Stanislavsky was beginning to be worried about the financial failure of the tour which might have spelt serious difficulties on their return to Moscow. Fortunately, the Crown Princess Cecilia, whose mother was Russian, came to see one of the performances, and next day came a telephone message from the Royal Palace asking for a copy of *Czar Fyodor*. A few days later, on a Sunday, came another message from the Palace asking for *Czar Fyodor* to be performed on Monday, as the Emperor Wilhelm II had expressed a wish to see it. It was pointed out that *An Enemy of the People* was billed for that evening and that a change of programme could only be made if the theatre received the permission to announce it as "by order of His Majesty". A quarter of an hour later a third telephone message from the Palace informed the directors of the theatre that His Majesty had no right to give orders to them but merely requested that such a change should be made. The handbills consequently bore the special notice : "At the special request of His Majesty Wilhelm II the play tonight will be *Czar Fyodor* and not *An Enemy of the People* as previously announced." This did the trick, and the house that night was packed with the cream of Berlin society. Wilhelm arrived in the uniform of a Russian dragoon regiment of which he was Colonel-in-Chief, which caused a flutter among the assembled diplomats as it was interpreted as an improvement in the Russo-German relations (the diplomatic world seems to be even more fantastic than the make-believe world of the stage). Wilhelm, of course, occupied the most conspicuous place in the Royal box, with his whole family grouped round him. He kept talking very animatedly all the time and now and again he leaned forward and motioned to the famous actors of his theatres in the stalls to pay attention to the Russian actors on the stage. A few times he applauded demonstratively. Stanislavsky, who observed him during the intervals through the peep-hole in the curtain, could not make up his mind whether Wilhelm was a good actor or whether he was really so fond of the theatre. After the performance Stanislavsky and Nemirovich-Danchenko were summoned to the Royal box where Wilhelm discussed the organization of their theatre with them very amiably. His first words were, "My wife and I disagree about the play. She's for Boris Godunov's party and I am for Shuysky's." Pointing to Ludwig Barnay, who was also in the box together with a few other prominent German actors, Wilhelm remarked jestingly, "I'm afraid our actors are not very pleased with your success. I've never seen such fine acting in any of our own theatres."

After Wilhelm's visit the theatre's receipts improved considerably and at the end of the Berlin visit, which lasted about six weeks, the artistic as well as the financial success of the theatre was assured.

At a dinner given in honour of the Moscow Art Theatre in Berlin by the veteran German actor Haase, Stanislavsky was presented to the leading actors of the Meiningen Company, which was also visiting Berlin at the time. But Stanislavsky had by now travelled a long way from his famous productions at the Society of Art and Literature and the Moscow Art Theatre, though *Czar Fyodor* was still there to remind him of his debt to Kronegk. In his account of this meeting with his old masters he merely remarks that he was very pleased to meet the actors of the "famous company" he had once "admired".

Stanislavsky and Nemirovich-Danchenko also paid a visit to Gerhardt Hauptmann, but unfortunately their conversation was "neither long nor eloquent", as Stanislavsky puts it, because their knowledge of German was not "good enough for discussing literary and artistic subjects".

In Wiesbaden, Wilhelm again went to a performance given by the Moscow Art Theatre and, inviting Stanislavsky, Nemiro-

vich-Danchenko and the leading actors of the company to his box
after the performance, distributed presents among them.

The last city visited by the theatre during this tour was Warsaw.
For political reasons the Poles ignored it completely and for the
first and last time in its history the Moscow Art Theatre had to
play to practically empty houses.

The Berlin visit of the Moscow Art Theatre had one rather
unexpected result by bringing two men into the theatre, each
of whom in his own way was of benefit to it. The two men, who
had sought refuge in Germany from the political storm in
Russia, were Nicolai Tarasov, who had just inherited a huge
fortune, and Nikita Baliev, a close friend of his, who had some
stage ambitions. Tarasov advanced the theatre 30,000 roubles
at a time when its funds, in spite of the success of its first tour
abroad, were dangerously low, and when the theatre eventually
offered to repay him his loan he refused to accept the money and
was made an honorary shareholder. Baliev was allowed to join
the company, no doubt in recognition of the generosity of his
friend, but he never became an actor, though in 1908 he was
given the responsible part of Bread in. Maeterlinck's *Blue Bird*.
After one performance Stanislavsky stopped Baliev and asked
him whether he liked the circus.

"Oh yes," replied Baliev.

"And clowns ? "

"I adore them."

"I can quite believe it," said Stanislavsky. "You're a real
buffoon. Not even a circus artist. Just a cheap buffoon."

Baliev must have taken the hint, for it was he who compèred
what was to become the famous annual variety entertainment of
the Moscow Art Theatre, the so-called "cabbage-soup" nights
which took place on the first Monday in Lent when the faithful
were forbidden to eat meat and their chief food was cabbage
soup. The whole theatre was put at Baliev's disposal a week
before the variety show and even Stanislavsky himself was at his
beck and call. Later Baliev, with Tarasov's financial support,
opened a variety show of his own in a cellar in Moscow under the
name of "The Bat," which under its French name of *Chauve
Souris* became famous in Europe and America.

Another incident that occurred during the Berlin visit of the
Moscow Art Theatre is characteristic of Stanislavsky's relations
with the actors at the period when he was still essentially a

producer-autocrat. Nina Litovtseva, the wife of Kachalov and one of the Moscow Art Theatre actresses who was later to become a producer working under Stanislavsky, had to play the part of Petra, Dr. Stockmann's daughter in *An Enemy of the People*. The part was new to her 'and she had no time to learn it properly. Stanislavsky said nothing to her but just remarked to Luzhsky, who was in charge of the Berlin production of the play, "Do you want this scene ? I don't. I suggest we cut it out." As it was almost Litovtseva's scene, the actress was very upset, but Stanislavsky refused to listen to any excuses or explanations. Soon afterwards Litovtseva fell ill. Stanislavsky took her illness very much to heart as he suspected that he was partly responsible for it. He kept making inquiries about her and then went to visit her himself and spent a long time at her bedside in spite of his morbid fear of catching an illness. When the company, including Kachalov, had to leave Berlin for Dresden, Stanislavsky, to whom the learning of a part was a real torment, especially if it was written in verse, insisted on taking Kachalov's part in *Czar Fyodor* so as to enable him to stay behind and look after his wife.

CHAPTER XL

STANISLAVSKY spent the summer of 1906 in Finland. Sitting on a cliff overlooking the Baltic, he cast his mind back over the twenty-five years of his activity on the stage and tried to bring his accumulated experience into some kind of order. He went over his old parts, trying to find out why certain places in them had given him so much trouble. He analysed the different stages of the process which had led to the conception and the consummation of his parts. He re-read the notes in his diaries. He recalled the advice of his friends and fellow-artists. What appalled him was the great number of bad theatrical habits he had acquired. It was clear to him that the only way of avoiding spiritual decay and the deadly repetition of the same old tricks of acting was some spiritual preparation before he went on to the stage to play one of his old parts. He had to know "how to enter that spiritual atmosphere in which alone the sacrament of creative art was possible."

This thorough analysis of his past experience on the stage led Stanislavsky to the conclusion that the state of mind in which an actor faced his audience was both unnatural and harmful. It had led to the invention of a large number of theatrical clichés for the expression of feelings of "an exalted kind." It was merely a way of showing what the actor did not feel ; it was make-believe of the crudest kind ; it was a physical and spiritual abnormality to which actors seemed to be doomed all their lives. Only the genius among the actors did not suffer from this abnormality. He was free from it because for some mysterious reason he did not acquire this state of mind which was so typical of the average actor. Instead he possessed on the stage what Stanislavsky called *the creative state of mind* which was indistinguishable from the normal state of mind of every ordinary man in real life. How then, Stanislavsky asked himself, was the average actor to attain this creative state of mind on the stage ? That was the first problem he set himself to solve, for he realized that such a state of mind was the only way through which an actor could achieve that congenial atmosphere which led directly to inspiration. Could it be achieved at will ? And if not, could this creative state of mind be produced bit by bit, put together from different elements after a series of carefully devised exercises ? An ordinary actor would of course never become a genius because he knew how to achieve the creative state of mind on the stage, but might he not come very close to the thing that distinguished a genius ?

The discovery of the creative state of mind and the elements of which it was composed now became what the actors of the Moscow Art Theatre called "Stanislavsky's latest fad". For the next three years he worked continuously on this problem, writing down his observations, reading any book he could get hold of that had any bearing on the subject of his inquiry, and taking every opportunity of discussing his ideas and theories with experts or friends. He was more than ever·appalled at his own ignorance and often spoke bitterly of the wretched education he had received as the greatest obstacle he had to overcome before he could apply himself with any hope of success to the task he had set himself. He had always been in need of what he called "encouragement," of understanding from those he knew intimately and on whom he could rely for support or sympathy. But what he needed most was a close friend in whose company he could feel completely unconstrained. He had had only one such friend in his life, "Fif" Kashdamanov, who had been his inseparable companion in the days of the Alexeyev Circle. And another such friend he now found in Leopold Sulerzhitsky. It is indeed questionable whether he would ever have undertaken so hard and uncongenial a task as the formulation of his "system", if he had never met the remarkable man who for over ten years was to be his closest friend and confidant.

Sulerzhitsky, or Suler, as Stanislavsky called him, whom Tolstoy had called "the purest man I have ever known", was about ten years younger than Stanislavsky. His life before he became closely associated with the Moscow Art Theatre as one of its producers was highly romantic and adventurous. As a boy he was always to be found behind the scenes of the theatre of his native town of Zhitomir. At the early age of twelve he tried his hand at producing *Hamlet*, a play with which he was to become closely associated with Stanislavsky and Gordon Craig. At the age of thirteen he left his secondary school for an art school. At sixteen he left his home and obtained work as an agricultural labourer and village teacher. A year later he went to Moscow and entered a school of painting and sculpture, where he met Tolstoy's daughter Tatyana. Through her he became acquainted with Tolstoy and became a faithful follower of his teachings. He was dismissed from the Moscow art school at the age of twenty-two in 1894 for making a revolutionary speech, and spent the next two years at sea, first as an ordinary seaman and then as a helmsman. In 1896 he refused to serve in the army on conscientious grounds, was placed in a lunatic asylum and a year later was exiled to Central Asia. To please his parents, however, he subsequently recanted, to the great disgust of the Tolstoyans, though not Tolstoy himself, and in 1898 he was again on the high seas. On his return in the same year, he accepted Tolstoy's offer to supervise the emigration to Canada of the persecuted sect of the Dukhobors and helped them to settle there. He was back in Moscow in 1900, where he was busy publishing those works of Tolstoy which were banned by the political censorhip. He met Gorky in the same year and at his request went to Switzerland to obtain an illegal press for printing revolutionary leaflets. In the same year he was working in Yalta as a stevedore and visited the Moscow Art Theatre for the first time. He met Stanislavsky in Moscow in 1901. A year later he was arrested, spent some time in solitary confinement and was then exiled to a remote province. In 1905 he was called up for the Russo-Japanese war as an orderly and sent to Manchuria, but was released from the army on his arrival there. He returned to Moscow and in the same year Stanislavsky made him a member of the company of the Moscow Art Theatre.

In his memoir on Sulerzhitsky, inscribed "Reminiscences of a Friend", Stanislavsky gives a moving description of Sulerzhitsky's character and personality. Their first meeting occurred quite unexpectedly after a performance of *An Enemy of the People*. Sulerzhitsky suddenly appeared in Stanislavsky's dressing room and, Stanislavsky writes, "we immediately knew each other although we had never met before. Suler," Stanislavsky continues, "sat down on the sofa, tucking one leg under him, and began talking excitedly about the performance. Oh, he could look and see in the theatre ! And that is not so easy, for to do that one must have a sharp inner eye. Suler was an excellent spectator and a first-class critic, too, without an axe of his own to grind."

That night Sulerzhitsky saw Stanislavsky to his cab, then suddenly jumped in himself and accompanied Stanislavsky to his home at the Red Gates, where they sat talking to each other till the small hours of the morning. It was in this unconventional way that Stanislavsky's second and last great friendship began. After his return from Berlin, Stanislavsky and Suler had a long talk together. Sulerzhitsky did not know what to do : whether to accept Stanislavsky's offer to become his closest assistant or whether to buy himself a plot of land and spend the rest of his life cultivating it. He had always wanted to live close to the soil and he warned Stanislavsky that even if he became his assistant in the theatre, he might at any moment leave him and settle on the land.

Stanislavsky accepted Sulerzhitsky's proposal and his trust in his friend was not misplaced. "Suler's rôle and significance in the theatre and the art of the stage," he writes, "were of the greatest importance."

What Stanislavsky liked so much about Sulerzhitsky was that he had brought into the theatre "an enormous supply of fresh and vital spiritual material straight from mother earth. He brought to the theatre," Stanislavsky continues, "the real poetry of the prairies, the countryside and nature as well as valuable artistic observations and original philosophic and religious ideas . . . a virginally pure attitude to art, without dividing it into separate compartments or into right- or left-wing movements. He was fond of studying the principles of art, but he was afraid of narrow-minded theorists and terms which are so dangerous to art, such as naturalism, realism, impressionism and romanticism. Instead of them he knew other words : beautiful and ugly, low and exalted, sincere and insincere, good and bad theatre. He drew his material only from life and nature, that is to say, he did unconsciously what Shchepkin taught us and what we are so passionately trying to achieve, and what is so hard to teach and learn. He could not tell you how certain parts had to be *played*, but he could himself live a part and show others how to do it. For only he who is an actor himself can be a producer.

"The rôle of the producer," Stanislavsky goes on, "is complex and many-sided. It comprises an æsthete, a poet, a psychologist, a teacher and theorist, a critic, an administrator, a man with

creative initiative, and so on. But Suler's nature, too, was complex and many-sided, and he, too, was an artist, a man of letters,
a singer, an actor, an administrator, a bit of a musician, he had
an excellent feeling for plastic art and dancing, he was interested
in philosophy, fond of psychology, and so on. And if to all this
you add an exceptionally good taste and an enormous capacity
for work, it will become clear why Suler so soon became a real
producer and a man of the theatre. In addition, he was an
excellent organizer, and he possessed a creative nature *par
excellence*. But what distinguished him most from other men of
the theatre was his great devotion to the service of art out of sheer
love of the people, of nature and of everything he had learnt
from Tolstoy and from his own hardships in life. Art was necessary to him because it allowed him to display the very essence of
his tender, loving and poetic soul, everything he believed in and
by which he brought happiness to people."

The first play Stanislavsky and Sulerzhitsky produced together
was Knut Hamsun's *The Drama of Life*. At the first rehearsal of
the play Sulerzhitsky was already present in his official capacity
as Stanislavsky's assistant.

"Let's begin ! " Stanislavsky said.

"Aye, aye, sir ! " Sulerzhitsky replied, sailor-fashion, in a loud
and cheerful voice.

"And," Stanislavsky adds, "I immediately believed in my new
assistant."

But he more than believed in him. His friendship with Suleiz-
hitsky grew into one of the greatest attachments of his life.
Sulerzhitsky was a diminutive man, his tiny figure contrasting
oddly with Stanislavsky's enormous size, and in spite of his saintly
nature, he was extremely touchy. Stanislavsky soon discovered
this weakness of his and the way he dealt with it shows how deep
his affection for "Suler" was. Their first serious quarrel occurred
during one of the rehearsals of *The Blue Bird*, about two years after
the beginning of their close collaboration. One day Sulerzhitsky
came home earlier than usual, looking very upset.

"What's the matter ? " his wife asked him. "Has the rehearsal
finished early today ? "

"No," Sulerzhitsky replied.

"Are you ill ? "

"No."

"Has anything happened ? "

Sulerzhitsky did not reply, but lay down on the sofa gloomily. "Let him produce it himself" he said suddenly after a few minutes. "Let him do as he likes."

But he did not lie sulking long. For presently the maid came in and announced that Stanislavsky was in the kitchen and asked if he might come in. Sulerzhitsky jumped up from the sofa and burst out laughing.

"Why in the kitchen?" he asked, Stanislavsky's humility taking even him by surprise.

And he rushed to meet him.

"My dear Suler," Stanislavsky murmured, clasping his friend's hand, "of course I don't insist. . . ."

There was no other person in the world to whom Stanislavsky would have behaved in such a way.

From the very beginning they realized that they had embarked on a new and great adventure. They not only saw each other at the rehearsals in the theatre, but also spent most of their free time together. When Stanislavsky was appearing in a play, Sulerzhitsky, too, went to the theatre to be in, Stanislavsky's dressing room at the end of the performance and to continue their never-ending discussion of the "system". They left the theatre together, Sulerzhitsky accompanying Stanislavsky home and sometimes staying the night at his friend's flat. The break between Stanislavsky and Nemirovich-Danchenko was not complete yet, but they no longer shared the same table during the production of a play, and with the exception of the three plays they were still to produce jointly, each of them had his own play and his own production. For the time being some sort of compromise between the two founders of the Moscow Art Theatre had been effected. This was perhaps made easier by the death in 1905 of Morozov, whom Nemirovich-Danchenko had disliked ever since he insisted on having a deciding voice in the affairs of the theatre. Now Nemirovich-Danchenko could count on having no one to oppose him in the administration of the theatre, for Stanislavsky took no part in it.

Writing of his relations with Nemirovich-Danchenko in the years preceding the final break between them in 1917, Stanislavsky is careful to point out that there was no divergence of views on fundamental principles between them. Their separation, he claimed, was a normal occurrence because every artist had sooner or later to go his own way. But it is, surely, significant that Stanislavsky never made any attempt to get Nemirovich-Danchenko to help him with his work on his system. He always remained loyal to Nemirovich-Danchenko ; he never forgot that without him there would most probably have been no Moscow Art Theatre ; he always felt a little guilty before Nemirovich-Danchenko, for as an actor he always seemed to deprive him of his due share of limelight ; and, above all, he could never forget that but for Nemirovich-Danchenko neither Chekhov nor Gorky would have come to the Moscow Art Theatre.

Stanislavsky's reaction from his own lavishly realistic productions led him naturally enough to the other extreme, and for the next few years he was preoccupied with what he called "irrealistic" plays. As it happened, those very plays proved to be the best possible medium for the first tentative application of his new theories of acting. For, dealing mainly with personified ideas and passions, they were an excellent testing ground for the more general principles with which Stanislavsky dealt first of all in his long and arduous quest for the laws governing the art of stage embodiment. His first experiment in "irrealistic" drama was his production of Knut Hamsun's play, the main theme of which was abstract "higher justice", which, like the "higher truth" in Hauptmann's *The Sunken Bell*, seemed to be unattainable to mere mortals. The note of sombre pessimism, which is so characteristic of this pretentious, pseudo-philosophic drama, appeared more strongly in *The Drama of Life*, which lacked the imaginative powers of *The Sunken Bell*, in which Stanislavsky had been so successful in the days of the Society of Art and Literature. The absence of the fairy-tale element in their plays was as a matter of fact what attracted Stanislavksy so powerfully to Hamsun and Andreyev, for this very effectively curbed the extravagant inventiveness of his own imagination and made it possible for him to concentrate on the bleak "fundamental tones" so beloved of the left-wing movement in the theatre, which in Stanislavsky's production of Knut Hamsun's play made the mountains so very mountainous, the tree-trunks so very perpendicular, and the line of the flowing river so very straight.

The rehearsals of the play, in which Stanislavsky played the main part of Koreno, the personification of the idealized seeker after justice who lives in a high glass tower so as to be nearer to heaven, began in the summer of 1906. As always when embarking on something entirely new, Stanislavsky infected everybody with his amazing vitality and enthusiasm. He alone never seemed to get tired. He kept the actors working till the stage had to be vacated for the evening performance and even then, if he himself was not acting that night, he would go on with the rehearsal in the green-room upstairs.

Having discovered the existence of the creative state of mind which alone protected the actor from the hateful stage clichés, Stanislavsky tried to induce it in his production of Hamsun's play by "the new principles of inner technique". Stanislavsky does not specify what those principles were, but it is obvious that at the time he was quite convinced that it was possible for an actor to express abstract ideas of human passions divorced from their individual manifestation in a living character by merely forcing the actor to "live" them. Thus, at one of the rehearsals of *The Drama of Life* Stanislavsky found Sulerzhitsky sitting astride Leonidov, who was lying on the floor growling and doing his utmost to squeeze out of himself the particular passion he was meant to represent.

"Go on ! Go on ! Give us more of it ! Put a little more force into it ! " Sulerzhitsky shouted, applying more and more pressure to Leonidov's recumbent figure.

It was disembodied passions in their pure and bare form that Stanislavsky tried to represent in this production. It seemed to him that to do this the actor only needed the help of his eyes and of his facial expression. He therefore forced his actors to "live" the particular passion each of them represented in the play by remaining absolutely still and relying entirely on their feelings and temperaments. In his enthusiasm for "the new methods of inner technique" he really believed that to represent his experience on the stage the actor had only to induce the creative state of mind in himself for everything else to follow automatically. He thought that the complete absence of gestures would free the actor from his bodily limitations and make it possible for him to concentrate all his attention on the inner life of his part. But what actually happened was that a compulsorily imposed immobility which remained unjustified from within, as well as an attention directed inwards at the behest of the producer, merely gave rise to a most paralysing tension of body and soul. It was then that Stanislavsky discovered in practice that any coercion of nature simply frightened away all genuine feeling and inevitably led to the emergence of all sorts of mechanical clichés so characteristic of the actor's, as opposed to the creative, state of mind. Only a short while before he had severely criticised a certain producer for treating his actors like horses, but now he was doing exactly the same thing. His methods were therefore no better than those he had been criticising so violently. The simple, bare expression of passion without any theatrical conventions appeared to be entirely beyond the capacity of the actors of the Moscow Art Theatre, as indeed it would have been beyond the capacity of any actor, though at the time Stanislavsky seemed to think that this failure was due to their faulty technique.

The Drama of Life, performed for the first time on February 8th, 1907, had a very mixed reception. The left-wing spectators applauded furiously, shouting, "Down with realism ! Down with crickets and mosquitoes (an unkind reference to Stanislavský's productions of Chekhov's plays) ! " while the right-wing spectators booed and shouted, "Shame ! Shame ! Away with all this nonsense ! Three cheers for the old theatre ! " The play was not a success (it ran for only twenty-seven performances), but so far as Stanislavsky was concerned it was a hopeless failure. For once again he discovered that, as with his first productions at the Moscow Art Theatre, the actors merely hid behind their producers, stage designers and, in this particular instance, the new composer of the Moscow Art Theatre, Ilya Satz, who had been taken over from the defunct Studio in Povarskaya Street and whose music was an integral part of the whole production. The methods of "inner technique" he had applied to the play proved entirely useless. His whole work had been wasted and he found himself again in a cul-de-sac. It took him a long time to realize that everything new on the stage had first to become a "habit" and be transformed into the actor's second nature. For only then could the actor make use of the new without bothering about its mechanics. The creative state of mind, too, could only be of use to the actor if it became his natural and normal state of mind ; for otherwise he would merely copy the external forms of the left movements in drama without justifying them from within. The question whether the so-called "left movements in drama" ever possessed anything except external forms did not seem to trouble Stanislavsky at the time. Indeed, having failed with Knut Hamsun's play, he immediately addressed himself to Leonid Andreyev's pretentious essay in dramatic mysticism.

Andreyev's "mystic" drama The Life of Man presents in a very abstract form man's life from birth to death in five acts : (1) the birth of Man and his mother's childbirth pains ; (2) love and poverty ; (3) a Rich Man's ball ; (4) Man's unhappiness ; and (5) Man's death. It has no ordinary characters ; instead there are only abstract figures : Man, his wife, his impersonal friends, his neighbours, and so on. Beginning with the prologue a mysterious "Someone in Grey, called He," passes through the play, holding a lighted candle, the symbol of life. The theme of the play is the utter senselessness of man's life.

From a play representing disembodied passions and ideas, Stanislavsky now turned to one representing vague, pessimistic symbols. Andreyev was at the height of his fame at the time, but Leonidov, who played Man in Stanislavsky's production, thought him utterly insincere. "He was very popular," Leonidov writes in his autobiography, "enormously successful, but his success was not very sound, for it had something of a tenor's success in it : female admirers, love letters, flowers, assignations—in short the whole thing was cheap and shoddy. He was a very handsome man : burning black eyes, though the fire in them was often of an alcoholic origin. While outwardly modest, he was deeply conscious of his own worth. But when 'under the influence' he became so vain and boastful that I never met anyone like him even among actors, and what actor does not think himself a genius ? Once we were driving in a sledge along Tversky Boulevard. It was late at night. Frosty. We had just been at a dinner party.

" 'Look out Dostoevsky !' Andreyev suddenly bawled at the top of his voice. He seems to have been engaged in writing *Anathema*[1] at the time and that was his way of warning Dostoevsky that he had been superseded.

"His inner world," Leonidov goes on, "was peopled with nightmares, horrors, mysticism ; but for all his passion and intenseness, he was pretentious and affected and, hence, false. Andreyev was fond of oceans, pyramids, titans, the universe. He knew the secret of pulling the wool over the eyes of his spectators and readers. He would stun them with one blow, but when you thought it over, you realized how cheap it all was. *The Life of Man*—what didn't he put in there ? Its characters did not so much talk as utter prophecies. The chief part of Man was given to me, an actor who cannot abide falsehood of any kind and, particularly, the

---

[1] Produced by Nemirovich-Danchenko in November, 1909.

predominance of the outer over the inner on the stage. But the play was successful, though its success did not satisfy me."

But to Stanislavsky the play was merely a vehicle for testing his latest theories, which in their initial stages were almost as crude as Andreyev's play itself. Besides, by the time the play had been chosen for production he had discovered his famous "black velvet trick", for which alone he would have chosen Andreyev's play. The trick was discovered accidentally. Stanislavsky and Sulerzhitsky were experimenting with new ideas of stage design for Maeterlinck's *Blue Bird* when a piece of black velvet Stanislavsky had had in his hand a minute before suddenly vanished. They searched the room, but could not find it. Then Stanislavsky saw it lying on a larger piece of black velvet. Eureka! A new principle was found, or so it seemed to Stanislavsky in the excitement of the moment. "Columbus was not so excited when he discovered America," Stanislavsky writes in *My Life in Art*, "as I was that evening. For what combinations of tricks could I not design with black velvet! I could show faces suddenly appearing and disappearing on a stage covered with black velvet. Whole groups of actors or pieces of scenery could vanish before the very eyes of the spectators just by covering them up with black velvet!" Even during his short disillusionment with the picture stage Stanislavsky remained a conjurer at heart. However, it seems that as usual, he let his imagination run away with him. The disappearance of actors and scenery on a stage was "too tricky a trick", suitable for the revue rather than for the legitimate stage. Besides, a whole stage swathed in black velvet transformed it into an eerie, grave-like expanse. Isadora Duncan, the American dancer whom Stanislavsky greatly admired, was present at one of these black velvet demonstrations and, according to Stanislavsky, she exclaimed in horror : *"C'est une maladie!"* Stanislavsky could not help feeling himself that the whole thing was really a bit too morbid, especially as it was only *black* velvet that possessed this magic quality of making things invisible. Still, the trick came in very useful in *The Life of Man*, for it was, he felt, very appropriate to place "the little life of man" depicted in the play on this sombre stage and to show it only in its ominous outlines by using differently coloured ropes to indicate the contours of the rooms, windows, doors, tables and chairs. The costumes of the characters were also merely outlined against the background of black velvet, so that the people wearing them seemed unreal, mere symbols, and their whole meaningless, phantom-like life appeared and disappeared in the unrelieved blackness of the stage.

Just as in his early production of *The Bells*, Stanislavsky used darkness in Andreyev's play for all sorts of grotesque effects, though in a more subtle and stylized form. In the scene of the Rich Man's Ball, Man was outlined in a golden contour, a ghostly orchestra played mournful music, two figures of young women whirled in a ghastly, macabre dance, and along the footlights, exactly as in *The Bells*, a whole row of monsters—rich old women, old millionaires : a whole gallery of smug, stupid, immobile faces. The last act of Man's Death was like a scene from a nightmare, and if not in execution, then in conception and sound effects, it approached most closely the last act of *The Bells*. The black figures of the three Fates in long cloaks, resembling three huge crawling rats with enormous tails, their senile whimpering, laughing and muttering creating an atmosphere of stark horror and imminent death ; along the footlights groups of drunken, reeling figures appearing and disappearing, coughing, wheezing and gesticulating wildly or standing stock-still in a drunken stupor, like figures in a bad dream, one moment filling the stage with their shrieks and then, suddenly, lapsing into silence and leaving behind them indistinct sighs and the heavy breathings of drunken men ; at the moments of Man's death, huge figures appear suddenly, rising eerily to the very ceiling while writhing and coiling serpents are outlined as they crawl from under the floor ; then a loud, ringing report and Man's life comes to an end—everything vanishes : Man himself, the phantoms, and the whole drunken nightmare ; and it is then that the huge, sinister figure of Someone in Grey reappears from the darkness and passes sentence upon humanity "in a relentless, steel-like voice".

All these effects Stanislavsky achieved with the help of black velvet, but it is doubtful whether he succeeded in thrilling his audience to the same extent as he had on the tiny stage of the Hunting Club in the last act of *The Bells* ten years earlier. Andreyev's play certainly did nothing to advance his theories of acting. In this play the actors contributed even less than in *The Drama of Life* to the final impression, which depended entirely on the scenery, such as it was, and on the light and sound effects. Stanislavsky did not succeed in finding the background for the actor which would have helped instead of hindered his complex artistic work. He realized that what he wanted was a simple background and that this simplicity should be the child of a rich and not of a poor imagination. But the simplicity of the scenery of *The Life of Man,* produced by the black velvet and coloured ropes, attracted more attention than the most lavish scenery of the old theatre, to which the spectator is so used that he no longer notices it. The result was of course that it distracted the attention of the audience and diverted it from what Stanislavsky now came to believe to be the principal aim of a performance, namely, the playing of the actors, who felt at a disadvantage against such a background and naturally gravitated towards the well-tried conventional methods of acting.

CHAPTER XLI

HAVING FAILED to learn anything from Meierhold, and deeply disappointed in his own experiments with "irrealistic" plays, Stanislavsky decided to turn for help to a man who was considered to be the most brilliant and original producer in Europe : he persuaded the Moscow Art Theatre to invite Gordon Craig to produce *Hamlet*. This did not mean that he had completely renounced the realistic traditions of the Moscow Art Theatre. Indeed, in the speech he delivered on the occasion of the tenth anniversary of the foundation of the Moscow Art Theatre shortly before Craig's arrival in Moscow, he astonished his hearers by declaring that the theatre would return to the realistic traditions of Shchepkin, but he uttered a warning against the banal and conventional interpretation of these traditions. Realism, he declared, must be sought in the reflection of "the life of the human spirit", a phrase that was to become the pivotal point of his system. "Of course," he wrote to Gurevich in connection with his production of *The Government Inspector* (performed for the first time on December 18th, 1908), "we have returned to realism, to a deeper, more refined and more psychological realism. Let us get a little stronger in it and we shall once more continue on our quest. That is why we have invited Gordon Craig. After wandering about in search of new ways, we shall again return to realism for more strength. I do not doubt that every abstraction on the stage, such as impressionism, for instance, could be attained by way of a more refined and deeper realism. All other ways are false and dead."

And in May, 1909, after Craig had already discussed with him the proposed production of *Hamlet*, Stanislavsky wrote to Gurevich : "Not only have we not grown disappointed in Craig, but we are now convinced that he is a man of genius. The entire theatre has been placed at his disposal, and I myself, as his closest assistant, have put myself entirely at his command, and I am proud of it. It will take a long time before even a few people begin to understand Craig, for he is half a century ahead of us all. He is a fine poet and a wonderful artist—a producer of the most refined taste and knowledge."

Craig arrived in Moscow in October, 1908. In the summer of the same year Stanislavsky had paid a visit to Maeterlinck at his old abbey in Normandy, having gone there from Homburg, where he had been taking his annual cure that year. He spent about a fortnight with Maeterlinck, discussing the production of *The Blue Bird* with him. Maeterlinck, he discovered, had most precise views about everything but not the slightest idea how to carry them out on the stage. He had, therefore, practically to act the whole play for him and demonstrate the different methods he had in mind for its production. At his departure, Maeterlinck promised to be present at the première of the play, but unfortunately (or fortunately, in view of Maeterlinck's subsequent criticism of Stanislavsky's production) he found himself unable to carry out his promise.

From Homburg Stanislavsky wrote a long letter to Nemirovich-Danchenko in which he reverted to his old plan of establishing a provincial touring company with the students of the Moscow Art Theatre. He visualized four kinds of plays for such a company : (1) plays which young actors were competent to produce ("I myself would gladly go to see them," he wrote, "and I should be quite willing to forgive a lot in such plays where the main thing is youth") ; (2) plays which are too difficult for young actors, but in which the leading parts could be taken by those actors of the Moscow Art Theatre for whom there were no suitable parts in the repertoire and who were just kicking their heels and feeling frustrated ; (3) plays which are "good theatre" and do not require fine acting ; and, finally, (4) plays which are interesting as plays and for the sake of which even a bad performance could be forgiven, but which, on the whole, are unworthy of the Moscow Art Theatre, though their authors show promise and ought to be supported.

In Moscow in the autumn Stanislavsky got everything ready for the arrival of Gordon Craig. In his autobiography Leonidov left this description of Craig's arrival : "I remember Craig arrived, wearing a light summer overcoat and a light wide-brimmed hat, and wrapped in a long woollen scarf, at a time when we were having a particularly hard winter with severe frosts. We got him a fur coat and a fur cap. From the station we took him straight to the theatre. That night we were giving *The Government Inspector*. Craig watched the play without understanding a thing and just kept saying, 'Curious!' After the theatre we took him to the 'Hermitage' restaurant, where we regaled him with traditional Moscow dishes and caviare. Then we all went to the 'Yar' to listen to the gypsies. From there to 'Mauretania' and from 'Mauretania' at daybreak to 'Jean's' in Petrovsky Park to eat crawfish, and, finally, in the morning to 'Yegorov's' where, in the famous Chinese Room on the second floor, they served the famous Yegorov pancakes. And so in just about twelve hours Craig got an excellent idea of Moscow night life."

Craig seemed at first to get on very well with Sulerzhitsky, who was to act as his second assistant in the production of *Hamlet*. Stanislavsky thought them "picturesque and sweet," both laughing and gay, Craig very tall with long hair and beautiful, inspired eyes, in his borrowed fur coat and Russian cap, and Sulerzhitsky, looking so diminutive beside him, in a kind of docktailed Canadian coat and "buckwheat" hat. Craig spoke a curious Anglo-German jargon and Sulerzhitsky a similar Anglo-Ukrainian, which gave rise to a lot of jokes and laughter.

After a short acquaintance, Stanislavsky felt that he and Gordon Craig had a great deal in common. Craig explained to him the fundamental principles of the art of the stage as he conceived them and his discoveries in "the art of movement". He showed him many sketches of the new art he had invented— some curious looking lines, scudding clouds and flying stones creating an irresistible impression of an upward movement, and Stanislavsky could not help feeling that it showed promise of development. He agreed with Craig that it was impossible to place the three-dimensional figure of the actor alongside a two-dimensional painted canvas and that what the stage needed was sculpture, architecture and three-dimensional objects. According to Craig, a painted canvas could be used on the stage only as a distant background in the gaps between architectural structures. The sketches of Craig's production of *Macbeth* and other plays apparently no longer satisfied Craig himself, for, like Stanislavsky, he was completely disillusioned about the picture stage and its scenery. Both felt that what they wanted was a much more simple background with which they thought they could create a multiplicity of moods by a combination of lines, spots of light, and so on.

But Craig's more advanced ideas did not strike Stanislavsky as practical and too often he found them rather vague and contradictory. Stanislavsky was as innocent of English as Craig was of Russian, so their discussions must have been conducted through an interpreter, a very unsatisfactory and often confusing way of discussing principles of art. So far as Stanislavsky could make out, Craig apparently claimed that every work of art must be made of inorganic matter, such as stone, marble, bronze, canvas, paper, and paints, and then fixed once and for all in one artistic form. He considered the actor's body as useless for creative work. Indeed, he went so far as to claim that actors were not wanted on the stage, particularly if they were not endowed by nature with striking personalities, that is, if they were not by themselves works of art, like Duse or Salvini. What Craig seemed to abominate most of all (and there Stanislavsky fully agreed with him) was the actor's and particularly the actress's love of limelight. "Women," Stanislavsky quotes Craig as saying, "ruin the theatre. They don't know how to wield their power over us men. They simply abuse their powers." Craig, therefore, dreamed of a theatre without men or women, that is to say, a theatre without actors. He would have liked to replace them with puppets and marionettes which, he contended, would have cleansed the atmosphere of the theatre and lent a more serious tone to the whole business of the stage, while with the dead material out of which they were made one could have attempted to create the Actor with a capital A who lived in Craig's imagination. But Craig's extreme views did not apparently prevent him from showing his delight at the slightest manifestation of true talent in an actor or an actress. The moment he became aware of it, Craig became transformed into a child, jumped up from his chair and rushed to the footlights, brushing away the wisps of long, greying hair that fell from his forehead. But the sight of a third-rater on the stage made him furious and he would again start dreaming of his marionettes.

Having made the acquaintance of the Moscow Art Theatre and its actors and directors, Gordon Craig agreed to join the theatre as producer for one year and was officially entrusted with the production of *Hamlet*. Most of the spring of 1909 they spent in going over the text of the play and discussing it scene by scene,

Sulerzhitsky as a rule making verbatim transcriptions of their conversation and Stanislavsky providing carefully reconstructed production notes of every scene in the play.

Stanislavsky, for instance, took very full notes of Craig's conception of the ghost of Hamlet's father, which Craig considered a highly important part, though he was not sure how it should be represented on the stage. One day he would insist that the ghost must not be theatrical. Let it be real, or in other words, let the attitude of the spectators towards it be real, that is to say, let them believe in its actual existence. "Do you think it can be done ? " Craig would ask Stanislavsky, as though afraid that what he was saying was something unpractical and silly and unsuitable for the stage. But there were times when, as though disappointed in the possibilities of such a real ghost and mindful of the difficulties of fabricating it out of some coarse material, Craig would insist most emphatically that the ghost was merely a tragic figure evoking pity or horror at one and the same time. Unfortunately, it was impossible to make it into a tragic figure such as is found in Greek drama because it spoke of things which were too mundane as well as of its life in the next world. It was therefore only a half-real tragic figure, of the middle ages rather than of ancient Greece.

Those considerations, Stanislavsky explains, led Craig to quite a different conception of the ghost. Now apparently he wished to convey the impression of tragedy inherent in the ghost by realistic means and hence lapsed into ultra-realism, trying with its help to create an abstraction. At such moments the figure of the dead King of Denmark presented itself to Craig in this form : it was straight because it was rigid as a corpse ; it was a skeleton devoured by worms ; bits of flesh were still adhering to its bones, as in a drawing of Death in medieval drawings ; it wore no armour, which the frightened soldiers merely imagined it to wear because they were used to seeing their king in all his martial glory either in battle or at tournaments ; the bones of its body gave out a mysterious, ghostly light, and, in their panic, the soldiers mistook it for the sheen of armour ; it was wrapped in a tattered, decayed and torn shroud, which entangled its legs and prevented it from moving about freely, though it was doomed to walk the earth till its wrongs had been righted ; this skeleton in its torn shroud and with bits of flesh hanging from it looked like some starving, ragged beggar—*sic transit gloria mundi* perhaps best expressed the appearance of that best of men in whom now only his beautiful, tormented soul lived.

The whole figure, Craig maintained, must be picturesque, the skeleton being supposed to convey a hint of its former kingly appearance. It must be tall and slender. "I repeat," Craig, according to Stanislavsky, kept exclaiming again and again as he clasped his long hair and threw himself back in his chair in despair, "it is a highly important and extremely difficult part, for it has to convey the idea of a human figure and at the same time appear supernatural in this realistic guise."

Stanislavsky did not object to Craig's conception of the ghost, but Craig and he disagreed violently about the interpretation of Ophelia's character. On April 24th, 1909, they had a long and lively discussion about Polonius and his family and the whole meaning of Act I, Scene 3, of the play. Craig began explaining that he would like the family of Polonius to be different from anything that had gone on before. "Laertes," he declared, "is only a little Polonius." And in reply to Stanislavsky's question how this difference should be expressed, Craig observed that it was a fatuous, stupid family.

Stanislavsky. "And what about Ophelia ? "

Craig. "I'm afraid she, too, is stupid. She must be beautiful and stupid at the same time. That's why it's such a difficult part."

Stanislavsky. "How do you mean ? Ought she to be a positive or a negative character ? "

Craig. "I rather think she ought to be neither the one nor the other."

Stanislavsky. "But aren't you afraid that the audience, which is used to regarding Ophelia as a sympathetic character, will say that the theatre is distorting it by making her out to be a stupid and unpleasant girl ? "

Craig. "I see what you mean."

Stanislavsky. "Don't you think it would be wiser to make her pleasant and sympathetic on the whole, but show her to be rather foolish in a few scenes ? Would such an interpretation be right ? "

Craig. "Well, I don't know. I can't help feeling that Ophelia and her whole family are rather despicable people, especially in this scene. It is only when she begins to go mad that she gradually grows into a more sympathetic character. I can't help thinking that the advice Laertes and Polonius give to Ophelia proves how utterly despicable they are."

This entirely new conception of Ophelia's character worried Stanislavsky, who was afraid that it might confuse a Russian audience, which was taught to accept the view of the great Russian critic, Belinsky, who regarded Ophelia as second only to Hamlet himself in importance and as one of those rare creations of Shakespeare's in whom simplicity, frankness and naturalness blended into one beautiful, vital and typical character. "Imagine," Belinsky wrote, "a meek, harmonious and loving creature, born to experience calm, untroubled but deep feelings, a gentle creature who is unable to endure great disasters, who will die if her love is rejected, or rather if her love is at first reciprocated and then scorned, but who will die not with despair in her soul, but with a blessing on her lips, with a prayer for the man who has brought about her ruin, and fade away as a sunset on a fragrant May evening—and there you have Ophelia. She is not a Desdemona who, though no less feminine and weak a creature, is strong in her weakness, whose love has swamped all her other feelings and loyalties and who, when she dies strangled in the claws of the African tiger, tells Emilia that she is herself to blame for her death and begs her to vindicate her in the eyes of her husband. No, Ophelia is not at all like that. . . ."

Stanislavsky was afraid that the audience of the Moscow Art Theatre would not only object to Craig's interpretation of Ophelia's character, but would be glad of the opportunity of showing how "well-read" it was and condemn the whole production because of it.

Craig. "But who, knowing Cordelia, can possibly consider Ophelia or Desdemona as poetic characters ? "

Stanislavsky. "But Belinsky, comparing Ophelia with Desdemona, thinks—"

Craig (interrupting). "I think both of them are a little silly."

Stanislavsky. "In that case there is no tragedy."

Craig. "Well, I don't think she has anything to do with the tragedy. I have no sympathy with Ophelia. The only Shakespearean women one can sympathize with are Cordelia and Imogen."

Stanislavsky. "But how does Shakespeare regard Ophelia ?"

Craig. "I think the same as I."

Stanislavsky. "I don't agree. If Ophelia were just a silly little girl, she would belittle Hamlet in the eyes of the audience."

Craig. "She is only wanted in the play to make the whole of

300

it a little more pathetic. That's all. The English critic, Mrs. Jameson, thinks that she has been a little simple since childhood. Perhaps she was frightened by some boy making faces at her from the top of a fence.

Stanislavsky. "If Hamlet rejects a silly little girl, it is not interesting, but if he dwells among the stars so much that he refuses the love of a pure and beautiful girl, then what we get is a tragedy."

Craig. "I don't see that. She's an insignificant little creature."

Stanislavsky. "But why then was he in love with her ? "

Craig. "He was in love with his own imagination, with an imaginary woman."

Stanislavsky. "I'm afraid, then, we shall have to explain it to the audience during one of the intervals."

The discussion then turned on the subject of Hamlet's relationship to Rosencrantz and Guildenstern. Craig argued that Hamlet regarded them as his friends, while Stanislavsky maintained that he never regarded them as such.

Craig. "One of the most poignant scenes in the play is the appearance of Rosencrantz and Guildenstern. Hamlet wants them to be with him. They were great friends at school. He sent for them because he wanted to renew his friendship with them."

Stanislavsky. "But Hamlet did not send for them. It was the King who sent for them."

Craig. "Well—but they were brought up together."

Stanislavsky. "What does it matter who you are brought up with ? To be brought up together does not necessarily mean to be friends."

Craig. "Quite right. When they learnt that Hamlet had not succeeded to the throne, they decided to throw in their lot with the King."

Stanislavsky then turned to Craig's main idea of the play, namely, the collision between two mutually destructive elements —spirit and matter. He wanted to know how the two were to be expressed on the stage. He thought that Polonius was a capable but base and despicable courtier, and that his make-up should be realistic and he should be played realistically, and that only in the presence of Hamlet should he and the rest assume a slightly tragic touch of caricature. Craig did not seem to think so, maintaining that the whole of Act I, Scene 3, should be played at a quick tempo as there was nothing of importance in it. He told Stanislavsky that he admired Italian actors, who were very good at rushing through an unimportant scene in order not to tire the audience and make sure that it reacted more strongly to the more important scenes in the play.

Stanislavsky. "That is your personal impression. I shouldn't have said that. Such a manner of acting is characteristic of touring companies. . . . It's an Italian way of acting."

Craig. "Yes, but I don't think it should be difficult to obtain such a way of acting."

Stanislavsky. "But in order to play a scene at such a quick tempo the actors would have to move about as little as possible. We'd have to let them sit throughout the whole of the scene."

Craig. "But they have already been sitting in the previous scene ! "

Stanislavsky. "Don't forget that the most difficult thing for an actor is to stand still in the middle of an empty stage."

Craig. "Yes, yes, I know that. But can't you really see Ophelia in this scene, crying and grimacing, but without any deep feeling, standing motionless in one place with hardly any movements ? "

Stanislavsky. "But do you know of a single actress who could carry it off? Duse alone perhaps could do it. What do you think ? "

Craig (laughing uproariously). "Oh, Duse would have been rushing about all over the stage."

Stanislavsky still maintained that what Craig wanted could be carried out only by an actress of genius. Craig thought Lilina could do it. (Lilina did not act in *Hamlet* when it was finally performed two and a half years later.) He insisted that the scene should be played as much as possible without any movements. And in this connection he expressed the opinion that, generally speaking, Shakespeare's plays contained no feelings or moods which could be read between the lines (a just criticism of Stanislavsky's own productions of Shakespearean plays, if Craig had only known it), but that everything was expressed in his dialogue.

Stanislavsky. "But we have to do something to make the audience hear the words."

Craig. "That's exactly why I propose to have such simple scenery and why I'd like the movements to be so few and simple."

Stanislavsky. "But why do you think we introduce so many movements in Chekhov's plays ? "

Craig. "Because they are inherent in the text."

Stanislavsky. "Well, yes, but Chekhov has not got any movements in his plays. We make the actors move about in order to force the audience to take notice and listen."

Craig. "Yes, yes ! "

Stanislavsky. "And the most difficult thing in the world is to put two actors on the stage and make them go through their dialogue without moving. This at once becomes theatrical in the worst sense of the word."

Craig. "But here the words are beautiful in themselves. The idea lies in the words."

To which Stanislavsky quite justifiably replied that the words had been translated and could not possibly be as beautiful as in the original and that, besides, to make an audience listen to beautiful words one must first know how to enunciate them beautifully, which (and here Stanislavsky spoke from experience) was not as easy as it seemed. But Craig was quite sure that a Shakespearean play did not demand a great variety of poses and movements and that its entire meaning must be sought in its dialogue. "To transmute the dialogue into movement," he said, "is only possible on one condition, namely, that there are as few as possible of these poses and movements."

The Russian text of the play, too, presented many difficulties, and it was during these preliminary discussions with Craig that Stanislavsky realized for the first time how faulty his particular translation of *Hamlet* was and that it was responsible for a number of important misunderstandings of some of the most vital passages in the play.

CHAPTER XLII

GORDON CRAIG soon left for Italy to work on the *mise-en-scènes* of *Hamlet*, and Stanislavsky began his rehearsals of *A Month in the Country*, the first play he produced according to his system.

Already in the previous year Stanislavsky had started using rather odd sounding terms at his rehearsals, such as "nail",[1] "circle", and "aids". These seem to have been the first terms he used when working out the main elements of the creative state of mind of the actor. While analysing his past experience on the stage during his Finnish holiday, Stanislavsky was struck by the fact that in his most successful part of Dr. Stockmann he had unconsciously endowed it with a number of external traits which he had observed in life and kept buried in his memory till the moment came for them to be combined in the delineation of a character with whom he felt a strong affinity. He at once realized the importance of these hidden memories, which he embodied in his system first under the name of "affective memories" (he had presumably been reading Th. Ribot's work *Problèmes de psychologie affective*) and later under the name of "emotional memories". It was also at the same time that he began to wonder what it was exactly that all the great actors he had studied seemed to possess in common, and he came to the conclusion that it was the absence of muscular tension. The "relaxation of muscles", therefore, became another indispensable element of his system. He further discovered that while he was completely absorbed in his work on the stage, he held the attention of the audience without any effort, and that led him to the discovery of the element he first called "the circle" or "the circle of attention". He then realized that the fullest possible concentration of the actor's physical and spiritual nature was one of the

---

[1] In Russian the word is used metaphorically like its equivalent French word *clou* (the metaphoric use of the word is in effect a Gallicism) in the sense of "the main attraction."

most fundamental laws of the actor's art, and so "concentration" was added to the other elements. As he went on with his experiments and observations, he found that the actor had to believe in what he did or said on the stage and that truth on the stage was merely what the actor believed in. The actor, no doubt, realized that he was surrounded by things that were not true, that in fact everything on the stage was a lie, but by saying to himself *if* those things were true he would be acting thus and thus, he transformed the lie into an artistic truth. The important thing, therefore, was that the actor should be aware of this imaginary truth, for this awareness possessed the magic quality of instilling belief and, consequently, transforming everything round it into truth. *If* thus became another important element of his system. All those elements, the feeling of truth as well as the relaxation of muscles and concentration, he discovered, were amenable to development and exercise. Indeed, it was only when he had discovered the importance of the feeling of truth, produced by the action of *if* on the actor's imagination, that he succeeded in attaining a genuine and natural state of concentration and relaxation of muscles.

Finding that his discoveries made little impression on the actors, some of whom, to his great distress, did not conceal their hostility to his "latest fad", Stanislavsky decided to select a small group of actors and actresses and produce a play according to the principles of acting he had already discovered, principles that were based on the premise that the actor was the chief creative artist in the theatre.

To produce *A Month in the Country*, Stanislavsky took a step that was unprecedented in the history of the Moscow Art Theatre : together with a small group of actors—the cast of Turgenev's play—he suddenly disappeared from the theatre for four months, thus breaking the by now firmly established tradition that every actor in the theatre, whether playing or not, had to be present at all the rehearsals, which were considered to be the actual school of acting in which the young actor of the company got all his practical knowledge of the stage. No one knew what Stanislavsky and his small group of actors were doing on the "small", that is, the rehearsal stage of the theatre. All that was known was that they were rehearsing *A Month in the Country* in a way that no play had ever been rehearsed before. For instance, the actors never spoke their lines, and if they did address each other, they did not even speak in a whisper but just moved their lips soundlessly. Even the limited space of the small stage was apparently too large, for Stanislavsky had it partitioned off into two or three tiny rooms where the actors used to retire and communicate with each other not with words but (so it was rumoured) only with their eyes.

Stanislavsky produced *A Month in the Country* as an experiment in his still far from complete system. Turgenev was not a playwright and his "play" is a masterly psychological study in the form of dialogue. It therefore lacks the usual "stage" atmosphere of the genuine dramatist, which fact was an added attraction to Stanislavsky at a time when ordinary conventional dramatic situations and, indeed, the whole structural form of a play began to pall on him. He saw at once that it was impossible to produce Turgenev's play by the traditional methods of stage representation. His problem consisted in finding the best possible way of laying bare the souls of the characters so that the spectators should be able to grasp at once what was taking place in them. Such a problem could not be solved by gesture, or the play of hands and feet, or indeed by any of the generally accepted methods of acting. What he had to get was some "invisible irradiation of will and feeling by means of a look in the eye of the actor, by means of hardly perceptible inflexions in his voice, by means of psychological pauses of great intensity." He had, besides, to be careful to remove everything that stood in the way of the spectator's perception of the most essential inner feelings and thoughts of the characters. He had therefore to apply methods almost identical with those he had already used with so little success in Knut Hamsun's *The Drama of Life*: almost complete absence of gesture and superfluous movement, which meant practically eliminating the producer's *mise-en-scènes*. He decided to repeat the same experiment in *A Month in the Country* because in Turgenev's play he was no longer dealing with passions in the abstract but with concrete and highly individualized passions of people who were familiar to him.

In *A Month in the Country*, Stanislavsky for the first time shifted the emphasis from the producer to the actor, and therein lies its importance as an experiment, a successful experiment as it turned out, in the famous "system".

"We have decided to treble the artistic demands on ourselves," Stanislavsky wrote to Lyubov Gurevich in May, 1909, "and throw overboard everything that has become vulgar on the stage.

No *mise-en-scènes*, no sounds. Everything now is based on simplicity and on the inner delineation of the part. Do you realize what it cost me to turn the whole cast at one stroke to what we have been trying to achieve gradually and systematically? But there is no evil but good may come of it. This forced everybody to sit up and take notice of my system, which during the last few years I have got sufficiently ready. It's hellish work, but fascinating. . . ."

Stanislavsky himself, who played Rakitin, Olga Knipper, who played Natalya Petrovna, and the other members of the cast could now show beyond a doubt whether or not the actor, as required by the system, was the chief person in the theatre. Here, therefore, Stanislavsky for the first time discovered another of the essential elements of his system, namely, that the actor must understand what was demanded of him, know what he himself wanted and what could fire his imagination creatively, and that out of the infinite number of these absorbing *problems* and *pieces the life of the human spirit of the part* was composed. This is one of the most essential propositions of Stanislavsky's system. In Turgenev's play these problems and pieces were easily found by Stanislavsky, though perhaps not so easily by the other actors, because the play dealt with the sort of people he knew and because the inner meaning of the play which, as a rule, is so difficult to perceive and which Stanislavsky later defined by the two terms of *ruling idea* and *through-action*, could be easily grasped and inwardly digested by him.

But the new methods devised by Stanislavsky were not so easily assimilated by the actors, who were bewildered by the terms he used and who had not been through the long and painstaking process of converting mere theory into practice so that in the end it became an unconscious habit. Olga Knipper, in particular, found it very difficult to get under the skin of her part of Natalya Petrovna, the heroine of Turgenev's play, who is torn between her duty to her husband, her affection for Rakitin and her love for the student Belyayev. One day at a rehearsal, despairing of ever being able to convey the fine psychological subtleties of her part, she burst out sobbing, told Stanislavsky that she could not possibly play the part, and went home. It was at a crisis like this that Stanislavsky showed how understanding and patient he could be in spite of his ruthless disregard of any opposition from his actors. In a very moving letter he at once wrote to Olga Knipper, he explained that he had not been to see her personally because he had not wanted to cause her more unpleasantness. "You must be so sick of me," he declared, "that I think I'd better keep out of your sight for a while. Instead of myself, I am sending you these flowers. Let them tell you how tenderly I admire your talent. It is my great admiration for it that forces me to be cruel to everything that might tarnish the beautiful gifts with which nature has endowed you.

"You are now going through a period of tormenting artistic doubts," Stanislavsky continued. "All deep feelings of suffering on the stage are born of such agonies. Don't think that I am indifferent to them. I am terribly worried about you, though I know that these agonies of yours will bear splendid fruit. Let not me but someone else explain to you what nature has given you. I am ready to watch patiently and from a distance how your talent, dispensing with everything it does not need and feeling free at last, will reveal itself in all its strength, suppressed only for a time by this damnable trade of the actor. Believe me when I tell you that what seems so difficult to you now is really of no importance. Have the patience to analyse, think over, and understand these trifles, and you will experience the greatest joy anyone can ever experience in this life. I promise not to frighten you any more with technical terms. I expect that must be where I went wrong. I implore you to be firm and courageous in your present artistic conflict, which you must win—not only for the sake of your talent, which I love with all my heart, but for the sake of our theatre which is the only thing I care for in life. Go over your part again and try to find out into what pieces it naturally falls. I am sorry for the pains I have caused you, but believe me they are unavoidable. Soon you will yourself achieve the real joy of art."

"This letter," Olga Knipper writes, "brought me much suffering, but it brought me great comfort, too, for I no longer felt lonely, and I realized that Stanislavsky had not abandoned me, that he supported me, and that I had to pull myself together for the sake of the play and be worthy of the theatre which was all Stanislavsky 'cared for in life'."

From the point of view of scenery, *A Month in the Country* also marked a considerable advance on Stanislavsky's last two productions. The abstract scenery of *The Drama of Life* and, particularly, of *The Life of Man*, was a failure because all its value lay in its novelty (a most ephemeral element in any art). Actually, it merely served the purpose of disguising the actor's inability to deal with mere abstractions on the stage. For *A Month in the Country*, Stanislavsky succeeded in obtaining the services of Mstislav Dobuzhinsky, a member of the famous group of Petersburg artists who, under Alexander Benois, had already won international fame in designing the *décor* of Diaghilev's ballet. Dobuzhinsky was at the height of his fame at the time, having distinguished himself particularly for his subtle understanding and fine rendering of the poetic and sentimental moods that were so striking a feature of the aristocratic culture of the period between the 'twenties and the 'fifties of the nineteenth century. Dobuzhinsky went to Moscow to design the scenery of *A Month in the Country*. He had a room in Stanislavsky's flat which was later known as "Dobuzhinsky's room", and there he worked with Stanislavsky on the scenery of Turgenev's play. He was present at all the rehearsals, and first of all produced a number of sketches of his first impressions of the different scenes and costumes, which Stanislavsky carefully collected and then hung on the wall so as to give the artist a clear idea of the gradual emergence of his designs. It was in this way that what Stanislavsky called "the architectural plan of the floor and scenery" was gradually evolved with the producer's constant and vigilant co-operation. Stanislavsky took great care that there should be no clash between the views of the actors and the stage-designer, for he realised that the harmonious collaboration between the actors and the stage-designer was an indispensable condition of the collective work of the stage.

The work on Turgenev's play and his other duties (he was, in addition, appearing in the part of Krutitsky in Ostrovsky's play *Even A Wise Man Stumbles*, produced by Nemirovich-Danchenko) so exhausted Stanislavsky that at the beginning of the season, which opened on October 2nd with Andreyev's *Anathema*, also produced by Nemirovich-Danchenko, he had to spend five days in bed. *A Month in the Country* was first performed on December 9th, 1909, and it was an immediate success. The play was remarkable for the entire absence of the so-called "external expressiveness" and for its astonishingly bare *mise-en-scènes*. In the third act, for instance, the actors sat almost all the time on a sofa which occupied practically the whole wall of the curved room the stage represented. In general, the rooms in *A Month in the Country* were merely indicated by the arrangement of the furniture. There was no trace of the succession of rooms in Stanislavsky's productions of Chekhov's plays that Valery Bryussov had found so amusing. Even the scene in the garden had only one seat and one three-dimensional tree against the background of a painted backcloth. These sets seemed definitely to help the spectators to accept the new form of the performance and its highly sensitive methods of "inner delineation of character." Here, then, Stanislavsky's theories were for the first time proved right, and he was justifiably happy and delighted with the 'result of his production. But what pleased him most was that it had led him to a more thorough examination of the methods of studying and analysing both his part itself and his state of mind in it. For it was then that he discovered the further truth that an actor must know how to work not only on himself, but also on his part.

The triumph of his theories naturally led Stanislavsky to his next task of putting them into practice in spite of the opposition of many members of his company. Here Sulerzhitský came to his help. Already on February 20th, 1909, Sulerzhitsky had drawn up a report on the marked deterioration in the acting of several of the principals in the popular *Blue Bird*, a play in which Stanislavsky once again showed how inexhaustible his imagination was in the production of fairy stories. Knowing from his own experience how stale even a successful part could become in the course of a long run, Stanislavsky added an important postscript to Sulerzhitsky's report, warning the actors not to overlook its serious implications. He pointed out that there existed two quite different ways of acting, one characteristic of the actor who looked on the stage as a profession and the other of the actor who looked upon it as an art. "The actors of our theatre and Russian actors, in general," Stanislavsky wrote, "will never be satisfied with being just competent stage hacks. For that you have to be a foreigner. The art of actors consists in living a part. Our actors must not only be able to live their parts, but must also know how to make themselves live their parts. And that is not enough, either. They must know how to accomplish the act of living their parts easily, without forcing themselves to do it. This can be done, and I am ready to teach this art to anyone who will himself show a desire to learn it. For without it the theatre, in my opinion, is superfluous, harmful and stupid. Now I am free.

During the coming season I shall be very busy. In future I shall refuse to work in accordance with any other principle. I therefore invite anyone who is interested in the art of living a part to spare me a few hours of his time. I shall resume my lessons next Monday. I shall be at the theatre every day at one o'clock to explain what the theatre has discovered after so much hard work and long study. I cannot, however, undertake the organization of the different groups and the arrangement of their time-tables.''

The uncompromising tone of this declaration, so characteristic of Stanislavsky when he became obsessed by an idea, frightened the actors and he had to select his own small team with which to produce *A Month in the Country*. During the next season Stanislavsky was too busy to resume his campaign for his newly discovered system, and in the summer of 1910 his first serious illness occurred which kept him away from the theatre for a whole year and brought about a postponement not only of the practical application of his system, but also of the production of *Hamlet* by Gordon Craig.

CHAPTER XLIII

IN SPITE OF HIS present disappointment with realism in the theatre, it was in the realistic portrayal of Krutitsky, the old General in Ostrovsky's comedy *Even A Wise Man Stumbles*, performed for the first time on March 3rd, 1910, that Stanislavsky achieved another of his great triumphs on the stage. He approached this part in his old manner of a study from life, and his make-up, too, was taken from life. But as with every part that did not come to him naturally, the first representation of Ostrovsky's blimpish character had something of the grotesque in it. It was only during the Petersburg season of the Moscow Art Theatre in the spring of 1910 that he achieved a complete blending of himself and Krutitsky and immediately scored a resounding success.

"Everyone ought to go and see one of our greatest actors in this part," a well-known Petersburg dramatic critic wrote. "I call Stanislavsky a great actor," he continued, "not because he has given us a most perfect portrayal of Krutitsky (which in itself is a remarkable feat), but because his Krutitsky is not only a highly individualized character, but also a universal type. That is not just fine acting, but the sort of creative acting only great actors are capable of."

Indeed, so complete was Stanislavsky's embodiment of Ostrovsky's character that even his friends fell entirely under the spell of the stage illusion when meeting him behind the scenes. Gurevich saw him in the wings one evening waiting for his cue in one of the scenes of *Even A Wise Man Stumbles*, and the impression she got of him was so uncanny that when he stretched out his hand to her she drew back in bewilderment. He looked a complete stranger to her—an old relic of a bygone age one still occasionally ran across in the street, stooping with age and be-whiskered, with a pair of stupid round eyes, a muffled, wheezy voice, and flabby hands.

Stanislavsky laughed when he saw how startled Gurevich was, but his laughter, too, sounded different to her.

"I'm awfully sorry," she said, half in jest and half in earnest, "but I don't think I've met you, General, and I really don't know what to say to you."

"What a bore it is to have to play stupid old men," Stanislavsky replied, laughing again.

But the illusion persisted.

"Yes, yes," Gurevich said quickly, "I know of course that you are Konstantin Stanislavsky, but I don't feel it and, anyway, I'm afraid I must go back to my seat."

And still looking startled and uncomfortable, she touched the "General's" flabby old hand and went away.

It was most probably during this season that Stanislavsky and Leonidov were invited to Tsarskoye Selo, the summer residence of the Czar, to a performance in the Chinese Theatre of Schiller's *Bride of Messina*, translated and produced by the Grand Duke Konstantin Konstantinovich, who was well known as a poet under the initials K.R. (Konstantin Romanov). The Grand Duke acted the leading part in the play and after the second interval, his *aide-de-camp* went up to Stanislavsky and told him that his Highness desired to discuss the production with him.

"But, surely," said Stanislavsky, "this is against all the rules of the stage. I never allow anyone to visit me in my dressing-room during a performance as I find that it distracts me. I feel very reluctant therefore to disturb his Highness before the end of the performance."

But the real reason of his refusal to see the Grand Duke Stanislavsky explained to Leonidov afterwards.

"Why should I go to him ? " he said. "I'd have had to discuss his performance which was terrible. I could hardly have told him the truth, particularly as he is an amateur and not an actor. And I should have hated to have to lie to him."

After the Petersburg season Stanislavsky went off for his annual cure to the Caucasus, and this time his wife and children again accompanied him. In Kislovodsk he continued to work on his system.

"It is harvesting time with me now," he wrote to Sulerzhitsky at the end of July. "For two months I've been sowing all sorts of ideas and questions in my head. They were ripening rather painfully during the summer and would not let me sleep, but now the first green shoots are appearing. I have barely time to write down what I dimly perceive, what is engendered in my brain and demands a more or less precise definition. If I don't succeed now in writing it all down, I shall have to start all over again next year, for everything is still so vague that I am afraid I may forget it soon. And, besides," he added, thinking no doubt of the production of *Hamlet* which was due to take place after Gordon Craig's return to Moscow in the autumn, "this year I shan't have time to write down everything that has matured in my brain unless I do it here in the Caucasus."

He was convinced at the time that all he needed for his system was a theory that he could put into practice by methods which had been carefully checked on the stage. He. had already discovered most of the "elements" of his system and worked out a whole series of exercises for them. He had experimented with them on the stage himself and found that they worked. But the reluctance of the actors of the Moscow Art Theatre to accept his findings and, particularly, his experience with Olga Knipper during the rehearsals of *A Month in the Country*, convinced him that he had still to discover some way of making the actor wish to put his system into practice. He was, therefore, now working on what he later called "the motive forces of inner life", that is to say, he was trying to discover the principles which set the "elements" of his system in motion. At the moment he knew that before an actor applied himself to his system he had to bring the processes which stimulated his will into action, and that, when given the text of the play, he had to begin his search for the various *problems* and *pieces* of his part by some kind of literary discussion ; but he did not know how the process of searching for the right problems was to be kept up and developed. He knew, too, how to stimulate the actor's desire to live his part (he had shown it in this production of Turgenev's play), but was not yet quite certain how to assist him in its *embodiment*. Still he thought that he had already explored the ground sufficiently and was near to the discovery of the right way in which to solve this particular difficulty. On the other hand, the processes which brought about the fusion of the actor with the audience and their influence upon each other seemed perfectly clear to him. The only thing he had to find now was some practical way of arousing the actor's imagination in all those different processes. Unfortunately, psychology seemed to have disregarded almost completely the workings of the artist's and, particularly, the actor's creative imagination, but after the success of *A Month in the Country* he was pretty sure that the system he had devised made good this omission. Moreover, he was convinced that his system could be taught to every actor and that, indeed, a producer could use it to write a "score" of a play just as a composer wrote a score of a symphony. It took him years of experience in the practical application of his system before he realized that it possessed no such qualities and that each part had to be created anew by every actor.

But Stanislavsky fell ill with typhoid fever in August and all his plans for the next season, including the production of *Hamlet*, had to be postponed indefinitely. In Moscow the news of Stanislavsky's serious illness was received with consternation, for it meant a sudden change in the theatre's programme for the 1910-1911 season. Nemirovich-Danchenko decided to put off the production of *Hamlet* for a year and set to work immediately on producing *The Brothers Karamazov*, the first adaptation of a long novel given by the Moscow Art Theatre. In the meantime, Sulerzhitsky hurried off to Kislovodsk without waiting for his leave of absence from the theatre, and stayed there till Stanislavsky was out of danger. By the middle of October, Stanislavsky had recovered sufficiently to be able to resume his correspondence. During his illness he was very worried by what was happening in Moscow and the news of the production of *The Brothers Karamazov*, which he received on October 14th, so delighted him that he sent off a telegram to Nemirovich-Danchenko, congratulating him on the great work he had done and expressing the hope that the adaptation of so vast a work of fiction would open up new perspectives for the theatre. He was dreaming, he told Nemirovich-Danchenko, of putting on an adaptation of *War and Peace* in two parts, *Peace* during the next season and *War* at the beginning of the 1912-1913 season during the centenary celebrations of the Russian victory over Napoleon. In a letter he wrote to Nemirovich-Danchenko on the same day that he sent his telegram, he declared that the day he had received the news of the production of *The Brothers Karamazov* was the happiest of his life. It was, indeed, a thrice blessed day, for it was on October 14th that the Moscow Art Theatre was opened and it was also the day of the 200th performance of *Czar Fyodor*. "Hurrah!" he wrote. "Our theatre is still alive and kicking, and its workers are talented, efficient and full of determination. If only half of our gigantic work is accomplished, I shall still shout hurrah, clap my hands like a madman, and be as happy as a sandboy ! "

Nemirovich-Danchenko was even more excited than Stanislavsky with the production of *The Brothers Karamazov*. He was convinced that he had not only broken new ground but had accomplished a veritable revolution in the theatre. "With Chekhov," he wrote to Stanislavsky, "the limits of the stage conventions have been widened, but with *The Brothers Karamazov* they have been abolished." Now, he asserted, there was no literary work of art that the stage could not tackle. Indeed, he had apparently not only abolished the conventions of the theatre, but had abolished the playwright as well. Why should a play have three or five acts ? He had divided Dostoevsky's novel into twenty acts, some lasting an hour and a half and others only a few minutes. Why write plays that took at most four hours to act ? He had presented *The Brothers Karamazov* on two successive nights. Soliloquies ? Why, some of his soliloquies lasted between twenty and thirty minutes, and, he added, a little too confidently as it turned out, the audience showed no sign of flagging interest. Development of plot ? He had introduced a narrator who told the audience all that had to be left out of the novel. Descriptive passages ? Well, why not employ a great artist to paint them and then let the narrator read the novelist's descriptions so that the audience could experience the double enjoyment of *seeing* and *hearing* beautiful landscapes ?

"I am waiting impatiently for a complete victory," Nemirovich-Danchenko went on. "Like a general who has captured an important position from the enemy, I am burning with the desire for a final conquest. But—I know that one mustn't be in a hurry, that one must gather new strength, get everything ready first and then inflict a crushing blow on the theatrical conventions. In future the history of the theatre will be divided from Ostrovsky to Chekhov, from Chekhov to *The Brothers Karamazov*, and from *The Brothers Karamazov* to—Greek tragedy ? No, I don't think so. From *The Brothers Karamazov* to the Bible ! "

All this was strictly in accordance with Nemirovich-Danchenko's theory of the "creative" producer and, one might add, with his idea of his own importance. It could not have escaped Stanislavsky's notice that with the exception of Ostrovsky, Chekhov and himself, Nemirovich-Danchenko did not mention any dramatist. Instead he had given him a long list of novelists whose works the Moscow Art Theatre ought to adapt in future. What worried Stanislavsky was that both the Press and the public appeared to be lukewarm, if not hostile, towards Nemirovich-Danchenko's proposed abolition of "the conventions of the stage". The receipts of *The Brothers Karamazov* had been very small. "You need not try to convince me about the adaptations of novels, or the Bible, or even Plato," he wrote to Nemirovich-Danchenko on November 15th from Kislovodsk. "There seems, however, to be one serious snag—the box-office receipts. For if the public is not particularly eager to spend its money on *The Brothers Karamazov*, which has created such a furore, it may be expected to be even less keen on spending its money on other adaptations. You're wise—I'm anxious to hear what you have to say to that."

But Nemirovich-Danchenko was apparently hurt by his partner's scepticism, for he did not reply to Stanislavsky's letter. After dismissing the whole question of adaptations of novels as still of only theoretical importance (he was later to take up an outspokenly negative attitude towards adaptations of long novels, especially after his own production of an adaptation of Gogol's *Dead Souls*), Stanislavsky, in his next letter to Nemirovich-Danchenko on November 25th, returned to the financial difficulties of the Moscow Art Theatre. Nezlobin, an actor and producer who had founded a private theatre in Moscow only two years before, was doing excellent business, perhaps just because he had "borrowed" many of Stanislavsky's earlier methods of production. "Nezlobin's scenery is so nice," Stanislavsky wrote, "his corners and foreshortenings so wonderful ! He has so many rooms on the stage and he puts on plays that are either too easy or too difficult to follow (both of which are good paying propositions). At the Maly Theatre, too, I am told they are simply coining money, while we don't seem to be able to get an audience. I can't help thinking," he went on bitterly, "that we are now faced with a real anti-Christ in our business—Nezlobin. Everything in his theatre is pretty and tasteless to the point of crudity, but this is apparently what the public wants and what our critics, with whom Nezlobin knows how to keep on good terms, like. Whatever the stupid critics, who do not understand our theatre at all, say about us, can be said with more justice about Nezlobin. Not a spark of talent, a luxury which to our taste is the very essence of tawdriness, though the critics think it is the real thing, and the most stale stage clichés that any hack-actor can easily acquire. Next year, I understand, Nezlobin intends to strengthen his company (strictly in accordance with the taste of the public, of course), and then everybody will be convinced that he has all the talents. And what about us? I'm afraid we hang by a thread. It is not reasonable that the fate of our theatre should depend on two men only. Why are we incapable of producing independent administrators and actors? Do we really suppress them so much? If that is so, then I'm ready to shoot myself rather than go on exerting so crushing an influence on people."

All these melancholy reflections (as a matter of fact, the budget of the theatre was balanced for the first time at the end of the current season), made Stanislavsky return to the idea of making the Moscow Art Theatre into a "People's Theatre". "This is a painful step to take," he wrote in the same letter, "since in such a theatre we shall not be able to keep up our high artistic standards, but on the other hand who are we devoting our lives to now? The rich people of Moscow? Is it really possible to enlighten them? Of course they will leave us for Nezlobin. We must do something or else we had better extract the last penny from the Moscow Art Theatre, pay off everybody, and start afresh on a much less ambitious scale. Oh, how important it is to get a really sensational success next season! You know what is beginning to worry me? I am afraid our public will not recognize Craig's genius and will just think him an eccentric. I can't help feeling that Nezlobin and the Maly Theatre have exerted so great an influence on our public, and the decadents have so wearied them with their innovations, that they have become corrupted and all they want now is nice scenery, and when they see *Hamlet* they will simply say, 'Oh, what a pity they have not done it the old way!'"

Apart from his worries about the future of the Moscow Art Theatre, Stanislavsky, like everyone else in Russia at the time, was greatly shocked by the death of Tolstoy on November 7th. Tolstoy's death may not have been such a personal loss to him as Chekhov's death was, but he felt it no less poignantly on that account. "I am completely overwhelmed by the beauty and the majesty of Tolstoy's spirit and of his death," he wrote to Nemirovich-Danchenko on November 10th. "The circumstances of his death were so unusual and so symbolic that I can't think about anyone save the great Leo, who died like a King, renouncing before his death all that is vulgar and unnecessary and only insults death. What great happiness it is to have lived at the same time as Tolstoy and how terrible it is to remain on earth without him, almost as terrible as to lose one's conscience and one's ideals."

And referring to the decision of the Moscow Art Theatre to found a school for peasant children in memory of Tolstoy, Stanislavsky wondered whether it would not have been better to select a group of actors and organize special performances of Tolstoy's play *The Power of Darkness*.

In a letter to Sulerzhitsky, written at the same time, he declared: "Tolstoy not only overwhelmed me by his greatness, he also gave me great æsthetic joy by the last days of his life. All this taken together is so beautiful that I feel afraid to remain in this world without him." And, finally, Stanislavsky added this characteristic confession of his belief in the existence of a life after death : "I, who have just been through a serious illness, cannot help feeling that with him I should not have been so afraid to go to that other life which lies beyond (for I am sure, that is, I *feel* that that *beyond* exists—somewhere)."

His illness had left Stanislavsky very weak and all he could manage was to climb up laboriously to the top of the tower of the boarding house where he was staying or go for short rides in a cab. He was forbidden to write, and the letters he did contrive to send off were all written in secret. Sulerzhitsky was about to leave for Paris just then at the invitation of the famous French actress Gabrielle Réjane, who had seen Stanislavsky's production of *The Blue Bird* during her visit to Moscow in October, 1910, and who was anxious to put on Maeterlinck's play at her Paris theatre according to Stanislavsky's *mise-en-scènes*. "I hate to give in to Réjane's impudence," Stanislavsky wrote to Sulerzhitsky. "I wonder what she would have asked us to pay if we had gone to Paris to get some of her secrets ? However," he added, "the French gave us a great deal that is good in the art of comedy and, I suppose, we can now repay part of our debt."

CHAPTER XLIV

IN THE AUTUMN of 1910, Gorky invited Stanislavsky to visit him on the island of Capri, where he had been living for some years because he was consumptive. "I want to see you, you great rebel," Gorky wrote. "I want to talk to you, I want to communicate certain ideas to you—add some fuel to your blazing heart, the flames of which I have always admired and shall continue to admire whatever you may be doing, my dear sir."

Stanislavsky was deeply touched by this letter, but was too ill to answer it. Sulerzhitsky wrote to Gorky that Stanislavsky often talked about him during his illness. "The Moscow Art Theatre," Sulerzhitsky reported Stanislavsky as saying, "has nothing to live on. It is being kept at its present high level artificially. It was alive only when Chekhov and Gorky wrote for it. There are no new playwrights and in another year or two our theatre will no longer be able to keep up its high standards. It is time to make an end of it and start a new one on popular lines. I shall work near it in a studio and perhaps put on a play for it occasionally and act in it, too, now and again. But I have no more strength left in me to go on fighting. I'd like to work quietly by myself."

Gorky's invitation to discuss his new ideas with Stanislavsky came at the right moment, for Stanislavsky, too, was anxious to ask his opinion of the first outline of "a grammar of dramatic art" he had completed. He met Gorky in February, 1911, when he went to Italy to recuperate from his illness. He spent a short time in Capri with Gorky, whose idea, which eventually led to the creation of the First Studio of the Moscow Art Theatre, was the establishment of a theatre of improvisation. Gorky had seen such a theatre in Naples and become a firm believer in its possibilities. Recalling Stanislavsky's Capri visit in 1930, Gorky said : "Twenty years ago I suggested to Stanislavsky that he should organize a studio in which the young actors, in addition to studying theatrical art, should create plays collectively." No record of Gorky's conversation with Stanislavsky in Capri has been preserved, but in a letter Gorky wrote to Stanislavsky on October 12th, 1912, he returned to the subject of a theatre of improvisation and explained his idea at some length. According to his plan, the playwright would first of all prepare a rough outline of the plot of the play and its characters. After that the actors would set to work on it, every actor developing his part independently and then discussing his idea of it with his fellow-actors, who were expected to criticise and complement it. "This," Gorky wrote, "would make the characters more alive and real and would suggest how each character should behave towards the others and what his attitude should be towards the subject-matter of the play, for the presence of firmly sketched characters must inevitably lead to some kind of dramatic collision between them." Gorky insisted that the actors should be allowed full freedom in their work on their parts, the producer merely making sure that they did not unconsciously make use of "literary" situations and expressions or try to make their particular parts into the leading parts of the play for reasons of self-display. In this way, Gorky thought, the text of the play would gradually emerge, and during the rehearsals it could be further improved on. The playwright himself would only be called in, if necessary, after the final version of the text had been agreed on in order to put the finishing touches to it.

The idea at first appealed to Stanislavsky, though of course he would have preferred Gorky to write another play for the Moscow Art Theatre. It made him think of the possibility of reviving in some new form the Italian *commedia del' arte*.

"In a talk I had with Stanislavsky in his dressing room after a performance," the critic Efros writes, "he told me at great length about these plans of his and discussed the ways in which they could be realized. What he wanted was a playwright who did not write his plays independently of the theatre, but took part in the collective work of the actors who would be the real authors of the play."

Nothing came of these plans so far as the Moscow Art Theatre was concerned, but Gorky's idea provided Stanislavsky with a method for overcoming the actor's reluctance to do the exercises for the different elements of his system. He did it by letting the actors improvise on the dramatic situation that was best suited as an exercise for a particular element. Gorky's suggestion helped him to infuse life into the dry bones of his theory of acting.

The summer of 1911 Stanislavsky spent in Brittany with his family. There he met Efros and his wife, Nadezhda Smirnova, a well-known actress of the Maly Theatre. At the time Stanislavsky was interested in Hindoo philosophy and especially in the yoga system of abstract meditation and mental concentration, which supplied him with one of the most important elements of his own system—the *circle of public solitude*, consisting of a number of large and small "circles" into which the actor has to withdraw in order to keep his attention concentrated on the stage and not on the audience. His studies of Hindoo philosophy also provided him with the numerous sayings of Indian sages with which he was fond of illustrating his talks to the actors.

This is how Smirnova describes her first meeting with Stanislavsky : "I saw Stanislavsky for the first time on the beach. I was in my bathing costume and I felt so awful at being introduced like that to a man who inspired a respect that amounted almost to superstitious fear. But afterwards I got so used to him that I was able to look at him with a critical eye. This remarkable man forced you to think always of the theatre. He himself was entirely preoccupied with the theatre. His ideas on any other subject were neither interesting nor particularly profound, but about the theatre he could not only talk, but also think deeply and originally."

Efros was of course a godsend to Stanislavsky, who at once enrolled him as his amanuensis, kept discussing the more intricate points of his system with him and made him write down his latest conclusions and definitions. This was much harder work for Stanislavsky than for Efros ; for his system was still too new and untried for him to be able to discuss it clearly and with that uninterrupted flow of logical reasoning and visual imagery in which he became so adept ten years later. In his talks with Efros in Brittany he found it very difficult to express himself. He would get excited, stammer, search in vain for the right words in which to define his still rather complicated theories of acting, and was often driven to despair by his inability to convey something that he had already established as an incontrovertible fact of the actor's experience. But his constant pre-occupation with his system did not prevent him from joining in the fun of a holiday by the sea. He did not bathe, but he paddled while the others bathed, and he would invent all sorts of spontaneous and rather childish practical jokes. One evening, left alone with Efros to discuss his theories, he suddenly interrupted their talk and proposed to hide in the bushes and waylay their wives and friends, pretending that they were hold-up men. He was genuinely disappointed when his prank did not come off because he was recognized at once. Another time they were overtaken by darkness on their return home along some precipitous cliffs. "Let's go in single file," the forty-seven-year-old Stanislavsky proposed, "hold on to each other and pretend to be blind. Close your eyes all of you—you can't see anything anyway—and I'll be your guide. Just like in Maeterlinck's *The Blind*. And afterwards let's tell each other what we felt." And he forced the whole company of middle-aged people to do as he wished just as if they were his actors and he were rehearsing a play with them.

They went to see an historical pageant in Dinan, but Stanislavsky kept jumping up from his seat and muttering, "Oh, if only I could have done it for them ! This isn't even amusing. Little children playing at soldiers are more amusing ! " Smirnova was just then studying the part of Lady Macbeth which she was to play at the Maly Theatre during the winter season, and when she and Stanislavsky found themselves in the Hall of Thick Columns on Mont St. Michel, the medieval castle perched on top of a high hill on a rocky island off the Breton coast, he began rehearsing her part with her.

"Remember all this," he said to Smirnova. "Breathe in this air. It was here that Lady Macbeth came down the spiral staircase round this column. She had a lighted candle in her hand. As she came down the stairs, she kept disappearing behind this column and reappearing at the bend of the stairs. The flickering candle lighted up her deathly pale face and threw a bright spot of light on the column. How much this picture will give you for your part ! "

He stopped her again on one of the outside staircases of the castle. "I'll stand and wait for you below," he told her. "You come down the stairs reading the letter you've just received from Macbeth describing his meeting with the witches. Come on now. Remember your lines ? Where else if not here can you receive the right inspiration for your part ? "

"Stanislavsky," Smirnova writes, "fired my imagination and I began to live the life of a lady in a medieval castle. I could already fancy myself as Lady Macbeth passing along its passages devoured by ambitious dreams. I was in the tower where King Duncan was killed, and in the Hall of the Knights where Macbeth was giving his banquet when Banquo's ghost appeared. From that day I became obsessed with the part of Lady Macbeth, and it was Stanislavsky who had initiated me into it. Thanks to him this part no longer seemed difficult to me. I felt happy when I worked on it and I was not afraid to play it after the great Yermolova."

And on their return to the mainland, Stanislavsky appeared to her a magician who was able to transport people into any age he liked and make them live in it.

CHAPTER XLV

STANISLAVSKY was always good newspaper "copy". The engagement of Gordon Craig to produce *Hamlet* immediately gave
rise to a crop of rumours of disagreements between him and the
English producer, and even as early as the spring of 1909 some
newspapers announced that their partnership was at an end and
that Craig had finally broken with the Moscow Art Theatre.
What gave rise to these reports is difficult to say. Quite probably
Stanislavsky's unpopularity with the actors just at that time,
caused by his rather rough and ready way of cramming his
system down their throats, had led some of them to exaggerate
the differences of view between Stanislavsky and Craig during
the initial discussion of the production. Anyway, Stanislavsky
immediately denied the rumours of a break with Craig. But the
crisis the Press had foreseen broke dramatically a few days before
the first night of *Hamlet*, on December 23rd, 1911. It arose out
of the growing personal disagreements between Craig and Sulerzhitsky, culminating in Craig's demand that Sulerzhitsky's name
should be removed from the handbills. As Sulerzhitsky had been
doing most of the donkey work on the play, he naturally resented
this final affront (unlike Stanislavsky who would never dream of
letting a personal grudge interfere with his work on the stage)
and disappeared from the theatre. The cat was out of the bag
now and the whole story, suitably embellished, was eagerly
reported in the Press.

Again, as during the rehearsals in Pushkino, personal vanities
and uncontrollable tempers threatened to wreck his work, and
again he was deeply grieved and bewildered.

"You have either fallen ill, in which case please let me know
how you are, or you are demonstratively protesting and are
angry, in which case I am sorry that the work which began so
joyfully, should end so sadly," he wrote to Sulerzhitsky on
December 22nd. "I feel," he went on, "that I must do something,

but I am not sure I know what has happened. Are you angry with Craig for the change in the lighting? I can't believe it. It is Craig, after all, who is responsible for the scenery and the whole idea of the production. Just as Peter Hansen, the translator of Ibsen, who thinks that *Brand* is his own play, is ridiculous, so should I have been ridiculous if I had claimed that the screens and the whole idea of the production of *Hamlet* were mine. There is nothing like success, and the 'mousetrap' scene was highly successful yesterday. Besides, did you not feel yesterday that Craig was right in deciding to play the scene in darkness and that in it (i.e. in the darkness) is our only hope of saving the performance? And, as a matter of fact, the darkness did conceal all the loose ends wonderfully. The last scene went off so well just because the darkness hid the operatic shoddiness of the costumes."

Stanislavsky then turned to the real reason of Sulerzhitsky's disappearance from the theatre. "It is rumoured," he wrote, "that you are offended because of the handbill. But I had nothing to do with it. Craig got on his high horse and rejected all suggestions. The theatre demands that Craig's name should be on the handbill because the row he made has become known all over the town. Craig demands my name on the handbill, that is to say, he is afraid of responsibility and wants to have me as a scapegoat in case he may need one. Amid all these absurd complications I have to reconcile Craig with you or you with Craig, for I can't possibly appear by myself on the handbill. I go to you for advice and you start talking to me about *The Blue Bird*. It is then that I just can't make anything out. Will our work, which began in so friendly a spirit, end like that? If that is so, then I must give up what I hold most precious in life—art, and run from its temple where it is no longer possible to breathe.

"One can't go on living like that and suddenly be offended without giving any reason. If you are cross with Craig, I can understand it, though I can't help being sorry, but—Craig is a great artist, he is our guest, and in Europe they are now watching us to see how we shall receive his art. I don't want to make a fool of myself, and, besides, I don't relish the task of teaching Craig. Don't you think it is much better to finish the work we have begun, particularly as there is only one more day left?

"Turn your anger to kindness and do not spoil a good beginning by a bad ending. Tomorrow at two o'clock we are rehearsing the appearance of the ghost in the bedchamber."

Sulerzhitsky's reply is interesting both for throwing light on his relations with Craig and for containing important criticisms of Craig's production.

"Craig," Sulerzhitsky wrote to Stanislavsky on December 23rd, the day of the first performance of *Hamlet*, "is a great artist and will always remain so to me. That he is our guest I also know and, I think, I have proved during the two years of my work with him that I can put up with the rudeness, irritability and confusion of this man and, in spite of it all, be fond of him.

"That Europe is watching him does not interest me in the least, for that will not alter my attitude to him or to anyone else. He can have any lighting he likes—he has a right to that—and I have nothing against it. I have helped him in the past, and today I shall work on the lighting in the bedroom scene, for there as well as in the play as a whole, the screens are not everything. You and I and our theatre put a lot of work into it, and if something has to be changed, I will change it, if that is the wish of the chief producer of the play, I mean you. And, generally, so long as *Hamlet* is not finished, I am ready to carry out Craig's instructions, even if they do not coincide with my own views, so long as you find that Craig is right.

"In the sphere of artistic work I cannot be offended— you know that very well, and you know why : because I have little faith in myself and in my own powers, and when dealing with you it would be both absurd and foolish to take offence. But it's different with Craig. When he goes on talking of lines, composition and even lighting, I feel that it is—Craig, but when it comes to the question of production I am not so sure that he is absolutely right, for he does not seem to be interested in the actor very much. Here I find that the lighting of the 'mousetrap' scene is wrong, and if it was successful at the dress rehearsal it was not because of the lighting but in spite of it. Everybody was complaining that they could not see Hamlet, and the first night audience will never forgive the theatre that.

"But such a sudden change does not and cannot offend me . . . though I cannot help regretting the fact that you gave in so easily, for you yourself spent ten minutes arguing with Craig and trying to prove to him that it was quite impossible to play in such darkness, and that it might be all very well for the screens but that it was not fair to the actors or the performance as a whole.

"As for Craig's refusal to have my name on the handbill, all

I can say is that after two years of hard work and endless sacrifice for Craig, who would never have completed his production without me, I certainly did not expect it. That's all. But I am not offended. Craig the artist I respect, but Craig the friend no longer exists for me. There can be nothing in common between him and me. It is not a question of any offence, but I shall never have anything to do with him again. I am simply not interested in having anything to do with such a man—that's all there is to it. I shall, however, always enjoy seeing his work, whatever it may be.

"But," Sulerzhitsky concludes, "I am certainly not cross with you, particularly as you don't even notice such incidents. If, however, there should be a great many such pinpricks, they would become a matter of serious concern to me and I am afraid that our good relations might be affected. But life is short and such unpleasant incidents do not often occur, so that there is no danger of that."

Stanislavsky himself was tremendously impressed by Craig's scenery, consisting mostly of "screens", which, he thought, showed Craig to be a producer of great genius as well as a fine artist. Unfortunately, not all Craig's ideas could be realised, which, curiously enough, Stanislavsky did not regard at all as a reflection on Craig's art as a producer. He ascribed it entirely to the inadequacies of the modern stage. Neither he nor Craig seems to have asked himself why Shakespeare was not troubled by such questions but accepted philosophically the limitations of his stage and shaped his art accordingly.

It would appear from Stanislavsky's account of the final form of the production of *Hamlet* that Craig had changed his mind about Ophelia and agreed to present her as "a girl with a pure soul". But the production as a whole was entirely in conformity with Craig's own symbolic interpretation of the play, an interpretation that was imposed on the actors. This did not at the time worry Stanislavsky, although *Hamlet* as well as the other plays he produced during this period, such as Tolstoy's *The Living Corpse*, Molière's *Le Malade Imaginaire*, and Goldoni's *The Woman at the Inn* were all rehearsed by him according to his system, and though, in fact, he had already reached the conclusion that the actor was the most important person in the theatre. These rehearsals soon disclosed a number of serious faults in the system, particularly between the inner incentives of the actor's creative feelings and their embodiment. Stanislavsky discovered, for instance, while demonstrating to Craig the different modes of diction, that when he thought he was expressing his feelings truthfully, he was in fact merely expressing them in the conventional manner he had unconsciously adopted from the bad type of theatre. That for a time shook his faith in his own theories and made him spend many more uneasy years in re-examining the main concepts of his system.

This re-examination had become all the more necessary because one of the chief "elements" of his system, that of problems and pieces, proved totally inadequate in *Hamlet*. For the division of the play into small pieces and their work on each piece separately, made them lose sight of the play as a whole.

The "element" of pieces always gave Stanislavsky and his followers a great deal of trouble. Stanislavsky himself certainly never meant it to be anything but a means to an end, though at the time of the production of *Hamlet* he may have treated it somewhat more rigidly, chiefly because he had found it so serviceable in *A Month in the Country*. Writing of this particular problem many years later, Leonidov expressed the view that the performances of the Moscow Art Theatre had degenerated into the representation of certain scenes of a play and not of the play as a whole. "I must say," he declares, "that recently I have failed to see a play as a whole on the stage of the Moscow Art Theatre. All I see are good or bad performers and, occasionally, brilliantly executed scenes, but I do not see the play as a whole. Neither the actors nor the producers seem to think about it. They are all following Stanislavsky's instructions that a play, a part, and a scene must be divided into small pieces, but they forget that Stanislavsky regarded such a procedure merely as a temporary expedient and that after having worked on the separate pieces, these must be joined together."

Another unforeseen result of the production of *Hamlet* was that the simplicity of its scenery proved to be an illusion. Indeed, Craig's screens and "operatic" costumes were even grander and more lavish than Stanislavsky's black velvet and coloured ropes in *The Life of Man*. Stanislavsky could not help reflecting again that the simpler one tried to make a production, the more pretentious it seemed to be. It did not occur to him that the simplicities of a producer of genius like Craig had a strident splendour of their own.

CHAPTER XLVI

THE OPENING OF the First Studio in January, 1913, was a direct consequence of the lukewarm, if not hostile, reception of Stanislavsky's system of acting by the actors of the Moscow Art Theatre. This was chiefly Stanislavsky's own fault. He did not seem to have realized that it was not enough to have invented a system, but that he had also to invent a method or methods of applying it in practice. He would call the actors together in the foyer of the theatre and tell them to do certain exercises without first convincing them that their acting would actually improve as a result of it. He would often lose his temper with them, appear, as the actors put it, "with a white face", if they did not show sufficient enthusiasm for the particular exercise he chose for them. "Bolder! Bolder!" he would roar. One day a stranger happened to be present in the foyer while Stanislavsky was putting the actors through their paces and he was so shocked by what he thought was his outrageous behaviour towards famous actors, that he went up to Stanislavsky and undid his tie, as if to say, "Well, is this bold enough for you?" Stanislavsky looked embarrassed, and saying, "Yes, something of the kind," retired to the other end of the room.

The trouble, of course, was that there was some justification for the unwillingness of the actors to accept Stanislavsky's assurances about the benefits his system would confer on them. For the odd thing was that ever since he had been preaching his system his own acting had perceptibly deteriorated. "He was a much better actor before he discovered that system of his," the actors whispered to each other. "And no wonder! He was acting then, and not fooling about!"

And it was true enough. His acting had become worse, for he was not so much acting as experimenting now, and his art as a performer and interpreter of his parts had suffered in consequence.

But in spite of the grave doubts this fact aroused in his mind, he refused to give up his theories. His obstinacy again asserted itself and made him more and more unpopular with the actors. A wall seemed to have sprung up between him and them. His attempts to interest the younger actors in his system also failed. It was then that he decided that Sulerzhitsky should begin teaching the system in one of the private dramatic schools in Moscow. The experiment proved successful and very soon several of Sulerzhitsky's students joined the Moscow Art Theatre and formed the nucleus of what was soon to become the First Studio.

One of Sulerzhitsky's students was Eugene Vakhtangov, who was to become one of the most brilliant younger producers on the Russian stage. He had accompanied Sulerzhitsky to Paris and assisted him in producing *The Blue Bird* at Réjane's theatre. Later he headed a group of young actors at the Moscow Art Theatre who were anxious to be trained in the Stanislavsky system, Sulerzhitsky supervising their exercises for entering the circle of attention, the relaxation of muscles, the attainment of the feeling of truth and belief, and so on. These exercises were periodically shown to Stanislavsky who, to the dismay of his followers, often repudiated some of the theories he had been propagating so passionately. "What fool taught you that?" he would sometimes ask them. But, on the whole, his system was beginning to take root among the young actors and, in spite of his disappointing experience with the Studio in Povarskaya Street, he decided to organize another studio for them outside the Moscow Art Theatre. Nemirovich-Danchenko came to his help and, as the administrator of the theatre, promised to advance the studio sufficient money to begin its work.

This small but promising beginning had an immediate effect on Stanislavsky's state of mind and, according to the testimony of his closest friends, he had not for a long time been so happy and contented as in the summer of 1912. He would often burst into song, "take off" all sorts of important personages, such as Jules Claretie, the venerable director of the Comédie Française, whom he represented as accepting the homage of a young decadent playwright. One day he paid a visit to the Summer Gardens in Moscow and watched the open-air entertainment, beaming with delight whenever a juggler or an acrobat appeared on the stage. "This is real art!" he kept saying to his companions. "This is beauty! Oh, if the actors would only understand the true meaning of this kind of precision of movement. An acrobat does nothing haphazardly. He leaves nothing to chance. He knows very well that he has only to make one slip and he will break his neck. That is why he is always working to perfect his body. Actors don't seem to realize that this is no less important to them ! "

In August he went for his summer cure to Kislovodsk and there he continued to work on his system. He had now decided to collate his own conclusions on the art of acting with the conclusions reached by the old European masters of stagecraft, and in a letter to Gurevich in September he asked her to go through all their works in the Petersburg libraries and have the relevant passages translated and typed out for him.

Throughout the autumn and the winter preparations were made for the opening of the Studio. A small flat, consisting of one large and two small rooms, formerly used by the cinema "Lux", was rented. It was, as it happened, on a higher floor of the very building in which the Society of Art and Literature had been inaugurated in 1888. Gorky kept bombarding Stanislavsky with letters expounding his proposal for a theatre of improvisation and sending him several outlines of plays for the members of the Studio to work on. He was sorry the first experiments would be made without him, he wrote to Stanislavsky on October 12th, 1912. "It would be nice," Gorky went on, "if you could come here with a dozen young students. In two months we should have tried out a comedy, a tragedy or a melodrama of the new type."

"People like you," Gorky wrote to Stanislavsky in another letter, "strengthen my faith in the future of our country. Don't take these words of mine as a compliment—why should I pay you compliments ? I realize that by now you must be thoroughly sick of them. But your beautiful and living soul I love tenderly. . . . Carry on with the good work. We shall live and work for our country joyfully each in his own way—you in Russia and I here. If we make mistakes, we shall not hesitate to point them out without losing our respect for one another. . . . I usually write : keep cheerful and have faith in life and the creative powers of man, but I need not write that to you, and that is what I like so much ! "

Sulerzhitsky kept Gorky informed about the work of improvisation the Studio was carrying out. On March 9th, 1913, he sent him a detailed report of some improvised sketches, adding that occasionally the dialogue of the actors was so good that he was tempted to write it down. "We never discuss the improvised scenes beforehand," he wrote. "Only afterwards do we put them together in a certain order so that they should not interfere with one another."

All this evidence proves conclusively that the Studio was originally intended as an experiment in improvisation. It is all the more surprising therefore that in his own account of the First Studio in *My Life in Art*, Stanislavsky completely ignores this particular aspect of the Studio's work. It is quite likely that the first experiments in improvisation proved so disappointing as a means of creating a play that Stanislavsky gave up the idea. On the other hand, he found the whole process of improvisation so congenial to the teaching of his system that he incorporated it as an exercise into the curriculum he prepared for the Studio. He began reading a course of lectures on his system to the students, while Sulerzhitsky conducted the practical exercises in the attainment of the creative state of mind, the analysis of parts either in improvised scenes or in scenes taken from plays, and in the stimulation of the actor's will-processes on the basis of the logical consistency of feelings.

The first signs of a radical change in Stanislavsky's approach to the actor—a definite break with his methods of producer-autocrat—make their appearance with the foundation of the Studio. He had the following notice displayed in the theatre : "Anyone wishing to read something, to appear in a scene from a play, to submit scale-models of sets, to demonstrate the results of his researches in stage technique, or to offer some literary material for the stage, should put down his name in a special book kept for that purpose in the hall of the Studio."

The first two plays performed by the new Studio—Heijermans' *The Loss of Hope* and Gerhardt Hauptmann's *The Festival of Peace*—were both successful, though the second play, produced by Eugene Vakhtangov, provoked a violent outburst from Stanislavsky and was nearly suppressed by him.

The first performance of *The Loss of Hope* took place on January 15th, 1913. At first the rehearsals of the play proceeded very slowly because the young actors were busy at the Moscow Art Theatre. Stanislavsky called a meeting of the Studio actors and told them that the performance would have to take place even if they had to do the impossible. "Remember," he said to them, "that your whole future depends on this performance. You must go through your own 'Pushkino,' as we had to go through it before the foundation of the Moscow Art Theatre. If you can't rehearse the play in the daytime, do it at night even if you have to work till daybreak."

When the play was eventually produced, Stanislavsky regarded its success as a triumph for his system. The acting of the young student-actors, he thought, revealed "a simplicity and depth of rendering" he had never known before. At the official opening of the new and larger premises of the Studio in October, 1913, Stanislavsky warned the actors that it was the duty of a theatre to exercise a beneficent influence on the spectators. "The theatre," he said, "can be very helpful to the spectators, but it can do great harm to them, too."

How well justified this warning was Stanislavsky realized when he saw Vakhtangov's production of *The Festival of Peace*, one of Hauptmann's naturalistic plays showing the decay of a German middle-class family. At the end of the performance, Stanislavsky was white with fury. The actors had never seen him so angry before. "In your interpretation of this play," he told Vakhtangov, "you took a stuffy cellar instead of a powder magazine for your starting point." What he meant was that Vakhtangov had so exaggerated the purely naturalistic elements of the play that he violated one of the most cardinal principles of his system, a principle he had learnt at the very beginning of his career on the stage, namely, that in presenting the dark sides of life, the producer and actor must always look for its brighter sides. What he saw in Vakhtangov's production, however, was hysteria and not life.

This production revealed two diametrically opposed tendencies in the Russian theatre, which were to become more and more pronounced and irreconcilable as the political events in Russia moved to a crisis, culminating in the revolution : the tendency of denunciation and exposure and the tendency of artistic truth. The first eventually led to Vakhtangov's temporary break with the Moscow Art Theatre. The second led Stanislavsky to adopt an intransigeant attitude towards all tendentiousness in art and to the conviction that tendentiousness could only be permitted on the stage if it were justified from within.

At first Stanislavsky refused to allow *The Festival of Peace* to be performed in public, and he was supported in his decision by Sulerzhitsky and Nemirovich-Danchenko. It was only after the actors of the Moscow Art Theatre, especially Kachalov, had pleaded with him to remove the ban on Vakhtangov's production that he changed his mind and gave permission for the play to be performed. The direct sledgehammer blows of Vakhtangov's production had an immediate effect : the play was a great success.

Gorky saw *The Loss of Hope* and *The Festival of Peace* on his return to Russia in 1914. He had violently attacked the two Dostoevsky adaptations produced by Nemirovich-Danchenko— *The Brothers Karamazov* and *Nicolai Stavrogin*—in 1910 and 1913 respectively, for he was fundamentally opposed to "the philosophy of suffering" which was perhaps unnecessarily emphasized by the producer. ("We were at the time," Nemirovich-Danchenko explains in his autobiography, "the idolaters of the movement in art which was anxious to proclaim its independence of life and politics.") But Vakhtangov's production of Hauptmann's play brought about a reconciliation between Gorky and the Moscow Art Theatre. After the performance Gorky went behind the scenes, where he burst out crying and kissed the actors of the leading parts. He thanked them for affording him real artistic pleasure and declared that the Studio was one of the most interesting theatres in Russia. This sort of thing was what he liked ; it was real art—the art of denunciation and protest.

Stanislavsky never even mentions *The Festival of Peace* in *My Life in Art*. He was at the time busy carrying out one of Sulerzhitsky's fondest wishes—a permanent home for the actors of the Studio in the country, where they could all live a communal life on the land, building their own houses, growing their own food and, as the element of the fantastic was always dear to Stanislavsky's heart, erecting a Theatre with a capital T. This last dream was never realized, but Stanislavsky bought a plot of land near Eupatoria in the Crimea, bounded on the one side by a lovely stretch of sandy beach and on the other by the flat, endless steppe, the monotony of the view broken only by a clump of wild olive-trees. There Sulerzhitsky and the actors of the Studio would retire for the summer and live a primitive life, and there Stanislavsky went to see them in the summer of 1914. He had arranged to meet Gurevich earlier at Lustdorf, a seaside resort near Odessa, as he was anxious to study the material on the history of the

European stage that had been translated for him in Petersburg. On meeting Gurevich on June 4th, he exclaimed : "I simply adore the sea ! As soon as I caught sight of it on my arrival here, I trembled all over with excitement." He had used almost the identical phrase in a letter to Gurevich in the previous year after the first visit of the Moscow Art Theatre to Odessa. This repeated avowal of love for the sea rather surprised Gurevich, who had been told that Stanislavsky was indifferent to the beauties of nature. She knew, of course, that he had no appreciation at all of flowers, although he always sent them to actresses, but that, she thought, was due to the fact that he was so used to receiving them that they no longer made any impression on him. His professed love of the sea, however, made her try to find out what his attitude to nature really was. "You see," said Stanislavsky, "every time I am planning to spend my holidays in a place famous for its beauty spots, I picture it so vividly in my mind that when I arrive there I am no longer impressed, for reality looks so much poorer to me than what I had imagined it."

Stanislavsky only spent a few days with Gurevich at Lustdorf, and as he was anxious to continue their studies, he invited her to join him in Marienbad where he intended to have his annual cure that year after his short visit to Eupatoria. Lilina was already there and in another fortnight Gurevich and Stanislavsky resumed their work on collating the views on the art of the stage of Stanislavsky's predecessors with his own. "I shall never forget the work we did together on the extracts from the old books on the art of acting," Stanislavsky wrote to Gurevich on March 4th, 1928. "I am referring to our daily meetings in Marienbad when the menacing war clouds were already gathering round us. This work clarified many things to me and helped me to lay out the facts I had learned from experience on the shelves of my mind."

"I can see him as though he were sitting before me now," Gurevich writes in her reminiscences of Stanislavsky, "on the terrace of the Marienbad restaurant, reading extracts from *Reflections on Recitation* by Luigi Riccoboni, the reformer of the Italian theatre, who in 1737 was already propagating the type of acting which Stanislavsky called 'the art of living a part'. He was so pleased to find in these *Reflections* what he himself had discovered long ago and had formulated in his theories of acting that he trembled with excitement. 'Oh, the darling, the darling ! I could embrace him ! I could kiss him ! ' he exclaimed in a voice of infinite tenderness, stretching out his arms as though he could actually see the old Italian actor before him and wished to press him to his heart.

"I am describing this scene," Gurevich continues, "and his words and movements with absolute accuracy because they took me completely by surprise by their child-like spontaneity and their passion. Such as I saw him then, I have never seen him either before or since."

Stanislavsky was equally enthusiastic about *The Art of the Theatre* by Riccoboni's son, Francesco Riccoboni, who, like himself, preached that "the actor must never rely on inspiration or go on the stage as an improviser, but must work, work, and work." He was also greatly interested in Diderot's views on the theatre, the methods of acting of the two famous French actresses, Léris Clairon and Marie Françoise Dumesnil, and the writings of François Talma. He liked, in particular, the extracts from the books of the famous German actor and theorist of the stage August Wilhelm Iffland. Once, when they were talking of the great German actor Konrad Eckhoff, founder of the Berlin Academy of Stage Art, who laid particular stress on the importance of rehearsals and the ensemble, Stanislavsky fell silent suddenly, his face looking "so solemn and beautiful" that Gurevich dared not ask him what he was thinking of. Then, as though recollecting himself, Stanislavsky said in an undertone, "It seemed to me that his spirit had walked past us," and he added after a pause, "Who knows? Maybe he felt that we were talking about him, that we understood him."

The imminent outbreak of the war threw Stanislavsky into feverish excitement. He already imagined the whole of Europe torn by war and the sheer folly of it all made him ill. He ran a high temperature and the doctor ordered him to bed. But he was too worried to remain in bed. He would dress and leave the hotel to find out the latest news. He persuaded Gurevich to join him and his wife in Munich and go with them from there to Switzerland. The official declaration of war caught him in Munich.

When Gurevich, who had stayed behind in Marienbad for a few days, arrived in Munich, she found Stanislavsky greatly changed. He looked very tired. His eyes were feverish. He had a high temperature. He sensed the hostile atmosphere in the city and the rising spy-mania. He told Gurevich excitedly that "detectives" had been to see him at the hotel and had examined his papers.

Stanislavsky described his nightmarish journey through Germany after the outbreak of the war in an article under the title "A Prisoner of War in Germany", which he published shortly after his return to Russia. What impressed itself on his mind at the railway station in Munich was the gloomy silence that seemed to hover over the crowds of Russians who were anxious to leave Germany. They stood in small, silent groups, afraid to utter a word lest they should attract attention, watching the countless trains with soldiers and guns. "I got the impression," Stanislavsky writes, "that I was surrounded by a wall of steel. Even the monotonous field-grey uniforms of the Bavarian soldiers seemed to be made of steel. I glanced at the glass roof of the station, and the sky, too, was steel-like." An hour and a half later as he looked up again at the glass roof the sky was ominously red. "It seemed to me," he declares, "that death was hovering everywhere."

And his feeling seems to have been justified, for an hour after their train had moved out of the station (they were bound for the Swiss frontier station of Lindau where they hoped to get a steamer across the lake to Switzerland), it was stopped and a German officer came into their carriage and addressed Stanislavsky "in a menacing voice".

"What nationality ? "

Stanislavsky drew himself up to his full height and replied with calm dignity,—

"Russian ! "

His calmness apparently angered the German, who turned round, bared his sword and, waving it wildly in the air, shouted in a thin, shrill voice, "*Heraus ! Heraus !* "

They got out on the platform, Stanislavsky holding on tightly to his precious attaché-case in which he carried all his manuscripts. But they were ordered to leave all their things on the platform and were immediately surrounded by armed soldiers. Lilina, who was the last to leave the carriage, was hustled out by an officer who brandished a revolver in her face. Followed by a large hostile crowd who threatened "the Russian spies" with their fists, they were marched off to one of the refreshment rooms on the station. "The room," Stanislavsky writes, "had two large windows which covered almost the entire space of one of the walls, and the crowd outside pressed against them, climbing on top of one another, the whole window practically covered with faces, but those faces were no longer human : they were the faces of wild beasts, on the left mostly German reservists, on the right women's faces which looked no less brutish."

The soldiers in the refreshment room were for some reason re-arranging the tables, and it looked to Stanislavsky as if there were some horrible purpose behind it all. His worst fears seemed to have been confirmed when they were all lined up against the panelled wall. Were they going to be shot ? But, surely, thought Stanislavsky, they were not going to ruin such a fine panel ! "Then I began to think," Stanislavsky writes, "that if there were many soldiers in the firing party, death would be instantaneous, but if only six men were to shoot fifty, it would be an execution no longer, but a shambles. It occurred to me, though," he adds, "that they would never shoot us in the panelled room, but would take us out into the street, through the yelling crowd, which was still peering through the windows."

However, having indulged for a moment in this flight of fancy (his sense of drama was as keen in life as on the stage), he suddenly remembered the document he had been given at the Russian consulate in Munich in which the fact was mentioned that he had once played in the presence of Wilhelm, and he handed it to one of the German officers, who examined the paper and gave it to the other officers to read. "It seemed to us," Stanislavsky writes, "that the attitude of the Germans towards us changed and became more friendly."

After their documents had been examined, they were again placed in a train which, however, moved off in the opposite direction from the Swiss frontier. It was a very slow train. Their fourth-class carriage was lit only by a candle-end in a lantern. Through the window they could catch a glimpse of some distant hills silhouetted against a bright moonlit sky. Stanislavsky bent over to Gurevich. "The men," he whispered, "will probably be shot." Then he began telling her that the events of the last few days had convinced him that human culture was still only skin-deep and that what they wanted was quite a different kind of life, a life in which human needs were reduced to a minimum and in which the artist could work for the benefit of the people, at least for those, he added to Gurevich's great surprise, who had not as yet been entirely engulfed by "bourgeois culture".

At Kempten the train was stopped again. They were ordered out on to the platform, drawn up in fours, and once more taken to one of the refreshment rooms, where the soldiers started re-arranging the tables again. Stanislavsky heard one of the soldiers say to an officer that they did not have enough ammunition. "But," Stanislavsky writes, "our nerves had become so blunted by that time that we were not afraid of anything any more, and even the word 'ammunition', which they evidently wanted for our execution, did not dismay us."

Soon, however, they were informed that they would be allowed to continue their journey to Switzerland in the morning and would be kept as prisoners-of-war only if Switzerland refused to admit them. The refreshment room was full of Russians, including a group of Jewish artisans who had fled from Russia during the pogroms and had now to return there. Some of them went up to Stanislavsky and started talking to him in broken Russian. He listened to them courteously and did his best to calm their fears. On returning to his table, he sat down beside his wife for a moment and then got up again.

"I don't think I was friendly enough to those poor fellows," he said. "I must go and return their visit."

And he went off to their corner of the room and spent a long time talking to them.

In the morning they were off again, this time bound for the Swiss border. At Lindau, however, the women and children were allowed to proceed to Switzerland and the men (Lilina insisted on remaining with Stanislavsky) were marched off to the local barracks where they were kept for a few hours till the order came through permitting them to enter Switzerland. Through the open door of the shed Stanislavsky watched the evolutions of the German soldiers in the barrack square. He stood beside a tall, lean Prussian officer, who reminded him of a cartoon from the German comic paper *Simplicissimus*." "It seemed to me," Stanislavsky writes, "that he was watching me all the time to see what impression the marching soldiers made on me. A moment of keen delight was in store for him. A squad of twelve soldiers was just marched past him. As they drew alongside, they raised their legs as one man, turned their heads to the right and fixed their eyes on the officer. They stood stockstill in that unnatural position till the officer, having sustained the pause, put his finger to his peaked cap. This scene, I could see, filled his heart with great pride. I expect what the soldiers did was considered to be the highest achievement of military drill."

On arrival in Switzerland, Stanislavsky and his wife decided to return to Russia by sea via Marseilles and the Dardanelles. Between Malta and the Ægean they were struck by the great number of English and French warships. "The nearer to the Dardanelles," Stanislavsky writes, "the greater the number of warships." At Smyrna and Constantinople the atmosphere was very tense. As they passed through the Bosphorus shots were fired across the bows of their ship. It was a signal for them to stop. Suddenly a huge warship loomed out from the distance. It was the notorious German battleship *Goeben*, which was returning from a cruise in the Black Sea. The *Goeben*, which everyone still called by her German name, was surrounded by a large number of cruisers and destroyers. She seemed to bear straight down on the Russian passenger boat, which was already pressed hard against a minefield and was in imminent danger of being blown up. "The *Goeben*," Stanislavsky writes, "seemed determined to ram us, and it was only when a collision seemed inevitable that she turned and passed within a few inches of us. We had a good chance of examining the crew of the battleship. The officers wore German naval uniforms. Evidently they no longer thought it necessary to keep up the masquerade. As soon as she came alongside us, her whole crew, as if at a word of command, turned their backs on us and made an improper gesture. In this childish fashion the Germans showed their contempt for us Russians."

With this "symbolic" salute from the German navy Stanislavsky ends his account of his experiences as a prisoner-of-war in Germany.

CHAPTER XLVII

THE WAR PRODUCED a repertoire crisis in the Moscow Art Theatre. The Russian stage was inundated with cheap patriotic plays, and while refusing to follow the example of the other theatres, Stanislavsky felt that the Moscow Art Theatre ought to produce plays that would be consistent with the patriotic feelings that were sweeping the country. It was decided to put on a series of plays by Russian classical authors and the choice finally fell on Pushkin's three little tragedies—*The Stone Guest*, which had given Stanislavsky so much trouble during the first year of the existence of the Society of Art and Literature and in which he did not appear this time, *The Feast during the Plague*, and *Mozart and Salieri*, in which Stanislavsky played the part of Salieri, the second-rate composer who in the play poisons Mozart.

Salieri was actually the *last* part Stanislavsky was ever to play (the only other *new* part was that of Shuysky in *Czar Fyodor*, which he played during the European and American tour of the Moscow Art Theatre in 1923 and 1924). And again his inability to speak verse proved almost an insuperable obstacle to his tackling a Pushkin part. This time he turned to a man he regarded as the greatest master of the spoken word— the famous Russian singer Fyodor Shalyapin. They spent hours together, Shalyapin reading Salieri's opening soliloquy and Stanislavsky listening intently to the cadences of his voice.

"I find my work extremely hard," he wrote to Gurevich on December 2nd, 1914. "Acting is devilish work. I can't sleep, I am in a state of constant alarm, and I am haunted by nightmares. But I mustn't complain. Indeed, I count myself happy when I consider what other people have to put up with."

He was carrying on with his work on the system. He had now discovered the element which seemed to him to provide all the necessary stimuli for setting the actor's subconsciousness free to take an active part in the embodiment of the character he was representing on the stage—the *through-action* of the part, welding all the other elements of his system together and directing it towards the ruling idea of the play.

"My work in art goes on," he wrote in the same letter to Gurevich. "I have evolved a great deal that is new, especially in the sphere of the subconscious and the methods of stimulating the activity of those feelings which are beyond the reach of the conscious mind."

At the First Studio Sulerzhitsky was producing an adaptation of Charles Dickens's story *The Cricket on the Hearth*, which was destined to become one of the Moscow Art Theatre's most resounding successes during the war years. In his *Reminiscences of a Friend*, written after Sulerzhitsky's death in 1916, Stanislavsky paid a warm tribute to his friend's devoted work for the Studio. "He loved the Studio," he declared, "because he saw in it the realization of one of his chief purposes in life : to bring people together, to create a common interest in life, to fight vulgarity, violence and injustice—to serve love and nature, beauty and God." The highly idealistic conception of the aims of the theatre of the Tolstoyan Sulerzhitsky exercised a great influence on Stanislavsky and led him to share his friend's dream of "creating something like a spiritual order of actors," whose members should be "people of lofty ideas, who know the human soul, who aspire after noble artistic aims, and who are ready to sacrifice themselves for their ideals." Later on he realized that such an exalted view of an actor's position in society justified the accusation that he was aiming at transforming the actor into an anchorite. That, he claimed, was not true. All he wanted was that the actor should realize that his talent "already doomed him to the heroism of creative work," and that a creative artist had no alternative but to sacrifice everything for his art. That, however, did not mean that the actor had to renounce life or give up its joys and pleasures. The opposite was true : an actor's heart must be wide open to life's troubles, struggles and conflicts.

Sulerzhitsky put his whole heart into the production of *The Cricket on the Hearth*. In September, 1914, the Studio showed it to Stanislavsky and Nemirovich-Danchenko. Stanislavsky felt at once that in this play he could catch for the first time perhaps those deep, heartfelt notes of "superconscious feeling" which his system aimed at producing. Unlike Nemirovich-Danchenko, he spent hours with the actors after the performance discussing different points of their acting with them. The through-action of the play, he told them, could be summarized in the sentence : "To awaken in people a sense of human-kindness." And he warned them especially against the dangers of "stage smiles".

"Get rid of the stage smiles," he wrote in the Studio's commonplace book, "for they prevent the actor from believing in the reality of his feelings."

The great success of *The Cricket on the Hearth* in Moscow was repeated in Petersburg during the Studio's visit in 1915. But by that time Sulerzhitsky's illness (he was suffering from chronic nephritis which he had contracted while settling the Dukhobors in Canada) was progressing rapidly to its fatal end. He spent the summer in the Crimean settlement of the Studio where Stanislavsky visited him. In the autumn he returned to Moscow. But his condition was hopeless. Stanislavsky went to see him at the hospital daily. "I went to the hospital to see him," he wrote to Benois after his last visit, "and it seems he had just had a severe attack. After it Suler was no longer there. All I saw was a terribly emaciated, lifeless body. He could not utter a word. Only his expressive eyes still seemed to speak. He wanted to say something to me, but couldn't. He died quietly. At midnight his body was taken to the Studio and placed in the foyer. The two days during which it remained there were very moving. Everyone seemed to realize what Suler was and what the Studio and the theatre had lost. The student-actors carried him to the cemetery. I thank you again for your sympathy with our great sorrow."

Sulerzhitsky had been working on another adaptation of a Dickens story—*The Chimes*. And even during his last hours when he could no longer speak he clung desperately to the cheap popular edition of Dickens's story which he would not let out of his hands. "At last," Stanislavsky writes in describing this scene, "the crumpled book fell out of his hand and—his connection with art was severed for ever."

Sulerzhitsky's death left a great gap in Stanislavsky's life, a gap that was never filled. A few months before his own death, twenty-two years later, Sulerzhitsky's wife came to see him. He was not feeling well and he told her sadly that the four books on his system he still wanted to write would never be written. As she got up to leave, he said, "There is not a single day on which I do not think of Suler. Believe me, it is so."

As the war progressed, so the repertoire of the Moscow Art Theatre got more and more disorganized. "Life in art is very hard," Stanislavsky wrote to Gurevich on January 5th, 1916. "The season is dead. We are expecting more call-ups. We simply don't know what play to put on and whom to put it on with. From the financial point of view the season has exceeded all our expectations. The house is sold out every night, but that does not give me any pleasure." And on April 12th he wrote : "I am in the same neurasthenic condition as I was in Berne. We shan't go to Petersburg this year and we are glad, although it will mean a considerable financial loss to us. Why not ? Because a visit at this time would have nothing to do with art, but would be a purely business venture. That is trade, not art. This year we could do nothing because of the constant call-ups. All the plays are in a terrible muddle, the ensemble has been destroyed, our nerves worn to rags. Under such conditions it is impossible to play. We'd much rather stay at home and work on *The Village of Stepanchikovo* and *The Rose and the Cross*."

The Rose and the Cross, a neo-romantic play by the great Russian symbolist poet Alexander Blok, first conceived as a ballet on a medieval theme, was rehearsed by Stanislavsky for almost two years (from March 1st, 1916, to December 31st, 1918), but was never put on. Stanislavsky, however, used it for further experiments in simplified stage designs with the help of black velvet, especially for creating the illusion of distance on the stage.

The Village of Stepanchikovo was the only new play put on by the Moscow Art Theatre during its 1917-1918 season. It was the same adaptation of Dostoevsky's humorous novel as that in which Stanislavsky had been so successful in the part of Colonel Rostanev when he produced it for the Society of Art and Literature in 1891. But this time it led to a crisis in the theatre, culminating in the final break between Stanislavsky and Nemirovich-Danchenko and in Stanislavsky's giving up playing any new parts.

To understand the cause of this truly tragic event in Stanislavsky's life, it is necessary to remember how highly he prized discipline in the theatre and how much the part of Rostanev meant to him. Though the play was produced jointly by Stanislavsky and Nemirovich-Danchenko, it was the latter who was in charge of the production. Besides, when playing a leading part Stanislavsky, as a rule, placed himself entirely in the hands of Nemirovich-Danchenko. When, for instance, Nemirovich-Danchenko was in charge of the production of *Even A Wise Man Stumbles*, the actors were amazed at the humility with which Stanislavsky accepted his instructions. He stood like a timid neophyte among the other actors, listening to the producer's criticisms of his acting and taking down every remark of his in his note-book like a conscientious schoolboy. But in *The Village of Stepanchikovo* Nemirovich-Danchenko's interpretation of Colonel Rostanev's character, his "literary" analysis of it, cut right across Stanislavsky's intuitive approach to it. Like Dr. Stockmann in *An Enemy of the People*, the fusion of Stanislavsky and Colonel Rostanev came about naturally and without the slightest effort. When playing the part, he felt like Colonel Rostanev ; he *was* Colonel Rostanev. He tried loyally to carry out Nemirovich-Danchenko's conception of his part, but nothing came of it. By the time the dress rehearsals came, the acting of the part in make-up was sheer agony to him. He would keep everybody waiting, and they all knew that he was late because he had been crying like a child in his dressing room. In the end, Nemirovich-Danchenko took the part away from him and gave it to another actor. The news stunned the actors. The thing was unheard of. They were all wondering what was going to happen. But nothing happened. Stanislavsky did not dream of challenging the producer's decision. The actors never heard a murmur from him, though many of them thought that his acting in this part was as good as, if not better than, in many another part that had made him famous. But the fact that he did not complain did not mean that he did not feel deeply hurt. Three years later when Gurevich asked him what new part he would be rehearsing shortly, his face became suddenly overcast.

"I shall never act in a new play again," he said. "I don't suppose you've heard what happened. . . ." And he went on to tell her that Nemirovich-Danchenko had said something to him at a dress rehearsal of *The Village of Stepanchikovo* that made it impossible for him to carry on with his part so that it had to be given to another actor. "He said to me that I have not succeeded in giving birth to the part. Since then I just can't play any new parts."

Gurevich could not help noticing that when Stanislavsky

used the rather odd expression—"I had not succeeded in giving birth to the part"—his lips quivered and his voice sounded dull and hollow. But even then Stanislavsky did not utter a single harsh word against Nemirovich-Danchenko, though he no longer worked with him in the theatre and though he could never forget the injury done not to his prestige (that would not have worried Stanislavsky in the least) but to what he considered to be the most precious part of himself as an artist—his capacity for a direct and intuitive realization of a stage character.

The crisis which confronted the Moscow Art Theatre during the first years of the war became more acute with the outbreak of the revolution. During its 1916-1917 season it produced only one new play (*The Village of Stepanchikovo*) and no new plays at all during its 1917-1918 season. But apart from this crisis in its repertoire, the theatre was also undergoing an acute ideological crisis. The revolution had split the Russian theatrical world into two hostile camps : the right wing group, to which the Moscow Art Theatre and the former Imperial theatres belonged, and the so-called "front of revolutionary theatres", which united all the "new" movements and clamoured for the immediate closing down of the "academic" theatres, particularly the Moscow Art Theatre. There were street demonstrations with red flags and all the usual paraphernalia of revolutionary pressure was used to force the Government, especially after the October Revolution, to take drastic measures against the "reactionaries". But the Soviet Government remained firm in its determination to preserve the great cultural inheritance of the past and showed no sign of giving in to the hysterical mob of the so-called "reformers" of the stage.

"There was a stormy moment of the revolution," Stanislavsky said, speaking of those turbulent days at the thirtieth anniversary of the foundation of the Moscow Art Theatre on October 27th, 1928, "about which Lenin said that the revolution could do nothing to assist the development of the arts. At the moment we had to save our cultural treasures, we had to save our theatres and steer them safely through the Scylla and Charybdis of the revolutionary storms. In those days the Government came to our help and thanks to it our theatre was able to weather the storm. . . . But," he went on with the frankness and sincerity that was so endearing a feature of his character, "our Government earned my deepest gratitude for something

347

quite different. When the political events in our country had caught us—the old actors of the Moscow Art Theatre—unawares and rather bewildered, when we still failed to understand the real meaning of what was happening, our Government did not force us to dye ourselves red and pretend to be what we were not. We came gradually to understand the times in which we were living, and we began to adapt ourselves to the new conditions. Otherwise we should have been forced to become turncoats from purely selfish motives. But we were anxious that our attitude towards the revolution should be different ; we were not interested in watching people marching with red banners, but in getting a real insight into the revolutionary soul of our country. To this science, to this art, to this important consciousness which was constantly developing within us, we dedicated all our time in the quiet of our studies, and for letting us do that I thank our Government most warmly."

Stanislavsky had always striven to get the common people into the theatre. He had always regretted the necessity of sacrificing the original "popular" character of the Moscow Art Theatre and even as late as 1910, in his letter to Nemirovich-Danchenko quoted earlier, he reverted to the same idea. The revolution at last made his old idea of a national theatre on the lines advocated by Alexander Ostrovsky in 1882 a practical proposition. In his paper on the establishment of a national theatre Ostrovsky expressed a view that Stanislavsky was now to accept wholeheartedly. Ostrovsky wrote : "Poetry as expressed in drama is nearer to the common people than any other branch of literature. Every other literary work is written for educated people, but tragedies and comedies are written for the whole people. This closeness to the common people does not degrade dramatic poetry; on the contrary, it adds to its strength and prevents it from becoming vulgar and trivial." In 1918, Stanislavsky was to find out the truth of Ostrovsky's words. "The working class spectator," Stanislavsky declared, almost echoing Ostrovsky's statement, "is anxious to go where he can laugh and cry real tears that come from his heart. What he wants is not some highly refined form of art, but the life of the human spirit expressed in a simple, unartificial, intelligible, strong and convincing form. . . . Our 'now', " he told the actors, "is seeking for a key to life in art, while our 'yesterday' was only interested in art as an entertainment. What does the theatre give us today ? First of all, it must not give us a bare reflection of life, but must reflect everything in life in its inner heroic tension, in the seemingly simple forms of the ordinary day, but in reality in precise and luminous images in which all feelings are alive and in which all passions have been ennobled. And what must you, modern actors, be? You must first of all be living people and you must carry about in your hearts all those new qualities which ought to help us all to achieve a new kind of consciousness. What kind of consciousness? The kind in which life for the good of all should no longer be the subject of idle dreams and unrealizable fantasies. . . ."

Stanislavsky's conception of the actor as a man who is wholly devoted to his art has now been amplified by the conception of the actor-citizen who takes a personal part in the building of a new and better life, the actor, too, who is "a son of his people," and whose work on the stage is closely bound up with the best aspirations of his people.

The revolution also introduced great changes in the routine of the Moscow Art Theatre. For a time Stanislavsky and his company had to give performances in the large Solodovnikov Theatre where he had scored his first successes as actor and producer. And during the years of famine and civil war he and the other actors were forced to overlook the strict rule of the Moscow Art Theatre not to accept any outside engagements. "My life has greatly changed," he wrote to Gurevich at the time. "I have become a proletarian and am not actually in want so far because I am playing outside the theatre on all my free evenings. I have not yet fallen so low as to give up my artistic standards and that is why I am appearing only in plays that can be produced outside the theatre. I am ashamed to say that my old friend *Uncle Vanya* comes invariably to my rescue. In a couple of days I shall be appearing in Goldoni's *The Woman at the Inn*. I am afraid my wife finds life very hard. It depends on her entirely whether we have enough to eat or not, and but for her we should have been starving. This is very important for the children. Whatever we earn, we spend on food. Everything else we have to do without. We all look shabby. The hall, the drawing room and the dining room have been taken over by the Studios, one room we let, and the rest of the flat we occupy ourselves. Our artistic work is still in full swing, though we are not putting on anything new. . . ."

Stanislavsky was, in fact, very busy training the young actors

349

of the Studios (the Second Studio of the Moscow Art Theatre was founded in December, 1916), and supervising their productions. At the beginning of 1918 the First Studio scored a great success with *Twelfth Night*, produced under the direct supervision of Stanislavsky. "The play," he wrote to Gurevich, "was successful in spite of the fact that we had to make it up of all sorts of odds and ends." Actually, however, it is much more likely that the play was a success *because* he had to make it up "of odds and ends". It was the first and only time he had been successful in a Shakespearean production and it was also the only time he did not indulge in unnecessary elaborations of the text and scenery.

But more and more of his time Stanislavsky now devoted to the Opera Studio of the Moscow Bolshoy Theatre, which he had founded at the request of the authorities in 1918. He had always had a hankering after opera, and his ill-starred attempt to become an opera singer himself at the time of the dissolution of the Alexeyev Circle had not killed his affection for an art which had first attracted him to the stage. He had already tried his hand at producing scenes from operas in the spring of 1897 and 1898 at the instigation of his elder brother Vladimir. And now, twenty years later, Vladimir joined his famous brother as assistant of the Opera Studio. Stanislavsky's sister Zina, who had so excelled in playing opposite him in the musical comedy *Lili*, joined her two brothers, and the three of them were to spend the rest of their lives together as trainers of opera singers and producers of opera.

Stanislavsky would usually begin his work at the Opera Studio with some new "element" of the actor's "inner technique", either "communication", or "given circumstances", or any other of the "elements" of his system.[1] He was always careful not to make his talks into lectures. He used to say that he learnt to hate lectures as a boy and that in the art of the stage, that is to say, the art of action, it was by graphic examples that the principles of acting must be inculcated. His method can be illustrated by the following examples.

One day a new student, a well-known opera baritone, sang Valentine's aria from *Faust* in the way it is usually sung on the

---

[1] The talks on the wider ethical and aesthetic implications of his system, delivered by Stanislavsky at the Opera Studio between 1918 and 1922, have recently been published in Moscow as well as in an English translation in London under the title *Stanislavsky on the Art of the Stage*.

opera stage. Stanislavsky complimented him on his voice, but declared that he did not understand anything.

"Am I not enunciating the words clearly enough?" asked the baritone.

"Yes, you are," replied Stanislavsky, "but I don't get the meaning of your song and I don't see why you are singing it. First of all, whom were you addressing your song to?"

"To you, sir."

"To me? But am I the deity? Your text says: 'Almighty God, God of Love.' Your object then is God and your aria is a prayer."

The baritone agreed.

"Don't you know how to pray?" asked Stanislavsky. "Did you never say your prayers as a child or did you never see anyone do it?"

"As a child I used to kneel in the corner of the room and address myself to the icon."

"Well, do so now. Forget all about us. Kneel down with your back to us. Don't you feel now that you shouldn't have sung so loudly?"

It was in this way that the meaning of an aria was made clear to the singers, with the result that after a short time it sounded quite different.

The singers often complained that they found it very difficult to carry out the demands of the vocalist, the musician, and the producer. Stanislavsky always claimed that the art of the opera was much easier than the art of drama, because the opera singer was given his "rhythm" by the composer, while the actor had to create his own "rhythm" for every part. But he readily agreed that opera was more difficult than drama in the sense that the singer had to deal with three different arts. Once, however, he had become the master of them all, he could hold the attention of the audience much more easily than the actor. Shalyapin, Stanislavsky thought, was a good example of the perfect combination of the three arts.

"I have copied my system from Shalyapin," he observed one day. "When I told him my views on the art of acting, Shalyapin yelled, 'Help! I've been robbed!'"

In the spring of 1921, Stanislavsky considered the work of the Opera Studio sufficiently advanced to give a public performance of scenes from three operas, and before the end of 1922, he rehearsed two whole operas, Chaykovsky's *Eugene Onegin* and

Massenet's *Werther*, which were performed in Moscow during the Moscow Art Theatre's tour abroad.

The rehearsals of *Eugene Onegin* began shortly after Stanislavsky had moved into the house in Leontyev Lane. It was an old house, separated from the street by a large front garden with old poplar trees, flower beds and a lawn. The Studio was on the first floor—a large, old-fashioned drawing-room with a painted ceiling, divided into two by four thick marble columns which formed a kind of portico. An antique bronze chandelier with crystal pendants hung from the ceiling. The entrance to Stanislavsky's flat was straight through the Studio, which communicated with his own study—a smaller room with a similar painted ceiling and bronze chandelier. His study was furnished very simply : a few armchairs with loose covers, two writing desks, which he never used, a grand piano, a sofa, on which he usually sat, a cupboard and some open bookcases. The constant noise in the Studio never worried him. On the contrary, as soon as it stopped, he always sent someone to inquire why they were not working. This time he had the theatre always next door to him.

It was about this time that Gurevich, who had just arrived in Moscow, met Stanislavsky in the street. He was walking along deep in thought, looking very happy and carrying a huge bundle (costumes for one of his studios) on his back by the crook of his walking-stick which he held over his shoulder. In spite of his age (he was about fifty-eight at the time), he walked very erect and with the springy gait of a young man, as though he did not feel the weight of his big bundle at all. Gurevich called to him and he rushed up to her and began telling her about the changes in his life.

"Our private possessions keep disappearing one by one," he said to her laughingly, "and somehow it makes me feel a much freer man. A little more and I shall be as free as a bird and be able to go somewhere far, far away ! "

Next day Gurevich had dinner with Stanislavsky and his family. She was struck by the fact that their living quarters were very cramped, but the dinner, not as sumptuous as in the old days, was still a dinner, though there was no sugar for their black coffee at the end of it. But Stanislavsky went out and brought back two tiny lumps of sugar, putting one on Gurevich's saucer and one on his own.

"I'm afraid," he whispered apologetically, "I can't work unless I have some sugar in my coffee."

The only play Stanislavsky produced for the Moscow Art Theatre before his European and American tour was Byron's *Cain*.

In June, 1919, about a year before the first performance of *Cain*, part of the company of the Moscow Art Theatre, including such leading members of it as Knipper and Kachalov, were cut off in Kharkov by the anti-Soviet forces of General Denikin, and, faced with a disaster that threatened to destroy what was left of the ensemble of the theatre, Stanislavsky was looking for a play with as few characters as possible. In addition, he felt that in view of the political events he had to have a play "of great inner and social significance," and his choice finally fell on Byron's "mystery" which seemed to him to fulfil these two conditions. Besides, Byron's prestige in Russia seemed likely to overcome the difficulties a play on so avowedly religious a theme might otherwise have encountered at a time when religion was not exactly a popular subject on the stage or on the political platform. In this Stanislavsky was mistaken. In the final form in which he produced it, the play turned out to be more in the nature of a biblical legend than a tract against divine authority. It may be doubted, too, whether Lucifer's injunction to the human race "to think and endure" possessed the right kind of social significance, as Stanislavsky seemed to think it did. The play was a failure. In spite of its one hundred and sixty rehearsals, it survived only eight performances. But it is significant as marking an important milestone in Stanislavsky's career as producer : it finally convinced him that so far as the mere mechanics of mounting a play was concerned, he had nothing to learn any more and that all his researches must henceforth be directed towards the inner life of a part and its realization by the actor. Indeed, in spite of the great ingenuity of the two separate designs he had contrived for *Cain*, the "architectural" one and the "sculptural" or "constructional" one, he soon discovered that both were merely variations of the principles of stage-design he had perfected during the last years of the Society of Art and Literature and the first "realistic" period of the Moscow Art Theatre. In his "architectural" design he placed the entire action of the play within a medieval cathedral and made the monks into the performers of the "mystery". Here it was the light and sound effects that played a great rôle in working on the imagination of the spectator : the illusion of stars in the Abyss of Space was created by the countless lighted candles carried by the monks, while the dying planets were suggested by the dim lights of the lanterns carried by the vergers ; the mysterious glitter of the altar, hidden away in the depths of the nave, and the soft strains of the organ, indicated the presence of the angelic hosts, while the procession of the monks at the end of the service was to evoke the feeling of the proximity of Paradise ; in the last scene the differ-ent coloured lights streaming through the stained-glass windows were to evoke all sorts of strong emotional responses from the audience, just as in the last act of *The Bells* in which Stanislavsky used similar effects with the glass door of the mayor's bedroom.

Nothing, surely, shows up Stanislavsky's lack of political sense more glaringly than this "architectural" plan he devised for *Cain* in the first years of the revolution when anti-religious propa-ganda was at its height. He himself claims that the reason he abandoned it was the high cost of such a production, but it is more likely that he was induced to give it up by some of the more politically minded members of the theatre. Be that as it may, in his second "constructional" plan he again merely reproduced the different principles of stage-design he had used earlier, particularly in *The Sunken Bell*, combined with the additional effects produced by the black velvet trick he had used in *The Life of Man*. Thus, in the scene in Hades the huge statues representing the "mighty phantoms" of a former universe, which emphasized Cain's "petty portion," were merely a repetition of Simov's device of placing a huge rock in front of the stage in the first act of *The Sunken Bell* to make Stanislavsky's figure look small in comparison ; again, the immense colonnade round the Land Without Paradise, placed at the end of a gigantic staircase with enormous steps, of which the lower part only was shown, the rest being left to the imagination of the spectator, was also merely a variation of one of Simov's devices in Hauptmann's play. The black velvet effects in *Cain* were mainly used to create the illusion that Cain and Lucifer were suspended in mid-air in the Abyss of Space as they wandered among the dying planets (extras swathed in black velvet carrying lanterns on long black sticks).

The failure of *Cain* placed Stanislavsky and the Moscow Art Theatre in an impossible position. Stanislavsky refused to have anything to do with the Soviet plays of that period because he failed to find any living human being in them, but just black and white figures of melodrama. In the summer and autumn of 1921 he was rehearsing Tolstoy's *The Fruits of Enlightenment*, the play with which he had scored his first success at the Society of Art and Literature in 1892. But again he searched in it in vain for a key to the revolutionary spirit of the time and he decided not to put it on. The other play he was rehearsing, *The Government Inspector*, was performed for the first time on October 8th, 1921. It was the last play he produced before the Moscow Art Theatre left for its tour of Europe and America. The truth is that, as in 1906, the Moscow Art Theatre had reached an impasse : at a time when tendentiousness was rampant on the stage Stanislavsky was helpless. He regarded the mad frolics of the "revolutionary" producers with keen distaste. He was not daunted by their screams, and their acrobatics merely disgusted him. The "new" theatre, he maintained, had not produced a single original playwright or actor. They had not discovered a single original method that contained even a hint at a new approach to the solution of the problems of the actor's inner technique. They all used a jargon that was reminiscent of the mumbo-jumbo of witch-doctors. "I do not recognize any laws of the stage," declared Tairov, the founder of the Kamerny Theatre, in his *Notes of a Producer*, published in 1921, "except the law of inner harmony born of the rhythmically active structure of a performance." Meierhold had not advanced a step since the days of the Studio in Povarskaya Street. The trouble was that while the external methods of production and acting had been developed to an extent undreamt of before, the inner possibilities of the actor's art were either completely forgotten or ruthlessly suppressed. And the result, of course, was that the vacuum in the actor's soul was filled with the junk of outworn stage clichés, which were ingenuously given out to be the newest achievements of the Russian stage. But Stanislavsky could not find the right solution to the problem of adjusting the Moscow Art Theatre to the new conditions created by the revolution or give a convincing answer to the accusations hurled against him by "the front of revolutionary theatres". The only convincing answer, of course, would have been the success of his new productions. But *Cain* was a dismal failure in spite of the hard work he had put into it. In the circumstances the best thing he could do was to take the Moscow Art Theatre for a tour abroad both to escape the hysterical shrieks of his detractors and to keep his actors away from the infectious atmosphere of the people who, masquerading as revolutionaries, were destroying dramatic art in Russia.

Before he left for his European and American tour Stanislavsky suffered a grievous loss by the death of his most promising pupil—Eugene Vakhtangov.

After his disagreement with Stanislavsky over the production of *The Festival of Peace*, Vakhtangov had left the First Studio and opened his own school of dramatic art. In 1920, however, he had rejoined Stanislavsky, and his school became known as the Third Studio of the Moscow Art Theatre. In 1921, Vakhtangov was working on his most famous production—an "improvised" version of Carlo Gozzi's fairy tale comedy *Turandot* (he had gone on experimenting with Gorky's idea of a theatre of improvisation). Stanislavsky was present at the dress rehearsal of *Turandot* on February 27th, 1922. Vakhtangov was already stricken by a fatal illness at the time, and during one of the intervals Stanislavsky went to see him at his home which was only a few minutes walk from the theatre. He came back looking broken-hearted.

"My best pupil is dying ! " he murmured in a choked voice. "My best pupil is dying ! "

CHAPTER XLVIII

THE MOSCOW ART THEATRE left for its second tour abroad on
September 14th, 1922. The tour lasted two years, the theatre
giving a total of 561 performances of eleven plays from its old
repertoire, including the four Chekhov plays (*The Three Sisters,
The Cherry Orchard, Ivanov* and *Uncle Vanya,* but not *The Seagull,*
which after an abortive revival in 1905 was never put on again),
Gorky's *Lower Depths,* Alexey Tolstoy's *Czar Fyodor,* Ostrovsky's
Even A Wise Man Stumbles, Ibsen's *An Enemy of the People,* Goldoni's
The Woman at the Inn, Turgenev's *A Provincial Lady,* and scenes
from the adaptation of *The Brothers Karamazov.* The company
was led by Stanislavsky who, in addition to his old parts which
had made him famous, played Shuysky in *Czar Fyodor.* He was
fifty-nine when the tour started and of late his eyes had been
giving him a great deal of trouble—his eyesight was failing perceptibly. He took an active part in all the preparations for the
tour, and his conscientiousness and the realization of the great
responsibility of his theatre's mission, kept him all the time in a
state of high nervous tension. Nemirovich-Danchenko, to his
great chagrin, was left to hold the fort in Moscow. To be out of
the way, he had gone to Wiesbaden for a holiday, and, in a
letter to Stanislavsky, he told him not to worry about the success
of the tour in Europe. "I should like to tell you again," he wrote,
"that you need not worry about the 'backwardness' of our art.
They have, no doubt, gifted actors here, but, generally speaking,
all their stage novelties are merely technical tricks. Your way of
creating the actor is the newest thing there is. I am not wanted
either in Berlin or Prague," he went on, "but you might have
needed me badly in Paris where I could have delivered one or
two lectures (in French of course) before your arrival, but this
would have been rather costly. They need me in Moscow badly."

As it happened, the two met after all at the frontier station at the very start of the tour, Nemirovich-Danchenko's train arriving just at the moment when Stanislavsky was having a rather violent argument with a customs officer. (Stanislavsky and Rayevskaya, the oldest actress of the theatre, were travelling by land, while the rest of the company went to Germany by sea via Leningrad and Stettin.) Nemirovich-Danchenko soon succeeded in calming both the refractory official and Stanislavsky, but he had only time for a short business talk with his fellow-producer.

In Berlin Stanislavsky was given an official welcome in grand style : milling crowds, mountains of flowers, press photographers. From now on the American theatrical manager, Morris Gest, who was arranging the tour of the Moscow Art Theatre in the United States, took over : he had sent his brother and an American correspondent to look after Stanislavsky and his company during their European tour and to provide all the preliminary publicity for the American Press. Stanislavsky sensed the vulgarity of it all the moment he entered his apartment in one of the best Berlin hotels : the large drawing-room had been converted into a florist's and confectioner's shop, baskets and wreaths of flowers being heaped in rising tiers on the floor and the tables groaning under the weight of enormous boxes of sweets and innumerable cakes with Gest's monogram on them. "Stanislavsky," his secretary records, "was somewhat crushed by all this pomp, for he loved simplicity above all, but felt that he would have to make the best of it. Many a time during the tour he sighed at the terrible discomfort of the life he was forced to lead, but he just waved his hand in a gesture of despair and quoted the Russian proverb, 'If you call yourself a mushroom, you mustn't grumble if people shove you into a bag.' "

The second Berlin season of the Moscow Art Theatre was an even greater success than its first one in 1906. The plays were practically the same : *Czar Fyodor*, performed on the opening night on September 26th, *The Lower Depths*, *An Enemy of the People*, *The Cherry Orchard* (not performed in 1906), and *The Three Sisters*, performed on the last night on October 10th. The last performance was transformed into a grandiose public tribute to Stanislavsky, the stage being strewn with flowers, representatives of the German theatres delivering speeches, and Stanislavsky expressing in a few appropriate words the thanks of his company and himself.

In Prague the theatre was welcomed by tumultuous crowds.

They opened their season on October 20th with *Czar Fyodor* and wound it up on October 30th with *The Three Sisters*, giving an additional performance on October 31st at reduced prices. On November 2nd, Stanislavsky and the leading members of the company appeared in a concert hall where they gave readings to a large and enthusiastic audience. Their next stop was Zagreb, where the enthusiasm of their audiences exceeded anything they had yet experienced, their last performance (*The Cherry Orchard*) ending in a battle of flowers, the audience bombarding the actors with bouquets and the actors throwing flowers back at the audience. It was in Zagreb that Stanislavsky introduced a system of doubling the more important parts, himself playing the part of Shuysky for the first time and creating a real furore by the remarkable delineation he gave to this character.

The Moscow Art Theatre arrived in Paris on November 30th and in spite of the lateness of the hour (their train drew into the station at one o'clock in the morning), they were officially welcomed by representatives of the Paris stage, and Stanislavsky had to pose to Press photographers and give Press interviews at his hotel. On December 4th, on the eve of the opening of the Paris season at the *Théâtre des Champs Elysées*, a special soirée was given to the Moscow Art Theatre by the leading French actors and producers, including André Antoine, the doyen of the French stage and founder of the *Théâtre Libre*, and Jacques Copeau, the director of the theatre *Le Vieux Colombier*. Antoine referred in his speech to "the mission of the Moscow Art Theatre in the renaissance of the French stage," emphasising the fact that, as the doyen of the French stage, he had to learn from the Moscow actors because Stanislavsky had been successful in what he had set out to do, while he had not been able to bring the reform of the French theatre to a successful end. Stanislavsky made a suitable speech in reply, announcing, incidentally, that in spite of the delay in the arrival of the scenery, the first performance of the Moscow Art Theatre would take place as arranged.

The theatre opened its Paris season with *Czar Fyodor* on December 5th. Again they scored a great success. "Just imagine," Antoine remarked to a French dramatic critic, "at six o'clock their scenery had not arrived and yet they gave us this splendid performance. What must their play be like at home !" And on December 11th Antoine wrote in *Information* :

359

"A few days after the beginning of the performances of the Moscow Art Theatre it became clear to me that our theatre has still a great deal to learn from the Russians. The wonderful perfection of their *mise-en-scènes*, the splendid finish of their scenery and costumes, where everything had been thought out to the last detail, the high level of their acting, the self-denying discipline of the actors and their love of the theatre make us acutely conscious of how much our theatre has still to do to restore its old prestige. . . . To achieve such remarkable results," Antoine concluded, "a discipline is required which no longer exists on the French stage."

The last performance of the Moscow Art Theatre in Paris (*The Three Sisters*) took place on December 20th, and on December 24th Stanislavsky and several actors appeared on the concert platform in scenes from *The Brothers Karamazov*, *A Provincial Lady* and dramatised versions of two Chekhov short stories. On December 27th Stanislavsky and his company left Paris for Cherbourg where they embarked for New York on the White Star liner *Majestic*. Stanislavsky described their voyage and arrival in New York in a long letter to Nemirovich-Danchenko.

He found everything on the liner very luxurious and tasteless. (They travelled cabin class, the American manager, no doubt, being loath to spend too much money on their passage before he was quite sure that their American tour would be a financial success.) "People were watching us from the first class," Stanislavsky wrote. "We did not look like Europeans ! I was wearing goloshes, Vishnevsky a fur cap; while the Europeans were wearing summer clothes and, just as we went aboard, evening dress after dinner. I was taken to be introduced to one of the directors of the White Star Line. He said something to me in English, I bowed and said something to him in French. Silly ! In the second class it was much more cosy and simple. Nothing very striking, but comfortable. A small cabin with two berths (I keep my bags on the top one and sleep on the bottom one). A cupboard, a wash-basin, coat hangers, central heating. A basket of flowers with a message of welcome from the shipping company. I had a wash. Went to the dining room. A huge room with columns. The people very poor—emigrants of all nationalities. Can't order anything myself. Had to appeal to Knipper and to the others of our English-speakers. Sholem Asch (a playwright, a Jew) came up. After dinner a jazz band played in the lounge, and people danced their horrible modern dances. The rest looked on without showing any special interest."

The passage was stormy and Stanislavsky had to spend two days in bed. "I was told," he wrote in his letter, "that the American papers had reported that the *Majestic* was in-danger. But I have a strong suspicion that this is only another of Morris Gest's publicity stunts."

There were two "outstanding events" during the voyage. The first was (to quote the official programme) "A grand concert in aid of Seamen's charities by the members of the Moscow Art Theatre Co. (under the direction of Konstantin Stanislavsky) on Monday evening, January 1st, 1923, commencing at 8 o'clock."

"It is a custom," Stanislavsky wrote, "that actors on board a liner should play or sing in aid of the sailors. We had to do something, too. The concert took place in the huge second class dining saloon. The programme included : (1) Boris Godunov (Pushkin)—Vishnevsky and Burdzhalov—not a single word could be heard because of the racket made by the ship's screw ; (2) Brutus and Antony, myself and Kachalov—we yelled at the top of our voices and were heard ; and (3) Moskvin and Gribunin in the dramatised version of Chekhov's short story, *The Surgery*, which everyone understood, especially as the comic bits were acted rather broadly."

The other event was Stanislavsky's meeting with Coué, the French psychologist who was very popular at the time.

"Coué," Stanislavsky wrote, "is a great celebrity. He paid me a visit because he was interested in my theory, but actually it was he who did most of the talking, while I listened. What I found so important in his talk and what proves the correctness of my methods is that one must never force people to do things, but always seek to influence them through their imaginations. Coué was accompanied by one of his American followers, a beautiful woman, though not very young.

"I had to return their visit," Stanislavsky continued, "but the procedure of getting from the second class to the first class is very complicated. The Americans and the English are great sticklers for form. I am grateful to Sholem Asch, who helped me to get to the first class. Everything there is just as it is on the photographs, and perhaps even a little more luxurious. I wanted to have a look at the bathing pool, but it was reserved for the ladies just then. No matter! They told me to go in. Unfortunately (! ! !), there was no one there."

They arrived in New York late on Wednesday, January 3rd, and "next morning," Stanislavsky continues with his story, "we were awakened at eight o'clock and taken to one room. The journalists arrived. Just like a flock of rooks. They started photographing me—one way, then another, and so on.

"I forgot to tell you that while we were in Paris a whole hullabaloo started. A letter from the American National League appeared in the New York papers warning the public that we were arriving for propaganda purposes and that one third of our receipts would be sent off to Russia for some secret purpose. I was interviewed about it in Paris, and now of course they were all eager to cross-examine me as if I were in a court of law.

"The formal examination that followed was just a farce. Questioned by officials as to the purpose of my visit. Examination of passports, etc.

"Because of the Press interviews I missed the Statue of Liberty. Saw only the waterfront, the houses covered with snow. The view reminded me of the Volga. In the distance lots of squat buildings looking like workshops—the landing piers. At the end of one of them a crowd of people waving handkerchiefs. I recognized Baliev, Boleslavsky (a former member of the First Studio), Rachmaninov's wife and daughter (Rachmaninov could not, unfortunately, come himself as he was away on a three months' concert engagement), and Morris Gest himself with his staff.

"From that moment a real vaudeville began. Gest came on board. He had made arrangements to be photographed with me without my knowing it. Then I was photographed alone in the act of waving to a huge crowd (which was not there). And there was a frightful meeting still to come. Gest insisted that I should be met by the local Russian bishop (or some other priest)—in full canonicals! But the bishop himself, thank goodness, refused to come. Then the mayor was supposed to have handed me the keys of the city, but that should have taken place on the 3rd. On the 4th they had an important meeting in the City Hall and no one turned up. Representatives of local organizations should have given us an official welcome, but it seemed that the boat took a long time to get to the pier, and as they are all very busy people, they could not wait. That was why the presents they should have handed me were all piled up in the car which was waiting for me. Then the presents were taken away to be photographed. Where they are now I don't know. Perhaps they were on hire ! ! !

"The Police Commissioner sent a smartly uniformed police officer to escort me from the boat. And so I rode off like a convict under police escort. The policeman stood on the foot-board of our car, blowing his whistle and warning all police-men to stop the traffic, while we drove through the streets at terrific speed (I expect they were taking motion pictures of us all the time). Gest, of course, was sitting beside me. . . .

"I live in a sort of semi-hotel and semi-boarding house. The theatre in which we are playing is Al Jolson's Theater on 59th Street.

"At seven o'clock we had all to attend a performance at Baliev's theatre. I arrived half an hour earlier to be introduced to the millionaire Otto Kahn (I expect it is he who is financing our tour). On my arrival there were of course ovations and flowers. I had to make a speech—in Russian, and Gest trans-lated. I thanked them for the reception and for sending food parcels to our actors last year.

"The programme (of Baliev's *Chauve Souris*) was excellent and the scenery showed good taste. . . . In the intervals I met Nazimova (she has grown old, but is very sweet), Rachmaninov's wife and elder daughter, Léon Bakst, and, last but not least, my nephew Koka. Quite an unexpected and very affectionate meet-ing. We even kissed in public (shocking !). He has aged and looks very English. That day I had dinner with him at a Russian restaurant. Apparently Gest usually dines there, too. Anyway, he found me there and was very upset that I should have shown myself in public before my first appearance on the stage. Koka and he had a quarrel about it. I think the whole thing is just absurd."

Stanislavsky liked Al Jolson's Theater. He spent the whole of the Sunday there supervising the assembling of the scenery and rehearsing the extras. He admired the efficiency of the American stage-hands. "They all work cheerfully and with a will," he wrote to Nemirovich-Danchenko in the same letter. "Their industry, patience and endurance is quite amazing. They told us Russians a few times to smile and not to look so gloomy. The electrician here is a real artist. We have already given him an ovation. Perhaps everything seems to go so well only at the beginning—touch wood ! But for the time being the atmosphere in the theatre and all around us is very friendly, and that is a great help. We experienced the same sort of thing in Zagreb. And, as a matter of fact," he concluded his letter, "I like New York and its inhabitants very much. The city is rather tawdry, but comfortable. It is not true that there are only skyscrapers here (they are quite rare, in fact). There are lots of small houses. The traffic is not as bad as I was told. It is not very different from Paris. . . . The only trouble is that I don't know the language. . . ."

The Moscow Art Theatre opened its New York season on Monday, January 8th, 1923, with a performance of *Czar Fyodor*, scoring quite an exceptional success, in spite of a little *contretemps* when the curtain went up too soon revealing the clergy rushing to their places holding the tails of their cassocks, which made Stanislavsky throw a fit (he was terribly nervous the whole of that day) and in a brief speech to the actors implore them to do their best to save the performance. After the play Stanislavsky and the actors were presented with laurel wreaths and flowers (all, as they later learnt, at their own expense) and had to take innumerable calls. The stage was then invaded by a host of excited people, Mrs. Morris Gest, to Stanislavsky's consternation, kissing his hands. Among them was America's veteran theatrical manager, David Belasco, who kept shaking Stanislavsky's hands and bowing low to him ("Just as if he were a miracle-working icon," the actors thought).

"We have never had such a success in Moscow or anywhere else," Stanislavsky declared in his first letter to Nemirovich-Danchenko. "No one here seems to have had any idea what our theatre and our actors were capable of. I am writing all this," he added, "not in self-glorification, for we are not showing anything new here, but just to give you an idea at what an embryonic stage art is here and how eagerly they snatch up everything good that is brought to America. Actors, managers, all sorts of celebrities join in a chorus of the most extravagant praise. Some of the famous actors and actresses seize my hand and kiss it as though in a state of ecstasy. Such an attitude, which we perhaps don't really deserve, is very touching all the same."

Stanislavsky then gave this description of how he spent his day in New York : "At nine o'clock my telephone rings and I order my breakfast. In comes a nice, though rather stupid negro with a huge orange cut in two and sprinkled with sugar (I don't know what they call it here[1]). It's quite an extraordinary fruit. It's worth while living in America because of it. You have only to eat it first thing in the morning and your stomach becomes a chronometer. Then they bring in my coffee and bacon. At twelve or one o'clock—rehearsals. Before that an interview or a meeting. At five, dinner at the hotel or in a restaurant where everything is roasted on a spit. Then I have my afternoon nap and after that to the theatre to play or to make sure that everything is in order. Then again introductions, interviews, and so on. After the performance tea at my hotel or in a restaurant.

"No," he concluded, "it is not so easy to be the representative, producer, director and actor all rolled into one of a group of sixty people with their wives, husbands and children. But I am not complaining. Our journey is very interesting."

The theatre remained in New York for three months, most of the time playing to full houses. In addition to *Czar Fyodor*, they gave on alternate weeks, *The Lower Depths*, *The Cherry Orchard*, *The Three Sisters*, and *A Provincial Lady* together with scenes from *The Brothers Karamazov*. In March, however, their receipts showed a considerable falling off during the repeat performances, due mainly to the fact that the American public was not very conspicuous among their spectators, most of whom were either Russian emigrants or educated Americans who were interested in Russian literature and drama.

Stanislavsky was not happy in New York. He had just turned sixty and he found the hard work at the theatre very tiring. He was, besides, very lonely at his hotel and his ignorance of English kept him indoors. The food, in spite of the miraculous properties of his morning grapefruit, disagreed with him and he was involved in a farcical interlude with an American film company which wanted him to produce *Czar Fyodor* in an up-to-date Hollywood version. Nothing came of it in the end, but he kept having conferences with the two directors of the company, who rejected his scenario, but of whom one was still in favour of making such a film and the other against. The whole thing caused a lot of unnecessary excitement and loss of time and effort.

In March, Stanislavsky found time to write another long account of his impressions of America to Nemirovich-Danchenko. "It is certainly a great thing to be successful in America,"

[1] This seems to have been Stanislavsky's first acquaintance with a grapefruit.

he wrote, 'but—anyone who has seen their theatrical managers or knows anything about their theatrical trusts, which are all working for the benefit of the owners of the theatres, will understand what a terrible thing it is—what a ghastly catastrophe it is —not to be successful here. I tremble to think what Gest, Schubert or Otto Kahn would have done to us if we had not been successful and if we had incurred losses. Having realized it both with my brain and with my heart, I should like to warn everybody against the danger of being unsuccessful here.

"It is a great mistake to suppose," Stanislavsky continued, "that they don't know good actors here. They have seen the best that Europe could give them. Perhaps that is why America values personality so much. The whole theatrical business in America is based on the personality of the actor. One actor is a man of talent and the rest are nonentities. Plus the most lavish production, *such as we don't know*. Plus the most marvellous lighting equipment, about which we have no idea. Plus stage technique which we have never dreamt of. Plus a staff of stage hands and their foreman, we don't even dare to dream of. (We begin *The Three Sisters* and *The Cherry Orchard* at 8.5 p.m. sharp and finish at 11.10 p.m. ; *Czar Fyodor* we begin at 8.5 p.m. sharp and finish at 10.25 p.m. ; the interval before the second act of *The Cherry Orchard* is 8 minutes, before the fourth act of *The Three Sisters* 10 minutes. And that on a stage only 26 feet deep ! !)

"So that we cannot hope to surprise America in every sphere of our art. Such an actor as David Warfield, whom I saw in the part of Shylock,[1] we have not got. And Belasco's production of *The Merchant of Venice* exceeds in sheer lavishness anything I ever saw, and as for its technical achievements, the Maly Theatre could envy them. John Barrymore's Hamlet[2] is far from ideal, but very charming. Such a Peer Gynt as Schildkraut we have not got in Russia. And they have many more well-known actors we have not seen yet. The opera, so far as voices are concerned, is incomparably better than any theatre in Europe. Nor will you be able to find in Europe such conductors or such symphonic orchestras as they have here. To tell you the truth, I have often wondered why the Americans praise us so much. Our ensemble ! Yes, that impresses them greatly. But what impresses them most of all is that our company should possess three or four

---

[1] Stanislavsky saw *The Merchant of Venice* on February 1st.
[2] Stanislavsky saw *Hamlet* on January 25th.

individual artists whose presence is at once detected. The rest, they say, is merely the work of the producer. That they, too, can do with their ordinary actors. But three or four artistic personalities—that's what surprises them so much. It is true that they have overlooked a number of actors in our company, but those who are in the first class they picked out immediately and appreciated them more than in Europe."

Stanislavsky went on to express his unfeigned admiration for the American people. "The people here," he wrote, 'are very charming, friendly, good-humoured, naïve, eager for knowledge, not at all stuck up, lacking European snobbery, looking you straight in the eyes and ready to accept everything that is new and real."

It was in March that Stanislavsky began his work on *My Life in Art*, having accepted after a great deal of hesitation an offer from an American publishing house to write an account of his experiences on the stage. He wrote pages of it in his free time and then dictated them to his secretary. "Stanislavsky," his secretary records, "did not seem to know the meaning of fatigue. We wrote page after page. During our work he would snatch a few minutes to drink a glass of sour milk and then go on dictating. At two o'clock in the morning or even later he was still fresh and ready to go on with his work, but would interrupt me with the words, 'A pity, but I'm afraid we must stop.' "

His work on the book was interrupted when the theatre went on tour to Chicago, Philadelphia and Boston. They stayed three weeks in Chicago and a fortnight in Philadelphia and Boston respectively, giving the same four plays in each city (*Czar Fydor, The Three Sisters, The Cherry Orchard*, and *The Lower Depths*). After the last performance in Boston on May 19th, he felt ill and tired, and he still had to appear in New York during the last "farewell" weeks. On June 2nd the Moscow Art Theatre gave its last performance in New York and on June 7th Stanislavsky embarked for France on the Cunard liner *Laconia*. During the return journey he resumed his work on his book. He worked most of the day and sometimes far into the night. Writing to Gurevich from Freiburg, where he spent the summer of 1923 with his family, he complained about the slow progress of his work. "Oh, how terrible it is to be an author!" he wrote. "I simply must carry out my contract. I have to go on writing, though I am forced to write things I should not have written in normal circumstances.

But my chief worry is my eyes. I can't work more than three hours a day. So willy-nilly I have to crowd all my writing— the book and my letters—into these three hours. If I don't carry out my contract, I shall forfeit part of my royalties."

He finished his book in time, but he spent over a year on its Russian edition and so thoroughly revised it that when it was published in 1925, it was practically a different work.

The Moscow Art Theatre began its second American season in New York on November 9th, 1923. This time they spent twelve weeks in New York, three weeks in Chicago, and one week respectively in Philadelphia, Boston, Washington, Pittsburgh, New Haven, Hartford, Newark, Cliveden and Detroit. The new plays performed by them during this second season included *Uncle Vanya, Ivanov, Pazukhin's Death,* and a fuller version of the adaptation of *The Brothers Karamazov.*

During their week in Washington Stanislavsky and the actors of the Moscow Art Theatre paid a visit to the White House.

CHAPTER XLIX

ON HIS RETURN TO Russia in the autumn of 1924 (he had spent his summer holidays after his second American tour at a seaside resort near Nice), Stanislavsky found that during his absence Nemirovich-Danchenko had dissolved his studios. This was quite a logical step from Nemirovich-Danchenko's point of view : he did not possess Stanislavsky's fanatical zeal, nor did he enjoy his authority. His knowledge of the system, too, was inadequate. The First Studio, to Stanislavsky's great sorrow, formed its own theatre, which under the name of The Second Moscow Art Theatre existed till 1936. The Second Studio was incorporated into the Moscow Art Theatre. The Third Studio became known as Vakhtangov's Theatre, and the Fourth Studio, founded in 1921, as the Realistic Theatre.

Stanislavsky had to begin from scratch. But for the next four years he was busy with his productions for the Moscow Art Theatre and the Opera Studio, which in 1926 became known as Stanislavsky's Opera House. He was at the same time, of course, also appearing in his old parts on the stage. During this short time he produced seven plays, including Ostrovsky's *Ardent Heart*, Beaumarchais's *The Marriage of Figaro*, an adaptation of a French melodrama, *The Sisters Gerard*, and four plays by Soviet dramatists which were not crudely propagandist in character. In addition, he spent a long time on the rehearsals of an adaptation of Dickens's story *The Battle of Life*. During the same period he produced a number of operas, including *La Bohème* and *Boris Godunov*.

Stanislavsky's production of *The Ardent Heart*, first performed on January 23rd, 1926, marked a definite break with the "Chekhov traditions" of the Moscow Art Theatre. The "Chekhovian half-tones" in which he wanted the actors to play *Julius Cæsar*, had now finally been abandoned. The first night spectators were

369

amazed at the bright colours in which Stanislavsky had dressed Ostrovsky's Robin Hood melodrama, at the sharpness of the social satire, and at the rollicking fun of it all. Some people in the audience were genuinely shocked. "What's happened to Stanislavsky?" they were heard asking each other. "Doesn't he realize that Chekhov's seagull has flown from this vulgar music-hall?" But they never asked themselves why even Chekhov's *Seagull* had not been able to survive the enervating elegiac atmosphere in which the Moscow Art Theatre had been wallowing for so many years and which was now as out of date as the audiences of whom it was so characteristic before the revolution. Stanislavsky's greatness lay in the constant growth of his artistic sensibilities. He never hesitated to throw over the outworn enthusiasms of his past. At the age of sixty-three he could still astonish the world by his youthfulness. But it was a different kind of youthfulness : it was steeped in wisdom and experience and drew its inspiration from the living well of the human heart.

In *The Marriage of Figaro*, which was first performed on April 28th, 1927, Stanislavsky tried to devise a system which should prevent the attention of the spectator from being diverted from the general "line" of the development of the action of the play by the impingement of his private affairs on his consciousness. He did it by changing the scenes without drawing the curtain (for the first time taking full advantage of the revolving stage of the Moscow Art Theatre) and thus avoided the dangerous hiatus in the spectator's mind. He found that far from distracting the spectator's attention, this increased his interest in what was taking place on the stage.

By this time Stanislavsky left most of the work on the play to his assistants. He usually took the preliminary rehearsals and came on the scene again only after the play had been thoroughly rehearsed (detailed reports of every rehearsal were sent to him), when he went over the play again. In the meantime he discussed the sets with the stage-designers, saw to the costumes and, generally, supervised the entire technical side of the production.

The preliminary rehearsals of the plays were usually conducted by Stanislavsky in the study of his house in Leontyev Lane. The actors and their assistant producer first gathered together in the drawing-room with the columns. They were usually in a state of subdued excitement (no one knew whom Stanislavsky might not pick out as the guinea-pig for demonstrating one or another "element" of his system), talking in undertones, smoking and glancing nervously from time to time at the closed door of the study. When they were all assembled, the assistant producer would press the electric bell at the side of the door. After a while it was opened by the greyhaired housekeeper and they would be admitted.

Stanislavsky usually sat on a large sofa beside a little table on which there always lay the notes of his system. The assistant producer sat down beside him, the prompter took up his position by one of the windows, and the actors disposed themselves in the armchairs in a semi-circle round the sofa. The preliminary rehearsals usually began with a few "general" remarks. If Stanislavsky was in a good mood, he would put his pince-nez over his right ear, crack a few jokes, pay a few compliments, put a few ironic questions about the theatre, then give rather a formal smile, clap his hands, and say, "Well, ladies and gentlemen, let's begin ! "

The work began. Stanislavsky's face grew concentrated, his eyes narrowed a little, their pupils contracting, his lips and face moved in concert with the movements of the face and lips of the actor, till, suddenly, he would lean forward, cup his ear with his hand, and declare firmly : "I don't believe it ! " When the actor went over the particular piece again, Stanislavsky's face would assume a stern expression and his lips twitch nervously. "I beg your pardon ? " he would ask very politely. "Can't understand a word of it !" There followed a careful analysis of the whole "piece" in the play. Stanislavsky would then spend almost the entire rehearsal in search of what he called "the little truth", a most painstaking process which was usually accompanied by a discussion of a general nature. Thus, during the rehearsals of *The Battle of Life* performed for the first time on October 4th, 1924, Stanislavsky expatiated on the fundamental task of the theatre, which, he claimed, must be not to entertain the spectator, but to educate him and "to open his eyes to the ideals created by the people themselves." The thrill the spectator received from watching a play must never be merely a result of the producer's methods, but must come from the disclosure of the inner meaning of the play and the ability to subordinate all the means of theatrical expressiveness to that aim.

"It is impossible to live on the stage or to perform a play," he said in this connection, "for the sake of showing what a clever actor or producer you are. It is true you must and should be devoted to your profession, but not for the delights and laurels it brings you. You should love your art because it makes it possible for you to talk to the spectator about the things he cares most for in life, and to make him a more useful member of society by embodying certain definite ideas on the stage in artistically creative characters. If the spectator obtains an answer to what is engaging his thoughts, he will grow fond of the theatre and will learn to look on it as a necessity. But if all we do in the theatre is to entertain him, he will come and have a look at us and then go away. It is important to the spectator that the thoughts uppermost in his mind should agitate you and that the thoughts uppermost in your minds should agitate him. If you will realize what it means to find and follow the ruling idea of every play and make it interesting to the spectator, your work on the stage will always be vital and will always agitate the spectator, that is to say, it will always retain its youth."

The ruling idea of the play and its "through-action" was occupying more and more of his thoughts. In other words, he realized at last the great significance of the playwright's intentions as the basis for the producer's work on the stage. This was the logical result of his abandonment of the position of the producer-autocrat to whom his own interpretation of the play is what matters most. During the last year of his life, after his book *The Actor's Work on Himself* had already been written, he often expressed his regret that he had dealt with the ruling idea and through-action at the end of it instead of at the beginning. He regarded that as the greatest flaw of the system as formulated by him in the book. "When you read my book," he warned the actors, "you must keep in mind that at the time I wrote it I was not able to start at once with the ruling idea and through-action. That was my fault as an author. In a play," he went on, "you are given an extract of life, and the through-action *passes through* it like a fairway. Everything that goes along that fairway is important. Everything must lead to it and through it to the ruling idea. The general connection with it and the dependence on it of whatever happens in the performance is so great that the smallest detail, if it is not related to the ruling idea, becomes superfluous and harmful and is liable to divert the attention from the essential point of the play."

The producer's main concern, therefore, ought to be to discover the ruling idea of the play and then thread the through-action on it. "No producer," he said, "can produce a play unless he first finds its ruling idea. At present the producer of a play in our theatres and even in the Moscow Art Theatre does not care about its ruling idea at all, but builds up his production entirely on all sorts of clever tricks. This is the very negation of the art of the stage. It is true that such clever tricks are usually rewarded by a thunder of applause, which is all the actors want, but it was not for this that Pushkin or Shakespeare wrote."

And towards the end of his life Stanislavsky wrote : "The elements of the inner state of mind on the stage, polished and made ready for creative work but not linked by common action, are like pearls thrown haphazardly on a table. Thread them and put a rich clasp at the end and you will get a string of pearls. It is the same with our creative art and the actor's creative state of mind. We must link all the elements (the pearls) together into one whole, thread them on the general line (the string), which in our stage parlance we call 'through-action', and then strengthen them with the final and chief aim of the play (the clasp), which we call the 'ruling idea'. For without through-action and the ruling idea there can be no creative state of mind and no creative action, just as without a thread and a clasp there can be no string of pearls."

Producers and actors who know how to analyse a play thoroughly, pick out the right "problems and pieces", disclose "the logic of the action", find "the given circumstances", "aids", "communication", "the moments of truth and belief", and all the other elements of the system, but forget the most important thing of all, namely, through-action and the ruling idea, are, he once told Leonidov, "like a man who knows that to make an omelette he must get a frying-pan and eggs, that the eggs have to be broken and put into the frying-pan, and that he must put in a pinch of salt—he knows everything and he does it all, but he doesn't get his omelette because he forgets that the frying pan has to be heated."

This being his present attitude towards the playwright, what was now his attitude towards the actor and the producer ? In the last fourteen years of his life he had turned sharply against any imposition by the producer of his personal feelings and ready-made *mise-en-scènes* on the actor. "The old method of *mise-en-*

scènes," he wrote to a critic, "belongs to the producer-autocrat against whom I am fighting now."

And at one of the rehearsals in Leontyev Lane, he gave this detailed statement of his present position with regard to the tasks of a producer :

"Before, a producer planned his *mise-en-scènes* and the nature of the inner feelings of the *dramatis personae* in his own study. He then went to the rehearsal and told the actor to carry them out. The actor was quite naturally expected to copy his producer. But when I arrive at a rehearsal now, I am no more prepared than the actor and I go through all the phases of his work with him. The producer must approach the play with a mind as fresh and clear as the actor's and then grow together with him."

The whole development of the production of a play must, therefore, according to Stanislavsky, evolve during the process of the work on the play and with the maximum regard to the stage individuality and the creative abilities of each member of the cast. Far from belittling the position of the producer, such a conception of his duties, Stanislavsky maintained, presented him with an opportunity of solving a great many complex problems, for to foist on the actor a ready-made solution was much simpler than helping him "to find himself in his part and his part in himself." In his endeavour to avoid everything that might evoke in the actor premature and untimely conceptions of the character he had to represent on the stage, and in this way bring him straight to the final result, namely, the "acting" of feelings and an external and superficial delineation of character, Stanislavsky renounced his old principles of organizing the creative process of stage representation. "Before," he told his actors, "we stuffed the head of the actor with all sorts of lectures about the epoch, the history, and the life of the characters in the play, as a result of which the actor used to go out on the stage with a head full to bursting and was not able to act anything." Not that Stanislavsky now denied the need for studying the historical background of a play, but he proposed to do it in the course of the actor's work on his part and only when the actor himself felt an organic need for acquiring such information. In the end he even denied the advantages of a preliminary study of a play "at the table" and its division into small pieces and problems. Such an analytic method, he held, led the actor into the sphere of abstract reasoning, whereas it was the task of the producer-instructor to develop the active nature of the actor's creative work.

"Reasoning," he maintained, "has nothing to do with art. The best analysis of a play is to act it in the given circumstances. For in the process of action the actor gradually obtains the mastery over the inner incentives of the actions of the character he is representing, evoking in himself the emotions and thoughts which resulted in those actions. In such a case, an actor not only understands his part, but also feels it, and that is the most important thing in the creative work on the stage."

Stanislavsky, therefore, demanded that the actors should first of all act the plot of the play, concentrating on its physical actions. "Simple physical actions," he said, "form the firm basis of everything people do in life. Their value to our art lies in the fact that they are organic in any given circumstances. But the actor must never forget that physical actions are merely an excuse for evoking inner action. When you have learnt to create this line of action and when your whole attention is directed towards it, we shall be able to guarantee that on coming out on the stage you will always do that which is necessary and for the sake of which your art exists."

True to his new principles, Stanislavsky left the entire initiative to the actors themselves. He merely watched, examined and directed their work. One day, for instance, he asked a young actress what part she would like best to act.

"Hamlet," the actress replied.

"You mean Ophelia, don't you ? "

"No, I mean Hamlet."

"Very well," said Stanislavsky, "Let's see what you can do."

And for a time he took a personal interest in her work on the part of Hamlet, and in reply to the doubts expressed by some teachers of dramatic art who reminded him of his own statement in *My Life in Art* about the danger of permitting young and inexperienced actors to tackle difficult dramatic material, Stanislavsky said : "We must give them a chance and support their creative aspirations. We did not allow actors to take difficult parts till their youth was gone and their passions had died. Perhaps we made a mistake."

This incident, by the way, gave rise to the rumour that Stanislavsky was contemplating producing *Hamlet* with a young actress in the title part, a rumour often quoted as a fact abroad.

Stanislavsky never turned his back on what he now considered the fundamental principle of the art of the stage—the pre-eminent position of the art of the actor, a principle in which he merely followed Shchepkin and Ostrovsky. He now subordinated everything to the actor, asserting that the scenery and the various methods of the producer had a right to exist only in so far as they did not interfere with the actor. His methods had now only one aim in view : to awaken the actor's individual creative powers. He no longer "fabricated" a part, but let it grow up gradually in the actor's soul. He was very anxious to get the right "line" of the inner rhythm of an act in a play. He would no longer show the actors how to play their parts, but would help them instead to find the inner dramatic movement of the scene or act. He would use hardly any gestures or movements or mimicry. Just a slight change of posture and his huge figure would suddenly become transformed. Having found the rhythmic basis of the scene, he would try to get from the actors a definite delineation of their parts. He made each actor work out his own rhythm. He created, as one actor put it, a most complex counterpoint of the action and then, like a conductor, watched the inner rhythm of every individual actor until he got the delineation of his part absolutely right and until the inner image of the particular scene was clearly revealed.

In the spring of 1925, Stanislavsky and the Moscow Art Theatre went on an extensive tour of the Caucasus and Southern Russia, playing in seven towns, including Tiflis and Kiev. In the spring of 1927 and 1928, the theatre visited Leningrad. The year 1928 was one of the busiest in Stanislavsky's stage career. He was responsible for three new productions at the Moscow Art Theatre, and he was also rehearsing *Othello* (with Leonidov in the title part) and Moussorgsky's opera *Boris Godunov*. From a letter he wrote to Gurevich on March 4th of that year, it is clear that in 1928, too, he began writing his second book, in which he was to present his system not as a theory but as a practical guide to actors. But his constant pre-occupation with his rehearsals and his writing did not by any means exhaust his activities that year. For it was on October 27th, 1928, that the Moscow Art Theatre was celebrating the 30th anniversary of its foundation, and Stanislavsky had to prepare a long report on the activities of the theatre and, in addition, take part next day in the first act of *The Three Sisters* at a gala performance at which several acts from different plays were to be given. The composition of his speech gave him a great deal of trouble and he spent several sleepless nights in writing and correcting it. On the eve of October 27th he hardly slept. In the morning he went to the theatre, where he received messages of congratulations from all over the world. In the evening the official celebrations started very late because of the delayed arrival of a high personage who had to deliver an official address. Stanislavsky kept pacing his dressing room, getting more and more nervous and impatient. When the meeting started at last, he had to listen to endless speeches from all sorts of official bodies and foreign delegations, and by the time he got up to deliver his speech he was very tired. His speech was a dignified and courageous re-affirmation of the principles he stood for. He pleaded for the preservation of the traditions of the Russian theatre. "Ancient art," he declared, "was magnificent, but something has not been handed down to us and it has gone for ever. *Bel canto* was magnificent, but its secret has been lost for ever. To prevent the same thing from happening again to our art we must first of all preserve the traditions that have come down to us from such pioneers as Shchepkin." Lunacharsky, the Soviet Commissar of Education, had said in his speech that the time would come when Soviet playwrights would give a true reflection of the great times they were passing through. Stanislavsky would not gainsay it, but he affirmed that so far no such play had been written and that until it was written they would go on giving only what they themselves felt to be true. "For," he added, "if we force ourselves and do what we do not think is right, we shall fail, and art never forgives such failures. We shall grow and change gradually," he declared, "in a natural way." He then took up the challenge of his opponents who accused him of being "slow on purpose" and of still "lagging behind the times". "This is," he said, "because the revolution is not proceeding at the same fast pace inwardly as it does outwardly. Outwardly it is easy ; but one must experience it inwardly. During the first years of the revolution when we were looked upon as a backward theatre," he went on, "we all sat in our studies and did our best to systematise our art ; we tried to write a 'grammar' of dramatic art, and I am happy to say that thanks to the theatre and thanks to the help I received from my colleagues, I seem to have accomplished something of importance ; and I comfort myself with the hope that I shall have enough strength to deliver a course of public lectures this year in which I shall explain what I know and what is so dear to me."

But Stanislavsky never delivered this course of lectures. After the speeches were over, the guests were invited to a banquet in the foyer and Stanislavsky was on his feet most of the time, talking to everybody. He was too tired to stay for the dance which followed upon the banquet. Next morning he rang up Gurevich and talked to her for an hour, discussing the anniversary celebrations and telling her about the rehearsals of *Othello* and how wonderful Leonidov was in the leading part. "He is better than Salvini!" he exclaimed with youthful enthusiasm, and this coming from one who regarded Salvini as the greatest Othello he had ever seen, was praise indeed.

In the evening Stanislavsky played Vershinin in the first act of *The Three Sisters*. It was the last part he was ever to play. Towards the end of the act he felt sharp pains in the region of his heart. At first he paid no attention and went on playing. But the pains became fiercer and fiercer till he could scarcely prevent himself from running off the stage. It was only, as he later confessed, his inner artistic discipline and his fear of ruining the gala performance that made him carry on to the end. He just managed to stagger to his dressing room, where he lay down on the sofa without taking off his costume or make-up. His heart attack was getting more and more violent. A well-known physician, who happened to be in the auditorium and whose patient Stanislavsky had once been, was summoned to attend to him. He found that Stanislavsky was suffering from a violent attack of angina pectoris.

CHAPTER L

STANISLAVSKY did not leave his bed for the next three months. At first his condition was critical, but he got better slowly and painfully, leaving his house for the first time in May, 1929. He soon left for his favourite seaside resort near Nice where he stayed for a year and a half. As he was suffering from an incurable disease of the heart, a doctor was now permanently in attendance on him. His doctor found him a very difficult patient. He used to exaggerate his complaints, making his medical diagnosis more difficult. His ideas of medicine were very primitive. At first he tried homeopathic treatment, but soon gave it up. He was afraid to take certain medicines. When abroad he refused to consult specialists, as he disliked and mistrusted foreign doctors. But he was very meticulous in carrying out his doctor's orders and, having found out how many steps a day he ought to take, he carefully counted the steps from his seaside hotel to the seat in which he usually rested after his afternoon sleep, and never took one step more than necessary.

He spent most of his time at the seaside resort near Nice writing his *mise-en-scènes* for *Othello*, the production of which had been put off by his illness. (His rehearsals of *Boris Godunov* were so advanced by the time he had been taken ill that he had entrusted Moskvin with the final work on the opera.) Circumstances had compelled him to resort to a practice he now condemned. Away from his theatre, he had no choice but to adopt his old methods of producing a play by imposing his own plan of production on the actors. In *Othello* this reversion to past practices was made easy by the fact that he used the same faulty translation of the play he had used in 1896. His *mise-en-scènes* therefore were based entirely on the Russian text he had before him and his whole plan of production was influenced by it. His elaborations of the scenes in the play, which bear quite a striking resemblance to

379

his imaginative interpretation of the same scenes in his earlier production, are a direct consequence of his faulty text. Indeed, there can be no doubt that if he had known Shakespeare's text, he would never have written those production notes. Moreover, his second production of *Othello* had quite certainly been influenced by the lavishness of David Belasco's production of *The Merchant of Venice* which he had seen in New York. He therefore fell into another of his old errors, that of imitating someone else's style of production. He had, besides, already rehearsed Leonidov in the part of Othello, but was prevented by his serious illness from co-ordinating the final conception of this part with the other parts in the play. All this boded ill for the success of Shakespeare's tragedy, and indeed when it was finally performed on March 14th, 1930, it proved a failure, and was withdrawn after the tenth performance.

Stanislavsky returned to Moscow in the autumn of 1930. He looked as youthful as ever. "He wore his greatness without realizing or noticing it," is how Gurevich described him shortly after his return from abroad. His movements were as impetuous and as full of vitality as ever. He still welcomed his visitors with a bright smile. He put up with the inconveniences of his fame—the constant importunity of strangers who either came to see him or wrote to him from all over the world—without a murmur ; on the contrary, he was always eager to help anybody who was genuinely seeking his advice. He resumed his regular rehearsals, though most of his time was devoted to writing his book. He now decided to give it a semi-fictional character, but he was never satisfied with his work. He mistrusted his literary judgment, and for a time he persuaded Gurevich to act as his literary editor. His main trouble was that he frequently changed his ideas about the importance of certain elements of his system. Thus, at first he regarded the emotional memory of the actor as of paramount importance and treated it quite independently of the actor's imagination. It was only later that he began to regard the "magic if", that is to say, the actor's imagination, as of much greater importance, and this view, too, as already noted, he subsequently modified, so that by the time his book was already in print it was the ruling idea and through-action that became the cornerstone of his system. There were also a great number of purely scientific problems that Stanislavsky had neither the time nor the knowledge to deal with adequately and that had to be submitted to various experts for correction. All this made his work on the book a very slow and at times rather painful business, and it is perhaps not surprising that in the end Gurevich gave up her collaboration with Stanislavsky.

Shortly after his return from abroad Stanislavsky chose his next production for the Moscow Art Theatre : it was to be a stage adaptation of Gogol's great novel, *Dead Souls*. As was his practice now, he appointed two producers and let them carry out the rehearsals without interference. The producers decided to do the play in the most fashionable style of the time—the grotesque style of exaggerated caricature. Stanislavsky saw the dress rehearsal of the play in 1931 and found the whole idea of the production so unsatisfactory that he decided to scrap it and do it himself.

"The grotesque," he told them, "is perhaps the highest form of stage art, but to bring it off successfully one must first of all culti- vate the soil and the roots from which this quite remarkable living plant springs. But in your anxiety to pluck the flower, you did not think of the roots at all, and it is impossible to achieve anything that way. I remember," he went on, "seeing in Paris a remarkable comedian in some cheap comedy who took off his trousers and belaboured his mother-in-law with them. It was beautifully done, and I enjoyed every moment of it because the great actor had convinced me by the organic logic of his action that there was nothing else he could do. But to achieve such a result you must either possess great talent or put a lot of preliminary work into your acting, work on the growth of the roots out of which such a plant will gradually grow."

Stanislavsky decided to produce the play in his old realistic manner and he invited Simov to go back to the Moscow Art Theatre after a separation of twenty-five years and design the scenery for him. Simov found Stanislavsky very different from the man he had known : age had not dimmed the inventiveness of his imagination, but brought order and logic into it. A single touch, a gesture, a pose, an intonation, and the desired scene sprang to life. Occasionally, as he tried to explain something, he would interrupt his speech by the question, "Do you feel it ? " and pause, biting the back of his hand as he scrutinized Simov. He insisted that the mounting of the play should correspond to Gogol's literary manner, that is, that the scenery should blend harmoniously with the text.

The rehearsals of the play went on for a year and a half, but even when Stanislavsky at last allowed it to be performed (its first night took place on November 28th, 1932), he was not satisfied with it.

"It isn't a finished performance by any means," he told the actors, "but I am releasing it because I can see that the soil and the roots have been sufficiently cultivated. I can see small but living green shoots which, if you follow the right path, will grow and produce real flowers." And turning to the actor who played the leading part of Chichikov, he said : "You have now learnt how to walk on the stage, but you are still not acting like Chichikov. You are a living man, but you are still a child. Go on following this road and in another ten years you will be Chichikov, and in ten years more, you will really be able to play Gogol."

And in his final address to the cast of *Dead Souls* he said : "There are only about one hundred different technical ways in which the problems of a certain scene can be solved, but nature has a countless number of ways. Stage acting as expressed by the methods of an actor's technique is as different from living organic action born of the actor's intuition as artificial teeth are from real ones, a wig from natural hair, or a paper flower from a living plant."

In the summer of 1931 Bernard Shaw paid his visit to Moscow and a meeting was arranged between him, Stanislavsky and Lunacharsky, the Commissar of Education. Shaw is reported to have described Stanislavsky as "the most handsome man in the world." [1]

In October, 1931, a permanent nurse was engaged for Stanislavsky. Lyubov Dukhovskaya turned out to be a very able and sensible woman with whom Stanislavsky got on capitally, though at first she found it a little difficult to please him. He had a system for everything. Above all, his bed had to be made in a certain way. "I am used to sleeping that way," Stanislavsky told her. "It's such a nuisance to be a creature of habit. I've been terribly spoilt." At night everything on his bedside-table had to be arranged according to a once and for all established plan : the glasses, the medicine bottles, the bell—everything had its own appointed place, so that he could get everything he wanted at

[1] Bernard Shaw writes : "I cannot remember a word of what was said by Stanislavsky and Lunacharsky when we met. Probably we talked topical politics and not theatre shop.

"I certainly did not describe Stanislavsky as the most handsome man in the world. He was goodlooking, but not so notably as to call for such a remark."

night without switching on the light ; his notebooks, a bottle of eyedrops, a lamp with a blue lampshade, and a small tray were on a little bedside cabinet, and in its drawer were his pince-nez, his thermometer, and his favourite nickel watch. On the mantelpiece was his blue mug with his shaving things (he always shaved himself without using a glass). Three nightshirts were usually put over the back of his bed so that he could change into a new one whenever he perspired heavily.

During the first months of her attendance Dukhovskaya did not see Stanislavsky very often as he was always busy rehearsing and going to the theatre. At the beginning of 1932 he had another heart attack and spent three months in bed. After that he stayed indoors every winter, conducting his rehearsals in his study or the large drawing-room and writing his book. The summer of 1932 he again spent abroad, this time in the Black Forest spa of Badenweiler where he continued to work on his book. His wife and grand-daughter were with him. In Badenweiler he was in bed with influenza for a fortnight and he had another slight heart attack shortly before his return to Moscow.

In 1932 the Moscow Art Theatre was officially renamed The Gorky Moscow Art Theatre, and in a letter to Gorky, Stanislavsky wrote : "I am glad that our theatre, the close witness of your brilliant literary career for the past forty years, now bears your name. From now on we shall work together for the Soviet theatre which alone can sustain the decaying theatre in the rest of the world."

On January 10th, 1933, he received a reply from Gorky, who addressed him as "the greatest reformer of dramatic art," and stressed in particular Stanislavsky's work in educating a whole generation of great actors. "The cultural significance of this work of yours," Gorky wrote, "seems to me not to be sufficiently appreciated. And if you need any expressions of gratitude from the Soviet Union, they ought first of all to be made to you for creating the best artists of the theatre in the whole world. By this work you have proved again how rich and inexhaustible the creative energy of our country is. . . . You have done a great deal and you can do a great deal more for the happiness of our people and for its spiritual strength and beauty. Accept my deepest respects, great artist and indefatigable worker, the teacher of our actors."

Stanislavsky answered Gorky's "wonderful" letter on the same day. "I have been lucky in my life," he wrote. "Life herself has arranged everything for me. I am a mere tool in her hands. But such good luck puts me under the obligation to pass on what life has given me before I die. It is very difficult to share one's experience in so complex an art as the creative work of the actor. In personal communication with students it is possible to convey and to represent what cannot be so easily formulated in words. Representation is the actor's sphere. But when I pick up my pen the necessary words for the definition of what I feel fly away from me. Ever since our meeting in Capri, when you were so good as to run over my first essays in the form of 'a grammar of dramatic art', I have been doing my utmost to put down on paper what a young actor ought to know. Such a book is necessary, if only because it would put an end to all the silly talk about my so-called 'system', which in the form it is taught now merely cripples the actor.

"Besides, theatrical art, or rather the art of the actor, is dying out. One after another the great actors and technicians of the stage are disappearing, leaving after them only a memory and a few bad photographs. That is why I have decided to leave a written record of my experiences. But such a work can be undertaken only by a real writer, and to write about art 'scientifically' is a tedious and useless occupation. . . . Oh, if only I could throw off ten years of my life and get rid of my constant illnesses ! To get well one needs a warm climate, but in a warm climate one can't work, and if one can't work, what is the use of living ? "

On January 18th Stanislavsky was seventy. Telegrams of congratulations had been arriving all day from every country in the world. A wireless had been installed in his study so that he could listen in to the tributes paid to him over Moscow Radio. In the afternoon a reception was held in his study. Representatives from different theatres, famous producers, actors and opera singers came to congratulate him on his birthday (Nemirovich-Danchenko alone was conspicuous by his absence). He sat in his usual place on the sofa surrounded by enormous baskets of white lilac. Amid the white flowers and in the bright light of the bronze chandelier he looked like another Prospero—with his irresistible smile and white downy hair. Like Prospero, he had defeated his enemies, and now basked in the sunshine of his success, and, like Prospero, he could truly say :—

> —I have bedimm'd
> The noontide sun, call'd forth the mutinous winds,
> And 'twixt the green sea and the azure vault
> Set roaring war : to the dread rattling thunder
> Have I given fire, and rifted Jove's stout oak
> With his own bolt ; the strong-based promontory
> Have I made shake ; and by the spurs pluck'd up
> The pine or cedar : graves, at my command,
> Have waked their sleepers, oped, and let 'em forth
> By my so potent art. But this rough magic
> I now abjure. . . .
>   . . . I'll break my staff,
> Bury it certain fathoms in the earth. . . .

But, unlike Prospero, he did not drown his book "deeper that did ever plummet sound"—his book, on which he was still working, he always carried about with him in the precious attaché-case he had nearly lost at the outbreak of the first world war. He had it with him near his bed when he was sick, he took it with him abroad when travelling, and he kept it beside his table when rehearsing.

His guests went up to him one by one and handed him their presents. He shook hands with them and exchanged the traditional Russian greeting—an embrace and a kiss. The tables were piled high with presents when the door of the study was opened and two huge pasties, one filled with cabbage (Stanislavsky's favourite dish), were carried in as a special gift from his Opera House. The guests applauded and Stanislavsky himself burst out laughing, shaking hands with his opera singers and thanking them for their original present. At six o'clock he retired to his bedroom for a rest, returning again to his study later in the evening to the birthday party given him by his family, his wife, his sister Zina, his brother Vladimir and other relations.

A few days later he went to the Kremlin to receive the Order of the Red Banner from President Kalinin. All day long preparations were made for this solemn occasion. The large wardrobe in the bedroom was opened, the nurse took out one suit after another, and every time he would say, after examining it gravely, "Put it back, my dear." At last he chose a black suit, put it on, took some drops for his heart, as he was very excited, and drove off to the Kremlin, accompanied by his doctor. He came back looking very happy.

On January 23rd Stanislavsky sent a letter to the cloak-room attendants of the Moscow Art Theatre in which he thanked them for their birthday greetings. He addressed them as "My dear friends," and, faithful to the "aphorism" he and Nemirovich-Danchenko had adopted at the foundation of their theatre, he assured them that they, too, had contributed in no small measure to the theatre's fame. "Our Moscow Art Theatre," he wrote, "differs from every other theatre in that its performances begin from the moment the spectator enters it. You are the first to meet the spectators, and it depends largely on you whether or not they are in the right mood to receive the impressions from the stage. If the spectator is displeased, he cannot possibly enjoy the play, while if on entering the theatre he feels that he is received with respect, his attitude to the performance is quite different. That is why I consider your work so important."

The rest of the winter Stanislavsky went on working intensively (in addition to the opera he was rehearsing, he was rehearsing Ostrovsky's backstage comedy *Artists and their Admirers*, first performed on June 14th, 1933). Towards the end of the winter he again caught a cold, which was followed by pneumonia, and spent two months in bed. As soon as he got better, he resumed his work on his book, refusing to listen to his doctor's protests. "Believe me," he said, "I shall feel worse if I don't write."

In the summer Stanislavsky left for France with his wife, his daughter and grand-daughter, and his doctor. At first they went to the French spa of Royat, but Stanislavsky did not feel happy there (it rained most of the time), and they soon left for his favourite seaside resort near Nice. He felt well the whole of October and November, but when they were making ready to leave for Moscow, he had another attack of angina pectoris, and had to stay in bed for a fortnight. As the weather in December was very warm that year, they decided to postpone their return to Russia, but Stanislavsky's health did not improve and they spent three more months at the sea and another three months in Paris, returning to Moscow in the autumn of 1934.

In a letter to Dukhovskaya on March 4th, 1934, Stanislavsky described his life on the French Riviera as rather monotonous. "I get up at nine o'clock," he wrote, "and fling open the french window of my bedroom. Lying in bed I can see the enormous expanse of the sea as though it were only a few yards away from me, and the cloudless sky and the bright sun. Here I am not afraid of catching cold. Here I lie and write my book till twelve o'clock. Then I dress and go out on the roof on the fifth floor of the house in which we live. There I sit, protected from the hot rays of the sun by a large umbrella, almost the whole day, eating and writing, mostly letters in connection with my first book which has just been published in a French edition, and very handsomely published, too. Now I am conducting negotiations for the publication of my book in Sweden. I am also engaged in a correspondence with an American university about my second book which I am on the point of finishing, but, somehow, cannot finish. All this takes up a great deal of my time. . . . It is here on the large roof that I also take my constitutional for my heart and legs, that is, I walk between 700 and 800 steps. One thing is not so good, though—the fumes from the hundreds of chimneys which poison the air. That is why we got our flat so cheaply. It is a great nuisance. Fortunately, the wind this year is blowing mostly in a southerly direction, carrying the fumes away from us.

"We spend the time very happily till five o'clock, after which it gets terribly cold till about seven. During that time I seek safety indoors, turn on the central heating and sleep. Then we have dinner, and in the evening I read chapters from my book to my family, and they discuss and criticise them. At eleven we go to bed, but I never put out my light before one or even half past one in the morning.

"And so every day. All this time, that is, during the whole of the winter I have only been out on the beach four or five times. We hardly ever take a ride in the country. As you know I got stuck here by accident. I shall not start on my homeward journey till the weather has settled. I shall stop for a short time in Paris and Berlin and hope to be back in Moscow by the middle or the end of April."

It was while he was working on his second book in the South of France that he decided to found another studio, and the news from Moscow that his application for permission to open one had been granted pleased him greatly. On his return he was given a great reception at the station and arrived home in a car laden with flowers. All day long visitors came to welcome him back home and he spent a pleasant time with them, laughing a lot and recounting his experiences abroad.

"The theatre in Paris and Berlin," he told his friends, "is going downhill. The cinema alone seems to flourish there."

He devoted most of his time now to opera rehearsals (he only produced one play—Molière's *Tartuffe*—for the Moscow Art Theatre and it was performed after his death). Before his last journey abroad he was rehearsing *The Barber of Seville* and *Don Pasquale*, and on his return he went to a dress rehearsal of the second opera. The producers, who were watching his face intently, were surprised that he did not laugh as usual at Dr. Malatesta's pranks, though they could see that he liked the performance. Towards the end of the opera they saw him take out his handkerchief and brush away a tear. He was deeply moved and happy to find a grain of his art in their work. After the performance he told the actors that he now believed that his work would not die with him.

He spent the summer of 1935 at a sanatorium near Moscow, completing his programme for the new Dramatic and Operatic Studio.

"Our system," he told some of the members of the Studio who came to see him at the sanatorium, "has four storeys, four planes of perception. The actor who makes full use of its 'elements' (communication, problems, logic, etc.) has reached the first storey. If he knows how to establish the line of communication, the line of problems, and so on, and weave all these lines into one through-action, he has found the way of creating his part independently and has reached the second storey of the system. But if the actor has not discovered his own ruling idea, or, more correctly, his own ruling-ruling idea, he cannot be said to be a real artist. The ruling idea of a part can be understood in different ways. That depends on the ruling-ruling idea of the actor-man himself. Tolstoy, for instance, strove for self-betterment and self-purification and all his creative work is permeated by that ruling idea. Chekhov's works are permeated with a passionate desire for a new and better life. Dostoevsky sought for the borderline between man's divine and satanic origin, and so on.

"The fourth storey of our art is the sphere of the subconscious. It can only be reached when the actor has become the master of his technique to such an extent that he need no longer think of it and can give himself up entirely to inspiration and intuition. The wave from the ocean of the subconscious reaches us only occasionally, rolling up to us only in moments of the highest creative enthusiasm, but the actor of the future, having mastered the technique of his art, will be able to bathe in this ocean freely. We

must create schools which will educate these future masters of the
art of the stage. We must never forget," he went on, "that our art
is based entirely on the actor who is exchanging living currents
with the auditorium, and no external technique can alter that.
In the theatre of the future actors will come out on the stage
without the aid of scenery or make-up, and they will be able to
establish real organic communication between themselves. If
real life is born on the stage, the audience does not demand anything else—it is entirely in your power. It is such a theatre you
should strive to create. Now, however, it is impossible to do that :
we must first have actors who are complete masters of their art."

He disliked the cinema chiefly because it destroyed this direct
communication between the actor and the audience. For he
maintained that the audience was the sounding-board of the
actor's creative experiences and immediately reflected the emotional currents sent out from the stage.

"A machine," he told his students, "however perfect, kills what
is most important and most rare in our art."

Stanislavsky stayed on at the sanatorium till the beginning of
winter and on his return to Moscow began his work in the new
Studio. He appointed as his assistants pupils of his sister Zina.
"The lot has fallen to you," he told them. "I am throwing you
into the water, and if you start drowning, I shall hold you up."

Talking to his new students about his latest methods of working
on a part, he said : "Everything we did before, we shall do now
the other way round. We usually began by suggesting to the
actor that he was an old man, or that he was lame, or that he
wore a gaily coloured waistcoat, and so on. We stuffed his head
with all sorts of information about the historical background of a
play and the everyday life of its characters, with the result that
when he walked on the stage he could not do anything. He knew
everything about what sort of person he was supposed to be, but
he did not know the main thing : he did not know what he had
to do, so that he almost invariably ended by overacting. We tried
to draw feeling out of him and he exerted himself to the utmost
in his attempts to represent feeling. But now we shall proceed
differently. We shall create the line of his action, the life of his
body, and then the life of his spirit will be created indirectly by
itself. Before, we coached the actor how to play his part, but
now we shall try to find out how he himself acts. Once the
strong roots of his part have been formed, this 'how' will emerge

by itself. Before, we tried to squeeze the actor into the *mise-en-scène,* while the *mise-en-scène* should be born as a result of his work and his adaptation to his partner and the object. In the theatre of the future we shall work without any fixed *mise-en-scènes* so as to preserve the freshness of all the organic processes. If we deprive the actor of the *mise-en-scène,* he will have to think more of the circumstances of his part."

In his programme of the new Studio Stanislavsky hoped to introduce quite a new method for the study of the historical background of plays. He intended to have special exhibitions, illustrating different historical periods, and let the actors devise their costumes themselves, the aim of the study of history, in his view, being to teach the student how to act in the different conditions of each historical era. For the study of literature he proposed to set up a repertoire for the next twenty years so as to enable each student-actor to choose his part freely and defend his choice before a meeting of the members of the Studio.

In teaching the art of movement, Stanislavsky laid particular stress on plastic art, which, he claimed, ought to teach the actor to pay particular attention to his body. "Dancing lessons," he pointed out, "cannot be separated from the creative process and they must be dramatized—a ball in different historical periods, and this dramatization might even be given a plot of its own. In their study of plastic art, the student-actors must make use of antique sculpture, bringing to life and justifying the different poses of the statues."

When his assistants presented him with the programme of the first course of the Studio beginning with the words : "The development of the elements of inner technique in the students," Stanislavsky stopped them angrily.

"I can't understand a single word of it," he said. "How can anyone get any idea of our work from such headings ? About our art one must talk only in the language of art. Our art is based on action, so let them come and see how we act."

"But," his assistants protested indignantly, "we have been asked to compose a programme. What kind of programme are we to write then ? "

"You musn't write anything," Stanislavsky replied. "You must *show.* We'll have to compose a performance-programme in which we shall show everything we do in our Studio."

And he began to work on an illustrated programme of his

Studio which was only completed and presented after his death.

Lilina took a great interest in his work and he was glad to enrol her among the teachers in his Studio. The programme of the Studio included a special item which, for want of a better word, Stanislavsky called "tra-la-la-ing." The purpose of this exercise was to concentrate the entire attention of the actor on intonation and make him explain himself not with words, but only with "tra-la-las."

"But, darling," Lilina said to her husband one day, "I understand everything perfectly and I realize how important it all is, but what do you want your tra-la-las for ? I'm afraid no one will ever be able to understand it."

"You're always like that," Stanislavsky replied a little testily. "At first you always object to any new thing I introduce, but after a time you understand it better than anyone else."

"No," Lilina replied firmly, "I shall never understand this tra-la-la-ing of yours ! "

CHAPTER LI

STANISLAVSKY'S search for discoveries in the art of the stage went on during the last three years of his life, and even while he was seeing his book on the system through the Press, he kept looking for flaws in it and trying to perfect it. But in a sense his work was done. He might change his mind about the importance of one or another of the "elements" of his system, but the system itself, as he kept insisting, was not something rigid or indeed the only system on the art of acting that could achieve the results he sought. What he deplored most was a pedantic approach to his teaching. What dismayed him most was the idea that *anyone* could be taught to act in accordance with it. "Stanislavsky's only mistake in his book," Leonidov wrote, "was his insufficient emphasis on the fact that it is designed only for actors of talent. He, no doubt, took it for granted, but many of his readers do not realise it. They think that they have only to learn his system to become great actors. But Stanislavsky himself wrote at the end of his book : 'You have only to want badly, you have only to carry out such work in your life, you have only to learn to know your own nature and how to discipline it and, *provided you have talent*, you will become a great actor.'

"What is the main point of Stanislavsky's system ? " Leonidov continues. "What is he trying to achieve ? What he is after is great artistic truth—the truth of Homer, Sophocles, Shakespeare, Pushkin, Gogol. He does not want to hear vulgarity from the stage. He does not want theatrical clichés to reign on it. He wants to raise and develop the actor's taste ; he wants to teach him to work and to create ; he wants to train him to work hard all his life, however talented he may be, for without such hard work no actor can achieve anything ; he wants, as he used to say, to raise art on a high tower so that it should become the property of all and not only of a few chosen ones. He does not recognize form as something important in itself. He lets a producer choose any form he likes, provided that this form does no violence to the subject-matter of a play.

"Stanislavsky's art does not stand in need of any clever tricks or pretentious scenery among which it is impossible to move or speak naturally. He has something to say from the stage without such tricks. He wants the theatre to move the spectator deeply and not merely to entertain him. He wants art to be exciting and stimulating.

"Stanislavsky's system," Leonidov concludes, "does not force anything on anybody. He merely offers suggestions ; he merely wants to be of assistance to the actor. If you have your own method, use it by all means. He knows one thing only, namely, that the spectator must never be allowed to be indifferent. The spectator must always take an active part in the performance."

This analysis of Stanislavsky's system, coming from one of the greatest actors of the Moscow Art Theatre, whose advice and opinion Stanislavsky valued and often sought, shows that it was essentially complete. It is because its main proposition is that nothing ought to be imposed on the actor from without and that everything must come from within the actor himself, that Stanislavsky was so eager to establish his last Dramatic and Operatic Studio. But his work during the last three years of his life was continually interrupted by illness. He suffered from insomnia and his nurse Dukhovskaya used to sit for hours by his bed reading to him. On April 26th, 1936, he had another bad heart attack and for ten days his condition was serious. His sister Anna, who had taken so prominent a part in the Alexeyev Circle, died of a heart attack on May 1st, but it was decided that he should not be told of it. One night Dukhovskaya was reading a newspaper report of the successful tour of his Opera House in Stalingrad in which Stanislavsky's great achievements were praised.

"Aren't you proud of your fame ? " she asked him. "Doesn't it make you happy ? "

"No."

"Why not ? "

"Because they are not praising me for the things I should have liked them to praise me for. They praise me for something I no longer believe in. Why then should I be proud ? Sometimes I feel like swearing at actors for their performance, but the public praises them for what I no longer want to own. I have no followers. And what a reception they used to give us in Leningrad ! It was something unimaginable. In Paris, when I felt that we were taking the town by storm, I was happy. In America it was just a bacchanalia, madness. The reception they gave us there exceeded anything we had ever experienced. They used to carry us out of the theatre, kiss our hands. . . ."

"But aren't you sorry you no longer appear on the stage ? That you no longer see the enthusiasm of the crowds ? "

"No, I no longer believe in that sort of fame."

"But what you've done is a revolution in art. It will never die. And your fame will live for ever."

"But they will distort the truth I've taught them. I don't know when they will recognize it. You will see how they will attack me when my system is published. The names they will call me. The fight I shall still have to put up."

Lilina told him about the success of the examinations in the Studio and he was greatly pleased.

"I have great hopes of them," he said. "A new, fresh, young theatre is growing up."

On June 18th, Gorky died. As Stanislavsky had just had two violent heart attacks and was slowly recovering, he was not told of Gorky's death. The reporters who came to interview him were sent away.

When Dukhovskaya wakened him next morning, he asked her whether there was any news of Gorky.

"No," she replied.

"Haven't the papers arrived yet ? "

"Not yet."

A few moments later he again asked her for the papers.

"I'm afraid they haven't arrived yet," Dukhovskaya replied, looking rather embarrassed.

"Well, I will tell you then," said Stanislavsky. "Gorky is dead, isn't he ? "

"Yes."

Stanislavsky was silent. He looked very stern, then he suddenly said with a sad smile : "Well, now you can go on telling me lies."

"But how did you know that Gorky was dead ? "

"From your expression and from the way you spoke."

In a few moments he grew very agitated.

"I must write an article on Gorky for the papers," he said. "Help me. My head refuses to work."

"I don't think you ought to write it now," his nurse said. "Everyone knows that you are seriously ill."

Stanislavsky agreed. At the end of June his health improved sufficiently for him to be taken to a sanatorium near Moscow where he spent seven months. He returned on February 28th, 1937, but he was so weak that the car ride from the sanatorium brought on another heart attack. The moment he recovered, he resumed his work in the Studio. In July he went back to the sanatorium. His illness was progressing steadily now, and his heart attacks became more frequent. But on his return to Moscow in September, he resumed his work. The first time he re-entered the rehearsal room of the Studio, he walked very slowly, leaning heavily on his stick. But he held himself erect and looked confident. He was met by thunderous applause. He bowed and sat down in the armchair prepared for him, his nurse wrapping a rug round his legs.

He spoke to them of the importance of culture to an actor. What he meant, he explained, was that an actor ought not only to know how to wear his clothes or possess impeccable manners, but should be also cultured inwardly, be able to mix with people, respect the human personality, find the right value in everything, even in trifles, and look on art as one of the greatest gifts bestowed on man. "Very soon," he went on, "I shall no longer be with you, but if I am one of the links, however small, in the chain which is handed down by great men from century to century, I have the right to tell you : don't lose any time, and learn from me while it is not yet too late."

The whole of October he carried on with his work in the Studio and with his rehearsals, but in November he caught a cold which was followed by pneumonia. At the end of November he made another of his sudden recoveries. The elections to the Supreme Soviet were to take place just then and he was very anxious to cast his vote. As he was confined to the house during winter, he sent out his nurse, dressed himself, put on his hat, gloves and felt overshoes, opened the window and sat down in front of it. One of his assistant producers happened to pass the house at the time and, seeing the window of his bedroom wide open, he rushed upstairs. He asked Stanislavsky what he was doing.

"Oh," replied Stanislavsky, "I am just rehearsing. You see, I haven't been out for a long time and the elections are the day after tomorrow, so I am just trying to get used to the frosty air."

The window was immediately closed, but it was too late : Stanislavsky had a relapse and spent a few more weeks in bed. He applied to the returning officer of his district to be allowed to vote at home, and on December 12th the ballot-box was brought to his bed and he cast his vote.

All the theatres in Russia took part in the celebration of Stanislavsky's seventy-fifth birthday on January 18th, 1938. He received the different delegations in bed. He clinked glasses with them, sipping his champagne, and chatted to them about the affairs of their theatres. Among the actors and actresses who came to congratulate him were Kachalov and his wife, Olga Knipper, and Yablochkina, now a famous actress of the Maly Theatre, with whom he had had such a jolly time in Yessentuki in 1901

On the same day the Soviet Government conferred the Order of Lenin on Stanislavsky, and Leontyev Lane was renamed Stanislavsky Street.

Next day he had a slight temperature and felt very weak. He spent a few days in bed and got up feeling much better. He then went through the thousands of birthday messages he had received, anxious to reply to every one of them. A few days later he was lying in bed after dinner, when he suddenly said to his nurse :

"I shall die this year."

She looked up startled, and he repeated it.

"How do you know ? " she asked.

But Stanislavsky had his own signs and portents in which he firmly believed.

"I have good reasons for thinking so," he said.

In February he felt so well that he resumed his rehearsals of *Tartuffe*, the last play he was to produce for the Moscow Art Theatre, and *Rigoletto*, the opera he was producing for his Opera House. He also resumed work with his Studio. On April 13th Shalyapin died. His death was reported in the papers—a few lines on the back page. Stanislavsky was very upset.

"Oh, Fyodor, Fyodor ! " he murmured. "He was a born genius," he said to his nurse. "He seemed to know the secret of singing. It took him a long time to find it, but one day he rushed into my room like a madman, shouting, 'I've found it ! I've found it ! ' When I asked him what he had found, he kept repeating, 'Here ! Here ! ' and pointing to his throat. He never regarded himself as a finished artist and he always tried to achieve perfection. He should have taught voice production because he knew the secret. What a shame he left no school behind him ! He was so witty and original, but completely unrestrained."

In May, Lilina went to Leningrad with the Moscow Art Theatre. Stanislavsky continued dictating his system, conducting his rehearsals, teaching at the Studio, and keeping in constant touch with his theatres by telephone. It was with difficulty that he was persuaded by his doctor to take a rest every second day.

In the Studio he was rehearsing scenes from *Hamlet*. When, a little earlier in the year, a delegation of young producers who had just finished their course of studies at the State Institute of Dramatic Art asked him what was the substance of his recent researches in the application of his latest method of physical actions, he had taken *Hamlet* as an example.

"Suppose," he said, "you are working on the part of Hamlet. What are you to start with ? You can, of course, do what we used to do and begin your work with a study of the middle ages, conjure up in your imagination the gloomy old castle at Elsinore with its draughty vaulted corridors, and imagine yourself as a pale, dishevelled prince, wrapped in a cloak, walking slowly along one of these corridors. Can such a picture ever excite you ? Well, perhaps it can. But we prefer to go another way. If I were asked to play Hamlet, I should start with the proposition that I am Hamlet and not the man who is wandering about the castle. When ? Now, and not in the middle ages. Where ? Here in Moscow, in Leontyev Lane, and not in Elsinore." Stanislavsky looked round as though confirming the reality of his being in the rehearsal room with the columns at that very moment. "Now I am told," he went on, "that from behind that column (which in time may be transformed into a ledge of a cliff or a column of a medieval castle) my dead father appears, my father who died some time ago and at whose funeral I was. What should I do ? Not feel, but do, that is, act physically. I don't know. For the time being I can't do anything, but the question which has been put to me has already aroused my imagination and awakened my creative nature. Action is the very basis of our art, and with it our creative work must begin. Many things are still not clear to us. For instance, at what stage the actor ought to be first permitted to use his text and how that text should be made his own. Somewhere a more perfect and shorter way to the creation of a part lies hidden. At least, we have to re-examine everything afresh."

And at the rehearsal in the Studio in the spring of 1938, Stanislavsky returned to the problem of the text. He compared the art of the actor who has to deliver his dialogue on the stage with that of a sculptor. "Suppose," he said, "you have come to a great sculptor. A huge piece of clay lies before him. He takes a piece of it, kneads it, pounds it, moulds it, and, finally, there is one of the legs of Venus before you. He puts it in front of you—'Here you are ! Look at it ! Admire it !' Then he takes other pieces of clay and, without hurrying, relishing his work, moulds the other leg, then the arms and hands, the trunk—and puts it all before you. He then lovingly models the eyes, puts all the pieces together and in front of you is the figure of Venus. It is just like that that you have to approach the problem of dialogue. A word must be 'put in' and not 'spilt'. If I speak to someone and want to convince him, I demand to be heard, I put a greater emphasis on every word I use. The moment I deepen the given circumstances, I get a different rhythm of my dialogue. Until the phrase begins to ring, there is no speech."

It was not enough for an actor to convey the logical meaning of a play, Stanislavsky maintained. To influence his partner by his words the actor must, in Stanislavsky's phrase, "place under each word the moving pictures of his imagination," that is to say, each word an actor utters on the stage must be preceded by a succession of visual images in his mind. "When a word does not express a visual image of some sort," Stanislavsky said, "it is uselesss." And to make the enunciation of words correspond to their visual significance, Stanislavsky demanded that the visual images should be precise.

"But Shakespeare," a student-actor objected, "is very difficult to play. He forces you to resort to pathos."

"But what is pathos ? " Stanislavsky asked. "Sing-song enunciation, tremolo, unnatural intonations—that's the cause of all this beastliness. The first sign of pathos appears in an actor when he speaks without seeing anything. To destroy pathos, one must *act*. If an action requires pathos, it will come by itself, but it will be quite a different kind of pathos. It will not be the kind of pathos with which an actor fills his spiritual emptiness."

And as an example of how to play Shakespeare, Stanislavsky reproduced in a slightly exaggerated form, but with amazing accuracy, the monotonous, conventional enunciation of Shake-speare's verse by a performer of the part of Romeo :

> Alas ! that love whose view is muffled still,
> Should, without eyes, see pathways to his will.

"Don't you feel," he went on, "that your intonation is like a record that goes round and round in the same groove ? You pronounce sixteen words in the same tone of voice, while there should not be two words in the same tone."

What an actor ought to do, Stanislavsky urged, to avoid a repetition of the same intonation was to look for new "visual images" and not for new inflexions.

"It is impossible to learn voice production without music or singing," he said. "The actor must study musical speech in drama as well as in opera. Only when you have learnt to be masters of your words, when your voice production technique is perfect, your diction good and your breathing correct, can you play Shakespeare."

Stanislavsky then asked two student-actors to repeat the scene of the first meeting of Romeo and Juliet. The chairs in the studio were re-arranged to represent the hall in Capulet's house. Romeo rushed in with light, furtive steps, looking round him apprehensively. Then Juliet ran out, looking radiant and gay.

"What are you doing ? " Stanislavsky asked the actor.

"I am admiring Juliet's beauty," the actor replied.

"The word 'admire' must not exist in the actor's vocabulary, " said Stanislavsky, "for it expresses a state of mind and not an action. Before you begin to admire Juliet's beauty, you must examine and appraise it. What is your attitude to Juliet now ? "

"I am madly in love with Juliet," the actor replied.

"Not madly in love," Stanislavsky corrected, "but madly attentive to Juliet. Love first of all expresses itself in exceptional attention to a person. You can only play the feeling of love on the stage by conventional methods of acting. In a theatre one must never *act* feeling or an action or a character. That is the horrible 'professional' way of acting from which I am trying to do all I can to protect you. Don't rush after feeling, but learn to act correctly, and the correct desire will evoke the correct feeling. For action always evokes correct desires and correct desires will evoke the necessary emotions. It is much easier to overact on the stage than to act and speak truthfully."

"Why can anyone communicate with anyone he likes in life,

while not everyone succeeds in being truthful on the stage?" an actor asked.

"That happens," Stanislavsky replied, "because in life all people can be normal people, while on the stage not everyone succeeds in being normal. In life everyone has organic lines, the actor on the stage alone has not got them. It is only on the stage that an actor can think of anything under the sun while singing a passionate love aria to the audience and at the same time clasping the leading lady to his heart without even bothering to look at her. When an actor makes a declaration of love on the stage he puts his hand on his heart, rolls up his eyes, sighs, and so on. If you ever tried to do the same in real life, the girl you were in love with would certainly take offence and send you packing, but for some reason that sort of thing is considered quite normal on the stage."

In all his rehearsals at the Studio during the last months of his life, Stanislavsky applied his new method of "physical and verbal action", which was to form the central theme of the second book of his system—the actor's work on his part. By this method he hoped to arm the actor with an entirely new technique for the correct application of the organic processes of his work, leading to the discovery of the new methods of representation. In June the work of the Studio was sufficiently advanced for the students to give a public performance of scenes from plays to a few select spectators. But Stanislavsky was beginning to show signs of great fatigue. After one such performance he swayed unsteadily as he walked back to his rooms. "I'm afraid I'm tired," he told one of his assistant producers who rushed to his help. "I just can't go on any longer."

When one of the editors of his book brought him the page proofs, she found him looking very ill. He could not move his right arm. He asked her a few questions about the paper and the binding (he was very anxious that the cover of the book should not be expensive as he wanted everybody to be able to afford to buy it).

"May I take the book and just turn a few pages?" he asked her suddenly in the middle of their conversation.

She gave him the book and, as he took it, his face coloured and his fingers trembled. At that moment he seemed to be sure that he would live to see it published. But the book only came out after his death.

On June 16th the Studio gave a performance of some excerpts from an opera before the members of the State Arts Commission. At eleven o'clock Dukhovskaya wakened Stanislavsky. She asked him how he was and he replied that he was not in pain but rather weak. He got up at four o'clock and went to his study. His visitors soon arrived and they all went in to the rehearsal. During the intervals and at the end of the rehearsal Stanislavsky and his visitors drank tea in his study and discussed the performance. Stanislavsky was very pleased that the members of the Commission were satisfied with the performance they had seen. At nine o'clock the visitors left, and he spent some time talking happily to his nurse and daughter. At last he was persuaded to go to bed. He told his nurse that he was very happy at the result of the rehearsal.

"I have great hopes of them," he said. "A new theatre is growing up, a young, vigorous, strong theatre."

Next day he woke up feeling quite well. His nurse read the papers to him. Suddenly he felt very weak and began gasping for breath. His doctor was sent for and gave him an injection of camphor. That night he could not sleep and Dukhovskaya read to him till daybreak, when at last he fell asleep. He was still interested in the theatrical notices in the papers, but he was too weak to dictate the notes for his new book.

"I'm terribly weak," he told his nurse. "I'm not getting stronger at all. Fresh country air is my only hope."

He was waiting impatiently for Lilina to return from her Leningrad tour. However, his condition improved steadily, his pulse grew firmer and his voice recovered some of its old strength. He resumed his daily telephone talks with the managers and producers of his theatres. At last the telegram announcing his wife's return came.

After his morning coffee, the nurse would place his attaché-case on his bed and he would take out his notes and start dictating his new book. He thought of nothing else now. When he felt strong, he would go on dictating for hours, but quite often he was too weak to carry on.

"I can't go on any more," he would say to his nurse with an apologetic smile. "My head refuses to work. I just can't get what I want. . . ."

One morning when his nurse asked him how he felt, he replied "I don't know. I feel so strange : can't tell whether I am asleep or not. Can't understand a thing. My head seems to go on working all the time. Can't stop it."

He could only manage to walk from his bed to the washbasin, and even that required so big an effort that he slumped down in the armchair, gasping painfully for breath. But he bore it all very patiently, letting his nurse give him his injections without a murmur. He was fighting a losing battle, but he fought hard and stubbornly. It was a very hot summer, and the heat added greatly to his discomfort. He was no longer strong enough to hold up his manuscript and he often sank into semi-consciousness. His nurse sat reading to him almost all day long. She was reading the memoirs of a well-known actress and he recognized the names of many famous people he had known.

"Duse," he said, "was a fascinating woman."

"How do you mean ? "

"She was so feminine. Everything about her was feminine, from the straying wisps of hair at the nape of her neck to the tip of her nose. When she looked through the window of a railway carriage, it was just like a painting in a frame. She had a most violent temper, and when she was in a rage she would fight like a cat. But, as a rule, she was very gentle and quiet and sweet as an angel."

During the last days of his illness he spoke very little, but even when he was too weak to dictate, his precious attaché-case was always beside him on the bed and one of his manuscripts in his hands.

He pinned all his hopes of recovery on his departure for the sanatorium. After Lilina's return they discussed it a long time. They began getting ready for the journey. Stanislavsky supervised the packing of his things and spent a long time deciding which of his manuscripts to take. They were to leave for the sanatorium on August 2nd. Two days before Stanislavsky got a barber to shave him and cut his hair. On the day when they were due to set out Dukhovskaya woke him and asked him how he felt.

"Not so good," he replied, but would not postpone the journey.

At two o'clock he had his lunch and lay down for a rest. When he woke up everything was ready. Two cars were waiting outside. The doctors and ambulance men were in his bedroom. But when they began to dress him, he suddenly fell back on the pillows and lay motionless with closed eyes. His pulse was weak

and irregular. He had a very high temperature. The journey
had to be cancelled.

When Stanislavsky came to, he looked round him in surprise.
"What does it mean?" he murmured. "Can't understand
anything. Nurses, doctors, ambulance men. What's all this
for?"

He did not remember anything. He had even forgotten about
his intended journey to the sanatorium.

In the evening he still ran a high temperature. He was
delirious. Every day he was getting weaker. When he was asked
whether he felt any pain, he replied, "No, I feel no pain, only I
can't think. . . . It's as though I were asleep all the time. . . ."

He slept and slept. He lay quietly with his eyes closed, his
chin propped on his left hand.

When delirious he would describe movements in the air, as
though turning over the pages of a book.

"What are you doing?" his nurse asked him.

"I'm reading. Turning over the pages of a book."

One of his producers who came in to inquire how he was,
found Dukhovskaya's room empty. Stanislavsky's bedroom
door was open. He peeped in and saw Stanislavsky propped up
high on pillows. His eyes were closed and he was breathing
stertorously. Occasionally words would burst from his lips :
"Silence ! I don't believe it ! Can't hear your words ! Repeat
it !"

On August 4th, his temperature fell and he felt much better.
He spoke to his doctors and answered their questions. He had
no pain, but he felt very weak. His condition continued to be
satisfactory, but his pulse was fast and irregular. On the morning
of August 7th he seemed to take a greater interest in things and
he spoke a little to his wife and nurse. Most of the time he lay
quietly with closed eyes. It was only a short time before that the
woman had come to see him with the page proofs of his book.
She had asked him who Fif was, whom he mentioned in his
Artistic Notes. He had told her that he was the best friend of his
youth. He had few real friends, but Fedya Kashdamanov was
one of them, just as later Sulerzhitsky was another. Fif and Suler
—they had been his only friends. And yet there was another
man in his life who had played the most decisive part in his
career on the stage, a man who never became his friend—
Nemirovich-Danchenko. Why was that? What was it that had

always stood between them? He had always taken Nemirovich-Danchenko's part. He had always felt that he was perhaps much more to blame for their estrangement than Nemirovich-Danchenko. Yes, certainly more, for was it not he who had always been in the limelight? People even spoke of the Moscow Art Theatre as Stanislavsky's theatre. That was not fair. He corrected them whenever he could. But should he not have tried to break down the wall that was growing up between them? Lilina came up with his medicine in a spoon and gave it to him.

Suddenly he asked her :

"Who's taking care of Nemirovich-Danchenko? He's all alone now. He isn't ill, is he? Has he enough money? "

"Don't worry, darling," Lilina replied. "He's all right. He's abroad and he has plenty of money."

"Would you like me to say something to your sister? " Dukhovskaya asked. "I shall be writing to her today."

"I've lots to say to her, not just something," Stanislavsky replied. "But not now. I'm sure to get it all mixed up."

Those were his last words. His sister Zina and Nemirovich-Danchenko were the last persons he spoke of. Zina who was carrying on with his teaching, and Nemirovich-Danchenko who was carrying on with his theatre. His temperature rose and he sank into semi-consciousness. At two o'clock, Lilina retired to her room for a rest. The doctor on duty was in the study. Dukhovskaya gave Stanislavsky some water to rinse his mouth and he swallowed a little. Then he sank back on the pillows and lay there with a concentrated expression on his face. His eyes were closed and he was breathing quietly. Dukhovskaya sat down at his bedside and watched him all the time. At a quarter to four she bent over him, intending to take his temperature, when suddenly he gave a violent start.

"What's the matter, dear? " his nurse asked.

A spasm passed over his face. He grew deathly pale and his head sank down lower on the pillow. He was dead.

His funeral was attended by thousands of people. The whole of Moscow seemed to have turned out to bid a last farewell to the great actor and producer. He was buried in the Novodevichy Monastery, the same old monastery he always advised young actors to visit again and again before playing the parts of Ivan the Terrible or Boris Godunov.

INDEX

405

C

O

P

R

S

The rift between Stanislavsky and Nemirovich occurred dramatically at the dress rehearsal of the revival in 1917 of Stanislavsky's adaptation of Dostoevsky's early novel *The Village of Stepanchikovo*. It resulted inevitably from the irreconcilable differences between Stanislavsky and Nemirovich about the actor's place in the theatre. Nemirovich was a typical producer-dictator whose idea of directing a play was based on a literary man's "psychological" analysis of its characters and a ruthless suppression of any attempt by the actor to deviate from his instructions; Stanislavsky, a man of the theatre, had, on the other hand, already begun to evolve his revolutionary new "system" of the actor's art aimed at awakening an actor's creative potentialities to enable him to create the character he represented on the stage as *he* and not the director conceived it to be.

At the end of the dress rehearsal Nemirovich, who directed the play, appeared before the curtain and to everybody's surprise announced that he had decided to take away the part of Colonel Rostanev from Stanislavsky and give it to another actor. "We all gasped with dismay at this announcement," one of the actresses wrote later, "and waited with bated breath to see what was going to happen. Nothing happened. Stanislavsky accepted Nemirovich's decision without protest."

Three years later Lyubov Gurevich, a former editor of a Moscow literary monthly and a close friend of Stanislavsky's, gave quite a different account of what Stanislavsky's real feelings were at Nemirovich's announcement of his dismissal from the play. "When I asked him [Stanislavsky] what new role he had in mind to be working on shortly," she writes in her reminiscences, "his face suddenly darkened. 'I cannot bring myself to begin working on any new role,' he said. 'I don't suppose you know what happened.' And he began to tell me in a choked voice how at the dress rehearsal of *The Village of Stepanchikovo* Nemirovich had said something to him which made it impossible for him to carry on with his part. 'He said to me that I had failed to give birth to the role.' As he uttered those peculiar words: 'failed to give birth to the role' his voice sounded hollow, his lips quivered. Even then he did not express any resentment at Nemirovich's decision, but I could not help feeling painfully that an incurable wound had been inflicted on him. I did not dare ask him any more questions either then or at any other time. How highly he had thought of the part he had created in 1891 in his own production of the play can be gathered from what he wrote about it himself in his autobiography *My Life in Art*. Several people who were present at the dress rehearsal in 1917 told me that his performance was quite amazingly beautiful and moving. . . . So greatly shaken was he, however, that with the single exception of the part of Ivan Shuysky during the American tour of the Moscow Art Theatre he really never did appear on the stage in any new part again."

The rift between Stanislavsky and Nemirovich widened after the October revolution when Nemirovich became a member of the Communist Party and, as a reward, was appointed Director of all the Classical Theatres in the Soviet Union and thus became a de facto boss of Stanislavsky. No longer able to defy his new master, Stanislavsky decided on a policy of non-cooperation with him, which eventually led to a complete severance of their relationship.

In January 1921 Stanislavsky moved to the house in Leontyev Lane where he was to conduct his seminars with the actors, his rehearsals, and write the two volumes of his famous "system" of the art of acting. His world reputation was so firmly established by his tour in the United States that on his return in Moscow he was allowed to continue his work without interference. But he never forgot the part Nemirovich had played in the foundation of the Moscow Art Theatre. Nemirovich never came to visit him during his last illness, but shortly before his death he suddenly turned to his wife and asked excitedly: "Who is taking care of Nemirovich now? Now he is left alone by himself. . . . He is not ill, is he? Has he any money?" His wife assured him that he need not worry, for Nemirovich was not in any financial difficulties. Her reply calmed him. He died an hour later.

London, April 1975.   D.M.